To Mary Elizabeth,
    With gratitude for all you've done.
        Best Wishes,
            Glenn Altschuler
            Faust Rossi

TEN GREAT AMERICAN TRIALS: LESSONS IN ADVOCACY

GLENN C. ALTSCHULER + FAUST F. ROSSI

Cover design by Tahiti Spears/ABA Design.
Interior design by Betsy Kulak/ABA Design.

Printed in the United States of America.

20 19 18 17   5 4 3

Library of Congress Cataloging-in-Publication Data

ISBN 978-1-63425-592-9

Discounts are available for books ordered in bulk. Special consideration is given to state bars, CLE programs, and other bar-related organizations. Inquire at Book Publishing, ABA Publishing, American Bar Association, 321 N. Clark Street, Chicago, Illinois 60654-7598.

www.ShopABA.org

Contents

Acknowledgments

THE GENESIS OF THIS BOOK was the week-long "Great American Trials" course for Cornell University alumni we have taught every other summer for well over a decade. We prepared lectures on about sixty courtroom cases, thoroughly enjoyed the experience, and responded enthusiastically to the suggestion made by Kevin Clermont, Faust's colleague in the Cornell Law School, that we turn ten of our trials into a book.

We are grateful to over a dozen Cornell law students and several American Studies undergraduates who did research on various aspects of each of our cases. Charles Jermy, associate dean of the School of Continuing Education and Summer Sessions at Cornell, took a number two pencil to our prose—and improved it immensely. John Palmer, our editor at the American Bar Association Press, has been an insightful, responsive, and responsible professional. The talented people at Creative Services Associates proved to be skilled and thorough copy editors.

Charline Rossi, Faust's wife of fifty-four years, brought patience, judgment, editorial, and keyboarding skills to *Ten Great American Trials*. On one occasion, she raced from a hospital bed to a desk at home to help us meet a deadline. Without Charline, this book would not have been completed. The research and revisions done by Chris Rossi, Faust's son, who took time from his own work, were also indispensable. John Niederbuhl and Lyndsey Clark, administrative aides at the Law School, proved to be more than adequate to the not inconsiderable challenge of deciphering Faust's scribblings and turning them into readable texts.

Beth Beach, Glenn's administrative assistant, ran down our research requests, managed the tracked changes that whizzed back and forth from Ithaca to Bethesda, formatted the final drafts of each chapter, and helped us secure photograph permissions with the good cheer, grace, and consummate skill that characterize everything she does. Don Lebow, a graphic designer at the School of Continuing Education and Summer Sessions, identified photographs for each chapter, and used his expertise to manage the formatting of the digital files. Pat Burns listened to Glenn's daily summaries of information uncovered and interpretations crafted with patience, love, and, on occasion, genuine interest.

Our greatest debt is owed to the many authors who have written about our trials. Their essays and books have enhanced our understanding of what happened and why it was and is important. We have listed key sources in the first footnote of each chapter.

Finally, we thank each other. Collaborations sometimes end friendships. Anything but a trial, our collaboration on this book has deepened our already deep respect and affection for one another.

Introduction

TEN GREAT AMERICAN TRIALS PROVIDES chapter-length accounts of some of the most highly publicized—and fascinating—court cases of the twentieth century. Embedded in each of our narratives is an analysis of the use by prosecutors and defense attorneys of trial advocacy techniques (involving discovery, pretrial motions, jury selection, direct testimony, cross-examination, the introduction of forensic exhibits, and summations) to craft compelling stories about what happened. We also assess the impact of cultural, social, and political values on the proceedings and the outcomes.

We selected the cases, several of which have been dubbed "the crime of the century," because they are dramatic, suspenseful, emotional, intellectually powerful, and have become part of American culture. Uncertainty about motives, guilt, or innocence, it is worth noting, still haunt several of our trials. And every one of our cases has inspired a full-length movie, a television series, and/or a documentary.

All ten of our trials—*Sacco and Vanzetti; Leopold and Loeb; Scottsboro Boys; Alger Hiss; Sam Sheppard; Skokie, Illinois Neo-Nazis; Dan White* (the killer of Harvey Milk and George Moscone, the mayor of San Francisco); *Claus von Bülow; McMartin Preschool;* and *O. J. Simpson*—shed light on one or more "hot button" issues: xenophobia, the death penalty, race, anticommunism, free speech rights, homosexuality, and child abuse.

We recognize that our selection criteria were idiosyncratic and our cases are not "representative." After all, the overwhelming majority of indictments are settled and do not come to trial. And "great," "hard," and sensational cases rarely make good law. That said, one of our trials (Scottsboro) resulted in a landmark decision by the United

States Supreme Court that extended defendants' due process rights (previously reserved for federal government proceedings) to actions taken by the states—and added momentum to initiatives to guarantee fair representation of blacks on juries. Other cases in this book (*Sheppard*, *McMartin*, and *O. J.*) stimulated a public discussion of jury selection and sequestration, the value of the testimony of experts in psychology, prejudicial pretrial media coverage of crimes, and the circus atmosphere created by the presence of television cameras in the courtroom.

Our trials also serve as opportunities to examine the strengths and weaknesses of our adversarial system of justice. In contrast to the unfortunately named "inquisitorial" system of adjudication that prevails in most of the rest of the world (outside of the United Kingdom and former British colonies), where judges take an active role in investigating facts, appointing experts, and interrogating witnesses, the American system assigns evidence gathering and fact presentation to prosecutors and defense attorneys. The system treats the judge, in essence, as an umpire, intervening only when necessary to maintain a level playing field that is necessary to decide a case "correctly."

At its best, the system works well in the United States. In our "winner take all society," lawyers have incentives to find evidence that supports their clients—and to present clear and convincing narratives designed to persuade juries and judges to see things their way. As we will see, defense lawyers Clarence Darrow (*Leopold and Loeb*), Samuel Leibowitz (*Scottsboro Boys*), Alan Dershowitz (*von Bülow*), and Johnnie Cochran (*O. J. Simpson*) performed brilliantly as advocates under extraordinarily difficult circumstances. Prosecutor Thomas Murphy did a first-rate job of using the "pumpkin papers" of Whittaker Chambers and the Woodstock typewriter on which State Department documents had been copied to secure the conviction of Alger Hiss for perjury.

The adversarial system, however, does not always produce just outcomes. District attorneys, prosecutors, and defense lawyers often use trials to advance their own agendas, reputations, and career interests, including reelection, a race for higher office, a cause they support, or an opportunity to attract lucrative cases. And so, as John Mason Brown reminds us in *Through These Men*, lawyers "are almost always duty bound" to present blemishes as wounds; ask questions not only to learn but to lead and unsettle witnesses; read guilt into innocent, inconsistent, or incomplete answers; present lapses of memory as attempts to hide misdeeds; and deploy "feigned and wheedling politeness, sarcasm that scalds, intimidation, surprise, and besmirchment by innuendo, association or suggestion."

There is conclusive evidence, moreover, that clients who retain the best lawyers money can buy are far more likely than less affluent folks with court appointed or less accomplished attorneys to get the outcome they desire. Claus von Bülow's money, for example, made it possible for Alan Dershowitz to recruit a team of superb students from Harvard Law School, hire experts to reexamine the apparently incriminating forensic evidence, and draft an extraordinarily sophisticated appeal of a murder conviction. The wealthy parents of Leopold and Loeb hired Clarence Darrow who, against all odds, avoided a death penalty verdict against the young men. And, of course, prosecutors Marcia Clark and Christopher Darden were no match for O. J. Simpson's expensive "dream team" of lawyers, including Robert Shapiro, DNA expert Barry Scheck, F. Lee Bailey, Johnnie Cochran, and Alan Dershowitz. On the other hand, the ACLU, through its representative, David Goldberger, provided free legal services for the Neo-Nazis in the Skokie litigation in order to preserve "free speech for those we hate." And court-appointed attorneys Dean Gits and Danny Davis did yeoman work for the McMartin defendants.

Our cases also reveal that judges often play an active role in trials, belying the view that they are neutral, largely passive umpires. Webster Thayer, judge of the Superior Court of Massachusetts, did not hide his contempt for Sacco and Vanzetti. In private conversations, he allegedly called the defendants "Bolsheviki," vowing to "get them good and proper." And he denied virtually every motion made by Fred Moore, their lawyer, telling reporters "No long-haired anarchist from California can run this court."

At the other end of the ideological spectrum, James Edwin Horton, a judge on the Eighth Circuit Court in Alabama, who presided over the retrials of the Scottsboro Boys (only two of whom were under age sixteen), made the highly controversial decision to set aside the conviction and death penalty handed down against one of the defendants. He proclaimed that the accusations of rape were uncorroborated, improbable, contradicted by other evidence, and made by two women so "that their selfish ends may be gained." After ordering a new trial, Horton was taken off the case; he subsequently lost his bid for reelection as a judge and retired to his farm.

As we will indicate in the final chapter of this book, Lance Ito, judge of the Superior Court of Los Angeles County, California, had a substantial impact on the trial of O. J. Simpson. Perhaps because he relished his own appearances in the media limelight, Ito permitted live television coverage of the trial. In deference to the role prescribed for judges in the adversarial system, he allowed the two sides to try the case as they wished, permitting numbingly long and at times irrelevant speeches and interrogations of witnesses. He agreed to so many requests from lawyers to approach the bench that the word "sidebar" entered the English language as a synonym for unnecessary delays.

Judge Ito also made several important, perhaps pivotal, and certainly contested decisions on the admissibility of evidence. He ruled on a defense motion to prove its claim that Los Angeles Police Department detective Mark Fuhrman committed perjury by entering into evidence tape recordings in which he used racial epithets forty-one times, and on motions by prosecutors to exclude or limit the testimony on this issue to reduce the possibility of producing "undue prejudice" in members of the jury. Ito also had to decide whether to allow prosecutors to use O. J.'s 1989 no-contest plea to wife-beating charges and the 911 tapes in which she pleaded for help while Simpson was raging inside the house, in the face of objections by the defense that knowledge of prior convictions would unduly influence the jury.

As we focus on lawyers and judges, we examine as well the influence of politics and ideology on the content and context of trials, all of which have become touchstones of American culture, consciousness, and conscience. The behavior of Judges Thayer and Horton indicates one way in which prevailing beliefs and behaviors entered the courtroom. Three additional examples, elaborated on in detail in *Ten Great American Trials*, should suffice for this introduction.

Accusations by Whittaker Chambers, a senior editor at *Time* magazine, that in the 1930s Alger Hiss had delivered classified State Department documents to the Soviet Union (which Chambers had made before) may not have gotten traction in 1948; nor might Hiss have felt compelled to deny that he had ever met Chambers if millions of Americans had not been deeply fearful that vast networks of spies were operating inside the government of the United States. That the Un-American Activities Committee of the House of Representatives was conducting investigations, and politicians, including Richard Nixon, were exploiting the "Red Scare" to make their reputations as zealous Cold War anticommunists made a difference as well.

Less obviously, allegations in 1983 that about 400 young children had been subjected to sexual abuse, sexual encounters with animals, Satanic rituals, and travel in hot air balloons by Virginia McMartin, Raymond Buckey, and several teachers at the McMartin Preschool in Manhattan Beach, California, probably would not have resulted in arrests and the longest and most expensive trial in American history had there not been widespread hysteria about an epidemic of child abuse in the United States. Fueling the panic, moreover, was a mass media that tended to accept uncritically reports of predatory behavior, despite the absence of physical evidence—the only "confirmation" emanating from the suggestive questioning of children and unlikely claims about repressed and recovered memory. Before the panic subsided and the charges against the defendants were dismissed, several states passed laws allowing children to testify on closed-circuit television to avoid the trauma associated with facing the individuals they had accused.

And it now seems obvious that what might have been an "ordinary" murder trial of O. J. Simpson was transformed by the persistent and potent realities of racism, racial polarization, and celebrity culture in America into a spectacle digested and debated by tens of millions of people throughout the world.

Successful courtroom lawyers are skilled storytellers. They recognize that stories are essential to all of us as we learn, interact with others, and try to understand the world around us. They realize that facts do not speak for themselves; they must be interpreted. Operating within the formal rules, regulations, and norms of the adversary system (and willing, at times, to test its boundaries), lawyers weave the evidence that has been gathered into a clear, concise, and convincing narrative; frame the issue; and punch holes in the competing narrative offered by the other side. Using ordinary English, they demonstrate mastery of facts but do not get lost in details, never forgetting the observation of actor and director Kenneth Albers that "a great story is like a well-crafted joke—deliciously brief, immediately memorable, eminently repeatable, and virtually impossible to dismiss."

Successful trial lawyers generate sympathy for and trust in their clients, their witnesses, and themselves. They highlight weakness in the character, contentions, and credibility of their opponents. Aware of the backgrounds, beliefs, and biases of each juror and the judge, they use anecdotes, verbal expressions, body language, and, if appropriate, simple outlines on blackboards or flip charts to connect with and convince their listeners. They appeal to reason and emotion. They do not dispute facts that are (or should be) beyond dispute. They never ask a question unless they know the answer the witness will give and what to do in the event of a surprise. They understand that members of the jury form opinions quickly and often discount or reject evidence that contradicts their first impressions. They have learned that getting the last word—and making it count—can have an enormous impact on jury deliberations. Most important, they tell the story of the case in such a way that it arouses in the judge and jury a sense that justice will and must be served by a decision that favors the person or people they represent.

In *Ten Great American Trials,* we tell the stories of courtroom storytellers, evaluate the stories they told, and the axes and axioms they ground. Our cast of characters is large and varied. Our lawyers sometimes do—and sometimes do not—exhibit mastery of the techniques of trial advocacy. Our judges sometimes do—and sometimes do not—act impartially and in accordance with the precepts of our adversarial system. And our plaintiffs and defendants sometimes do—and sometimes do not—get what they deserve.

We have tried to make our narratives at least as accessible, dramatic, and thought-provoking as the fictionalized and documentary renditions of them; capture and assess what really went on inside the courtroom; re-create the mood of the times; and convey the ways in which our cases illuminate continuities and changes in the law and in the beliefs and behavior of Americans. We hope—and we think—that *Ten Great American Trials* has something to say about our legal structures and institutions, our history, and ourselves.

ONE

Sacco and Vanzetti: Martyrs or Murderers?[1]

---

1. This chapter draws heavily from the transcript of the record of the trial of Nicola Sacco and Bartolomeo Vanzetti in the courts of Massachusetts and subsequent proceedings, Name of Compiler or equivalent, comp., Official Name of Transcript, Volumes I through V (New York: Henry Holt & Co., 1928), hereafter referred to as "Transcript." The description of the case also relies on secondary sources including in particular Felix Frankfurter, *The Case of Sacco and Vanzetti: A Critical Analysis for Lawyers and Laymen* (Little Brown and Co., editions 1927, 1955, 1961), which is a republication of Justice Frankfurter's article in *The Atlantic Monthly*, March 1, 1927, available in four parts at http://www.theatlanticmonthly.com/magazine/archiv...03/the-case-of-sacco-and-vanzetti/306625/: Brian Jackson, *The Black Flag: A Look Back at the Strange Case of Nicola Sacco and Bartolomeo Vanzetti* (Routledge and Keegan Paul Ltd., 1981); Francis Russell, *Sacco and Vanzetti: The Case Resolved* (Harper and Row, 1986); Francis Russell, *Tragedy in Dedham: The Story of the Sacco-Vanzetti Case* (McGraw Hill Book Co., 1961, 1971); Bruce Watson, *Sacco and Vanzetti: The Men, the Murders, and the Judgment of Mankind* (Penguin Books, 2007); Susan Tejada, *In Search of Sacco and Vanzetti: Double Lives, Troubled Times, and the Massachusetts Murder Case That Shook the World* (Northwestern University Press, 2012); G. Louis Joughin and Edmund M. Morgan, *The Legacy of Sacco and Vanzetti* (Harcourt Brace and Company, 1948); Alan M. Dershowitz, *America on Trial: Inside the Legal Battles That Transformed Our Nation* (Warner Books, 2004); Francis X. Busch, *Prisoners at the Bar* (Bobbs-Merrill Company Inc., 1952); Robert Grant and Joseph Katz, *The Great Trials of the Twenties, The Watershed Decade in America's Courtrooms* (Sarpedon 1998); William Young and David E. Kaiser, *Postmortem: New Evidence in the Case of Sacco and Vanzetti* (University of Massachusetts Press, Amherst 1985); Douglas Linder, "Famous American Trials: The Trial of Sacco and Vanzetti," http://law2.umkc.edu/faculty/projects/ftrials/SaccoV/s&vaccount.html. This chapter is a revised and expanded version of an article written by coauthor Professor Faust Rossi titled "Sacco and Vanzetti: Martyrs or Murderers?," published in the *Cornell Law Forum* (July 2000).

IN 1921, IN THE MASSACHUSETTS State Court, Nicola Sacco and Bartolomeo Vanzetti were convicted of murder and robbery. They were Italian immigrants and radical anarchists. Six years later, still protesting their innocence, they were sentenced to death and executed. Vanzetti's words were recorded in an interview shortly before his death:

> If it had not been for this, I might have lived out my life, talking at street corners to scorning men. I might have died, unmarked, unknown, a failure. Now we are not a failure. This is our career and our triumph. Never in our full life can we hope to do such work for tolerance, for justice, for man's understanding of man, as we now do by accident.
>
> Our words, our lives, our pains; nothing. The taking of our lives, lives of a good shoemaker and a poor fish peddler; all. That last moment belongs to us; that agony is our triumph.[2]

His words were prophetic. In 1977, on the fifty-year anniversary of their execution, the state of Massachusetts apologized. Massachusetts Governor Michael Dukakis proclaimed August 23rd as Nicola Sacco and Bartolomeo Vanzetti Memorial Day. He declared that any stigma and disgrace should be forever removed from their names. Speaking for the state, he called upon its citizens to reflect upon these tragic events, to draw from their historic lessons the resolve to prevent forces of intolerance, fear, and hatred from uniting to overcome the rationality, wisdom, and fairness to which our legal system aspires.[3]

In 1997, Mayor Thomas Menino of Boston, the city's first Italian-American mayor, dedicated a bronze sculpture memorial of Sacco and Vanzetti. The sculpture depicted the two men facing distorted scales of justice. At the ceremony, the mayor said, "The city's acceptance of this piece of artwork is not intended to reopen the debate

---

2. The quotation is from "The Letters of Sacco and Vanzetti"; Russell, *The Case Resolved*, 222; Jackson, *The Black Flag*, 168–9; Russell, *Tragedy in Dedham*, 387.
3. Jackson, *The Black Flag*, 88–90.

about guilt or innocence. It is intended to remind us of the dangers of miscarried justice, and the right we all have to a fair trial."[4]

The case of Sacco and Vanzetti ranks as one of most significant of the twentieth century. The trial and its aftermath was an international sensation. It inspired bombings, demonstrations, songs, films, and thousands of pages of written material. It is worthy of study for three reasons. First, like the *Dreyfus* case in France in the late nineteenth century, it bared the soul of a nation. It forced America into a debate about its identity. Who do we define as "outsiders"? How should they be treated? The case also raised a host of political, cultural and legal issues; the dangers of xenophobia and prejudice, the immigration debate, the ethical and legal responsibilities of judges and prosecutors, and the advisability of capital punishment.[5]

Second, the sheer mystery at the heart of the case continues to fascinate. Did Sacco and Vanzetti do it? Did they rob and cold-bloodedly kill a paymaster and his armed guard? The trial was tainted and the process may not have been fair, but the question of their guilt remains. There have been dozens of books and articles written in support of Sacco and Vanzetti, but almost none of them venture a firm opinion on this factual question. Literature tells of a historian who was once asked by a philosopher, "Is immortality desirable?" The historian answered, "I almost think it is, if only to get at the truth of the Sacco-Vanzetti case."[6]

Third, the case exposes defects in the criminal justice system of the 1920s, and reveals how and why the law has changed. We cannot definitively answer the hard question: Were Sacco and Vanzetti innocent? Instead, we offer two opinions. The first is almost indisputable: under today's standards of criminal procedure, Sacco and Vanzetti could not have been convicted. The second is debatable: their trial was unfair even under the rules existing in the 1920s.

---

4. Richard Kreitner, "Menino: The Mayor Who Welcomed Sacco and Vanzetti," *Boston Globe*, November 23, 2014, http://www.bostonglobe.com/ideas/2014/11/23/menimo-mayor-who-welcomed-sacco-and-vanzetti/ovdxh5W4NvAXDbDaRvhMD1/story.html.
5. *Id.*
6. Russell, *The Case Resolved*, 138. The question was posed and answered by historian Ferris Greenslet.

One could argue that Sacco and Vanzetti were afforded not just due process, but undue process. They had a six-week trial, and the jury of twelve that convicted them had been culled from a panel of some 750 citizens. The attorneys representing the defendants were paid from a substantial defense fund raised by political allies. The defense was heard repeatedly and at great length on six separate applications for a new trial. They had two appellate hearings before the Supreme Judicial Court of Massachusetts. There were applications to and rulings by several federal judges. The governor of Massachusetts appointed a special advisory committee headed by the then president of Harvard University, Abbott Lawrence Lowell, to make an impartial review of the trial record.

All that is true, but as the well-known evidence scholar Professor Edmund Morgan of Harvard Law School indicated years ago: "The defendants had a trial according to all the forms of law but it was not a fair trial. The machinery of justice as it then existed was fully available and fully utilized; but it misfunctioned."[7] To understand why Sacco and Vanzetti could not have been convicted today, and should not have been convicted in 1921, we must look first at the political and social climate in the year leading up to the trial, and then at the facts: the proof presented at the trial and in particular the three pieces of evidence that formed the crux of the prosecution case.

In the aftermath of World War I, the nation entered a period of upheaval, dislocation, and fear. In 1919, there was rampant inflation. As many as one out of every five workers was involved in a labor strike. Race riots erupted in dozens of cities. It was also the time of the "Red Scare." The Russian royal family had been overthrown and murdered, and the Bolsheviks had taken power. Lurid press headlines reported on the Bolshevik mission to conquer America and on the pervasiveness of "Reds" in New England. The American Communist Party was formed that same year, and 90 percent of its members were immigrants from Eastern Europe. Anarchist groups were committed to the notion that government is the root of all evil and must be eliminated, through violence if necessary—for only then

---

7. Joughin and Morgan, *The Legacy of Sacco and Vanzetti*, 157.

could every individual be free. The anarchists were predominantly Italian, Spanish, or Slavic immigrants. In April and June of that year, explosions were reported in a number of cities on a single day. Many of these mail bombs were sent to public officials with leaflets that read, "Class war is on . . . we have aspired to make a better world, and you jailed us, you clubbed us, you deported us, you murdered us . . . we mean to speak for the proletariat with the voice of dynamite, through the mouth of guns."[8]

In 1920, the government began a brutal campaign to crack down on these dissident groups. These acts of oppression were led by the attorney general of the United States, A. Mitchell Palmer, assisted by a young J. Edgar Hoover, who headed up an antiradical organization in the Department of Justice. From November 1919 to January 1920, Palmer launched a series of raids to rid the country of what he called "Reds" and "Alien filth."[9] Throughout the United States, local police and federal officials rounded up many people based merely on their affiliation with what were deemed "subversive" political groups. Homes were entered, property was confiscated, and mass arrests were made without warrants. The possession of radical literature alone was considered an act of sedition. Aliens who had never been charged or convicted of any crime were deported. On New Year's Day in 1920, 6,000 alleged communists were arrested and thrown in prison. Complaints by civil libertarians were met by Palmer's statement that "[e]ach and every adherent of this movement is a potential murderer or potential thief, and deserves no consideration."[10]

There was little public outcry. The feeling against immigrants from southern Europe was strong. The words "alien," "radical," and "terrorist" were often used interchangeably. Walter Lippmann called it a time when "right thinking men were scared out of their wits." The fear of foreign radicals was especially strong in Massachusetts, where many white Protestants resented the influx of Irish and Italian Catholic immigrants.

---

8. Tejada, *In Search of Sacco and Vanzetti*, 111.
9. *Id.*
10. *Id.*

On April 15, 1920, there was a payroll robbery and two murders at the Slater and Morrill shoe factory in South Braintree, Massachusetts. Frederick Parmenter, the paymaster, and his guard, Alessandro Berardelli, were carrying a factory payroll of $15,770 in two metal boxes. As they walked along the main street going from the company offices to the separate factory building, two strangers were leaning casually against a fence. A third man was stretched out lazily near a pile of bricks. As Parmenter and Berardelli neared the shelter of the factory, the strangers leaped forward, pulled out guns and fired. Berardelli was shot and fell to his knees. One of the assailants straddled him and fired four more shots into his back. Parmenter dropped his payroll box and bolted for safety. He didn't make it. Two shots dumped him in the middle of the road. A large, dark Buick touring car bearing two other men arrived on the scene. Joined by the third man from the brick pile, the assailants snatched up the boxes, threw them into the getaway car, jumped in the Buick and roared off. Berardelli died at the scene and Parmenter expired 15 hours later. The bandit car was later found abandoned in the woods, the stolen money having been transferred to another automobile.

Three weeks later, on May 5, 1920, Sacco and Vanzetti, two Italian immigrants with no criminal record, were arrested while riding on a streetcar. They were arrested almost by accident.

Some months before the South Braintree robbery, there had been a similar but unsuccessful robbery attempt in the neighboring town of Bridgewater. The police chief there, Michael Stewart, had become convinced that both robberies were the work of a gang of Italian anarchists. He suspected a man named Boda. Having determined that Boda's car was being kept at the garage of Simon Johnson for repairs, Chief Stewart arranged for Johnson to call the police when someone came to pick up the car. On the evening of May 5, four Italians—Boda; his friend, Orciani; Sacco; and Vanzetti—came to the Johnson garage to pick up the car. Mrs. Johnson called the Bridgewater police. The car did not have license plates for 1920 and so the Italian group had to leave without it. Boda and Orciani, who were never arrested for any crime, left on a motorcycle. Sacco and Vanzetti walked some distance and boarded a trolley for Brockton.

At a certain point, police officer Connolly boarded the streetcar and arrested them.

Sacco and Vanzetti were not told that they were suspects in the South Braintree crimes. The police told them they had been charged as "suspicious characters."

When they were arrested, both men were armed. Sacco had a fully loaded 10-shot .32-caliber Colt automatic tucked into his belt. In his pocket, he had twenty-three loose bullets. Vanzetti had a 5-shot .38 caliber—also loaded. In his pocket, Vanzetti had four 12-gauge shotgun shells.

When questioned by the police, Sacco and Vanzetti lied about where they had been, where they were going, where they had gotten the guns and how long they had known each other. The trial judge said their lies proved to be the most potent incriminating evidence, which ultimately doomed them.

Nicola Sacco (left) and Bartolomeo Vanzetti (right).
© Bettmann/CORBIS

Sacco and Vanzetti were foreign radicals. They had lied, they would claim later, to hide the fact that they were anarchists and were on their way to hide anarchist literature from the police. They knew that many others who shared their political views had been arrested, held in jail for months, and then deported. Just the day before their arrest, they had learned of the death of Andrea Salsedo, one of the leaders of the anarchist movement. After being held in isolation for over a month, he fell, jumped, or was pushed out of the fourteenth floor offices of the Federal Bureau of Investigation in New York City.

Because Sacco and Vanzetti lied, however, they would have to take the stand at their trial and explain why they lied. As a practical matter, this removed an important defense option—the right not to testify. Even for an innocent accused, subjecting oneself to cross-examination by an experienced prosecutor is a dangerous business. To do so when one speaks poor English and might misspeak or mis-understand a question is doubly dangerous. Much more significant, it exposes the defendants' unpopular radical views to the jury, views which would otherwise be irrelevant.

Some of their supporters idealized them as saintly and benign "philosophical anarchists"; nonviolent peace-loving men who at worst held unorthodox views. The truth is likely more complex. They carried weapons and may well have been willing to use violence, at least to defend themselves or their cause.

Still, Sacco was in many ways an admirable figure. He came to the United States from Italy when he was seventeen in 1908. He worked steadily and developed into a highly skilled, well-paid shoe-edger, earning as much as $80 a week at a shoe factory. At the time of his arrest he had saved $1,500, a very substantial sum in those days. His employer described him as an excellent worker and a dedicated family man. His neighbors said that he had three passions: his veg-etable garden, which he tended in early mornings and late evenings; his work at the shoe factory; and his family. His unpopular political views were considered by many, including his employer, as an idio-syncratic aberration. However, he did believe that World War I was a capitalist war in which no working man should fight. So, during the war, he and Vanzetti, along with a hundred others, went to Mexico rather than register for the draft.

Vanzetti was a drifter. He had no steady job, never married, and had no personal life. When he needed money, he peddled fish or took odd jobs. Anarchism was his passion. He read a great deal, especially history, literature, and philosophy. After his arrest and conviction, Vanzetti taught himself to speak and write English with flair and eloquence.

Their trial began on May 31, 1921, the day after Memorial Day. The courthouse was in Dedham, Massachusetts, the Norfolk County seat. As was common practice at the time, Sacco and Vanzetti were kept in a barred metal cage in the center of the courtroom. The presiding judge was sixty-four-year-old Webster Thayer, who had asked to sit on this case. It was well-known that Thayer despised foreigners and radicals. Vanzetti would later describe the judge as "a self-conceited narrow-minded little tyrant" and "part tiger and part ass."[11] The district attorney was Frederick Katzmann, an ambitious elected official with his eye on a higher state office. The chief defense counsel was Fred Moore, a California lawyer associated with radical causes. An outsider unfamiliar with Massachusetts court traditions, Moore was openly offensive in his manner. He was reported to be a womanizer and at one time, a cocaine addict. In his remarks to the jury, Moore confessed that in this courtroom he himself felt like an alien. He and Judge Thayer clashed repeatedly. Many thought his appointment to represent Sacco and Vanzetti was a mistake because it underscored the radical background of the accused. However, his value went beyond his courtroom performance. Moore worked tirelessly as a publicist and fund-raiser to move the case of the two Italian immigrants into an earthshaking event that appealed to intellectuals, liberals, and radicals all over the world. Historian Francis Russell wrote that without Moore, "there would have been no Sacco and Vanzetti case with its worldwide repercussions."[12]

11. Watson, *Sacco and Vanzetti*, 116.
12. Russell, *The Case Resolved*, 22, 91.

Judge Thayer Webster (center) presided at the trial.
Photo credit: © Bettmann/CORBIS

It took five days to empanel the twelve-member jury. Usually, about one hundred prospects are called from the voter registration rolls. Such a selection process tends to exclude immigrants, foreigners, noncitizens, and minorities because they do not vote. This time, however, the prospective panel numbered over 650, the largest number ever assembled. Moore used his fifty-four preemptory challenges to remove every businessman on the jury. He wanted to ask all jurors if they were opposed to organized labor, if they belonged to a union, and if they hired union help. Thayer refused to allow these questions to be asked. The attorney assisting Moore, Thomas McAnarney, said that whenever Moore addressed the judge, it was akin to "waving a red flag in front of a bull." More than once Thayer said, "Mr. Moore, such tactics might work in California but not in the Commonwealth of Massachusetts."[13] Finally, Thayer had his jury of twelve. None among them were Italian or a member of any other ethnic minority. There were two dealers in real estate, an ex-policeman, a photographer, a farmer, a grocer, a salesman, a stock keeper, and four industrial workers. All were patriotic American citizens with little sympathy for radical immigrants.

But this is not a case that lends itself to jury criticism. If bias or prejudice entered the courtroom, it was the fault of the keepers of the system: the judge, the lawyers, and the procedures that were followed. In the six-week trial, 173 witnesses testified, about 100 of them for the defense, and so there was enough evidence for a jury to reasonably acquit. But there was also sufficient evidence presented by the prosecution for a fair-minded jury to conclude that Sacco and Vanzetti were guilty beyond a reasonable doubt. The evidence the prosecution was allowed to present, however, was tainted and other evidence that favored the defense was withheld by the prosecution or not discovered until after the verdict.

The state's case for conviction had three major elements. First, there was the eyewitness testimony. The prosecution theory was that Sacco was the one who shot Berardelli while Vanzetti sat in the getaway car. Several witnesses who were at the South Braintree shoe factory on the day of the robbery identified Sacco as being at the scene. A key witness for the prosecution was Mary Splaine, a forty-three-year-old bookkeeper who was working on the second floor of the Slater and Morrill plant; she testified that she heard the shots, rushed to the window, and saw the car driving off with a man she later identified as Sacco inside it. Two other witnesses identified Vanzetti as being in the car.

The defense countered with eyewitnesses who saw the assailants and testified that the defendants were not among them, and alibi wit-

---

13. Watson, *Sacco and Vanzetti*, 115.

nesses who testified that on that day, April 15, they were with either Sacco or Vanzetti in some other place.

All the eyewitness evidence for both sides was probably not decisive in the minds of the jurors. Eyewitness identification of strangers weeks after a traumatic event is notoriously unreliable. It is even more so when it is a cross-racial or cross-ethnic identification. Equally important, all the witnesses had very limited opportunities to observe.

The defense alibi witnesses were mostly friends of Sacco and Vanzetti, almost all Italians, and in some cases anarchists themselves. Furthermore, they could be easily discredited by prosecutor Katzmann or any experienced trial lawyer who would ask standard memory-testing cross-examination questions, such as, "You say you were with Sacco in Boston on April 15 having lunch at three o'clock in the afternoon? You sure that lunch was on April 15? You remember that now, a year later? So tell the jury who you had lunch with on April 14? April 13? How about last month?"

The second pillar of the state's case was the so-called "consciousness of guilt." When Sacco and Vanzetti were arrested three weeks after the holdup, they lied to the police: they acted like guilty men who were *conscious* of their guilt.

The third major piece of the prosecution case was expert testimony, in particular, the ballistics experts. There was expert testimony that one of the fatal bullets taken from the body of Berardelli came from the same .32-caliber pistol that was found on Sacco when he was arrested. This, if true, would, of course, be devastating evidence. But the prosecution experts were not definite. And there was confusion resulting from the fact that all the witnesses said only one man was shooting a gun at Berardelli and that this man emptied his pistol. Four bullets were found in Berardelli's body; of the four bullets, three were obviously from a weapon not found on either Sacco or Vanzetti. Only one bullet was from a .32-caliber Colt. What's more, the two prosecution experts were contradicted by two defense experts who testified that none of the bullets matched Sacco's .32-caliber Colt. The important fact here is that in 1921, ballistics expertise was in its infancy. More specifically, the comparison microscope which would allow more precision in matching a bullet to the gun that fired it had not yet been invented.

By today's legal standards, none of the three parts of the prosecution case would be admissible and none of it—not the eyewitness testimony, not the consciousness of guilt, not the expert ballistics testimony—would have been heard by the jury. Moreover, even by 1921 standards, each of these three pieces of evidence was tainted in a way that should have been exposed to the court and jury but was not, because of bias, incompetence, or lack of ethics.

Since the 1920s, a series of U.S. Supreme Court decisions have resulted in fundamental changes in the protections afforded to criminal suspects.

First, in order to be admitted into evidence, identification testimony must be reliable and not tainted by pretrial suggestion. If, for example, a witness is brought to the jail after a crime, and shown just the suspect, or just his picture, later in-court identification is usually excluded. The appropriate procedure is to place the suspect in a lineup with others including some of the same race or ethnic background so as not to provoke identification through accentuation. This procedure is so important that a defendant is entitled to have his lawyer present at the lineup to ensure fairness.[14]

These protections are particularly important in a case like this, in which all the identifying witnesses were speaking from brief observation, made under confusing traumatic circumstances, about men of a "foreign race" who were previously unknown to them.

None of these procedures were followed. The key prosecution witness, Mary Splaine, who was on the second floor of the factory, heard the shots, ran to the window, looked down a distance of sixty to eighty feet, into a car moving fifteen to eighteen miles per hour, for about one to three seconds, and said she saw a man previously unknown to her. One month later, she was brought down to the police station to see Sacco in his cell. She spent five minutes walk-

14. United States v. Wade, 388 U.S. 218 (1967), specifically cites the Sacco-Vanzetti case as an example of unnecessarily suggestive pretrial identification procedures that can violate the due process of the accused in criminal cases. *Wade,* 388 U.S. at 228–9. See also Manson v. Brathwaite, 432 U.S. 98 (1977); Stovall v. Denno, 388 U.S. 293 (1967).

ing around him. The police asked Sacco to hold out his hand as if he were going to shoot, to crouch down, and to adopt various aggressive and threatening positions that mimicked what allegedly went on at the crime scene. Mary Splaine knew that Sacco had been arrested and that she had been called to make an identification. Today, these facts alone would be more than enough to exclude her in-court identification.[15] But even with this suggestive procedure, Splaine said at the jail that she was not sure if Sacco was the man she had seen in the bandit car on April 15: "I don't say positively." Shown a group of police photographs, she picked one and said it looked just like the man. It was a man who was in Sing Sing Prison at the time of the crime.[16]

Three weeks later, at a preliminary hearing to determine if Sacco and Vanzetti could be held for the grand jury, Sacco sat in the courtroom while Splaine was on the stand testifying under oath:

Q: You don't feel certain enough in your position to say he is the man?

A: I don't think my opportunity afforded me the right to say he is the man.[17]

Mary Splaine did not see Sacco again until the trial, one year later. By that time the jury heard not doubt, but certainty. She testified that she was positive that Sacco was the man. She also now claimed that in those few seconds looking down at a moving car, she had seen an enormous amount of detail:

The man in the car was slightly taller than me. He weighed about 140 to 145 pounds. He was muscular, an active looking

---

15. The entire direct and cross-examination of Mary Splaine is contained in Transcript, Vol. I, 220–5.
16. Transcript, Vol. I, 243–44; Tejada, *In Search of Sacco and Vanzetti*, 136; Watson, *Sacco and Vanzetti*, 111.
17. Compare Splaine denying then admitting her statement. Transcript, Vol. I, 233, 248–9; Jackson, *The Black Flag*, 21.

man, his left hand was on the back of the front seat. It was a good-sized hand. He had on a gray-like navy color shirt. The face was a clean-cut face. The forehead was high. The hair was brushed back and the hair was between two and two and one half inches in length. The eyebrows were dark. The complexion was peculiar—it looked greenish.[18]

During cross-examination the defense asked if she had seen Sacco since the preliminary hearing. She had not.

Q: In other words, you changed your mind as to whether he was the man without making any further examination of him, didn't you?

A: Yes sir.[19]

Widely quoted later was the comment of Dr. Morton Prince, a renowned Harvard professor of psychology:

The star witness for the government testified, honestly enough no doubt, to what was psychologically impossible. Miss Splaine testified that she had only seen Sacco at the time of the shooting from a distance of sixty feet for from one and one half second to three seconds in a motorcar going at an increasing rate of speed at about 15 to 18 mph; that she saw and at the end of year remembered and described sixteen different details of this person, even to the size of his hand, the length of his hair . . . and the shade of his eyebrows! Such perception and memory under such circumstances can easily be proved to be psychologically impossible. . . And what shall we think of the animus and honesty of the state that introduces

---

18. Frankfurter, *The Case of Sacco and Vanzetti*, 11–13; Watson, *Sacco and Vanzetti*, 110.
19. Transcript, Vol. I, 220; The evolution of Splaine's testimony from doubt to certainty is described in Grant and Katz, *The Great Trials of the Twenties*, 34–35; Watson, *Sacco and Vanzetti*, 112.

such testimony to convict, hoping the jury is too ignorant to disbelieve?[20]

Judge Thayer should have excluded this evidence, as it could not have been based on her personal knowledge. Defense Counsel Moore should have made the prosecutor sorry that he had chosen to put Mary Splaine on the stand, but he was not up to the task.

Louis Pelser, a shoe cutter, placed Sacco at the scene of the murders and said he had been a witness to the shooting. He pointed to Sacco in the courtroom and said, "I wouldn't say it was him, but it is the dead image of him." He also claimed to have seen the Buick approach and the shots being fired. He even got the car's license plate number. Previously, Pelser had told the defense he had seen a body lying on the sidewalk, and nothing else. But under cross-examination, Pelser admitted never having told the defense he saw the shooting because "I didn't want to tell my story . . . because I didn't like to go to court." "You think so lightly of your word," Moore asked him, "that in order to avoid being called as witness, you deliberately told a falsehood?" "Yes sir," Pelser replied.[21]

Another prosecution witness, Lola Andrews, said that she and a companion had seen a man working under a car outside the Slater and Morrill factory before the robbery. She asked the man for directions, and when he stood up she saw his face. She said the man was Nicola Sacco. Andrews was on the stand for three days and under cross-examination, discrepancies in her story became apparent. Two weeks later, five defense witnesses contradicted Andrews's testimony. One of these was Julia Campbell, Andrews's companion on the day she claimed she saw Sacco. Campbell said she was "positively sure" that Andrews had not spoken to a man working on the car.[22]

20. Morton Prince, "A Psychologist's Study," *Boston Herald*, October 30, 1926; Frankfurter, *The Case of Sacco and Vanzetti*, 13–14.

21. Transcript, Vol. I, 300; Watson, *Sacco and Vanzetti*, 113; Tejada, *In Search of Sacco and Vanzetti*, 134; Jackson, *The Black Flag*, 22.

22. Tejada, *In Search of Sacco and Vanzetti*, 133; Watson, *Sacco and Vanzetti*, 134–5; Jackson, *The Black Flag*, 20, 53.

This pattern was repeated with the other prosecution eyewitnesses. Each, at first, could not identify either defendant, and they told friends, coworkers, and initially the police that they could not. But as time passed, they came to say that one or the other "looked like" the assailant. By the time of the trial "looked like" had become "that's him."

Another change in criminal procedure law would have dramatically affected the Sacco and Vanzetti trial. It involves a combination of two principles announced by the U.S. Supreme Court.

The first principle concerns the Fourth Amendment right to be free from unreasonable search and seizure. The Court decreed that it limited the police power to stop, frisk, or arrest a suspect without a warrant. If the police arrest or search a person without a warrant, they must have probable cause to believe that the suspect has committed a specific crime. Even to stop a suspect or to detain him for a few questions before an arrest, the officer must have reasonable suspicion to believe a crime has been committed. If these procedures are not followed, anything the officer finds in the search or learns during the illegal detention cannot be used in court.[23]

The other doctrine is one we know from television and the movies; the *Miranda* warnings. Before the police can question a suspect while he or she is in custody, the suspect must be "Mirandized"; that is, he or she must be told four things: You have the right to remain silent; if you talk, anything you say can be used against you; you have a right to a lawyer; if you can't afford one, a lawyer will be appointed for you. If the police do not clearly give each of these warnings, then no confession or damaging statements made in response to police questioning can be used in evidence.[24]

Did the police have probable cause to believe that Sacco and Vanzetti had committed crimes when they were arrested on a streetcar on May 5, 1920? Almost certainly not. Being "suspicious characters" is not a crime and forms no basis for an arrest. The police officer

23. Arizona v. Gant, 556 U.S. 332 (2009); Brinegar v. United States, 338 U.S. 160 (1949); Mapp v. Ohio, 367 U.S. 643 (1961).
24. Miranda v. Arizona, 384 U.S. 436 (1966).

who arrested them on the streetcar had no knowledge of any specific crime. The most that can be said is that they were arrested because they were apparently friends or acquaintances of someone else who was a suspect but was never charged. Today, the guns found in the search of their person, the bullets in their pockets, and the answers they gave to questioning while being held illegally would have been excluded from evidence as "fruit of the poisonous tree."[25] There would have been no lies in evidence that required explanation. There would have been no need to discuss the defendants' commitment to anarchism. The trial then would have been, as it should have been, solely about robbery and murder and not about radicalism or loyalty to the United States.

But that was not the law in 1921. One certainly can't fault the police or the courts for not seeing into the future. The police, understandably, did not give Sacco and Vanzetti full *Miranda* warnings.

Was there any problem with regard to the law as it existed in 1921? Yes. It involved prosecutor Katzmann's cross-examination of Sacco. On direct examination, Sacco explained their radical activities, their pacifism, their flight to Mexico to avoid having to register for the draft, and their need for a car in order to collect and hide socialist and anarchistic literature. That was why, he said, they had lied to the police when they were arrested. Their lies had nothing to do with fear that they might be arrested or prosecuted for the Braintree robbery. In cross-examination, with the concurrence of Judge Thayer, Katzmann methodically and systematically played on the emotions of the jury. Katzmann exploited, emphasized, and highlighted the political beliefs and activities of the accused. His cross-examination was prosecutorial misconduct, then and now.

In assessing the behavior of Katzmann, it helps to understand that prosecutors are subject to stringent legal and ethical obligations. Unlike the private lawyer or defense attorney whose obligations are to be zealous advocates for their clients, the prosecutor is a quasi-judicial

---

25. Nardone v. United States, 302 U.S. 379 (1937) used this now well-established metaphor to describe evidence that is obtained illegally (the tree) as in the case of a warrantless arrest or search without probable cause. Then anything gained from it (the fruit) is tainted as well and not admissible in evidence.

official entrusted with the duty to seek justice as the representative not of a single individual but of the government and society as a whole. The American Bar Association Canons of Ethics long ago decreed that: "The primary duty of a lawyer engaged in public prosecution is not to convict, but to see that justice is done."[26]

If Katzmann had wanted to cross-examine in a relevant and appropriate way, he might have tried to show that Sacco and Vanzetti were not really so radical, that they had nothing to fear from their political activities and, therefore, no such reason to lie. Instead, he chose to demonstrate the full extent of their radicalism and their lack of patriotism.

Although the format is question and answer, the cross-examining attorney is in control. The questions are leading. They are assertive. They are challenging. Here is a short sample of Katzmann's cross-examination questions:[27]

On dodging the draft:

Q: So you left Plymouth in May 1917 to dodge the draft, did you?

Q: When this country was at war, you ran away so you would not have to fight as a soldier?

Q: You said yesterday that you loved a free country—did you go to Mexico to avoid being a soldier for this country that you loved?

---

26. American Bar Association Canons of Professional Ethics, "Canon 5: The Defense or Prosecution of Those Accused of a Crime" (1908); Lisa M. Kurcias, "Prosecutor's Duty to Disclose Exculpatory Evidence," *Fordham Law Review* 69 (2000): 1205, 1209–12; Frankfurter, *The Case of Sacco and Vanzetti*, 57–59.
27. Transcript, Vol. II, 1867–90; Jackson, *The Black Flag*, 29–47; Frankfurter, *The Case of Sacco and Vanzetti*, 46–57; Linder, "Famous American Trials"; Watson, *Sacco and Vanzetti*, 155–8; Tejada, *In Search of Sacco and Vanzetti*, 157–59; Grant and Katz, *The Great Trials of the Twenties*, 29–31; R.M.H., "Cross-Examination to Impeach," *Yale Law Journal* 36 (1926–27): 384, 389, 390.

Q: And would that be your idea of showing your love for your wife that, when she needed you, you ran away from her?

Q: Don't you think that going away from your country when she needs you is a vulgar thing to do?

Q: Do you think it is a cowardly thing to do what you did?

Q: Mr. Sacco, that is the extent of your love of this country, isn't it, measured by dollars and cents?

Q: Is standing by a country when she needs a soldier evidence of love of country?

On the radical literature that Sacco testified he and Vanzetti were going to hide:

Q: And the books which you intended to collect were books relating to anarchy, weren't they?

Q: Bolshevist books?

Q: Soviet books?

Q: Communist stuff?

Q: And you weren't going to destroy those books, were you?

Q: You were going to keep them, and when the [dangerous] time was over you were going to bring them out, weren't you?

This line of questioning went on and on. Then Katzmann did something cross-examiners seldom do. It is a basic rule to never ask an open-ended question because it gives the witness an opportunity to explain. But Katzmann knew his victim. So he asked Sacco, "Tell us what you believe." In effect, explain why you think the United States is not a great country. Tell us why you are a revolutionary.

And Sacco did. He gave a lengthy response in broken English, speaking nonstop about how the United States exploited the working man, how the poor are excluded from society, and how the war was a capitalist war. He said that the United States government was criminal because it imprisons, without cause, socialists and anarchists. He concluded, "That is why I destroy governments, boys. That is why my idea I love socialists."[28]

It was a rousing speech for a radical audience, but not for a patriotic American jury in 1921. Some observers concluded that this speech, given in response to a grossly improper question, sent Sacco and Vanzetti to the chair. Katzmann's cross-examination and Judge Thayer's tolerance of it led them to believe that Sacco and Vanzetti were convicted not for what they did, but for what they believed.

Still, Katzmann was not satisfied. He engaged in a long series of argumentative questions refuting Sacco's views, insisting that his complaints about life in the United States showed ignorance. Katzmann, the patriotic American, was educating Sacco, the anarchistic, ungrateful alien.[29]

The defense repeatedly objected on grounds of lack of relevance and of prejudice. Judge Thayer overruled all objections. His explanation was that the defense was claiming that hiding anarchistic literature had been done "in the interest of the United States." This claim opened the door to prosecution rebuttal by showing that protecting the United States was not the defendants' motive for lying when arrested. The defense, however, never made such a claim. A reading of the transcript makes it perfectly clear that the defendants actually claimed they lied from their fear that they would be prosecuted for *not* registering for the draft, for being anarchists, and for possessing radical literature. It is inconceivable that Thayer did not understand

---

28. Transcript, Vol. II, 1875–7; Jackson, *The Black Flag*, 41–43.
29. Transcript, Vol. II, 1877–84; Jackson, *The Black Flag*, 43–47; Frankfurter, *The Case of Sacco and Vanzetti*, 53–57.

the defense theory especially since it was repeatedly pointed out to him by attorneys Moore and McAnarney. In spite of the defects in Thayer's rationale, the Commonwealth, when faced with the danger of a reversal on a postconviction motion for a new trial, adopted his position, asserting in their brief to the Supreme Judicial Court that:

> the presiding judge could do no less than to give the District Attorney full opportunity and latitude to develop this field of inquiry to see whether Sacco's radical views and radical actions were real or feigned to meet this serious inference of guilt that arose from his falsehoods.[30]

No reasonable person reading the transcript of Katzmann's cross-examination could credit this justification. Katzmann never made any attempt to undermine the accused's claim of anarchism. Instead, he not only adopted their confession but exploited it. This episode alone should have been enough for a reversal of the defendants' conviction.

One can imagine how Katzmann's emphasis on the radicalism of the defendants affected the jurors. The prejudice was emphasized when Judge Thayer instructed the jury at the end of the trial:

> The Commonwealth of Massachusetts called upon you to render a most important service. Although you knew that such service would be arduous, painful, and tiresome, yet you, like the true soldier, responded to that call in the spirit of supreme American loyalty. There is no better word in the English language than "loyalty."[31]

Another change in criminal procedure adopted after 1921 would have dramatically affected the third piece of the prosecution's case. Today, the prosecution is required to deliver to the defense any documents, statements, or information that would tend to exonerate the

---

30. Brief for Commonwealth on first appeal before the Massachusetts Supreme Judicial Court at 72. Frankfurter, *The Case of Sacco and Vanzetti*, 61.
31. Transcript, Vol. II, 2239; Frankfurter, *The Case of Sacco and Vanzetti*, 64–65; Russell, *Tragedy at Dedham*, 207.

The riot squad of the Boston Police Department guards the
Norfolk County Courthouse, at Dedham, Massachusetts,
during the hearing of a motion for a new trial.
© Underwood & Underwood/CORBIS

accused. Under the adversary system, investigative material gathered in preparation for litigation need not be disclosed to the other side. The attitude is "do your own investigation, get your own witness statements, don't compensate for your laziness by trying to poke around in my litigation file. But the role of the public prosecutor has in theory always been different. The American Bar Association Canon of Ethics has always made clear that "the suppression of facts or the secreting of witnesses capable of establishing the innocence of the accused is highly reprehensible."[32]

A modern offshoot of this principle requires prosecution disclosure to the defense of any potentially exculpatory evidence it has uncovered.[33] If that principle had been the law in 1921, Katzmann would have had to inform the defense that a police expert had rejected

---

32. American Bar Association Canons of Professional Ethics, "Canon 5: The Defense or Prosecution of Those Accused of a Crime" (1908); Kurcias, "Prosecutor's Duty to Disclose Exculpatory Evidence," 1205.
33. Brady v. Maryland, 373 U.S. 83 (1963) holding that it is a violation of due process for the prosecution to fail to disclose material exculpatory evidence to the defense. See Tejada, *In Search of Sacco and Vanzetti*, 309 for a list of the exculpatory evidence that the prosecution failed to disclose to Sacco and Vanzetti.

his theory that the .32-caliber bullet that killed Berardelli came from Sacco's gun.

Captain William Proctor was head of the state police; prior to that he had been in the Department of Public Safety for twenty-three years. He had testified as a ballistics expert in over a hundred capital cases. In preparing for trial, Proctor test-fired Sacco's gun, made comparisons, and reported to Katzmann that there was no evidence of a match between the .32-caliber bullet from Berardelli's body and Sacco's .32-caliber pistol. This information was uncovered after the trial. If it was disclosed earlier, Captain Proctor would almost certainly have become a formidable defense witness.

In 1921, Proctor's ballistic findings may not have been required to be disclosed. But at the trial, Katzmann not only failed to note Proctor's reservations, he also prearranged that Proctor would answer a carefully worded question in a way that would avoid perjury but still convey the impression that there was a match between the fatal bullet and Sacco's gun.

Katzmann called Proctor as his witness, elicited his qualifications, a description of the ballistics tests Proctor had done, and then inquired:

Q: Have you an opinion as to whether Bullet III [the fatal bullet] was fired from the Colt automatic which is in evidence? [Sacco's gun]

A: I have.

Q: And what is your opinion?

A: My opinion is that it is consistent with being fired by that pistol.[34]

Proctor's statement was literally correct. It was also meaningless and added nothing to the evidence. He said only that since Sacco

---

34. Jackson, *The Black Flag*, 23; Watson, *Sacco and Vanzetti*, 127.

had a .32-caliber Colt pistol, a .32-caliber bullet might have come from it. The fact that it could have come from any *other* gun that fires .32-caliber bullets was deliberately left unsaid.

Everyone in the courtroom took Proctor's testimony to mean that he had found a match between the bullet that killed Berardelli and Sacco's gun. And in his summation, Katzmann boldly argued that Proctor had found a match. Moore did not use cross-examination to expose the ambiguity of Proctor's words. In all probability, he was concerned that if he asked Proctor what he meant by "consistent with," Proctor would have expanded at great length on why he was sure that the fatal bullet had come from Sacco's gun. Worst of all, Judge Thayer, in his summary of the evidence, reminded the jury that Proctor had given his opinion that it was Sacco's pistol that fired the bullet that caused the death of Berardelli.[35]

In an affidavit after the trial, Proctor acknowledged the arrangement he had made with Katzmann:

At the trial the District Attorney did not ask me whether I had found any evidence that the so-called mortal bullet passed through Sacco's pistol, nor was I asked that question on cross-examination. The District Attorney desired to ask me that question, but I had repeatedly told him that if he did I should be obliged to answer in the negative. . . . Bullet Number III, in my judgment, passed through some Colt automatic pistol, but I do not intend to imply that I had found any evidence that the so-called mortal bullet had passed through this particular pistol and the District Attorney well knew that I did not so intend and framed his question accordingly. Had I been asked the direct question: whether I had found any affirmative evidence whatever that this so-called mortal bullet had passed through this particular Sacco's pistol, I should have answered then, as I do now without hesitation, in the negative."[36]

35. Transcript, Vol. II, 2254; Frankfurter, *The Case of Sacco and Vaznetti*, 77.
36. Russell, *The Case Resolved*, 146; Tejada, *In Search of Sacco and Vanzetti*, 201–2; Frankfurter, *The Case of Sacco and Vanzetti*, 76–89.

In his response under oath, Katzmann did not deny the content of Proctor's affidavit except to say that he had not *repeatedly* asked Proctor whether he had found any evidence that the mortal bullet had passed through the Sacco pistol.

This points to yet another error that should have resulted in a reversal of the convictions, and would be another instance of prosecutorial abuse in knowingly utilizing false evidence to mislead the jury.

When the evidence of the Proctor-Katzmann deception was presented to Thayer in the postconviction motion for a new trial, he found the incident to be harmless. He reached this conclusion in an opinion that misconstrued the content of the Proctor affidavit. Thayer found that the questions put to Proctor were clear and must have been understood by him. Of course the questions were clear and were clearly understood by Proctor; that was the point of his affidavit. He knew the questions and answers would be prearranged and that by this subterfuge the court and the jury were intentionally misled.

Thayer simply ignored the illegal prearrangement and maintained that if Proctor had wanted to explicitly state that there was no evidence that the bullet came from Sacco's gun, he should have said so at trial. Again, the judge missed the point. Proctor did not want to say it. Rather, he wanted to help the prosecution, and with Katzmann's help they found a way to mislead the jury without explicitly lying. The judge went on to say that "It is not the duty of the court in charging a jury to deal with the weight of and probative effect of testimony of witnesses."[37] True enough. But it was his duty when describing evidence to do it accurately. Instead, he specifically said that Proctor's testimony was that the fatal bullet did come from Sacco's gun.

On July 14, 1921, the case of *Commonwealth v. Sacco and Vanzetti* went to the jury. At 7:30 in the evening that same day, after only a few hours of deliberation, the jury returned its verdict. Sacco and Vanzetti were found guilty of murder in the first degree. Before sentencing, the defendants were asked if they wanted to make a statement. Vanzetti said they were innocent. Then, looking toward the prosecution, he said:

---

37. Frankfurter, *The Case of Sacco and Vanzetti*, 82–88.

We were tried during a time . . . when there was a hysteria of resentment and hate against the people of our principles, against the foreigner, against slackers, and it seems to me- -rather, I am positive of it, that both you and Mr. Katzmann have done all what it were in your power . . . to agitate still more the passion of the juror, the prejudice of the juror, against us."[38]

Judge Thayer sentenced Sacco and Vanzetti to die in the electric chair. Protests erupted in Italy and South America. The American Ambassador's house in Paris was bombed. Judge Thayer received threatening letters and his house was put under guard.

For the next six years, the defense team submitted more than a half dozen motions for a new trial based on newly discovered evidence uncovered by Moore, McAnarney, and an addition to the defense team, William Thompson, a highly regarded, conservative Boston lawyer. The applications included evidence that Walter Ripley, the jury foreman, had brought bullets from his own pistol into the jury room to try to help the other jurors understand the ballistics testimony. This would be clear error since the jurors are required to consider only evidence brought out in open court under oath and subject to cross-examination. Also included in this application was evidence that before he had become a juror, Ripley had said, in conversation with a friend, that even if they were innocent, Sacco and Vanzetti should be "hanged anyway."[39]

This was followed by the so-called Gould motion. Present at the scene of the robbery and murders, Ray Gould claimed that he was shot at by one of the gunmen; that he was within five feet of the bandit car, and that when he was taken to see Sacco and Vanzetti in the lineup, neither one was in the automobile. He had given his name to the police but had not been contacted, and the defense had been unable to find him until after the trial.

---

38. Russell, *Tragedy in Dedham*, 360.
39. Watson, *Sacco and Vanzetti*, 261–2.

A number of motions with new information from prosecution eyewitnesses who had testified at the trial were also filed. Pelser retracted his identification of the accused, saying he was drunk and out of work when he first spoke to Katzmann. Lola Andrews, another prosecution witness, who had claimed to have seen Sacco working on a car at the crime scene, retracted her testimony in an affidavit. Then, within days after consulting with Katzmann, both Pelser and Andrews withdrew their retractions and claimed coercion by Moore. Prosecution eyewitness Carlos Goodridge was shown to have a criminal record and to have testified under a false name. His wife stated that he had said that "all the Italians coming over on the ships to America ought to be sunk in the harbors."[40] Then came an affidavit by Albert Hamilton, a ballistics expert and criminologist. He used a high-powered microscope to determine that there was no connection between the bullets used at the shooting and Sacco's Colt pistol. All these applications were denied by Judge Thayer. Except for the Proctor application, Thayer was perhaps correct in denying a new trial since much of this evidence was either redundant or inconclusive.

Then came a striking development. The defense discovered substantive new evidence that Sacco and Vanzetti were innocent of the charges. Confined in the same prison as Sacco was a young Portuguese man, Celestino Madeiros. While Madeiros's appeal from a murder conviction was pending, he sent Sacco the following note: "I hear by confess to being in the South Braintree shoe company crime and Sacco and Vanzetti was not in said crime."[41]

Sacco relayed this information to his lawyers and Medeiros gave an affidavit. His story was that in 1920, when he was eighteen, he had been part of an Italian gang that robbed freight cars in Providence. Some of the gang members asked him to participate in a payroll robbery in Braintree on April 15, 1920, and he did. His role, he said, was to wait in the back of the car with a revolver, along with a "light skinned man" (clearly not Vanzetti) who was the driver, while two other men stole the money and committed the murders. Defense

---

40. Ibid., 204.
41. Jackson, *The Black Flag*, 56.

Attorney Thompson was able to corroborate much of Madeiros's story. The car the gang used was a Buick—the same vehicle a witness at the trial had identified as the getaway car. There was a gang in the area at that time that fit Madeiros's description. The leader, Joe Morelli, physically resembled Sacco.

Madeiros was clear that he would not name his associates but would fully describe all other aspects of the crime. The details he provided fit the facts of the Braintree crime. More importantly, this information provided answers to some of the questions of the Sacco and Vanzetti prosecution, such as what happened to the money, who were the five men in the car, what was their motive, and what accounted for all the bullets found in the victims' bodies that did not match the pistols of Sacco or Vanzetti. At the time of the Braintree crimes, the Morellis were under indictment for stealing shoe consignments from Slater and Morrill, a South Braintree company. They were out of jail awaiting trial and badly needed money for their defense. Madeiros refused to name the gang members who were with him but said there were five men including himself in the murder car; three were Italian, while the driver was either from Poland or Finland. Joe Morelli had a .32-caliber Colt. Another man described by Madeiros had a pistol whose bullets matched the other bullets found in the victims. Gang member Mike Morelli was known to drive a Buick that disappeared immediately after April 15, 1920. Also, shortly after that, Madeiros had about $2,800 in the bank, which he used for a vacation in Mexico. This money may have been his one-fifth share of the payroll robbery, which totaled $15,776.51. The police in New Bedford, where the Morelli gang operated, suspected them of the Braintree crimes, but dropped their investigation after the arrest of Sacco and Vanzetti.

The confession of a prisoner like Madeiros who was facing the death penalty would normally be treated with suspicion; after all, he has nothing to lose. But in this case he did. An appeal from his murder conviction was pending and was ultimately successful in getting him a new trial. Nothing could have been more harmful to his effort to reverse his conviction than to admit guilt in another murder.

In light of the valuable information acquired in Thompson's investigation, it appeared more likely that the Morelli gang and not Sacco and Vanzetti had committed the robbery and murders. The Madeiros-Morelli scenario accounts for all five involved in the crime, while the Sacco and Vanzetti prosecution accounted for only two. The Morelli story accounts for all bullets found in the dead men: the Sacco-Vanzetti prosecution accounts for only one of six. The Morelli story provides the motive: a desperate need of money to provide for their legal expenses. The Sacco-Vanzetti prosecution never provided a credible motive for their involvement. The Morelli story accounts for Madeiros's possession of $2,800, his share of the stolen proceeds of the robbery; the prosecution never traced any of the stolen money to Sacco, Vanzetti, or anyone else. The Morelli story involves professional, experienced thieves who stole cars and had made prior daylight robberies, whereas the prosecution's unlikely premise was that Sacco and Vanzetti, who had never been arrested before, had robbed and killed and then while flush with nearly $16,000 found themselves wandering the streets trying to borrow a friend's automobile, riding a public streetcar and, although fully armed, surrendering meekly to a single police officer.[42]

The jury had none of the facts of the Madeiros-Morelli connection when it decided that Sacco and Vanzetti were guilty. In asking for a new trial, Thompson presented Thayer with affidavits given by Madeiros and a deposition of a hundred pages, which included cross-examination by the district attorney.

Here then was the third convincing reason for a new trial following the episodes of Katzmann's prejudicial cross-examination and the Proctor-Katzmann legal trickery. Taken together or individually, each was material fit for consideration by a second jury. But it was not to be.

---

42. Thompson presented these comparisons to the Supreme Judicial Court. Transcript, Vol. V, 4791–3; Brief of William G. Thompson and Herbert B. Ehrmann on behalf of defendants in Commonwealth v. Sacco and Vanzetti, January, 1927; Watson, *Sacco and Vanzetti*, 285–6; Frankfurter, *The Case of Sacco and Vanzetti*, Appendix A.

On October 23, 1926, Judge Thayer filed a fifty-five-page decision finding Madeiros not believable. The judge called him, "Without a doubt a crook, a thief, a robber, a liar." His decision read:

> I am forced to the conclusion that the affidavit of Madeiros is unreliable, untrustworthy and untrue. To set aside the verdict of a jury affirmed by the Supreme Judicial Court of this Commonwealth on such an affidavit would be a mockery upon truth and justice. Therefore . . . this motion is hereby denied.[43]

Thayer intimated, without any proof in the record, that the Sacco and Vanzetti Defense Committee may have bribed Madeiros. He said, "Is it not quite likely that Madeiros desired, before he made his confession, to ascertain whether or not this large [legal aid fund] had been raised . . . and was given to understand that he would receive the same aid if he had the power of this organization behind him?"[44]

A massive disappointment to the accused and their defense team, Thayer's opinion also received condemnation from a variety of sources. Harvard law professor Felix Frankfurter, who would eventually sit on the nation's highest court, had this to say:

> By what is left out and by what is put in, the uninformed reader of Judge Thayer's opinion would be wholly misled as to the real facts of the case. Speaking from a considerable experience as a prosecuting officer, whose special task for a time it was to sustain on appeal convictions for the Government, and whose scientific duties since have led to the examination of a great number of records and the opinions based thereon, I assert with deep regret, but without the slightest fear of disproof, that certainly in modern times Judge Thayer's opinion stands unmatched, happily, for discrepancies between what the record discloses and what the opinion conveys. His 25,000-word document cannot accurately be described oth-

---

43. Transcript, Vol. V, 4726–7, 4748; Watson, *Sacco and Vanzetti*, 280–1.
44. Transcript, Vol. V, 4745; Tejada, *In Search of Sacco and Vanzetti*, 217.

erwise than as a farrago of misquotations, misrepresentations, suppressions and mutilations.[45]

The well-known psychologist Dr. Morton Prince wrote that any psychologist reading the Thayer opinion "could not fail to find evidences that portray strong personal feeling, poorly concealed, that have no place in a judicial document."[46]

The accumulation of disturbing facts revealed after the Sacco-Vanzzeti convictions began to influence public opinion even among those who had believed that the accused should be executed. Two developments contributed to this change. The first came in a *Boston Herald* editorial. The *Herald* had long maintained that Sacco and Vanzetti had been given a fair trial, that the verdict was correct, and that additional delays in the executions were unjustified concessions to domestic and foreign radicals and leftist liberals. That opinion was shared by most Massachusetts newspapers. But three days after Thayer's opinion was released, the *Herald* shocked its readers by changing its position and called for a new trial. The now famous Pulitzer Prize winning editorial by F. Lauriston Bullard entitled "We Submit" read as follows:

> In our opinion Nicola Sacco and Bartolomeo Vanzetti ought not to be executed on the warrant of the verdict returned by a jury on July 14, 1920. We do not know whether these men are guilty or not. We have no sympathy with the half-baked views which they profess. But as months have merged into years and the great debate over this case has continued, our doubts have solidified slowly into convictions, and reluctantly we have found ourselves compelled to reverse our original judgment. We hope the Supreme Judicial Court will grant a new trial on the basis of new evidence not yet examined in open court. We hope the Governor will grant another reprieve to Celestino Madeiros so that his confession may be canvassed

---

45. Frankfurter, *The Case of Sacco and Vanzetti*, 104.
46. Ibid., 105.

in open court. . . . We have read the full decision in which Judge Webster Thayer, who presided at the original trial, renders his decision against the application for a new trial, and we submit that it carries the tone of the advocate rather than the arbitrator. At the outset he refers to "the verdict of a jury approved by the Supreme Court of this Commonwealth" and later he repeats that sentence. We respectfully submit that the Supreme Court never approved that verdict. What the Court did is stated in its own words thus: "We have examined carefully all the exceptions in so far as argued, and finding no error the verdicts are to stand." The Court certified that, whether the verdict was right or wrong, the trial judge performed his duty under the law in a legal manner. The Supreme Court overruled a bill of exceptions but expressed no judgment whatever as to the validity or the guilt of the defendants. Judge Thayer knows this.[47]

The second development was the publication of Felix Frankfurter's article, "The Case of Sacco and Vanzetti" published in the March 1926 issue of the *Atlantic Monthly*. The article that criticized the witnesses, the trial, the verdict and the Massachusetts judiciary, reached a nationwide audience. As the historian Francis Russell wrote:

> The stirrings in Europe, mutterings in New England had now become articulate. Frankfurter's article was like a lighted fuse leading to a powder magazine. Sacco and Vanzetti became familiar names in all forty-eight states, not just among urban left–liberals but in the suburbs and the small towns and women's clubs and little brick Carnegie libraries.[48]

For most of those who read it, Frankfurter's attack was their first factual introduction to the background of a case they had heard about

---

47. Russell, *Tragedy in Dedham*, 3343–4; Jackson, *The Black Flag*, 61–62; Watson, *Sacco and Vanzetti*, 281–2.
48. Russell, *Tragedy in Dedham*, 352–3.

only vaguely. Deftly and concisely, Frankfurter explained how the two men had been arrested, discussed the method of selecting the jury, Katzmann's harrying cross-examination of Sacco, Judge Thayer's rhetoric, and the later discrediting of witnesses.[49]

All Thayer decisions during the trial and his denials of a new trial were put before the Supreme Judicial Court, the highest appellate court in Massachusetts, in two appeals. In both instances the Court affirmed all his decisions.[50] How was that possible? The answer is that the Court lacked the power to reverse. Unfortunately for the accused, in 1920's Massachusetts, the scope of permissible appellate review was extremely narrow, narrower than in other states and narrower than it was before or afterwards in Massachusetts. The Court was not allowed to review the facts or to decide if the verdict was supported by the evidence or whether, in the interests of justice, newly discovered evidence required a new trial. The power of the Court was confined to a review of only two matters. It could reverse for a serious error of pure law or for an "abuse of discretion" by the trial court.

The Court deemed all controversial decisions of Judge Thayer to be within his discretion. An appellate finding of "abuse of discretion" was almost unthinkable in the twenties. Abuse of discretion in Massachusetts would require an appellate ruling that Thayer was incompetent, almost akin to saying the trial judge was unfit for office.

The standard of review announced by the appellate court in all Sacco-Vanzetti appeals was stated this way:

> The question is not whether we should take a different view of the evidence or should have made an opposite decision from that made by the trial judge. To sustain these exceptions it is necessary to decide that no conscientious judge acting intelligently could honestly have taken the view expressed by him.[51]

49. Ibid.

50. Commonwealth v. Sacco, 255 Mass. 369 (1926) and 259 Mass. 128 (1927).

51. The standard applied by the court in Comm. v. Sacco is taken from a civil case, Davis v. Boston Elevated Railway, 235 Mass. 482, 502 (1920); Jackson, *The Black Flag*, 178–9 (Report to Governor 1 (c) notes that "Both the language and purpose of this standard of review indicate that little short of proof of sheer incompetence or corruption would have persuaded the Supreme Judicial Court to reverse matters it considered discretionary."

The full extent of the limited power of the Supreme Judicial Court of Massachusetts was revealed in its affirmation of the denial of a new trial in the Madeiros matter: "It is not imperative that a new trial be granted even though evidence is discovered and if presented to the jury would justify a different result."[52]

Or as the *New York Times* described the action of the court: "The judge [Thayer] had the right to rule as he did but the Supreme Court did not deny the validity of the new evidence."[53]

The combination of the Supreme Court's generous description of what falls under the discretion of the trial judge, combined with its narrow definition of what constitutes abuse of that discretion, along with the rule that all new trial motions must be submitted to the judge who presided at the trial, guaranteed that Thayer would be protected from reversal.[54]

In effect, the legal rules in Massachusetts in the 1920s placed enormous power in a single individual—in this case, in Judge Webster Thayer. Driven by a strong sense of duty, he believed that a large part of that duty was to protect his country against alien and radical forces. Indications of this concern were seen before, during and after the Sacco-Vanzetti trial. Thayer asked the chief justice to assign him to their trial, a departure from judicial decorum that suggested an interest in the outcome.[55] Nine days after the Braintree robbery and murder, he presided over the trial of a defendant charged with violating the criminal anarchy statute. When the jury returned a verdict of acquittal, Thayer rebuked them, saying "How could you arrive at such a verdict? Did you not hear that he told the police officers who testified that he believed in bolshevism and that our

52. Watson, *Sacco and Vanzetti*, 289. The author describes this statement as one that "reads" like the trial scene in *Alice in Wonderland.*"
53. Louis Stark, "What Seven Years of Legal Struggle Have Developed," *New York Times*, April 17, 1927.
54. Joughin and Morgan, *The Legacy of Sacco and Vanzetti*, 177 states that "the most vulnerable spot in all the proceedings lay on the function and power of the trial judge in dealing with the motions for a new trial. . . . If the appellate tribunal had been clothed with the duty and authority to examine the whole case and to order a new trial for any reason that justice may require, these defendants would certainly have a had another trial." See also Tejada, *In Search of Sacco and Vanzetti*, 287.
55. Jackson, *The Black Flag*, 192.

government should be overthrown? Didn't you consider the testimony given by the police officers when you were deliberating?" The foreman responded that the jurors had concluded that a person who merely expressed his opinion but did not engage in violence was not guilty under the statute.[56]

Judge Thayer's bias against the defendants was no secret. Over the course of the trial and the six-year appeal process, he was heard making prejudicial comments about Sacco and Vanzetti. The humorist Robert Benchley stated that Thayer had told a friend of his at a Worcester golf club that "A bunch of parlor radicals are trying to get those Italian bastards off. I'll see them hanged and I'd like to hang a few dozen of the radicals too."[57] In November 1924, after having denied the first of the defense appeals, Thayer remarked to a friend, a professor at Dartmouth College: "Did you see what I did with those anarchistic bastards the other day? I guess that will hold them for a while. . . . Let them go to the Supreme Court now and see what they can get out of them."[58] *Boston Globe* reporter Frank Sibley reported hearing Thayer refer to Sacco and Vanzetti as "damn fools." He was reputed to have called Sacco and Vanzetti "bolsheviki" who were "trying to intimidate me." About Defense Attorney Moore, Thayer said, "I'll show them that no long-haired anarchist from California can run this court."[59]

These statements were included in a motion for a new trial on the ground that Thayer was prejudiced. As the rules required, they were heard by Thayer, who refused to withdraw or reassign the motion, which he then denied on procedural grounds.

Governor Fuller gave the accused one last hope. He appointed a three-man advisory committee to review all aspects of the Sacco-Vanzetti case. The chair was Abbott Lawrence Lowell, president of Harvard University, a tenth-generation descendant of a distinguished New England family. Also on the committee was Robert Grant, a

56. Jackson, *The Black Flag*, 192, 196; "Judge Scores Jurymen for Freeing 'Red'," *Boston Herald*, April 24, 1920, 1; Watson, *Sacco and Vanzetti*, 1117–8.
57. Jackson, *The Black Flag*, 73.
58. Jackson, *The Black Flag*, 72; Watson, *Sacco and Vanzetti*, 252.
59. Watson, *Sacco and Vanzetti*, 115; Grant and Katz, *The Great Trials of the Twenties*, 48.

retired probate judge, and Samuel Stratton, president of the Massachusetts Institute of Technology. Lowell was later characterized by Harvard law professor Alan Dershowitz as "an anti-Italian bigot and an avowed racist who introduced racial and religious quotas at Harvard" and "who was anything but objective on a matter pitting the fairness of Brahmin justice against the claims of Italian radicals."[60] Lowell's background included anti-union activity and energetic lobbying for anti-immigration laws and national origin quotas, which severely limited immigration from southern European countries.

Lowell's committee found no fault with any aspect of the Sacco-Vanzetti trial. Acknowledging that some of Judge Thayer's out-of-court comments were "a grave breach of official decorum," the committee maintained that they "had no effect on his conduct of the trial or the opinion of the jury." Based on this report and on his own investigation, Governor Fuller concluded: "I believe, with the jury, that these men, Sacco and Vanzetti, were guilty, and that they had a fair trial. I further believe that there was no justifiable reason for giving them a new trial."[61]

The governor's announcement was followed by demonstrations outside American embassies all around the world. Last minute appeals for clemency were denied and the six-and-a-half-year battle on the defendants' behalf was over.

Sacco and Vanzetti were executed on August 23, 1927. Both men were led to the death chamber, and as the prison guard strapped Sacco into the chair, Sacco cried, "Long live anarchy!" Vanzetti shook the warden's hand and thanked him warmly for all he had done. Then he turned to the witnesses present and spoke his final words: "I wish to forgive some people for what they are now doing to me." On their death certificates, their cause of death was listed as "Judicial Homicide," an unintentionally ironic but perhaps apt description.

The responses to the executions were immediate and violent. For the next two days, angry crowds picketed the Boston State house. Over 150 people were arrested, among them, the author John Dos

---

60. Dershowitz, *America on Trial*, 252.
61. Transcript, Vol. V, 5378h; Jackson, *The Black Flag*, 76.

Demonstration at Union Square.
© CORBIS

Passos and the poet Edna St. Vincent Millay. At the same time, riots erupted in Paris, London, and Buenos Aires. A hundred thousand people appeared at Sacco and Vanzetti's funeral on August 28. Sacco and Vanzetti were hailed as martyrs. For at least seven years after their execution, August 23 was celebrated as a kind of Memorial Day for anarchists. Gatherings in Sacco and Vanzetti's honor were held in the United States, Europe, Russia, and as far away as Vietnam. In 1932, Judge Thayer's home was destroyed by a bomb. The legacy of the case continued to grow. As the critic Edmund Wilson wrote: "[The Sacco-Vanzetti case] revealed the whole anatomy of American life, with all its classes, professions, and points of view, and all their relations, and it raised almost every fundamental question of our political and social system. It did this, furthermore, in an unexpectedly dramatic fashion."[62]

---

62. "Boston Besieged, Scores Arrested," *New York Times,* August 23, 1927.

The extreme limitations on the power of the Supreme Judicial Court have been abandoned. In 1939, the Massachusetts legislature provided that in a capital case, the Supreme Judicial Court must review both the law and the evidence and may order a new trial or direct the entry of a verdict of a lesser degree of guilt "if the verdict was against the law or the weight of the evidence or because of newly discovered evidence, or for any other reason that justice may require."[63]

In 1977, fifty years after the Lowell committee exonerated the Sacco-Vanzetti proceedings from any suggestion of unfairness, Massachusetts governor Michael Dukakis, asked his chief legal counsel, Daniel A. Taylor, to study the case and determine whether there were substantial grounds for believing that Sacco and Vanzetti were unfairly convicted and executed.

Taylor's "Report to the Governor in the Matter of Sacco and Vanzetti" concluded "that there are substantial, indeed compelling, grounds for believing that the Sacco and Vanzetti legal proceedings were permeated with unfairness."[64]

The supporting memorandum to the report describes a long list of prosecutorial abuses. Included under this heading was the Proctor-Katzmann subterfuge, which "had an immense impact on the trial's outcome." The report assailed the use of unfair and misleading evidence in the presentation of eyewitnesses who, without viewing a lineup, gave testimony influenced by suggestive techniques such as jailhouse visits that required defendants to assume the crouching and shooting positions of bandits. Also condemned was the withholding of exculpatory evidence, including not revealing the names of eyewitnesses who had clear views of the bandits and who indicated that Sacco and Vanzetti were not among them, and a Justice Department finding supplied to the prosecution that there was no evidence that the defendants or their associates had any funds that came from the Braintree robbery.

---

63. Jackson, note 1 at 181–182; Mass Gen Laws c. 278, Sec. 33E (1939); *Commwealth v. Cox*, 327 Mass. 609, 614 (1951).
64. M.G.L.c 278 33E; Joughin and Morgan, *The Legacy of Sacco and Vanzetti*, 177; Jackson, *The Black Flag*, 178–80.

The report noted the prosecution failure to investigate new exculpatory evidence concerning the Madeiros confession and the involvement of the Morelli gang. Added to the list of abuses was the appeal to the jury's prejudices. Katzmann's cross-examination of Sacco and his distortion of the defendant's political beliefs and avoidance of the draft were singled out as particularly troubling. And the Taylor report repeatedly enumerated the ethical standards that were violated by the prosecution and the judicial abuses by Thayer.

Most important, the Taylor report reviewed the disputed nature of the eyewitness testimony, the ballistics evidence, and the so-called consciousness of guilt actions. It found that serious questions remained as to whether guilt was proven beyond a reasonable doubt. And the report admitted that the limitations on the scope of judicial review of capital cases in the 1920s placed too much discretion in the hands of one trial judge.[65]

Based on the Taylor report, Governor Dukakis issued his proclamation declaring that any stigma or disgrace should be forever removed from the names of Nicola Sacco and Bartolomeo Vanzetti. Dukakis did not issue a pardon because doing so would suggest guilt. He did not declare the defendants innocent, only that they had been unfairly convicted and executed.

Uncertainty about Sacco and Vanzetti's guilt remains. New ballistics tests, conducted with modern equipment, were done in 1944, 1961, 1982, and 1983. The results of these were inconclusive. Some of the tests showed that the third bullet from Sacco's Colt revolver may have killed the guard, Berardelli. But other experts believe that a substitution of bullets had taken place, citing the comment in 1937 made by a sergeant on the Boston police force to a *Boston Globe* reporter: "We switched the murder weapon . . . we suspected the other side of switching weapons so we switched ours."[66]

Commentators have noted a final irony in this case. Sacco and Vanzetti, who may have been murderers, are still celebrated in proclamations, memorials, literature, and film. Their statements made in

---

65. Ibid., 177–8.
66. Tejada, *In Search of Sacco and Vanzetti*, 294.

court and after their convictions now appear in anthologies of great American speeches, alongside the words of Abraham Lincoln and Franklin D. Roosevelt; almost everyone else connected with the case has ended up with a tarnished reputation.

Judge Thayer is viewed as biased. Prosecutor Katzmann is seen as effective but unethical, and Governor Fuller is regarded as lacking the courage to make an unpopular political decision.

Not even A. Lawrence Lowell, the president of Harvard, escaped blame. For a time, Harvard was ridiculed as a "hangman's house." The comment by the syndicated newspaper columnist Heywood Broun was widely circulated: "What more can the immigrants from Italy expect? It is not every prisoner who has a President of Harvard throw the switch for him." [67]

---

67. Grant and Katz, *The Great Trials of the Twenties*, 49; Watson, *Sacco and Vanzetti*, 327.

TWO

Leopold and Loeb: Crime of the Century[1]

1. This chapter relies heavily on trial transcripts contained in secondary sources including accounts of the Leopold-Loeb trial in Hal Higdon, *Leopold and Loeb: The Crime of the Century* (G.P. Putnam and Sons, 1975); Alvin V. Sellers, *The Loeb-Leopold Case* (Clark Publishing Co., 1926); Maureen McKernan, *The Amazing Crime and Trial of Leopold and Loeb* (Notable Trials Library, 1989); Francis X. Busch, *Prisoners at the Bar* (Bobbs-Merrill Company Inc., 1952); Alan M. Dershowitz, *America on Trial: Inside the Legal Battles That Transformed Our Nation* (Warner Books, 2004); Simon Baatz, *For The Thrill of It: Leopold, Loeb, and the Murder That Shocked Jazz Age Chicago* (HarperCollins 2008); and Clarence Darrow, *The Story of My Life* (1932 reprinted in Bucaneer Books, 1992 and Da Capo 1996). Useful ideas and information were also provided by law review articles and Internet sources including Scott W. Howe, "Reassessing the Individualization Mandate in Capital Sentencing: Darrow's Defense of Leopold and Loeb," *Iowa Law Review* 79 (1994): 989; Paula S. Fass, "Making and Remaking an Event: The Leopold and Loeb Case in American Culture," *The Journal of American History* 80 (1993); J. Fordyce Wood, "The Loeb-Leopold Case (From the Standpoint of the Handwriting, Pen Printing, and Typewriting Expert)," *The American Journal of Police Science* 1 (1930): 339; Gerald F. Uelmen, "Symposium on Trials of the Century: Who Is the Lawyer of the Century?," *Loyola of Los Angeles Law Review* 33 (2000): 613; and Michael Hannon, "Leopold and Loeb Case," University of Minnesota Law Library (May 2010), http://darrow.law.umn.edu/trialpdfs/LEOPOLD_LOEB.pdf; Marilyn Bardsley, "Leopold and Loeb," Crime Library; Douglas Linder, "Famous American Trials: The Leopold and Loeb Trial: A Brief Account," http://law2.umkc.edu/faculty/projects/ftrials/leoploeb/Accountoftrial.html. Of particular value are verbatim transcripts of the final arguments of Clarence Darrow for the defense and of Robert E. Crowe for the prosecution contained in a book published by Wilson Publishing Company entitled *Attorney Clarence Darrow's Plea for Mercy and Prosecutor Robert E. Crowe's Demand for the Death Penalty in the Loeb-Leopold Case*, hereinafter "Transcript."

IT WAS CALLED THE CRIME of the century. The year was 1924. The place was Kenwood, a quiet Chicago suburb where many wealthy Jewish families lived. Nathan Leopold, nineteen years old, and Richard Loeb, aged eighteen, were the brilliant sons of two of Kenwood's richest families. Over a period of six months, these young men meticulously planned to commit the perfect murder. They did so, in their own words, for the "thrill" of it, and to embrace, as they understood it, Friedrich Nietzsche's philosophy of the superman. They hoped to prove that they were superior beings who were above the law and conventional rules of morality. But theirs could not be just any crime. It would have to be a murder. They planned to kidnap and kill one of their young neighbors, hide his body, and then demand and collect a ransom. The body would never be discovered. The crime would never be solved. Only they would know, and cherish, the fact that they had prevailed over ordinary human beings and the simpleminded legal system.[2]

It was more than a fantasy. On Wednesday, May 21, 1924, at five o'clock in the afternoon, Leopold and Loeb lured a fourteen-year-old boy, Bobby Franks, into their rented car. As he sat in the front seat, they clubbed him with a chisel, dragged him into the backseat, forced a cloth into his mouth, and let him suffocate and bleed to death on the floor of the car. They then drove to the Wolf Lake game preserve, a marshy area twenty miles south of Chicago. There they stripped Bobby naked, poured hydrochloric acid over his face and body to make identification difficult, and stuffed him into a concrete drainage culvert.[3] They threw away the chisel and cleaned the blood from the back of the car. That night they called the victim's parents, telling them that their son had been kidnapped but that he was alive and well. Using a fictitious name, they told Bobby Franks's parents to expect a ransom letter with instructions. The typed, special delivery letter arrived for Jacob Franks the next day:

---

2. Dershowitz, *America on Trial*, 257.
3. Linder, "Famous American Trials."

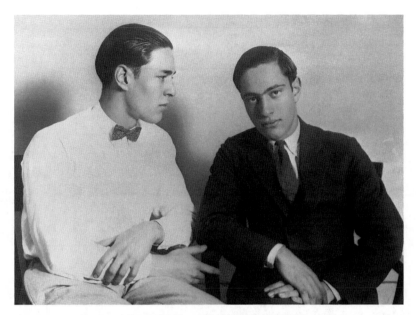

Richard Loeb (left) and Nathan Leopold (right).
© Bettmann/CORBIS

Dear Sir:

As you no doubt know by this time, your son has been kidnapped. Allow us to assure you that he is at present well and safe. You need fear no physical harm for him, provided you live up carefully to the following instructions and to such others as you will receive by future communications. Should you, however, disobey any of our instructions, even slightly, his death will be the penalty.[4]

The note ended with a demand for $10,000 in old bills and instructions on how the money was to be packaged. It also said that

4. Higdon, *Leopold and Loeb*, 41–42; Busch, *Prisoners at the Bar*, 148–9; McKernan, *The Amazing Crime and Trial of Leopold and Loeb*, 9–10; Sellers, *The Loeb-Leopold Case*, 12–13; Bardsley, "Leopold and Loeb."

the Franks should expect a telephone call with details on how the ransom should be delivered. It was signed "George Johnson."

Supermen are not supposed to make mistakes. Leopold and Loeb made many. Within ten days of the crime, they both confessed in elaborate detail. The public and the newspapers clamored for their quick trial and prompt execution. Execution in 1924 Illinois meant death on the gallows. The state's attorney who supervised the investigation and who would prosecute the case announced to the press, "I have a hanging case. The state is ready to go to trial immediately."[5]

At the time of the crime, the rights of the accused differed significantly from those of the accused today. Under current constitutional law, the police would have been required to advise the boys that they had the right to remain silent, that anything they did say could be used against them, and that they had the right to have a lawyer present during any interrogation. No such constitutional rights existed in 1924.[6] Leopold and Loeb were denied access to their families and to their lawyers until the state's attorney had finished amassing evidence against them. For two days after they confessed, without advice from defense counsel, the boys did themselves irreparable harm. They took the police around to locate evidence against them: where they discarded the murder weapon [the chisel], where they bought the hydrochloric acid, where to find the typewriter that was used to write the ransom letter, and where they had hidden the victim's bloody clothes. They were eager to broadcast their exploits to the police, to the reporters, to anyone who would listen. Loeb told the police captain "This will be the making of me. I'll spend a few years in jail and I'll be released. I'll come out to a new life."[7] Leopold told a reporter "Why, we even rehearsed the kidnapping at least three times, carrying it through in all its details, lacking only the boy we were to kidnap and kill. It was just an experiment. It was as easy for

---

5. Higdon, *Leopold and Loeb*, 112; Howe, "Reassessing the Individualization Mandate in Capital Sentencing," 997. A description of the meticulous planning of the murder and the completeness of the Leopold and Loeb confessions is described in Busch, *Prisoners at the Bar*, 154–60.
6. Miranda v. Arizona, 384 U.S. 436 (1966); Escobedo v. Illinois, 378 U.S. 478 (1964).
7. Higdon, *Leopold and Loeb*, 127.

us to justify as an entomologist in impaling a beetle on a pin."[8] The police took careful notes, and newspapers made hay with the story.

The state's attorney called it one of the most cold-blooded, cruel, and cowardly crimes ever committed. Prosecutors are not known for understatement. But the state's attorney was not merely bragging when he said, "We have the most conclusive evidence I have ever seen in a criminal case."[9]

Clarence Darrow was hired to defend these rich boys. Born in 1857 in Kinsman, Ohio, Darrow had already gained fame—and notoriety—for representing radicals in the labor movement and as a leading member of the American Civil Liberties Union. Leopold and Loeb and the Scopes "Monkey Trial" (1925) would make him a legend. Albert Loeb reportedly came to Darrow's house in the middle of the night and begged on behalf of his son and Leopold, "Get them a life sentence instead of death. That's all we ask . . . don't let them hang."[10]

For the public, the case was a sensation, a spectacle, and it dominated the national media for years. "The strangest and most baffling homicide in Chicago history" the Associated Press called it.[11] "The murder was a superlative crime," wrote the *Chicago Tribune*, "and it will be a superlative trial."[12] The paper even tried to get the trial broadcast live over its local radio station, but the public opposed doing so, because the sordid details were not appropriate for children.[13] The case eventually provided the content for four movies, *Compulsion* starring Orson Welles as Clarence Darrow, the Alfred Hitchcock movie *Rope,* and the more recent films *Murder by Numbers* and *Swoon.* Novels and at least half a dozen books have been written about it. Murders in Chicago in the 1920s were hardly unusual. Why such attention to this case? What was so special about it?

---

8. Higdon, *Leopold and Loeb,* 126; "Text of Loeb's Confession Putting Blame on Leopold," *Chicago Tribune,* June 8, 1924; Hannon, "Leopold and Loeb Case," 28.
9. Fass, "Making and Remaking an Event," 123.
10. Higdon, *Leopold and Loeb,* 123.
11. "Scion of Rich Man Murdered by Criminals," *South Bend Tribune,* May 23, 1924.
12. "Millions for Defense Trial to Rival Famous Thaw Case," *Chicago Tribune,* June 2, 1924.
13. Higdon, *Leopold and Loeb,* 158–9.

First, the case had the elements of Greek tragedy: hubris and the fall of the mighty. The wealth and social status of the defendants, their victim and their respective families provided great drama. Indeed, without the wealth of the parties, the *Leopold and Loeb* case would likely not have received much attention. It may not have had Clarence Darrow and the supportive testimony of psychiatrists. As wealth granted the defendants certain advantages, Darrow would argue, it also played a role in the emotional and mental disorders of Leopold and Loeb.

Second, the crime had no comprehensible motive. A random killing, it was every parent's nightmare. A child goes off to school and never returns. He is killed for no reason; his death is a frightening reminder of life's dangers. If it could happen here in this idyllic community, it could happen anywhere to anyone.

Third, the case had the addition of Darrow, the brilliant orator who agreed to defend the boys because he knew he would be speaking to a national audience. He also knew he would use it as his platform to address a favorite subject, his opposition to the death penalty.

And finally, the trial featured the presence of forensic psychiatrists, or alienists, as they were then called. Their testimony fueled a national debate on the causes of crime and personal responsibility.

The villains of this tragic drama were, of course, the two murderers: Nathan Leopold and Richard Loeb. Leopold, the son of a wealthy German Jewish émigré, was called a genius. He spoke at the age of four months. His IQ was so high it was not really measurable, although the Stanford-Binet test put it somewhere between 210 and 230. When he was sixteen years old, he had one of the finest collections of butterflies in the world. He was also a respected ornithologist who had written articles and several books on rare birds. Eight different departments in the federal government wrote to him for opinions. At age eighteen, he was the youngest person to graduate from the University of Chicago. He was fluent in five languages and read voraciously, especially philosophy, and in particular, the works of Friedrich Nietzsche. He identified with Nietzsche's concept of the "superman," the superior individual who existed outside the boundaries of the laws and codes of society to which "ordinary" men were bound.[14] Leopold had written to Loeb before the crime, "A Super-man . . . is, on account of certain superior qualities inherent within him, exempted from the ordinary laws which govern men. He is not liable for anything he may do."[15]

Richard Loeb's IQ was 160; he graduated from high school at four-teen and by the age of seventeen had graduated from the University of Michigan. Both young men were scheduled to enter Harvard Law School. But Loeb, unlike Leopold, was a charmer: handsome, outgo-ing, charismatic, a natural leader. However he was without moral sense and was the instigator of the idea of the perfect crime. Loeb domi-nated Leopold. There was testimony that they had a pact. Leopold agreed to engage in criminal acts to please Loeb. Loeb, in return, allowed Leopold to engage in occasional homosexual acts with him. As a defense psychiatrist would later report at the trial, "Their criminal activities were an outgrowth of a unique coming together of two peculiarly maladjusted adolescents, each of whom brought to the relationship a long standing background of abnormal life."[16]

And then there was the victim, four-teen-year-old Bobby Franks. The son of wealthy Kenwood parents, Bobby went to the Harvard School, the same well-regarded private school from which Loeb had graduated some years earlier. In fact, the Franks family knew the Loebs, and Bobby Franks sometimes played on the Loebs' tennis court.

Bobby Franks.
© Bettmann/CORBIS

14. Ibid., 19–20, 210; Hannon, "Leopold and Loeb Case," 5–6.
15. http://www.crimearchives.net/1924_leopold_loeb/html/bios.html.
16. Joint Psychiatrists Summary for the Defense described in Hannon, "Leopold and Loeb Case," 44.

The murderers chose to kill Bobby at the very last moment. They had planned everything in advance; only the identity of their victim had been left to chance. Even the ransom note had been prepared in advance, with the envelope waiting to be addressed. The salutation read simply "Dear Sir" because Leopold and Loeb had had no idea to whom they would be mailing their letter. So, on the day of the murder, Leopold was driving a car they had rented under an assumed name, with Loeb as his passenger, looking for someone to kidnap and kill. None of the possible prospects they had discussed were available. Then they saw Bobby Franks walking home from school. Bobby knew Loeb, so it was easy to entice him into the car. Bobby Franks was in the wrong place at the wrong time.

Was the *Leopold and Loeb* case really the crime of the century or the trial of the century? Probably not. The best one can say is that it is among the group of twenty or so great American cases of the 1900s. But one thing is clear. Of those great twentieth century cases, Clarence Darrow, the most prominent trial lawyer of his generation, participated in four of them, including the famous Scopes "Monkey Trial."

No lawyer of the twentieth century spoke as effectively to the social and historical context of the issues involved in the law. He influenced generations of the young to become lawyers. His exploits and oratory have been celebrated in many books, in films, and on Broadway.[17]

When Darrow was brought in to defend Leopold and Loeb, he was sixty-seven years old. He was a sophisticated attorney, well read in fields of literature, poetry, psychology, and philosophy. But his manner was that of a country lawyer. Although he began as a corporate attorney for the railroad, he quit that job at age thirty-seven and spent the rest of his life representing murderers, communists, socialists, and anarchists. Not for nothing was Darrow nicknamed "The attorney for the damned." Darrow liked to boast that none of his clients charged with murder had ever been executed. Would he still be able to say that after this case? Many thought it unlikely.

---

17. Michael Tigar quoted in Uelmen, "Symposium on Trials of the Century," 643.

The prosecutor was Robert Crowe, the state's attorney. A forty-five-year-old Irish politician, Crowe was ambitious, stubborn, and pugnacious. He was also a former judge with considerable skill as a trial lawyer. He had his eye on higher public office and was trying to establish himself as the top Republican in the Chicago area. Crowe was outraged that Darrow would seek to excuse or mitigate the brutal crime of these "fiends," as the prosecution team labeled Leopold and Loeb. Crowe's assistant was Joseph Savage, whose last name Darrow couldn't resist capitalizing on. In court, Darrow called Savage's plea for the death penalty a "cruel speech" and then in an aside he asked Crowe, "Did you pick him for his ability or just for his name?"[18]

Finally, there is the judge, a man who, to the surprise of many, ended up playing a pivotal role. Born in England, John Caverly was a sixty-four-year-old devout Catholic who had paid for his legal education by carrying water in steel mills for eighty-seven cents a day. He started as attorney for the city before becoming a municipal court judge. Caverly had been instrumental in establishing a juvenile court before he was promoted to the trial court of general jurisdiction.

Four significant aspects to this case were widely reported.

First, there was no doubt that the investigation and the gathering of evidence was superb, owing to the excellent work and supervision of State's Attorney Crowe. He was aided by several investigative newspaper reporters who on their own turned up important information. Media sources also helped by offering monetary rewards for any information leading to the identity of the killers. The case against Leopold and Loeb was wrapped up, remarkably, in less than two weeks.

The murder, though meticulously planned, was far from perfectly executed. Leopold and Loeb assumed that Bobby's body would not be found in the remote area in which they placed it and that in time it would decompose. But as luck would have it, a work crew discovered the corpse the very next morning. Within hours it was identified as Bobby Franks, the parents were notified, and so the ransom was

---

18. Hannon, "Leopold and Loeb Case," 68; Higdon, *Leopold and Loeb*, 236; Sellers, *The Leopold-Loeb Case*, 121.

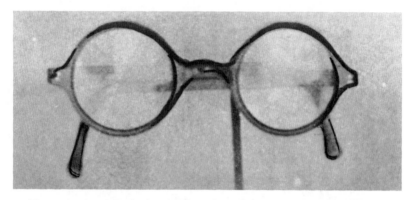

These eyeglasses, which were found near the body of Bobby Franks,
were traced to Nathan Leopold, Jr.
© Bettmann/CORBIS

never paid. The police then learned from a game warden at Wolf Lake
that the location where the body was found was also where Leopold often went to watch birds. This led to the first contact between
Leopold and the police. Leopold acknowledged that he and other
bird-watchers often went to the Wolf Lake area, but he denied any
knowledge of the crime. And at first, the investigators believed him.

Unfortunately for Leopold, as he was trying to hide the body, he
dropped his spectacles at the scene and the police found them there.
Since Bobby did not wear glasses, Crowe would call this discovery
"An Act of Divine Providence."[19] The prescription for these glasses
was common, but the hinge on them was unusual; eyeglasses with
this hinge were sold by only one Chicago optometrist, and he had
records showing that only three pairs had been sold in the last several
years. One was sold to a woman who still had her glasses. A second
went to attorney Jerome Frank, who, nearly fifty years later as a federal appellate judge, would deny the final appeal of Julius and Ethel
Rosenberg for a stay of their executions. The third pair of glasses
was sold to Leopold. Leopold then admitted that he had indeed lost
his glasses and he assumed they had likely fallen out of his pocket
while bird-watching at Wolf Lake. He had been unaware of their loss

19. Transcript, 129; Sellers, *The Leopold-Loeb Case*, 283; Linder, "Famous American Trials."

because he had not used the glasses except for a short period about six months earlier. It seemed a plausible explanation, and the police were again inclined to believe him.

The ransom note itself was a clue. It was flawless in form, grammar, and syntax, obviously written by a literate and well-educated individual. The note emphasized the "futility" of calling the police; it threatened the death of Bobby for the slightest "infraction" of instructions; it talked about the "execution" of the planned ransom exchange. Clearly the author was not the stereotypical criminal.

The note was found to have been typed on a portable Underwood typewriter. But the police could find no such typewriter in Leopold's possessions. At this point, two newspaper reporters joined the investigation. They discovered that Leopold belonged to a University of Chicago law student study group. From this group's members, the reporters learned that Leopold sometimes used an Underwood portable. Study sheets Leopold had typed were compared to the ransom note. There was a match.[20] In the face of this devastating evidence of guilt, Crowe was confident he had found their killer.

Leopold continued to deny any knowledge of the crime. When he was asked what he was doing on the day of the murder, Leopold said that he and Loeb were driving around all afternoon and evening in Leopold's car, and they had picked up some girls. That disclosure brought Loeb into the case as another suspect. He was questioned and confirmed Leopold's alibi. All the while, Crowe and his assistants kept digging. Then Leopold's chauffeur told investigators that on the day of the murder, he had worked on Leopold's car all day. It had never left the garage.

Confronted with this fact, Loeb confessed. When presented with the facts elicited from Loeb, Leopold also admitted everything. With the help of the defendants, Crowe then accumulated an abundance of physical evidence. The murderers' chisel was recovered. The Underwood typewriter was taken from the lagoon where the boys admitted they had put it. The clerk who sold the hydrochloric acid was found.

20. Higdon, *Leopold and Loeb*, 89–90; Wood, "The Loeb-Leopold Case"; Hannon, "Leopold and Loeb Case," 22–23.

Bobby Franks's discarded clothes were located. Crowe anticipated that insanity would be the only defense possible, and he sought to preempt it. He brought in three of Chicago's top psychiatrists to interview the boys. The doctors talked to Leopold and Loeb for about an hour and pronounced them perfectly sane. In short, Crowe had a slam-dunk, airtight case of murder one and kidnapping that he was certain would result in the death penalty; all this accomplished in ten days; all this accomplished before Leopold and Loeb were given access to their lawyers.

The second important aspect of the case was Darrow's creative lawyering. In particular, it was Darrow's decision to have the boys plead guilty.

Obviously, a factual defense, even for the great Darrow, was impossible. The boys did it, they admitted doing it, and there could be no doubt about it. Everyone, in Chicago and in the nation, expected a plea of not guilty by reason of insanity. However, Darrow knew that the traditional law on insanity, as applied in Illinois, had a rigorous right-wrong standard that required a showing that the defendants were so mentally defective that either they did not know what they were doing or that they did not know that what they were doing was wrong. Difficult and rarely successful in any case, not guilty by reason of insanity would not work for Leopold and Loeb.

The boys—or young men, as the prosecution would have it—were brilliant. Their crime had been carefully planned. They fully realized that what they were doing was wrong as a matter of conventional morality and legality. The fact that they regarded themselves as above such bourgeois constraints would not make for a very persuasive defense.

That said, most death penalty defense lawyers would probably have used the "not guilty because insane" plea in this case. They would have put before the jury all the psychological defects of the defendants in the hope that even if insanity was rejected, the jury would be influenced to mitigate the penalty from death to life imprisonment.

It was especially unusual for Darrow to plead guilty without first trying to make a deal with the prosecutors. One would have expected him to go to the prosecutor and say, "We'll plead guilty and save you a trial, if you agree not to ask for the death penalty." Instead, Darrow showed up in court and, without informing anyone of his intention, except the defendants and their parents, pleaded guilty. Why did Darrow do it this way?

He knew there was no possibility of a deal with Crowe. Crowe wanted a trial. There was no risk of an acquittal, and he wanted the defendants to hang, so much so that Darrow was afraid to even hint to Crowe that a guilty plea was possible. Darrow was afraid that if Crowe had advance warning of a guilty plea, Crowe would separate the charges of murder and kidnapping, each of which carried a maximum penalty of death. If he didn't get death on kidnapping, then he would proceed with the charge of murder and try again. Once Darrow pleaded guilty to both murder and kidnapping, a single penalty trial was guaranteed.

Even more importantly, Illinois law at the time provided that a plea of not guilty, or not guilty by reason of insanity, would be decided by a jury. If the case goes to a jury, the jury not only decides guilt, but also decides the penalty. But on a guilty plea, there is no jury. It is the judge who fixes the penalty. The media was clamoring for the death penalty. Most ordinary citizens knew the details of the crime. Their opinion was invariably that hanging was the only appropriate penalty. By pleading guilty, Darrow placed his clients beyond the reach of a jury pool that would surely have sent Leopold and Loeb to the gallows.[21] He left the boys' fate in the hands of Judge Caverly, a kindly and discerning man who had never before in his career had to decide himself whether a defendant lived or died. Caverly had sentenced convicted murderers to death in the past but only when a jury finding required him to do so. The judge also had a background in helping form a juvenile court. So Darrow counted on the fact that it would be hard for him to take full responsibility for killing two young men. With a jury, each juror could console himself with the thought that he was only one of twelve who voted for death. But when the judge is the sentencer, he cannot share his responsibility. It is his alone.

21. Darrow, *The Story of My Life*, 237; Hannon, "Leopold and Loeb Case," 45–46.

Darrow didn't hide his motivation. He expressed his reasoning openly to the court. Here is what he said:

> I am aware that a court has more experience, more judgment, and more kindliness than a jury. And then, your honor, it may not be hardly fair to the court, because I am aware that I have helped to place a serious burden upon your shoulders. And at that I have always meant to be your friend, but this was not an act of friendship. I know perfectly well that where responsibility is divided by 12, it is easy to say "away with him" but, your honor, if these boys hang, you must do it. There can be no division of responsibility here. You must do it. You can never explain that the rest overpowered you. It must be your deliberate, cool, premeditated act. . . ."[22]

Moreover, by pleading guilty, Darrow would not lose the opportunity to present evidence of his clients' mental abnormalities. What would follow now would be a trial solely on the issue of penalty. It would be a sentencing hearing or penalty trial. There would be witnesses and summations, but only one decision maker, the judge, and only one issue to decide, death or life imprisonment. Illinois law provided that evidence in mitigation or in aggravation could be presented to the judge. Today, Darrow's decision to forgo a jury and plead guilty is considered a masterstroke of trial tactics.

Both sides were now ready for a trial that started just three months after the commission of the crime. Each side had its psychiatrists and an arsenal of arguments.

The third important aspect or highlight of the *Leopold and Loeb* case is the most memorable. It is Darrow's summation. To call it a masterpiece is not an exaggeration. It is studied by trial lawyers. It is copied by death penalty defense advocates. It is included in every compendium of famous closing arguments. Professor Alan Dershowitz called it "one of the most remarkable legal arguments in the history of advocacy. . . . No lawyer, indeed no civilized person should

---

22. Transcript, 8–9; Sellers, *The Loeb–Leopold Case,* 121–2.

go through life without reading Darrow's eloquent defense of young human life."[23]

On August 22, 1924, in a "courtroom jammed to suffocation, with hundreds of men and women in the corridors outside,"[24] Darrow began his summation. In his baggy suit and string tie, gray hair falling over his forehead, he moved about the courtroom like a lion. Over the next two days, for a total of twelve hours, Darrow mixed poetry and prose, science, logic, and emotion. Darrow's plea for life is a classic model of persuasion. There are certain techniques that anyone engaged in the art of advocacy tries to use, and Darrow used them all.

Technique #1: There is the necessity for a single theory or theme.

This is a phrase, a sentence, a thesis that harmonizes all the undisputed facts into one well-reasoned, reasonable, and convincing theory. Of course, this theory must appeal to common sense. Rhetorical flights of fancy won't do it. Emotion alone won't do it. Trial lawyers know that before you can touch the heart, you must reach the head.

So what was Darrow's theme? It is embodied in one sentence: *"This terrible crime was the senseless act of the immature and diseased minds of children."* What explains the lack of motive? The boys are mentally sick. What explains the lack of remorse? They are mentally sick. Merely telling the story, reciting what happened, tells you they are mentally sick. Would normal boys do what they did? Never. They are sick; maybe not sick enough to meet the legal test of insanity, not sick enough to escape guilt, but sick enough to be spared the gallows. In Darrow's own words:

A boy with a beautiful home, with automobiles, a graduate of college, going to Europe, and then to study law at Harvard; as brilliant an intellect as any boy that you could find; a boy

---

23. Dershowitz, *America on Trial,* 256.
24. Linder, "Famous American Trials."

with every prospect that life might hold out to him; and yet he goes out and commits this weird, strange, wild, mad act, that he may die on the gallows or live in a prison cell until he dies of old age or disease. . . .

What else could it be? A boy in his youth, with every promise that the world could hold out before him, wealth and position and intellect, yes, genius, scholarship, nothing that he could not obtain, and he throws it away, and mounts the gallows or goes into a cell for life. It is too foolish to talk about. Can your honor imagine a sane brain doing it? Can you imagine it coming from anything but a diseased mind? Can you imagine it is any part of normality?[25]

Darrow then expanded on his theme:

I think all of the facts of this extraordinary case, all of the testimony of the alienists, all that your honor has seen and heard, all their friends and acquaintances who have come here to enlighten this court, I think all of it shows that this terrible act was the act of immature and diseased brains, the act of children. Nobody can explain it in any other way. No one can imagine it in any other way. It is not possible that it could have happened in any other way. And I submit, your honor, that by every law of humanity, by every law of justice, by every feeling of righteousness, by every instinct of pity, mercy, and charity, your honor should say that because of the condition of these boys' minds, it would be monstrous to visit upon them the vengeance that is asked by the state.[26]

In this penalty trial, Prosecutor Crowe called over eighty witnesses in order to reenact every detail of the crime: how the boys planned it, where they went, and what they did. All of this was rather

---

25. McKernan, *The Amazing Crime and Trial of Leopold and Loeb*, 274–5; Transcript, 60; Sellers, *The Loeb-Leopold Case*, 179; Linder, "Famous American Trials."
26. McKernan, *The Amazing Crime and Trial of Leopold and Loeb*, 291; Transcript, 73–74; Linder, "Famous American Trials."

unnecessary, as guilt was conceded, but Darrow did not object. In fact, he cross-examined only a few witnesses. Why should he object? Why should he cross-examine? The facts of the case fit his theory perfectly: *only a diseased mind would so act.*

Darrow made what are now familiar arguments: Life imprisonment is really worse than death; capital punishment is not a deterrent; the age of the boys, nineteen and eighteen, then below the age of majority. These militate against the death penalty. And he always returned to his theme.

Technique #2: Personalize and humanize your clients. Make them come alive as sympathetically as possible.

Although they were nineteen and eighteen years old, Darrow referred to them as boys or teenagers or lads or even children. He not only used his clients' first names, he used their childhood nicknames. Richard Loeb became Dickey. He called Nathan Leopold "Babe," his family name.

Technique #3: The art of rebuttal.

Trial lawyers are taught that you must concede weaknesses. You can't ignore them and wish them away. They must be addressed to maintain credibility with the judge.

He admitted the crime was terrible, that the boys deserved to be punished, that the parents of the victim deserved great sympathy, and that the mental defects of the boys might not constitute *legal* insanity. "I can imagine a psychiatrist," he said, "who might honestly think that under the crude definitions of the law, the defendants were sane and do know the difference between right and wrong."[27]

Also knowing that public opinion might influence the judge, Darrow treated it as seriously as any opponent. At the outset of his speech, he acknowledged the enormous publicity the case had

---

27. McKernan, *The Amazing Crime and Trial of Leopold and Loeb,* 258; Sellers, *The Loeb-Leopold Case,* 160; Linder, "Famous American Trials."

received. He derided the opinion of the masses. "When the public is interested and demands a punishment, no matter what the offense, it thinks of one punishment, and that is death." Sounding like a critic of today's strident opinion mongers, he continued, "In this land of ours, where talk is cheap, where newspapers are plenty, where the most immature expresses his opinion, and the more immature the stronger . . . a court couldn't help feeling the great pressure of the public opinion which exists in this case." By acknowledging the judge's dilemma in handing down an unpopular decision, Darrow also implies his obligations to be fair and just.[28]

So defense lawyers must face their problems. But beyond that simple advice is the reminder that the best defense is a good offense. The skillful advocate seeks to turn weaknesses into strengths; seeks to convert a seeming liability into an advantage. So it was that much of what Crowe argued in support of the death sentence, Darrow used in mitigation.

The prosecution called the crime cold-blooded. Well, said Darrow, prosecutors always say that:

> I have never yet tried a case where the state's attorney did not say that it was the most cold-blooded, inexcusable, premeditated case that ever occurred. If it was murder, there never was such a murder. If it was robbery, there never was such a robbery. If it was a conspiracy, it was the most terrible conspiracy that ever happened since the star chamber passed into oblivion. If it was larceny, there never was such a larceny. . . . Lawyers are apt to say that.[29]

Darrow first argued that all killing is cold-blooded, but here the victim did not suffer long. The defendants did not act out of hate or revenge or greed. This murder was not as cruel as many others, and

---

28. McKernan, *The Amazing Crime and Trial of Leopold and Loeb,* 213; Transcript, 5; Linder, "Famous American Trials."
29. Transcript, 10; McKernan, *The Amazing Crime and Trial of Leopold and Loeb,* 220; Sellers, *The Leopold-Loeb Case,* 123-4.

those others did not end in a death penalty. Then Darrow turned the argument against the prosecution.

> Cold-blooded, yes. But here are the officers of justice, so-called, with all the power of the state, with all the influence of the press, to fan this community into a frenzy of hate; with all of that, who for months have been planning and scheming, and contriving, and working to take these two boys' lives.
> You may stand them up on the trap-door of the scaffold, and choke them to death, but that act will be infinitely more cold-blooded, whether justified or not, than any act that these boys have committed or can commit. Cold-blooded! Let the state, who is so anxious to take these boys' lives, set an example in consideration, kindheartedness and tenderness before they call my clients cold-blooded.[30]

The prosecutor had emphasized that Bobby Franks should not die in vain. This allowed Darrow to talk about all boys, the boy defendants as well as the boy victim.

> No, Bobby Franks should not die in vain. But—would it mean anything if on account of that death, these two boys were taken out and a rope tied around their necks and they died felons? Would that show that Bobby Franks had a purpose in his life and a purpose in his death? No, your honor, the unfortunate and tragic death of this weak young lad should mean something. It should mean an appeal to the fathers and the mothers, an appeal to the teachers, to the religious guides, to society at large. It should mean an appeal to all of them to appraise children, to understand the emotions that control them, to understand the ideas that possess them, to teach them to avoid the pitfalls of life.[31]

---

30. Ibid.
31. Transcript, 65; McKernan, *The Amazing Crime and Trial of Leopold and Loeb*, 279; Sellers, *The Loeb–Leopold Case*, 185.

The prosecution pointed out that Leopold and Loeb came from wealth. They had all the advantages. This allowed Darrow to explain how wealth was one of the *causes* of the defendants' mental and emotional disease: "Your honor," he opined, "it is just as often a great misfortune to be the child of the rich as it is to be the child of the poor. Wealth has its misfortunes. Too much, too great opportunity given to a child has its misfortunes."[32] Then Darrow launched into a discussion of what went wrong in the family life of Leopold and Loeb.

Technique #4: The use of analogies.

Great trial lawyers, public speakers, and speech writers use analogies to persuade. Everyone loves a story. An apt anecdote or a personal illustration by the speaker accomplishes two things. It makes a point and at the same time it sympathetically humanizes the speaker.

One of the prosecution psychiatrists was Dr. William Krohn. The other prosecution medical experts testified the defendants were sane but conceded that the boys were abnormal and emotionally defective in one way or another. Dr. Krohn conceded nothing. The defendants were fine, he maintained, and they deserved to die.

Darrow in summation recalls Dr. Krohn's testimony in this way:

When Dr. Krohn testified my mind carried me back to the time when I was a kid, which was some years ago, and we used to eat watermelons. I have seen little boys take a rind of watermelon and cover their whole faces with water, eat it, devour it, and have the time of their lives, up to their ears in watermelon. And when I heard Dr. Krohn testify in this case, to take the blood of these two boys, I could see his mouth water with the joy it gave him, and he showed all the delight and pleasure of myself and my young companions when we ate watermelon. . . .[33]

32. Transcript, 47; McKernan, *The Amazing Crime and Trial of Leopold and Loeb*, 260.
33. McKernan, *The Amazing Crime and Trial of Leopold and Loeb*, 257; Sellers, *The Loeb–Leopold Case*, 160.

Darrow made his point. Krohn was a professional witness. He testified only for money. He was cruel. He was "Doctor Death." And, as a bonus, the judge was left with the endearing image of Darrow as a child eating watermelon with the other boys.

At another point, Darrow stressed that without considering the cause of a crime, one could not fairly decide on the punishment. Scientists, doctors, criminologists know this. But lawyers, alas, do not. Lawyers, especially prosecutors, think only of punishment. It rarely occurs to lawyers that crime has a cause just like a disease has a cause. And then came the analogy, the illustration:

> If a doctor were called on to treat typhoid fever he would probably try to find out what kind of milk or water the patient drank, and perhaps clean out the well so that no one else could get typhoid from the same source. But if a lawyer was called on to treat a typhoid patient, he would give him thirty days in jail, and then he would think that nobody else would ever dare to take it. If the patient got well in fifteen days, he would be kept until his time was up; if the disease was worse at the end of thirty days, the patient would be released because his time was out. As a rule, lawyers are not scientists. They have learned the doctrine of hate and fear, and they think that there is only one way to make men good, and that is to put them in such terror that they do not dare to be bad. They act unmindful of history and science, and all the experience of the past.[34]

Technique #5: Quantify for clarity and emphasis.

There is a device by which the advocate emphasizes a point or theme by subdividing it into parts. By quantify, we mean taking what might appear to be one argument and breaking it up into two or more. The result is that the major idea is emphasized and made

---

34. Transcript, 74–75; McKernan, *The Amazing Crime and Trial of Leopold and Loeb,* 292; Sellers, *The Loeb–Leopold Case,* 196.

TEN GREAT AMERICAN TRIALS

clearer. So, for example, the defense counsel in a criminal case will argue that there is reasonable doubt. He or she might say this is a case of reasonable doubt—but not just one doubt; there are ten reasonable doubts. One would be enough to acquit. However, here we have ten, and counsel then equates each weakness of the prosecution case or each favorable inference for the defense as a separate reasonable doubt.

Imagine that a tenant who rented property is suing the landlord because the tenant was injured by a defect on the property. The plaintiff's claim is that the landlord should have told the tenant about the defective condition. Plaintiff's attorney could say simply "the landlord never warned the plaintiff" and leave it at that. But it is more effective to say something like "the landlord never warned him. He didn't send him a letter telling him about the defect. He didn't call him on the phone and tell him about the defect. He didn't tell him face-to-face when they signed the lease about the defect. He simply never told him."

So when Darrow declared this act was the act of the diseased brains of children, he followed it by detailing, one after another, the acts of irrationality: killing for no reason; kidnapping in broad daylight in their own neighborhood where they were well-known and could be recognized; driving for miles around the neighborhood after the killing with a dead body in the car where even a minor accident would have exposed their crime and destroyed their lives; parking the bloodstained rented murder car overnight near the Leopold garage and then cleaning it in the presence of the Leopolds' chauffeur; burying the body in a place where Leopold frequently did his birding activities; and on to a dozen more instances of irrational and abnormal behavior.[35]

Similarly, Darrow argued that the true cause of this crime and of the defendants' abnormality were events beyond their control. He then dissected the testimony of the defense psychiatrists and listed in elaborate detail each of the possible causes of the boys' diseased

---

35. McKernan, *The Amazing Crime and Trial of Leopold and Loeb*, 235–8; Sellers, *The Loeb-Leopold Case*, 137–9.

minds. He started with their childhoods—the nanny who demanded too much, the childhood fantasies, the easy access to money, a too-early exposure to Nietzsche, and culminating in the fortuitous coming together of these two boys without which event there would have been no killing.

Technique #6: Universalize your cause.

It is also essential to maximize the importance of your cause, to make the case bigger than the parties, and let the judge know that his or her decision will affect future generations and make our nation—indeed, all humanity—better if you win and much worse if you lose. In other words, you make decision makers proud to find for you.

So in courtrooms one frequently hears lawyers telling juries to "send a message to the community." "Your verdict will be a pronouncement, a warning, to drunken drivers everywhere, or to manufacturers of shoddy products or to cheating store owners."

Trial lawyers are taught that even if they have a case so routine, so dull, so ordinary that it has absolutely no connection to anything of importance to anyone except the immediate parties, they should employ this technique, and say something like "Ladies and gentlemen of the jury, your honor, your decision in this case will be noted in the records of this courthouse and community forever."

Of course, Clarence Darrow had no difficulty universalizing his cause.

He began by tracing the history of capital punishment. He recalled times when nearly 200 different crimes were punishable by death in England; he pictured the public hangings of the nineteenth century. Now, he suggested, we look back at the past with horror as gradually, step by step, the criminal law has been modified and humanized. And what we found was less crime, not more. Barbarism breeds barbarism. With this background he universalized his cause:

> If these two boys die on the scaffold, which I can never bring myself to imagine, if they do die on the scaffold, the details of this will be spread over the world. Every newspaper in the

United States will carry a full account. Every newspaper of Chicago will be filled with the gruesome details. It will enter every home and every family. Will it make men better or make men worse? Would it make the human heart softer or would it make hearts harder? What influence would it have upon the millions of men who will read it?

Do I need to argue to your Honor that cruelty only breeds cruelty? That hatred only causes hatred; that if there is any way to soften this human heart which is hard enough at its best, if there is any way to kill evil and hatred and all that goes with it, it is not through evil and hatred and cruelty; it is through charity, and love, and understanding.

I am not pleading so much for these boys as I am for the infinite number of others to follow, those who perhaps cannot be as well defended as these have been, those who may go down in the storm, and the tempest, without aid. It is of them I am thinking, and for them I am begging of this court not to turn backward toward the barbarous and cruel past.[36]

Toward the end of his plea for mercy, Darrow returned to the significance and the importance of the judge's decision.

I know your Honor stands between the future and the past. I know the future is with me, and what I stand for here; not merely for the lives of these two unfortunate lads, but for all boys and all girls; for all of the young, and as far as possible, for all of the old. I am pleading for life. . . . I know the future is on my side. You may hang these boys; you may hang them by the neck until they are dead. But in doing it you will turn your face toward the past. In doing it you are making it harder for every other boy who in ignorance and darkness must grope his way through the mazes which only childhood knows. In doing it you will make it harder for unborn children. You may

---

36. Sellers, *The Loeb–Leopold Case*, 212–13; McKernan, *The Amazing Crime and Trial of Leopold and Loeb*, 249–51; Transcript, 37–38.

save them and make it easier for every child that sometime may stand where these boys stand. You will make it easier for every human being with an aspiration and a vision and a hope and a fate. I am pleading for the future; I am pleading for a time when hatred and cruelty will not control the hearts of men. When we can learn by reason and judgment and understanding and faith that all life is worth saving, and that mercy is the highest attribute of man.[37]

The fourth significant feature of this case was the use of psychiatry or, as the prosecution claimed, the misuse of it.

Some say that this trial was the first time psychiatric evidence was admitted not to establish a legal defense, not to show insanity, not to show "heat of passion" or "extreme emotional distress," in order to lower the degree of the crime or to avoid one of the legal elements of the charge. Here its sole purpose was reduction of the penalty.

It was "psychosocial evidence": defined as evidence that includes all information that might bear on the offenders "emotional and psychological makeup"; of the defendants' childhood upbringing, relationships, friendships, formative and traumatic experiences, personal psychology, present feelings, all circumstances in defendants' formative years.

This kind of evidence later moved from the penalty phase of the trial into the guilt phase. It was a forerunner of the "abuse excuse." A prelude to the victim trauma syndrome defenses, to modern-day defenses of battered woman syndrome, of child abuse syndrome—of defenses resulting from events that eliminate or minimize personal responsibility for violent acts.

What the defense psychiatrists said was not surprising. They concluded that Leopold and Loeb had severe mental and emotional disorders. Loeb suffered from an antisocial personality disorder. Leopold was obsessed with the idea that Loeb embodied Nietzsche's "Superman" and allowed himself to be completely dominated by his

---

37. Sellers, *The Loeb–Leopold Case,* 212–3; McKernan, *The Amazing Crime and Trial of Leopold and Loeb,* 304; Transcript, 84; Higdon, *Leopold and Loeb,* 241.

friend. The psychiatrists then went into the boys' backgrounds to explain what caused their abnormalities.

What is more interesting is how Darrow used this information to express his own theories about the causes of crime; what the prosecution called "Darrow's philosophy of anarchy."[38]

Darrow identified two views on human conduct. The traditional view assumes that those found guilty of crimes committed their acts intentionally and were therefore morally responsible. The other view, Darrow's view, was that individual decisions to act are determined by forces beyond the actor's control, a philosophy of determinism.

As Darrow put it:

> There is the old theory that if a man does something it is because he willfully, purposely, maliciously, and with a malignant heart sees fit to do it. . . . Very few half-civilized people believe that doctrine anymore. Science has been at work, humanity has been at work, scholarship has been at work, and intelligent people now know that every human being is the product of the endless heredity back of him and the infinite environment around him. He is made as he is and he is the sport of all that goes before him and is applied to him, and under the same stress and storm, you would act one way and I act another, and poor Dickey Loeb another.[39]

Darrow's emphasis on the philosophy of determinism came up again and again in his summation:

> Why did they kill Bobby Franks? Not for money, not for spite, not for hate. They killed him as they might kill a spider or a fly for the experience. They killed him because they were made that way. Because somewhere in the infinite processes that go to the making up of the boy or the man something slipped,

---

38. Higdon, *Leopold and Loeb*, 247.
39. Sellers, *The Loeb–Leopold Case*, 156; Linder, "Famous American Trials."

and those unfortunate lads sit here hated, despised, outcasts, with the community shouting for their blood.[40]

Then Darrow elaborated on the causes of crime:

Nature is strong and she is pitiless. She works in her own mysterious way and we are her victims. We have not much to do with it ourselves. Nature takes this job in hand and we play our parts. . . .

What had this boy to do with it? He was not his own father; he was not his own mother; he was not his own grandparents. All this was handed to him. He did not surround himself with governesses and wealth. He did not make himself. And yet he is to be compelled to pay. . . .

For God's sake, are we crazy? In the face of history, of every line of philosophy, against the teaching of every religionist and seer and prophet the world has ever given us, we are still doing what our barbarous ancestors did when they came out of the caves and the woods!

Your honor, I am almost ashamed to talk about it. I can hardly imagine that we are in the nineteenth or the twentieth century. And yet there are men who seriously say that for what nature has done, for what life has done, for what training has done, take the boys' lives.[41]

The psychiatric evidence allowed Darrow to show and to speculate about what influences, what factors, for which they were not responsible, controlled Leopold and Loeb and made them what they were.

Prosecutor Crowe was outraged. Darrow's arguments for sparing the lives of Leopold and Loeb called into question the entire notion of personal responsibility. If the Darrow theory was accurate, then

---

40. McKernan, *The Amazing Crime and Trial of Leopold and Loeb*, 232; Sellers, *The Loeb–Leopold Case*, 133–4.
41. Transcript, 52, 54; McKernan, *The Amazing Crime and Trial of Leopold and Loeb*, 265–7.

all criminal punishment was suspect. He was asking for a fundamental change in the system of criminal justice and punishment.
"This," Crowe said, "is the weird and uncanny philosophy of the paid
advocate for the defense, whose business it is to make murder safe in
Cook County."[42]

Then, in a flourish of oratory, Crowe lectured the judge:

> I want to tell your honor that it would be much better if God
> had not caused this crime to be disclosed; it would be much
> better if it had gone unsolved, and these men went unwhipped
> of justice; it would not have done near the harm to this com-
> munity that will be done if your honor, as chief justice of this
> great court, puts your official seal of approval upon the doc-
> trines of anarchy preached by Clarence Darrow as a defense
> in this case.
>
> Society can endure, the law can endure, if criminals escape;
> but if a court such as this court should say that he believes in
> the doctrines of Darrow, that you ought not to hang when
> the law says you should, a greater blow has been struck to our
> institutions than by a hundred, aye, a thousand murders.[43]

If there was a weakness in the content of Darrow's summation—
and even masterpieces have flaws—it was his overreaching theory of
determinism. No sentencing judge could accept it. But it is a tribute
to Darrow's persuasiveness that Judge Caverly did not reject it outright. He simply said, "I am not supposed to choose between competing theories of personal responsibility. It is simply not my function. It
is for the legislature." So he said that all this psychosocial evidence,
Darrow's theories of determinism, and the causes of crime may be
deserving of legislative but not judicial consideration. This case cannot be affected by it.

---

42. Transcript, 89; Higdon, *Leopold and Loeb*, 242; McKernan, *The Amazing Crime and Trial of Leopold and Loeb*, 309.
43. Transcript, 147; Higdon, *Leopold and Loeb*, 247; McKernan, *The Amazing Crime and Trial of Leopold and Loeb*, 370; Sellers, *The Loeb–Leopold Case*, 315.

We might wonder whether Judge Caverly really ignored it. When faced, as he was, with making a discretionary decision, one may find it hard to ignore any plausible argument. Maybe Darrow knew that. And although this psychiatric testimony was ultimately not a big part of Judge Caverly's decision, its use became more prevalent after Leopold and Loeb. As time went on, and awareness of the psychological factors that motivate behavior grew, there was an increased reliance on this kind of testimony during trial and as mitigating evidence during the sentencing phase.

On Wednesday, September 10, with the trial and arguments over, Judge Caverly announced his decision. Delivered to a courtroom jammed with journalists and amid the flash of camera bulbs, his statement was brief.

First, Caverly made clear that this was not, as in the usual case, a negotiated plea between the defendants and the prosecution. Guilt was a foregone conclusion. Insanity as a defense would not have worked. So the defendants gave up nothing by pleading guilty. Nor was the plea any benefit to the state. It did not shorten or eliminate a trial, since the testimony in aggravation and mitigation was as detailed as if the case had been tried before a jury.[44]

Second, although the psychiatric evidence, the life history of the defendants, and their present mental, emotional, and ethical condition will be of great interest to criminologists, a similar analysis of any accused criminal would probably reveal all manner of abnormalities. And the broad questions of human responsibility and legal punishment are in no wise peculiar to the individual defendants. They may be deserving of legislative but not judicial consideration, but the judgment in this case cannot be affected by this evidence or by these theories.[45]

Third, the crime was one of singular atrocity. It was abhorrent.

But then the judge announced his sentence of life imprisonment. As justification for his decision he gave only one reason: the age of

44. Transcript, 149; Baatz, *For the Thrill of It,* 401; McKernan, *The Amazing Crime and Trial of Leopold and Loeb,* 377; Sellers, *The Loeb–Leopold Case,* 318–9.
45. Transcript, 150; Baatz, *For the Thrill of It,* 401; McKernan, *The Amazing Crime and Trial of Leopold and Loeb,* 378; Sellers, *The Loeb–Leopold Case,* 319–20.

the defendants. He simply declined to impose the death penalty on persons who were not of legal age. He said:

> This determination appears to be in accordance with the prog-
> ress of criminal law all over the world and with the dictates of
> enlightened humanity. More than that, it seems to be in accor-
> dance with the precedents hitherto observed in this state. The
> records of Illinois show only two cases of minors who were put
> to death by legal process. . . . to which number the court does
> not feel inclined to make an addition.[46]

For each of the boys, Judge Caverly gave a sentence of life imprisonment for murder and ninety-nine years for kidnapping, and he
expressed the hope that the defendants would never be paroled.

After the verdict, Leopold and Loeb were transported to Joliet
Prison. After serving twelve years, Loeb died as a result of being
slashed with a razor over fifty times by another inmate, James Day,
while in the shower. Day's defense was that he killed Loeb to fend
off a homosexual advance. A *Chicago Daily News* reporter allegedly
opened his story with this merciless line: "Richard Loeb, despite his
erudition, today ended his sentence with a proposition."[47]

Leopold fared better in prison. He served thirty-three years and
then in 1958, at age fifty-two, he was paroled. He probably would
have been released much earlier except for the combination of
media attention and politics. At his parole hearing in 1958, Leopold
reflected on his crime. "I committed my crime because I admired
Loeb extravagantly, because I didn't want to be a quitter and because
I wanted to show I had the nerve to do what he insisted on doing.

---

46. Transcript, 151; Baatz, *For The Thrill of It,* 402–3; McKernan, *The Amazing Crime and Trial of Leopold and Loeb,* 379–80; Sellers, *The Loeb–Leopold Case,* 321.
47. Fass, "Making and Remaking an Event," 942; Compare Linder, "Famous American Trials," with Higdon, *Leopold and Loeb,* 298 where the quote is, "Richard Loeb, a brilliant college student and master of the English language today ended a sentence with a proposition." See *U.S. News and World Report* article at http://usnews.com/opinion/blogs/
john-farrell/2009/12/01/Leopold-Loeb-and-the-curious-case-of-the-greatest-newspaper-
lead-never-written which describes various versions of the lead sentence and indicates that
none of them are verifiable and that all of them may be apocryphal.

They are admittedly, not very reasonable motives. They don't even make sense to me."[48] His life in prison was a study in rehabilitation. Leopold organized the prison library and started a successful correspondence school for prisoners. He taught himself braille so that he could teach a blind inmate to read. He participated with a leading Chicago sociologist in a study to predict parole success and then published the results of his work, "Parole Prediction as a Science." He also worked during World War II on experiments seeking a cure for malaria and published a scientific paper based on this study.

Leopold lived as a free man for thirteen years before he died of heart disease. During those years he lived in Puerto Rico, where he worked for a church, studied leprosy on the island, taught at the university, and got married.

Today, death penalty opponents point to Leopold as an example of the contributions that can be made by murderers who escape capital punishment.

What remains to be said about the *Leopold and Loeb* case? As did the *O. J. Simpson* case, it raises the issue of the effect of money on the criminal justice system. But in this instance, the wealth of the defendants was a mixed blessing. Darrow's talent saved the defendants from the death penalty. And that talent was available because the parents of Leopold and Loeb could afford to buy it.

On the other hand, if Leopold and Loeb had been poor, if they had been slum kids, and if the victim, for example, had been a member of a rival gang, then they may not have needed Clarence Darrow. Had their crime been another run-of-the-mill Chicago murder buried on the inside pages of the newspaper, the defendants would likely have been allowed to plead guilty to homicide in exchange for life imprisonment. Without mass media attention, they likely would have been paroled earlier.

Darrow's plea for life in 1924 included a prediction that the future could bring the abolition of the death penalty. A fitting conclusion to this chapter would be the knowledge that his prophecy has come true. But, Clarence Darrow would be disappointed to

---

48. Hannon, "Leopold and Loeb Case."

Clarence Darrow (1857–1938).
Photograph taken during the
Scopes trial.
© CORBIS

discover, the United States is the last remaining western democracy that retains capital punishment. In 1999, seventy-five years after his prophecy, ninety-eight persons were executed. High crime rates in the 1970s and 1980s affected popular opinion enough so that polls showed 80 percent support for the death penalty. During this period it was politically wise for prosecutors to seek the maximum penalty and for state governments to support capital punishment.

However, in the last few years, there are signs that Darrow's prophecy may yet come to pass. After years of indifference, the United States Supreme Court has revealed a willingness to examine and regulate state death penalty practices. It has held that death sentences may not be imposed on the mentally challenged or on juveniles under the age of eighteen.[49] It has also prohibited states from making death mandatory for all murder convictions.[50] The states are now constitutionally required to provide discretionary options in mitigation. In other words, much like the situation in *Leopold and Loeb,* the judge or jury must consider not only the offense but also the nature of the

---

49. Roper v. Simmons, 543 U.S. 551 (2005) (unconstitutional to impose death penalty on defendant under age 18); Atkins v. Virginia, 536 U.S. 304 (2002) (unconstitutional to impose death penalty on mentally challenged defendant).
50. Woodson v. North Carolina, 428 U.S. 280 (1976).

offender. State statutes permitting death for nonhomicidal crimes such as child rape were stricken as unconstitutional.[51]

Since the year 2000, seven states have abolished capital punishment. In thirteen of the thirty-two states that have the death penalty, there have been no executions in at least the past five years. At the same time there has been a steady decline in popular support for the death penalty. Reasons for the change include the availability of the "life without parole" option, the declining crime rate, the cost of housing death row inmates for the many years that elapse between sentencing and execution as well as the bad publicity and moratoriums resulting from botched executions, and the concern over wrongful convictions.

The discovery of wrongfully convicted inmates on death row has cast doubt on the reliability of the capital justice system. Proof of innocence is now obtainable from the emergence of sophisticated technologies for evaluating DNA and other types of forensic evidence.[52]

All these factors have led to fewer executions, fewer death sentences, and a growing sense that the Supreme Court may be poised to move from the regulation of death penalty practices to their outright abolition.

---

51. Coker v. Georgia, 433 U.S. 584 (1977) and Kennedy v. Louisiana, 554 U.S. 407 (2008) (nonhomicidal rape of a child; states may not impose death penalty for a crime "where the victim's life was not taken").
52. Statistics cited are from the Death Penalty Information Center, available at www.death-penaltyinfo.org.

THREE

The Scottsboro Trials: A Legal Lynching[1]

THE TRAGIC SAGA OF THE "Scottsboro Boys," the nine black youths accused of the rape of two young white women in Alabama in 1931, ranks as one of the most infamous miscarriages of justice in our nation's history. For two decades the young men struggled against racial prejudice and the unresponsive legal system of the American South. In the course of their ordeal, together or separately, the boys endured sixteen trials, two United States Supreme Court reversals, four series of death sentences and prison terms ranging from six to nearly seventeen years. Their lives were irretrievably ruined. For

---

1. This chapter draws heavily on court transcripts and judicial opinions, newspaper articles, and secondary sources, including materials from the impressive website of Professor Douglas Linder on "Famous American Trials." http://www.law.umkc.edu/faculty/projects/ftrials/scottsboro/SB_acct.html.

  Particularly helpful was the highly acclaimed book by historian Dan T. Carter, entitled *Scottsboro: A Tragedy of the American South* (Louisiana State University Press, 2007), as well as *Stories of Scottsboro* (Pantheon Books, Random House, 1994), by James Goodman; James R. Acker, *Scottsboro and Its Legacy: The Cases That Challenged American Legal and Social Justice* (Praeger, 2007); and Kwando Mbiassi Kinshasa, *The Man from Scottsboro: Clarence Norris and the Infamous 1931 Alabama Rape Trial, in His Own Words* (McFarland & Company, 1997). The chapter is also a modified version of coauthor Professor Faust F. Rossi's two-part article "The First Scottsboro Trials: A Legal Lynching," published in the Winter 2002 and Spring 2003 editions of the *Cornell Law Forum*.

blacks, the case was the reflection of centuries of mistreatment by white Americans. Communists and radicals in the 1930s saw it as the result of an economic system based on class exploitation. For liberals, it was a symbol of the virulent racism that plagued the South. By contrast, many white southerners viewed *Scottsboro* as meddling by arrogant outside agitators that threatened to subvert their way of life by encouraging racial insubordination. The case, then, had all the ingredients to become a "cause célèbre" that produced villains, heroes, sectional strife, and two landmark United States Supreme Court decisions.[2]

The setting for this tragedy is 1931 Alabama. To understand what happened, we need to be reminded of three major aspects of life in the Deep South at that time.

First, rural areas in the South were particularly hard-hit during the Great Depression. Unemployment was rampant, for both whites and blacks, who often lived together in so-called hobo jungles on the fringes of larger southern cities. Women millworkers who became unemployed often resorted to prostitution in order to survive. In the constant search for jobs, the cheapest and most prevalent method of transportation was to hop a freight train and ride the rails. The two alleged white rape victims came from this milieu.

Second, ruthless oppression of black people prevailed in the Deep South. Most white citizens were not overtly cruel in their daily lives but they expected blacks, who they regarded as inferior and perhaps even a separate species, to "keep their place." There was also a common conviction that young black males, if not controlled, were prone to rape white women. Even well-educated southern moderates of that period, who opposed violence and lynching, endorsed segregation and thought it perfectly reasonable that blacks could neither vote nor serve on juries. And they resented northern troublemakers who meddled in their affairs.

Third, on a national level, the law was largely unresponsive to the plight of black people. In 1868, the Fourteenth Amendment to the federal Constitution mandated that "no state shall deprive any

---

2. Carter, *Scottsboro,* Preface p. xi; Linder, "Famous American Trials."

person of life, liberty, or property without due process of law, nor deny to any person the equal protection of the laws." These constitutional guarantees were designed to commit the national government to enforce legal equality between blacks and whites. Following the end of Reconstruction in the 1870s, when the last federal troops were removed from the South, however, the federal government and the courts, including the U.S. Supreme Court, failed to enforce these principles. The words were there, the promise was there, but they were not implemented.

Yes, black people were now formally entitled to vote, but somehow they were denied access to the ballot box through intimidation, violence, grandfather clauses, and poll taxes. Yes, blacks were now entitled to sit on juries, but somehow jury commissioners never called on them to serve. Courts justified inaction by distinguishing between acts of individual discrimination, which they claimed were not prohibited by the Fourteenth Amendment, and state discrimination. Without an admission by state officials that they were intentionally discriminating, the federal courts declined to second-guess procedures regarding civil rights and especially voting, which were regarded as prerogatives of the states. Court decisions reflected the tendency of the rest of the nation to let southerners handle race questions as they pleased.[3]

In addition, the protections afforded to criminal defendants, white or black, were not clearly defined in the 1930s. The Fourteenth Amendment imposes limitations on the states, but they are phrased in the somewhat vague terms "due process" and "equal protection." By contrast, the Bill of Rights, the first ten amendments to the Constitution enacted in 1791 when the United States Constitution was adopted, are more specific. The Sixth Amendment speaks of the right to the assistance of counsel in a criminal case, the right to confront witnesses, and the right to trial by jury. But the Bill of Rights was framed to limit federal power, not state power. Thus, the question was whether these specific protections were included in the Fourteenth Amendment phrase "due process" or in the meaning of "equal protec-

---

3. Carter, *Scottsboro*, 321–2.

tion." In 1931, the answer was not clear. In many instances, the U.S. Supreme Court had not yet decided which portions of the specific guarantees of the Bill of Rights were "incorporated" into the Fourteenth Amendment's "due process." It was unclear, in other words, which of the limitations on the federal government and on federal courts applied to state governments and state courts.[4]

The *Scottsboro* tragedy began on March 25, 1931. A freight train left Chattanooga, Tennessee, on its way to Memphis. Scattered among the cars were some two dozen people, some white and some black. The train followed the course of the Tennessee River, traveling west and then dipping south into rural northern Alabama. Its path would take it through the small towns of Stevenson and Paint Rock as well as Huntsville until it turned north again to Memphis.

After the slow-moving train crossed the Alabama border, a white youth walked across the top of a railroad car and stepped on the hand of an eighteen-year-old black man named Haywood Patterson. A fight broke out between the whites and the blacks. The larger group of blacks got the better of it and forced all but one of the whites off the train. The whites who were ejected complained at a nearby depot that they had been assaulted by a gang of blacks. The stationmaster telegraphed ahead to the Paint Rock Station. Word reached the county sheriff, who deputized every man in Paint Rock who had a gun and lined them up along the tracks at the depot. This posse was ordered to arrest every black person on the train when it stopped at Paint Rock.

The train arrived and was searched. The posse found nine black males ranging in age from twelve to twenty years old. Only four of the nine had known each other before they were arrested. Then came a surprise. Two young white women, dressed in men's overalls with caps covering their hair, were also found on the train. They were unemployed millworkers named Victoria Price and Ruby Bates. They claimed to have gone to Chattanooga in search of work, but having found none were now returning home to Huntsville.

---

4. Powell v. Alabama, 287 U.S. 56 (1932): Carter, *Scottsboro*, 161–2; Goodman, *Stories of Scottsboro*, 85–89; Kinshasa, *The Man from Scottsboro,*, 7–8.

As the blacks were being tied together, one of the girls told a deputy that she and her companion had been raped by all nine of them. Everyone was transported to Scottsboro, the county seat. In the jail, the older of the two females, Victoria Price, identified six of the nine blacks as her assailants. The guard concluded that "if those six had Miss Price, it stands to reason the others had Miss Bates." When one of the accused, Clarence Norris, protested and called Victoria Price a liar, a guard hit him with a rifle butt. The women were promptly sent downtown to be examined by two local physicians.[5]

Farmers from the nearby hills began gathering, and by dusk a crowd of several hundred had surrounded the dilapidated two-story jail. There were shouts of "Give them to us" and "If you don't, we'll come in and get them!" The sheriff called the governor in Montgomery, and the governor ordered the National Guard to Scottsboro. There would be no lynching that night.[6]

In the days that followed, newspaper editors had already made up their minds. The *Jackson County Sentinal* headline read, "All Negroes Positively Identified by Girls" and "One White Boy Who Was Held Prisoner with Pistol and Knives While Nine Black Fiends Committed Revolting Crimes." The paper went on to say that "the fiends roped them . . . beating them when they struggled." It proclaimed that, "The two girls were found in the freight car in a terrible condition, mentally and physically, after their experience at the hands of the black fiends." Other media accounts described the crime as "a wholesale debauching of society . . . so horrible in its details that all the facts could never be printed" and "a heinous and unspeakable crime that savored of the jungle." The prosecutor announced that he would seek the death penalty.[7]

Now events moved rapidly. With the National Guard's constant presence and manned machine guns on the courthouse steps deter-

5. Carter, *Scottsboro*, 3–7; Goodman, *Stories of Scottsboro*, 3–5; Linder, "Famous American Trials."
6. Carter, *Scottsboro*, 7–10; Goodman, *Stories of Scottsboro*, 5–6. Linder, "Famous American Trials."
7. "Nine Negro Men Rape Two White Girls," *Jackson County Sentinel*, March 26, 1931; Linder, "Famous American Trials"; Carter, *Scottsboro*, 13; Goodman, *Stories of Scottsboro*, 11–13, 15–16.

ring a hostile mob, the nine young black men were hustled to trial twelve days after their arrest. That a capital case could be tried less than two weeks after the crime was highly unusual even by the prevailing standards of 1931.

Of the nine defendants, one was twelve years old and away from home for the first time and another was thirteen. A third was practically blind, and a fourth was suffering from a venereal disease that would have made intercourse extremely painful and in fact needed a cane in order to walk. All of the defendants were illiterate, far from their homes with no access to their families. They were not asked if they had or could get a lawyer or if they had relatives who might be able to hire a lawyer for them. Nor were they told that a lawyer could be appointed to defend them.

Just before the proceedings began, the judge asked if the case was ready for trial.

Yes, said the prosecutor. No one answered for the defense. A Tennessee real estate lawyer, Stephen Roddy, who was not a member of the Alabama bar and was unfamiliar with Alabama law, stood up and said he was not representing the defendants but was willing to advise them. He also informed the court that he was unprepared for trial. Later he advised the judge that the defendants might be better off if he played no role in the proceedings.[8] An elderly local lawyer, Milo Moody, who had not tried a case in many years, agreed to advise Roddy. Although it was never clear whether either of these "advisors" actually represented the accused, Roddy did participate on their behalf in a manner of speaking. He was allowed twenty-five minutes to confer with them. No time was provided for a reasonable investigation of the alleged crime or of the backgrounds of the alleged victims. There was no time to find witnesses. The trials began.

The defendants were tried in four groups. Clarence Norris and Charlie Weems were tried first because they were the oldest. Next came Haywood Patterson whose hand had been stepped on. The third trial involved a group of five defendants: Ozie Powell, Willie Roberson, Andy Wright, Eugene Williams, and Olen Montgom-

---

8. Linder, "Famous American Trials."

ery. The fourth and final trial was that of the twelve-year-old, Roy Wright.

Before each of the four juries, the key prosecution testimony came from the alleged victims, Victoria Price and Ruby Bates, as well as the two local doctors, Drs. Bridges and Lynch. Both physicians testified to having found semen in the vaginas of the two women. Roddy did not try to question or refute the medical testimony. He did not make a detailed or substantive opening statement and, incredibly, saw no purpose in giving a summation. Worse still, because he did not have the opportunity to speak to his clients at length, he could not prepare them to testify. He called them to the stand nonetheless. As might be expected, some of them said, in effect, "Not me and not my two or three friends, but yes, these other guys were the ones that did it." No single lawyer can or should represent multiple clients if one or more of them blame another defendant or defendants for the crime charged. To do so constitutes a gross conflict of interest. But these "technicalities" went unnoticed or were ignored. In short, the defense, insofar as it existed at all, was a disaster.

These four rapid-fire trials were over in three days. Most took five hours or less. The jury deliberations for most of them averaged about thirty minutes. The verdict for eight of the nine accused was "guilty of rape," and the penalty in each case was death. The exception was the trial of twelve-year-old Roy Wright; his case resulted in a hung jury. Because Wright was twelve, the prosecutor asked for life imprisonment instead of the death penalty. This decision disappointed the jury, a majority of which held out for the death penalty. As a result, they could not render the required unanimous verdict. From the time of the arrests to the time of the death sentences, only two weeks had passed.

The "Scottsboro Boys," as they came to be known, did not die in the electric chair. Not then and not later. Who saved them? There were heroes, individuals and groups who intervened in their behalf, with skill or courage or commitment.

The initial media response to the convictions was limited to a few brief stories in several newspapers. There was no national media presence at the trial. Soon after the convictions, however, the American

Communist Party (ACP) became the first group to offer assistance to the Scottsboro Boys. The ACP knew a good issue when they saw it. The convictions, they argued, were a dramatic example of capitalist repression of the poor. Obviously, one motive in helping the Scottsboro Boys was propaganda. Idealism was another. In any event, their motives seem far less important than their actions. When you are powerless and facing death, when there is no one else aiding your cause, you take what help you can get. The ACP had the will and the capacity to mobilize mass protests that brought the case national and even international attention. Within days, protest demonstrations arose throughout the United States as well as in Germany, Spain, and Moscow. Moreover, the communists' legal team, the International Labor Defense (ILD) and its chief lawyer, Joseph Brodsky, were experienced, competent, and dedicated.

The second assist came from none other than the United States Supreme Court. After the verdicts were affirmed by the Alabama courts, they were appealed to the Supreme Court, and in the landmark decision of *Powell v. Alabama*[9] the Court reversed the *Scottsboro* convictions.

There was no question that the justices regarded the legal representation of the Scottsboro Boys to be inadequate. It was never clear whether the Tennessee lawyer, Roddy, actually had been appointed to represent the defendants. The colloquy in court between the judge and the advisors was confusing and inconclusive. As the Court stated in its opinion:

> The defendants, young, ignorant, illiterate, surrounded by hostile sentiment, hauled back and forth under guard of soldiers, charged with an atrocious crime, regarded with especial horror in the community where they were to be tried, were thus put in peril for their lives within a few moments after counsel, for the first time charged with any degree of responsibility, began to represent them.[10]

9. Powell v. Alabama, 287 U.S. 56 (1932).
10. Goodman, *Stories of Scottsboro*, 85–86; Powell v. Alabama, 287 U.S. 56, 58, 59 (1932).

The Sixth Amendment right to counsel would have served as a legal basis for reversal except, as we have seen, it applied only against the federal government, not against the states. The Fourteenth Amendment's "due process" did apply to the states, but what does due process entail? There was no precedent that said the right to counsel applies to the states through the operation of Fourteenth Amendment due process. No precedent until *Powell v. Alabama* created one in 1932. The Court concluded that even if more time to prepare had been provided, the failure of the trial court to make a clear, effective appointment of counsel was a denial of due process within the meaning of the Fourteenth Amendment.[11]

This decision is a legal landmark because it extended and clarified the meaning of "due process." Being the basis of the decisions that followed, it established the seminal right to counsel. In *Powell*, the Court read the right to counsel into the due process clause. This guarantee would now apply to all state trials. *Powell* also applied that principle to the *Scottsboro* trial and found that due process was lacking. That ruling saved the Scottsboro Boys from execution, at least for the time being.

To understand the long-term significance of this decision, it helps to know that the actual holding was a narrow one. The Court said that the Fourteenth Amendment due process requires the effective right to counsel in this case because the defendants were young, uneducated, and illiterate; a mob atmosphere surrounded the trial; and it was a capital case. The Court left open a host of questions that would be answered later. Does the right to counsel apply to all capital cases—even if the defendants are mature and educated and there are no mobs? Yes, said the Court in a later decision. Does the right to counsel apply to noncapital, serious felony cases? Yes, said the Court some years later. Does the right to counsel apply to all felonies, whether serious or not? Yes, the Court subsequently decreed. When in the trial process does the right to counsel attach? Only at the time of trial? No, earlier—at least at the time of indictment, answered the Court.

11. Powell v. Alabama, 287 U.S. 56, 71 (1932).

Why not even earlier than that, such as at the time of initial arraignment? Good point, the Court decided, and it so held. Why not still earlier? The Court ultimately held that the right to counsel attaches at the time of custodial interrogation, even before arrest. If the police detain a suspect and the suspect asks for a lawyer, at that point all interrogation of the suspect must stop. But how will a suspect know he has this right to counsel? Three decades after the initial *Scottsboro* trials, the Court held in *Miranda v. Arizona* that if the police take suspects into custody, they must be advised that they have the right to a lawyer and that if they cannot afford one, the state will appoint counsel for them. Thus over the course of thirty-five years, in decision after decision, the Supreme Court expanded the right to counsel in state as well as federal trials. It began with *Powell v. Alabama*.[12]

The Supreme Court decision, however, did not mark the end of the *Scottsboro* story. The nine defendants were returned to the Alabama courts to be tried again. And back in Alabama, not much had changed.

The ACP and the ILD now realized that in order to make their case for racial oppression, they needed to prove that the boys were innocent and somehow get acquittals from an all-white Alabama jury. It would require a superb, even perhaps a miraculous, defense. At this point, the ILD hired Samuel S. Leibowitz, who by 1933 had become one of the leading criminal lawyers in the nation, to represent the *Scottsboro* defendants. Only thirty-seven years old, Leibowitz was a New York City trial attorney who had defended murderers and organized crime figures, including Al Capone, as well as corrupt policemen. He was regarded as "the next Clarence Darrow." In seventy-eight trials he had won seventy-seven acquittals and one hung jury.

Leibowitz agreed to represent the defendants without a fee. He was politically ambitious and believed that his reputation would be

---

12. For the developments from Powell v. Alabama, 287 U.S. 56 (1932), see Gideon v. Wainwright, 372 U.S. 355 (1963); Escobedo v. Illinois, 378 U.S. 478 (1964); Miranda v. Arizona, 384 U.S. 436 (1966).

Chief Defense Attorney Samuel Leibowitz speaks with
Haywood Patterson, one of nine defendants charged with the rape
of two women on a train.
© Bettmann/CORBIS

greatly enhanced by this endeavor, more so than by his previous successes in representing nefarious clients.

And he would also command a national stage. Leibowitz made clear to the media that he was not a communist and that he disagreed with the communist philosophy. He was taking the case for one reason only: to get justice for the wrongly accused and convicted Scottsboro Boys.[13]

Leibowitz deserved his outstanding reputation. He was always thoroughly prepared and, with his charismatic courtroom presence, showed enormous skill as a litigator. However, like many successful trial lawyers, he could be overconfident and he had a large ego, which sometimes made him insensitive to risk. Not taking fully into account the intensity of racial bias in Alabama, Leibowitz was certain that he could secure acquittals. Also, he entered the fray with enormous disadvantages. He had been hired by the extremely unpopular Communist Party, he was a northerner, a New Yorker, and a Jew. He was representing young black males charged with defiling southern white womanhood and would be defending them before an all-white jury. Faced with three forms of prejudice—racial, religious, and regional—Mr. Leibowitz had his extraordinary talent, enough time for careful preparation, a well-financed investigation, a cause that was just, and one unexpected stroke of luck. The southern judge that was assigned to the retrials respected the rule of law.

Judge James Edwin Horton may well have been the most courageous figure in the Scottsboro tragedy. The descendant of an old Alabama family and steeped in southern traditions, Judge Horton was tall, thin, Lincolnesque, and better educated than his peers in the Alabama bar. Gracious and relaxed, he almost never raised his voice and was well liked by virtually everyone. He accepted segregation, tolerated all-white juries, and probably began the trial believing the defendants were guilty. But above all he was fair. He believed in the law. He believed in the legal process.[14]

Haywood Patterson was the first defendant to be tried. He seemed to white southerners to be the meanest, most fierce-looking of the accused. Appearing for the prosecution was the attorney general of Alabama, Thomas Knight. It was unusual for the state's attorney general to be the one who actually prosecutes. But Knight

13. F. Raymond Daniell, "Observers Leave Scottsboro Trial," *New York Times*, April 3, 1933.

14. Goodman, *Stories of Scottsboro*, 173–4; Carter, *Scottsboro*, 193–4; Linder, "Famous American Trials."

Judge James Edwin Horton (left) talks with Samuel Leibowitz (right).
© Bettmann/CORBIS

wanted to be governor and thought this case would give him favorable exposure to the voters of Alabama as a man who had vanquished communists, rapists, and northerners. What more could a southern politician want?

Leibowitz began by moving that the indictments be quashed because of the systematic exclusion of blacks from both the grand jury and the pool of trial jurors. He called to the stand the editor of the local newspaper, who admitted that he had never seen or heard of a black person sitting as a juror. For an entire day, witnesses testified about the absence of black jurors. Some were jury commissioners who denied discrimination but could not remember a single black person who had sat on a jury. Well-qualified black citizens with college degrees testified that they had never been called to serve. Leibowitz's motion to dismiss was denied, but now he had a good record for appeal, should an appeal be necessary.

The prosecution's case depended on (1) the testimony of Victoria Price about how she had been raped by Haywood Patterson and the others, a story she had told four times in the first set of trials, and (2) the medical testimony of Drs. Bridges and Lynch that semen had been found in Victoria Price and Ruby Bates. Leibowitz would have to undercut the testimony of these witnesses on cross-examination. Ruby Bates, the younger alleged victim, had disappeared. The prosecution could not find her and would have to do without her testimony.

Victoria Price testified that on the night before the train ride, she had stayed with Ruby Bates at Mrs. Callie Brochie's 7th Avenue boarding house in Chattanooga.

She hopped the train the next morning and had stayed in an open gondola car, sitting or lying with some white youths, on top of the cargo of gravel stones. Then, she claimed, a group of blacks had jumped down from an adjoining tank car and had thrown the whites off the train. One after another, the six blacks, including the defendant, had raped her, brutally and constantly, until the train reached the posse at Paint Rock. Convinced that Price was lying, Leibowitz set about destroying her on cross-examination. And he had the ammunition.

First, no one had been able to find Callie Brochie or the boardinghouse she allegedly ran. Mr. Leibowitz had a witness, Lester Carter, a young white man, who would testify that he had been with Vickie Price the day before she boarded the train. He would reveal as well that Vickie's boyfriend, one Jack Tiller, Lester himself, and Ruby Bates had all spent the night at a hobo swamp near the rail yards. During that night, Lester would testify, "I had sex on the ground with Ruby while Mr. Tiller had sex with Vickie right next to us."[15] That, of course, was crucial evidence. Not only would it show that Victoria Price was a liar, but it would negate the medical testimony by providing an alternative explanation for the presence of semen.

Leibowitz wanted to go further and attack Miss Price's character. He wanted to expose her as "white trash" and to some extent he did. Miss Price was about 21 years old, twice married, and had

15. Carter, *Scottsboro*, 205, 209; Linder, "Famous American Trials," http://law2.umkc.edu/faculty/projects/ftrials/scottsboro/Cartertestimony.html.

been convicted and jailed for adultery and fornication. Judge Horton properly excluded some of the evidence but the jury did hear many seamy details.

Leibowitz also intended to show that when the defendants were found by the posse in Paint Rock, some of them were in railroad cars nowhere near the gondola car where Miss Price claimed she had been raped. For this purpose, Mr. Leibowitz had the Lionel Corporation construct an exact scale replica of the original train.

He also planned to expose the absurdity of Miss Price's testimony that she had been hit on her head and forcibly raped by six men without respite while lying on rough gravel. She had also testified at the previous trial that her back, her head, and her genitals were bloody and that her ordeal had come to an end only when the train had pulled into the Paint Rock station. But her testimony of physical injury was not supported by the doctors who had examined her soon after the alleged rapes.

How then did his cross-examination go? It depends on whom you ask. Victoria Price might have been just as Leibowitz saw her: a woman of the underclass from the world of hobos and casual sex. She was certainly uneducated but just as certainly "street-smart." She was tough and fierce under cross-examination and absolutely refused to concede anything, even the most basic facts. She consistently answered Leibowitz's questions with "I don't know," "I can't say," "I won't say," or "I don't remember." She spat out her answers and was evasive, combative, sarcastic, and angry. She vehemently denied having sex with Tiller the night before the train ride. When asked if she had ever been convicted of any offense, she answered "Absolutely not," despite court records of her convictions. When asked to explain the evidence of her convictions, she said, "I don't know. It's wrong." When asked to describe Mrs. Brochie's boardinghouse, she could not remember anything about it: Where was it? Was it two stories or one? "I never paid attention to that."[16] Usually, when witnesses say,

16. Carter, *Scottsboro*, 209; Linder, "Famous American Trials," http://law2.umkc.edu/faculty/projects/ftrials/scottsboro/price.html.

Victoria Price and Ruby Bates, alleged victims in the *Scottsboro* case.
© Bettmann/CORBIS

"I don't know" or I can't remember," they are apologetic; Vickie Price was blatantly aggressive.

For three hours, Samuel Leibowitz dueled with Victoria Price. If a witness refuses to answer or refuses to concede the obvious, then the cross-examiner has difficulty getting leverage to expose the lies. But if a witness denies knowledge of matters that the witness must know, facts that any reasonable person would remember, then the witness self-destructs. No impartial person will believe a consistently and self-evidently evasive witness. So by any objective standard, the cross-examination was very effective. Leibowitz asked all the right questions, and Miss Price's refusal to answer should have totally discredited her. Headlines of news accounts in the northern press claimed, "Victoria Price Destroyed by Brilliant Cross-Examination" and "More Like a Dissection of a Life than a Cross-Questioning."[17]

---

17. Linder, "Famous American Trials," http://law2.umkc.edu/faculty/projects/ftrials/trial-heroes/essayhorton.html.

But the southern audience and the audience who counted, the jurors, saw it differently. They were furious at Leibowitz. Yes, Victoria Price was not a model of southern womanhood. Yes, Victoria Price might also be a hobo, a drunk, and a prostitute. Nevertheless, the locals did not want a Jewish lawyer from New York, especially one hired by the Communist Party, treating their women, even their poor white trash, so cavalierly and contemptuously. One courtroom spectator was heard whispering to another "It'll be a wonder if Leibowitz leaves town alive."[18] An editorial in a Decatur newspaper no doubt spoke for many of its readers:

> One possessed of that old southern chivalry cannot read the trial now in progress in Decatur and publish an opinion and keep within the law. Mr. Leibowitz's brutal cross-examination makes one feel like reaching for his gun while his blood boils to the nth degree.[19]

The testimony of Dr. Bridges, a key part of the prosecution's case, came next. He and his colleague, Dr. Lynch, had examined Price and Bates about ninety minutes after the alleged rapes. As he had at the first trial, Dr. Bridges testified on direct examination that there had been semen in the vaginas of both women. Because Dr. Bridges was an honest witness, Mr. Leibowitz on cross-examination was able to turn him into a witness for the defense. He asked about the manner of the alleged victims. Were they upset? Hysterical? Were they crying? Not at all said the doctor; they were completely composed and calm. Bridges also acknowledged that although Vickie Price had allegedly been raped repeatedly, there was barely enough semen found to make a smear slide. He went on to explain that the semen that was found was nonmotile or dead. He conceded that these facts made Price's story of recent successive rapes unlikely because spermatozoa normally live in the vagina for at least 12 hours and sometimes

18. Carter, *Scottsboro*, 210, 223; Goodman, *Stories of Scottsboro*, 138; Linder, "Famous American Trials," supra note 17.
19. Ibid.

as long as two days. Miss Price had also testified that she had been bleeding from her vagina and from the cut on her head, but the doctor testified that there had been no visible sign of blood.

Attorney General Knight declined to call Dr. Lynch to the stand on the grounds that his testimony would just repeat that of Dr. Bridges. However, sometime later, Dr. Lynch asked to speak to Judge Horton privately. When they were alone, he said, "Judge, these women were not raped. When I examined them, I told them they were lying and they just laughed at me." Judge Horton said, "My God, you have got to testify." Dr. Lynch replied, in substance, "Judge I can't. I graduated from medical school four years ago and now have a fair number of patients. If I testify for those boys, I'll never be able to practice medicine in Jackson County. I'll have to start all over."[20]

Horton was shaken. Should he have forced Lynch to testify? Horton could have done so. A judge has the power to call witnesses. Or he could have forced the doctor to repeat his assertions in the presence of Mr. Knight and Mr. Leibowitz. That's what Judge Horton should have done, but he did not do it. Perhaps he consoled himself by concluding that the strong defense case would result in an acquittal.[21]

The testimony of Lester Carter further strengthened the defense case by providing the explanation for the dead semen. He confirmed what Vickie Price had denied; that she had had sex with Jack Tiller in the freight yard the night before the train ride and at the same time that Ruby Bates had had sex with Lester himself.

Then came the most dramatic moment of the trial. To the astonishment of everyone, the courtroom doors opened and in walked a well-dressed Ruby Bates, the missing prosecution witness. But this time, Miss Bates, the other alleged victim and the friend of Victoria Price, stepped forward to testify for the defense.

Under oath, Ruby Bates recanted all the testimony she had given in the first set of trials. She now maintained that neither she nor Miss Price had been raped on the train. She explained that she had lied

---

20. Carter, *Scottsboro*, 214–6, 452–3; Goodman, *Stories of Scottsboro*, 175–6.
21. Ibid.

GLENN C. ALTSCHULER AND FAUST F. ROSSI

because Victoria had told her that otherwise they themselves might be jailed for vagrancy or crossing a state line with men for immoral purposes. Miss Bates confirmed that she had had consensual intercourse with Lester Carter before boarding the train, and at that same time and place Vickie Price had had intercourse with Jack Tiller. Bates also denied Price's claim that they had spent the night before the alleged attack in a Chattanooga boardinghouse. Why had Ruby Bates disappeared and where had she been? She explained that she had gone to New York, met with a minister, and told him about all her lies. He had urged her to return to Alabama and tell the truth. One might imagine that her testimony would have destroyed the state's case, but it did not.

Knight's cross-examination was devastating. He extracted from Miss Bates an admission that her beautiful clothes, her travel north, her lodging, and upkeep had all been paid for by what appeared to be representatives of the Communist Party. He succeeded in insinuating that she had been bought and paid for by the ILD and enticed by their New York City lawyers into giving false testimony.

Either Leibowitz or the ILD had badly miscalculated. It was a mistake to overdress her. It was a mistake to keep her in New York rather than in Alabama. It was a mistake not to have prepared her better for cross-examination. Ruby Bates, the surprise witness, was no help to the defense.

The State's summation was, in large part, an appeal to the deeply ingrained prejudice of the jury. Lester Carter was referred to as "Carterinski," a tool of the communists. The assistant prosecutor, Wade Wright, finished his summation by exhorting the jury to "Show them, show them that Alabama cannot be bought and sold with Jew money from New York." Judge Horton, Mr. Wright, and Attorney General Knight seemed embarrassed, but the point had been made.[22]

---

22. F. Raymond Daniell, "New York Attacked in Scottsboro Trial," *New York Times*, April 8, 1933; Carter, *Scottsboro*, 235–6; Goodman, *Stories of Scottsboro*, 143–4; Linder, "Famous American Trials," http://law2.umkc.edu/faculty/projects/ftrials/scottsboro/SB_bKNIG.html.

Judge Horton's charge to the jury was eminently fair. It was a plea for tolerance and an exhortation to jury members to decide the case based solely on the evidence.

> Take the evidence, sift it out and find the truths and untruths and render your verdict. It will not be easy to keep your minds solely on the evidence. Much prejudice has crept into it. Do not go off on side issues. You are not trying whether or not the defendant is white or black—you are not trying that question; you are trying whether or not this defendant forcibly ravished a woman. You are not trying lawyers, you are not trying state lines. You are here at home as jurors—a jury of citizens under oath sitting in a jury box taking evidence and considering it, leaving out any outside influences.
>
> We are a white race and a Negro race here together—we are here to live together—our interests are together. The world at this time and in many lands is showing intolerance and hate. It seems sometimes that love has almost deserted the human bosom. It seems that only hate has taken its place. It is only for a time, gentlemen, because it is the great things in life, God's great principles, matters of eternal right, that alone live. Wrong dies and truth forever lasts, and we should have faith in that.
>
> Do your duty.[23]

The jury was given the case on Saturday afternoon and delivered the verdict on Sunday morning: "We find the defendant, Haywood Patterson, guilty as charged and fix the punishment at death in the electric chair." Just a few minutes after getting the case, the jury had voted unanimously for a guilty verdict. It took them until the next morning to set the punishment because one juror at first thought that life imprisonment might be the more appropriate penalty.

---

23. Linder, "Famous American Trials," http://law2.umkc.edu/faculty/projects/ftrials/scottsboro/HORTONSINSTRUCT.html.

Leibowitz was shocked. He had expected to win. Instead, for the first time in has career, he had lost. The very next day, demonstrations began in the North and he appeared before a crowd of thousands in Harlem. The defeat had made him angry, and the roaring welcome seduced him into making rash statements.

In describing the jury that had convicted Haywood Patterson, he said, "If you ever saw those creatures, those bigots whose mouths are slits in their faces, whose eyes pop out like frogs, whose chins drip tobacco juice, bewhiskered and filthy, you would not ask how could they do it." Two weeks in Alabama made him feel that he needed a "moral, mental and physical bath."[24]

Leibowitz had eight other clients still to be tried in the same courthouse before the same community he had just trashed. His words were widely reported in the South, particularly in Alabama. Newspapers reacted with angry editorials.

As it turned out, Leibowitz's insults did not hurt his clients. Judge Horton announced that he did not know if Mr. Leibowitz had been quoted accurately or not, but that the publicity and the community response had persuaded him to postpone the remaining trials.

The Haywood Patterson trial was not yet finished. The defense made a motion to set aside the jury's verdict, arguing that it was against the weight of the evidence. Leibowitz had not convinced the jury; he had not convinced the community. The big question now was whether he had convinced Judge Horton.

Horton was still very much a southerner; his ancestors had fought for the Confederacy. He owed his judgeship to the community, and he knew that if he set aside the verdict he would never be reelected. With all this in mind and after deliberating for weeks, he rendered his verdict.

The vital question, said Judge Horton, is whether there was sufficient credible evidence upon which to base a guilty verdict. He then began a meticulous review of the testimony. He dissected Victoria

---

24. Carter, *Scottsboro*, 244; Goodman, *Stories of Scottsboro*, 147–8; "Negroes in Riotous March on Broadway, Welcome Defender in Scottsboro Case," *New York Times*, April 11, 1933; "Leibowitz Calls Alabama Jury Typical Bigots," *New York Herald Tribune*, April 11, 1933.

Price's account of the rapes. Most of her story was contradicted by the objective facts. Her physical condition could not be reconciled with the gang rape she claimed to have suffered. She asserted that she was bleeding from her head where she had been hit by the butt of a pistol and that her back was bruised by the sharp gravel on which she was lying during the assault. But the doctors who examined Price ninety minutes after the alleged rapes had found neither blood nor bruises on her head or back. Her vagina showed no signs of blood or tearing as might be expected after repeated forced intercourse. There was no semen on her pubic hair. Her respiration and pulse were normal, and she was not hysterical or even crying when she arrived at Paint Rock nor was she upset during the medical examination of Drs. Bridges and Lynch. The small amount of dead sperm found in her vagina was more plausibly explained by the consensual sex she had with Jack Tiller the night before, as testified to by Lester Carter. Price had denied Carter's testimony and had instead sworn that she had spent that night at Callie Brochie's boardinghouse. But she could not describe the house or where it was located, and the prosecution was unable or unwilling to produce Mrs. Brochie as a witness. Moreover, if Miss Price did not have sex with Jack Tiller on the eve of her train trip, why was Tiller not produced for the jury to support her contention and to contradict the testimony of Lester Carter?

Victoria Price testified that both Willie Roberson and Olen Montgomery were among those who raped her. Judge Horton asked, "Is it likely that Willie Roberson, the Scottsboro boy shown to have been suffering at the time from painful swelling and genital sores caused by a venereal disease and unable to walk without a cane, lept into the gondola and joined a sexual assault? Is it probable that Olen Montgomery, blind in one eye and nearly so in the other, helped throw white boys off the train and then committed rape?"

Rape, Judge Horton pointed out, is usually a crime committed secretly. Here the State had claimed that rapes were committed on a bright and clear day around noon on an open gondola railroad car filled with gravel within eighteen inches from the top and that the assaults continued in plain sight as the train moved slowly through a succession of country towns until, by "fortuitous coincidence," they stopped just as the train entered Paint Rock where a posse had been assembled. All parties on the train were found fully clothed, with no indication of wetness, blood, or semen on the clothing of Victoria Price or Ruby Bates or any of the Scottsboro Boys.

Finally, the judge noted that Victoria Price, instead of testifying with candor and sincerity, had been evasive on the witness stand and had refused to answer many relevant questions.

Judge Horton concluded:

> The law declares that a defendant should not be convicted without corroboration where the testimony of the prosecutrix bears on its face indications of improbability or unreliability, and particularly when it is contradicted by other evidence. The testimony of the prosecutrix in this case not only is uncorroborated, but it also bears on its face indications of improbability and is contradicted by other evidence, and in addition thereto, the evidence greatly preponderates in favor of the defendant. It therefore becomes the duty of the court under the law to grant the motion made in this case.
>
> It is therefore ordered and adjudged by the court that the motion be granted; that the verdict of the jury in this case and the judgment of the court sentencing this defendant to death be set aside and that a new trial is hereby ordered.[25]

Judge Horton's summary of the evidence appeared not only to discredit Miss Price's testimony but to affirmatively establish the innocence of the nine defendants. It was probably Judge Horton's hope that his opinion would be so convincing, so logical that the State would decide to drop all charges and not continue the prosecution of the Scottsboro youths. It was a vain hope. Neither the state

---

25. The entire opinion of Judge Horton appears as an appendix to the decision of Street v. National Broadcasting Company, 645 F.2d 1227, 1237 (1981) and in Appendix E in Kinshasa, *The Man from Scottsboro*, 195–209; Carter, *Scottsboro*, 265–9; Goodman, *Stories of Scottsboro*, 176–82; Acker, *Scottsboro and Its Legacy*, 95–97; Linder, "Without Fear or Favor: Judge James Edwin Horton and the Trial of the Scottsboro Boys," *UMKC Law Review* 68 (2000): 549.

of Alabama nor Attorney General Knight was ready to give up. And a year later, Judge Horton was defeated in his bid for reelection and never again held public office.

For the retrial of Haywood Patterson and Clarence Norris, Attorney General Knight had Judge Horton replaced by seventy-year-old William Callahan. Leibowitz again sought a dismissal because of the exclusion of blacks from the jury, but all motions were denied. Judge Callahan systematically undermined the defense presentations during these trials. He overruled almost every defense objection but sustained almost every objection made by the prosecution. He also excluded much of the defense case, whether or not Knight objected.

A few examples: Judge Callahan refused to allow any cross-examination of Victoria Price about her background or the fact that she had had sex with Jack Tiller the night before the alleged attack. He did not allow Lester Carter to testify that he had actually seen them in the act. As a result of these erroneous rulings, the jury never had an alternative explanation of the semen that had been found in Price and Bates. In addition, the judge refused to allow a brief delay so that the deposition of Ruby Bates, who could not travel to Decatur, could be taken and presented to the jury. Nor would he permit a recess so that the testimony of a Chattanooga doctor could be presented by the defendants. In his charge to the jurors, Judge Callahan explicitly allowed them to "presume that no white woman would ever have sex voluntarily with a Negro."[26] He told the jury the form in which they should report a guilty verdict. He neglected to tell them how to report an acquittal until that error was called to his attention by Leibowitz.[27] Patterson and Norris were convicted and sentenced to death.

All appeals through the Alabama courts failed, but once again the United States Supreme Court came to the rescue of the *Scottsboro* defendants. On April 1, 1935, the Court overturned the convictions of Patterson and Norris, holding in *Norris v. Alabama*[28] that the sys-

---

26. Carter, *Scottsboro*, 297; Acker, *Scottsboro and Its Legacy*, 123.
27. Carter, *Scottsboro*, 299; Acker, *Scottsboro and Its Legacy*, 124.
28. Norris v. Alabama, 294 U.S. 587 (1935).

tematic exclusion of blacks from sitting on the juries was a denial of equal protection.

Norris v. Alabama was another landmark case. The significance of the decision was not the legal principle itself; the Court had held years before that blacks could not be systematically and arbitrarily excluded from juries. But this principle was difficult, perhaps even impossible, to enforce because one had been required to prove intentional, systematic, and arbitrary exclusion. It had been difficult to show a discriminatory intent on the part of state officials who made up the jury lists, and the Supreme Court had been reluctant to overrule findings of the southern state courts that discrimination had not been shown. However, in *Norris v. Alabama,* the Court refused to accept the facts as found by the Alabama appellate court. It declared that the testimony showed that no black person had served on a jury in recent history, and that there were well-qualified black people in Jackson County who had never been called to serve. That was enough to indicate discriminatory exclusion.

Leibowitz's oral argument before the Supreme Court was unusual in one respect. After the *Scottsboro* trials, the commissioner of jurors, or a member of his staff, added the names of six black men to the rolls in an attempt to show that blacks were not excluded from consideration. The individual who attempted this fraud had had to squeeze the names into the small space that was left on the page for the year 1931. Leibowitz accused the State of having fraudulently added the names. "Can you prove it?" asked one of the justices. "Yes, your Honor," Leibowitz replied, as he presented to the Court the 1931 Jackson County jury roll. One by one, each of the justices looked at the relevant pages with a magnifying glass while Leibowitz waited to continue his presentation. It was a decisive moment and, some say, the first time the Supreme Court was presented with demonstrative evidence during an oral argument.[29]

---

29. Norris v. Alabama, 294 U.S. 587, 591–3, (1935); Carter, *Scottsboro,* 322–4; Goodman, *Stories of Scottsboro,* 243.

Sympathizers gathered to protest the jury verdict
against the Scottsboro Boys.
© Underwood & Underwood/CORBIS

The rest of the story is anticlimactic. Alabama prosecutors had
grown tired of the *Scottsboro* cases. The trials had not only been costly
but had earned Alabama terrible worldwide publicity.

In 1936, again before Judge Callahan, Patterson was convicted of
rape for the fourth time and was given a prison sentence of seventy-
five years. Never in the history of Alabama had a black man convicted of raping a white woman not been given the death penalty. The
following year, Clarence Norris was convicted of the same crime and
sentenced to death, but the governor commuted that to life imprisonment. Soon after, Charlie Weems was convicted of rape and given
ninety-nine years, and Ozie Powell got twenty years for assaulting
a sheriff. Then suddenly, at a press conference, the prosecution team
explained the dropping of all charges against Eugene Williams, Roy
Wright, Willie Roberson, and Olen Montgomery.

After careful consideration of the testimony, every lawyer connected with the prosecution is convinced that the defendants

Willie Roberson and Olen Montgomery are not guilty. The doctor who examined Roberson the day after the commission of the crimes stated that he was sick, suffering from a venereal disease and that in his condition it would have been very painful to have committed that crime, and that he would not have had any inclination to commit it. He has told a very plausible story from the beginning; that he was in a box car and knew nothing about the crime. Olen Montgomery was practically blind and has also told a plausible story, which has been unshaken all through litigation, which put him at some distance from the commission of the crime. The State is without proof other than the prosecutrix as to his being in the gondola car, and we feel that it is a case of mistaken identity.

The prosecution team all entertain the same view as to these two black people and in view of the doubt generated by the fact that their physical condition was as stated above, we feel that the policy of the law and the ends of justice would not justify us in asking a conviction of these two cases. Two of the defendants were juveniles at the time this crime was committed. According to a careful investigation by the Attorney General's office, we are convinced that at the time of the actual commission of this crime one of these juveniles was 12 years old and the other one was 13, and while they were in the gondola car when the rape was committed, counsel for the State think that in view of the fact they have been in jail for six and a half years, the ends of justice would be met at this time by releasing these two juveniles, on condition that they leave the state, never to return.[30]

Over the course of the next ten years, the rest of the imprisoned Scottsboro youths, except Haywood Patterson, who had managed to escape, were paroled. Brutalized by years in prison, they had difficulty adjusting to the outside world. Some violated parole or committed other crimes and ended up back in jail. Only Clarence Norris

---

30. Goodman, *Stories of Scottsboro*, 308–9; Carter, *Scottsboro*, 376–7.

made a successful return to society. He moved to New York, married, and had a steady job. He lived in freedom for forty-five years until his death in 1989 at age 76.

By 1976, all the Scottsboro Boys had died except for Clarence Norris. That year he received a full pardon from the state of Alabama. A major supporter of his pardon was the state's new attorney general, William Baxley. After a review of the *Scottsboro* case, Baxley wrote to the governor, "We have concluded that it is impossible that Victoria Price was raped as she alleged." Baxley urged the pardon board to "swiftly grant to Clarence Norris a full and complete pardon, which would remove the unjust stigma of a crime that the overwhelming evidence clearly shows he did not commit."[31]

The governor who signed the pardon and personally delivered it to Clarence Norris was none other than George Wallace, who in his 1963 inaugural speech had proclaimed ". . . segregation now, segregation tomorrow, segregation forever." A personal vindication for Mr. Norris, the pardon was also a reflection of how much the South had changed since the 1930s. Further evidence of this change came on April 19, 2013, when Alabama Governor Bentley signed a posthumous pardon for all nine Scottsboro Boys. Bentley acknowledges, "We cannot take back what happened. But we can make it right moving forward." Alabama's Speaker of the House added, "The Legislature's unanimous passage of this important legislation and the Governor's signature show that today's Alabama is far removed from the Alabama that caused such pain for so many so long ago." The ceremonial signing took place at the Scottsboro Boys Museum and Cultural Center in Scottsboro, Alabama.[32]

The *Scottsboro* cases, trials, convictions, and the years of imprisonment for the nine defendants, much of them spent on death row, were a tragedy, not only for the Scottsboro Boys but for the South and for the state of Alabama. Did anything worthwhile come out of it? Lawyers and historians point to two accomplishments. First, the

---

31. Carter, *Scottsboro*, 425–7; Goodman, *Stories of Scottsboro*, 387.
32. Alan Blinder, "Alabama Pardons 3 Scottsboro Boys After 80 Years," *New York Times*, November 21, 2013.

Scottsboro cases produced two landmark Supreme Court decisions that advanced racial justice and protected the rights of the accused. Second, *Scottsboro* is considered by many to have helped stimulate and spark the civil rights movement. In the *Scottsboro* trials, whites joined blacks in a demand for racial justice that had rarely been in evidence since the abolition movement. The American Communist Party was an animating force in fostering the interracial alliance, but as the trials continued into the 1930s, Scottsboro Defense Leagues were formed. Whites and blacks, rich and poor, men and women, the same kind of coalition that would serve American society so well in the 1960s and '70s, came together to protest the gross injustice that had been visited upon the Scottsboro Boys.

FOUR

United States v. Alger Hiss: A Cold War Confrontation[1]

UNITED STATES V. ALGER HISS is one of the greatest political trials of the twentieth century.

In the summer of 1948, Whittaker Chambers, a senior editor from *Time* magazine and a self-admitted ex-communist spy, appeared before the House Un-American Activities Committee (HUAC). During the session, Chambers identified several federal officials as having been members of a secret communist cell whose purpose was

---

1. This chapter relies heavily upon transcripts of HUAC hearings and of the Hiss trials as well as secondary sources, particularly including the best account of the Hiss-Chambers confrontation by Allen Weinstein in *Perjury: The Hiss-Chambers Case* (3rd ed. Random House, New York, 2013) and the beautifully written first book on the Hiss case by Alistair Cooke, *A Generation on Trial: U.S.A. v. Alger Hiss* (Greenwood Press Reprint, 1982). The authors have also relied on the lectures, essays, and oral presentations on this case by Professor Irving Younger that appear in *The Irving Younger Collection: Wisdom & Wit from the Master of Trial Advocacy* (ABA Section of Litigation, 2010); "Was Alger Hiss Guilty?," *Cornell Law Forum* Vol. 2, No. 4 (Fall/Winter 1975), which is a short version of his article in *Commentary Magazine* (August 1975). This chapter is an elaboration of an article by coauthor Professor Faust Rossi under the same title published in the March 2001 issue of the *Cornell Law Forum*.

to infiltrate the United States government. Among those accused was Alger Hiss, a respected lawyer and government official. Three months later Chambers elaborated on his accusation, testifying that Hiss, while in the State Department a decade earlier, in 1938, had taken secret government documents and turned them over to Chambers for delivery to Communist Russia. Hiss replied swiftly to these charges. He said that he was never a communist and never knew Whittaker Chambers, at least by that name. Later, Hiss did recognize Chambers, as a "deadbeat" acquaintance whom he barely knew then and could recognize now only with difficulty.

The accusations against Hiss shocked a nation already entangled in the politics of the Cold War. The stage was set for a sensational American trial.

Deciding which man's story was the truth and which was a lie was no easy task. But a federal grand jury in the Southern District of New York did exactly that when it indicted Alger Hiss on two counts of perjury. The jury's finding was based on the fact that Hiss denied under oath that he had passed official secret documents to Chambers in 1938, as well as claiming he had not seen or conversed with Chambers after January 1, 1937. There could be no finding of espionage, as that crime had occurred in 1938, and the three-year statute of limitations had run out.

For the charges brought against Alger Hiss, there was not one, but two trials. The first one ended in a hung jury on July 7, 1949, with the jurors deadlocked 8 to 4 for conviction. In the second trial, which began on November 17, 1949, and ended on January 21, 1950, the jury was unanimous. Hiss was convicted on the two counts of perjury and sentenced to five years in prison.

The historical significance of the Alger Hiss case lies in the momentous way it aroused and divided the nation. On one side were Democrats who viewed Hiss as a symbol of the young liberals who went to Washington in the thirties to join the New Deal crusade. To conservatives, many of whom were Republicans, Hiss was emblematic of the liberals' romance with socialism and their feckless response to the threat posed by the Soviet Union. Whether one believed Hiss or Chambers became a political litmus test.

The legacy of the *Hiss* trials further underscored their impact. But for the *Hiss* case, Richard M. Nixon might have remained an obscure congressman from California. And, as the historian Allen Weinstein has written, "More than any other factor, Alger Hiss's conviction gave Senator [Joseph] McCarthy and his supporters the essential touch of credibility, making their charges of Communist involvement against other officials headline copy instead of back page filler."[2]

Whittaker Chambers as he begins testifying before the House Un-American Activities Committee.
© Bettmann/CORBIS

For lawyers and other legal professionals, the case continues to inspire passion and analysis. For the court to arrive at a fair verdict after sorting through the convoluted histories of two public figures, navigating the blizzard of documents, high-profile witnesses, and a rabid media in a politically charged climate was no small feat. The major players in both trials, the judges and the lawyers, all did excellent, often brilliant work. To many, the *Hiss* case serves as an example of a moment when the system truly worked. To some, it remains a miscarriage of justice.

The *Hiss* trials featured a pair of experienced judges. In the first, there was Samuel Kaufman, a diminutive man, about five feet tall, but with an outsized personality. The second trial was presided over by Henry Goddard, the senior judge in the district. He was less exu-

---

2. Weinstein, *Perjury*, 531.

berant than Kaufman and more inclined to allow the jury to hear whatever either party considered relevant.

Prosecuting both trials was Thomas Murphy. He was not a famous lawyer but was considered a consummate professional by his peers. Murphy was neither loud nor flamboyant. At six foot five, weighing a muscled 250 pounds, and sporting a walrus mustache, he rarely needed to raise his voice to command attention.

Defense attorney Lloyd Paul Stryker was regarded as the best criminal lawyer of his time. Stryker was charismatic, witty, dramatic, and, pound for pound, a worthy opponent for Thomas Murphy. For the second trial, Stryker was replaced by Claude Cross, a very able, big-firm Boston trial lawyer.

All these men lived up to their reputations. The openings, cross-examinations, and summations were models of effective advocacy. Their legal innovations have found their way into the casebooks that law students study today. There may be no other trial in American history that relied on character and reputation witnesses as extensively as did the Hiss defense. The trial also marked the first time a psychiatrist was allowed to impeach the credibility of a witness—Whittaker Chambers—whom the psychiatrist had never examined or even met.

Another reason this case continues to fascinate is the sheer force and intensity of the confrontation between Chambers and Hiss. Clearly, one of them was lying; elaborately, completely, and continually. There was no failure of memory at play, no faulty reconstruction of old events, no rationalizing oneself into believing something that was not true. As F. Edward Hebert, a Democrat on the HUAC, told Hiss, "Either you or Mr. Chambers is lying . . . and whichever one of you is lying is the greatest actor that America has ever produced."[3]

If one were to choose between these two men, based on their known past life and reputation, there could be no question that Chambers was the malevolent liar. Alger Hiss, after all, was the golden boy.

---

3. The testimony of Alger Hiss before HUAC on August 16, 1948: Douglas Linder, "Famous American Trials," http://law2.umkc.edu/faculty/projects/ftrials/hiss/8-16testimony.html; T. Michael Ruddy, *The Alger Hiss Espionage Case* (Thomson 2005), 92.

Born in 1904 to a good Baltimore family, Hiss was Phi Beta Kappa at Johns Hopkins before graduating from Harvard Law School at the top of his class. A protégé of soon-to-be Supreme Court Justice Felix Frankfurter, Hiss became a clerk for Justice Oliver Wendell Holmes and then joined a prestigious New York law firm. During this time, Hiss married Priscilla Hobson, a Bryn Mawr graduate. Eager to help the downtrodden and dispossessed during the Great Depression, the couple became active in progressive social causes. In 1933, Hiss went to Washington. He was appointed to important positions in Franklin Roosevelt's New Deal administration: assistant general counsel of the Agricultural Adjustment Administration, legal counsel to the Senate Committee Investigating the Munitions Industry, and then special attorney in the Office of the Solicitor General. In a letter of recommendation to Assistant Attorney General O'Brian, Felix Frankfurter described Hiss as "not only a first-rate lawyer, but a man of unusual cultivation, charm and prematurely solid judgment."[4] Hiss also became the personal assistant to the assistant secretary of state, Francis Sayre. In the 1940s, Hiss was a principal advisor to President Roosevelt at the Yalta Conference. After the war, he helped create the United Nations and was appointed acting secretary-general of the United Nations. In 1948, Hiss became the president of the Carnegie Endowment for International Peace.

Hiss's resume was impeccable, and throughout the trial, Lloyd Stryker made the most of it. The trustees of the Carnegie Endowment, "who are not stupid men," Stryker proclaimed, had "selected the best man they could get in America, the most trustworthy man."[5]

Then Mr. Stryker raised his right arm, as if to swear an oath: "I will take Alger Hiss," he cried, "by the hand, and I will lead him before you from the date of his birth down to this hour even, though I would go through the valley of the shadow of death, I will fear no evil, because there is no blot or blemish on him."[6]

---

4. Weinstein, *Perjury*, 91.
5. Cooke, *A Generation on Trial*, 115.
6. Cooke, *A Generation on Trial*, 115; Kurt Ritter, "Drama and Legal Rhetoric: The Perjury Trials of Alger Hiss," *Western Journal of Speech Communications* (1985): 87.

Whittaker Chambers was, in almost every way imaginable, Hiss's opposite. In contrast to Hiss's tall frame and elegant, patrician presence, Chambers was short, overweight, and unkempt. While Hiss's résumé was marked by a striving for professional excellence and positive social change, Chambers's was tainted by rebellion, contrarianism, and failure. Born in Philadelphia in 1901 and raised on Long Island, Chambers's disreputable behavior started early. Chosen by his high school peers to deliver the class prophecy, he drafted a speech that was so offensive that the principal forbade Chambers from delivering it. Chambers wrote a second speech but delivered the first one instead, and as a result never received his diploma. At eighteen, Chambers left home, drifting from Baltimore to Washington, D.C., and to New Orleans, using false names and working as a day laborer. Eventually he returned to New York and enrolled at Columbia. Expelled for writing a controversial play about Jesus Christ, he lied his way back in. But Chambers never graduated from Columbia or any other college. He got by through a succession of odd jobs, one of which was at the public library. When an investigation turned up sixty-four stolen books in his locker and at his home, he was fired. During this time his brother Richard proposed that they commit suicide together. While Chambers thought it over, his brother killed himself. Chambers fell into a depression and stayed in bed for months. In 1925, Chambers joined the Communist Party. He gave false information on applications for passports, driver's licenses, and employment forms until he broke with the party in either 1937, as he first said, or in 1938, as he later remembered. In 1939, Chambers got a job with *Time* magazine. A gifted writer, he became a senior editor earning a yearly salary of $30,000, a substantial sum in 1948. In May 1942, the FBI interviewed Chambers about his communist background. Although he did not mention instances of espionage or stolen documents, he did identify Alger Hiss.

In his opening statement for the prosecution at the first trial, Thomas Murphy told the jury, "If you don't believe Whittaker Chambers, we have no case." This admission played into the defense's strategy. Stryker would be delighted to have the jury ignore the other evidence and to consider only the credibility of the two adversar-

ies. So Stryker pounced on Murphy's words, and never let the jury forget them. As he sketched for the jury his indelible, contrasting biographies of each man in his opening statement—Hiss the dignified statesman, and Chambers, the slanderous failure—he articulated his theme: "Who can you believe, the saint or the sinner?" And he described the accuser:

> He chose to join a conspiracy to overthrow the United States by any means, especially by lying. For twelve long years this man Chambers, alias Adams, alias Crosley, alias Cantwell, alias a great many other things . . . was a member of this low-down, nefarious, filthy conspiracy . . . against the land that I love and you love. He cheated his government on income taxes and filed no returns for the money he was being paid for the prostitution of his soul. He wrote a filthy despicable play in college, about Jesus Christ, and was dismissed. And how did he get back? By lying.[7]

Stryker ended his opening statement with this analogy:

> In the warm southern countries, you know, where they have leprosy, sometimes you will hear on the streets among the lepers a man who walks ahead to give warning. His cries ring out down the street, "Unclean, unclean," at the approach of a leper. I say the same to you at the approach of this moral leper.[8]

As Alistair Cooke has reminded us in *A Generation on Trial*, the *Hiss* case was unique because it judged a man "in one decade, for what he was said to have done in another."[9] And how different these decades were.

---

7. Cooke, *A Generation on Trial*, 115.
8. Cooke, *A Generation on Trial*, 118; Ritter, "Drama and Legal Rhetoric," 88.
9. Cooke, *A Generation on Trial*, 3.

The changed climate was a prescription for misunderstandings. Murphy said as much to the jury in the second trial: "I am going to ask you to sort of throw yourselves back to those years, 1937, '36, '35, '34. Because unless you do that, you can't quite grasp what the thinking was at that time."[10]

In the 1930s, the nation was battling the twin monsters of economic depression at home and the rise of fascism abroad. In America, many people believed that capitalism was failing. Banks, corporations, and captains of industry, the heroes of the '20s, were now the villains, and the economic alternative for some was communism. Some Americans contrasted Soviet opposition to German fascism with the appeasement of England and France. To them, helping Russia was not unpatriotic; on the contrary, it was helping to bring about world peace and to aid the American people.

They overlooked what Stalin was perpetrating on his own people. The disillusionment of Soviet sympathizers began with the shock of the Nazi-Soviet pact in 1939. Implying that these "fellow travelers" had been willfully ignorant, George Orwell wrote in 1940 that "the sin of the American left in the 1930s was to have wanted to be anti-fascist without being anti-totalitarian."

By 1948 and 1949, the United States was in the midst of a cold war, with Russia the enemy about to successfully test an atomic bomb and China about to fall to the communists. The House Un-American Activities Committee was obsessed about the infiltration of the American government by communist subversives. And polls showed American citizens holding more punitive views of communists in their midst.[11]

The national mood shift did not bode well for Alger Hiss. In the courtroom, however, it was the prosecution's problem. How could the jury believe anything Chambers, the admitted communist, said? How could the prosecution get a jury to believe Hiss would betray his country by delivering secret documents to the Russians? Murphy

---

10. Ibid.
11. Douglas Linder, "Famous American Trials," http://law2.umkc.edu/faculty/projects/ftrials/hiss/hissaccount.html.

had to convince this 1949 jury that Hiss, the 1930s idealist, was not what he seemed; he could indeed commit espionage and still think he was acting nobly.

The Chambers-Hiss confrontation began on September 2, 1939, nine days after the Nazi-Soviet pact, when Whittaker Chambers met with Assistant Secretary of State Adolf Berle. Chambers told Berle that he had been a communist, had left the party, and now felt it was his duty to report that a number of government officials were members of an underground communist cell. Chambers named names and one of them was Alger Hiss. Berle made some notes and put them in a file. Nothing came of this meeting, or so it seemed.

Six years later, in March of 1945, the chief security officer of the State Department interviewed Chambers. Chambers explained, as he had to Berle, that the Communist Party had recruited an underground group of promising young men with advanced social and political ideas. Their assignment was to advance to high government positions in order to shape legislation favorable to the Communist Party. Chambers said that the leaders of this underground were, in order of importance, Harold Ware, Lee Pressman, and Alger Hiss. The information was summarized in a memorandum, placed in a file, and no further action was taken until August 1946, when the security officer again sought out Chambers. It was a similar conversation, but this time Chambers mentioned that he had asked Hiss back in May of 1938 to break with the party and that Hiss had refused. These accusations did not become public knowledge until the House Un-American Activities Committee held high-profile hearings.

Formed in 1938 to investigate possible communist infiltration of the Roosevelt administration, HUAC was chaired by J. Parnell Thomas of New Jersey. Among the other members, and soon to play a key role, was a freshman congressman from California named Richard Nixon. Robert Stripling was the committee's chief investigator. Asked by Stripling to testify, Chambers was reluctant. He had told his story to Berle in 1939 and again to the security officer in 1945 and 1946. He believed he had done his duty and was not inclined to relive the past in a public forum. HUAC was under pressure to produce results, and 1948 was a presidential election year, with President

Truman in a tight race against Thomas E. Dewey, and the House Committee had yet to come up with much evidence of communists in government. So a subpoena was issued to Chambers, and he testified first in a brief closed session and then in public on August 3, 1948.

Chambers's accusations were a media bombshell. Of the nine names mentioned in the session, Hiss's drew the most attention. The day after Chambers's testimony, the front-page headlines read, "Former Spy Names Alger Hiss" and "*Time* Editor Charges Carnegie Endowment Head was Soviet Agent."

Hiss had been alerted to Chambers's accusations by a Baltimore newspaper. That very evening, he fired off a telegram to the committee, denying everything and demanding to be heard, immediately and in public:

> My attention has been called by representatives of the press to statements made about me before your committee this morning by one Whittaker Chambers. I do not know Mr. Chambers and insofar as I am aware have never laid eyes on him. There is no basis for the statements made about me to your committee. I would appreciate it if you would make this telegram a part of your committee's record, and I would further appreciate the opportunity to appear before your committee to make these statements formally and under oath. I shall be in Washington on Thursday and hope that that will be a convenient time from the committee's point of view for me to appear.[12]

Hiss's request to appear was promptly granted. On Thursday, August 5, 1948, he appeared in open session before the committee and read the following statement:

> I am here at my own request to deny unqualifiedly various statements about me which were made before this committee by one Whittaker Chambers the day before yesterday. . . .

---

12. Cooke, *A Generation on Trial*, 60.

I am not and never have been a member of the communist party. I do not and never have adhered to the tenets of the communist party. I am not and never have been a member of any communist-front organization. I have never followed the communist party line, directly or indirectly. To the best of my knowledge, none of my friends is a communist.

To the best of my knowledge, I never heard of Whittaker Chambers until in 1947, when two representatives of the Federal Bureau of Investigation asked me if I knew him and various other people, some of whom I knew and some of whom I did not know. I said I did not know Chambers. So far as I know, I have never laid eyes on him, and I should like to have the opportunity to do so.[13]

Hiss ended his testimony with an unequivocal declaration: "The statements made about me by Mr. Chambers are complete fabrications. I think my record in government service speaks for itself."[14]

Following Hiss's statement, the questioning began. At one point, Stripling placed before Hiss a photograph of Chambers and asked, "Do you recognize this man?" For the first time since the hearing began, Hiss seemed to hedge a little. "I cannot swear that I have not seen that man," he said. "I would very much like to see this man face-to-face. Then I would know. At this point, for all I know, this could be a picture of the committee chairman."[15]

Hiss was so impressive that some members of the committee worried that they might be made to look foolish and HUAC might be irreparably damaged for pursuing Chambers's charges. So they treated Hiss with elaborate courtesy. At the end of the hearing a congressman asked him, "Mr. Hiss, do you feel you have had a free and fair and proper hearing this morning?" Hiss replied, "I think I

13. The testimony of Alger Hiss before HUAC on August 5, 1948: Linder, "Famous American Trials," http://law2.umkc.edu/faculty/projects/ftrials/hiss/8-5testimony.html; Ruddy, *The Alger Hiss Espionage Case*, 33–36; *Hearings Regarding Communist Espionage in the United States Government, Before the House Committee on Un-American Activities*, 80th Cong., 2nd Sess. 642–3, 646–7 (1948).
14. Ibid.
15. Ibid.

have been treated with great consideration by this committee." There were then expressions of gratitude to Hiss for his "very cooperative attitude" and his "forthright statements."

On August 7, the committee recalled Chambers for a closed session with no publicity and no reporters. Richard Nixon did the questioning, asking him if the photograph placed before him was "the man you have been talking about":

> He sure is! It's Alger Hiss. He was and may still be a communist. He was in my cell of the underground. I knew him well. In fact I knew him very well. My wife and I stayed overnight with Hiss and his wife a number of times, we spent time together over several years, we took a vacation together. We visited them. They visited us. Believe me, there is no mistake.[16]

Chambers provided a wealth of intimate knowledge about Hiss. He knew Hiss's nickname for his wife, and Mrs. Hiss's nickname for Alger. He knew what the Hisses called their children, details about their servants, their pets, their various addresses, and descriptions of furniture. Chambers knew what schools the Hiss children attended, and he knew that the education of Alger's stepson was paid for by the child's natural father. Chambers talked about Hiss's hobbies and his taste in books and food. At one point, Chambers mentioned that Hiss was an avid bird-watcher and was excited one day because he had seen a bird rarely seen in the Washington area, a prothonotary warbler, on the banks of the Potomac.

On August 16, Hiss was asked to return for another appearance before the committee. It was a private session and the questioning was more direct this time. Hiss was shown old photographs of Chambers, as he appeared in the thirties. Nixon asked him, "How about now, do you know this man?" Hiss replied, "I do not recall any person with distinctness and definiteness whose picture this is. But it

---

16. Ibid., Ruddy, *The Alger Hiss Espionage Case*, 42–48; *Hearings Regarding Communist Espionage in the United States Government, Before the House Committee on Un-American Activities*, 80th Cong., 2nd Sess. 662–7 (1948).

is not completely unfamiliar." Nixon began to check on the accuracy of Chambers's testimony. "What do you call your wife? What's her nickname for you?" Nixon asked. Hiss protested, "Look, if I give you details, they might leak to Chambers and help him to build a very persuasive case by claiming that he knew these things before." The committee assured Hiss that there would be no leaks and that Chambers was already fully on record. So Hiss answered, and Chambers's detailed memories were confirmed. When Hiss revealed that he was an amateur ornithologist, the committee chair said innocently, "Have you ever seen a prothonotary warbler?" "Yes," Hiss said, "I saw one right here on the Potomac."

Hiss, however, was not finished:

> It begins to dawn on me that this fellow Chambers may be a casual acquaintance from back in 1934 or 1935. A man named George Crosley. He was a freelance writer hoping to sell articles on the munitions committee. I was counsel to the senate committee investigating munitions transfers. So I talked to him. He had blondish hair, very bad teeth, married to a strikingly dark person with one child, a baby. [Hiss recalled that he rented an apartment to this family; that they had stayed with the Hisses in their new house for a few nights until their furniture arrived.] I didn't know the man very long because he turned out to be a deadbeat. He didn't pay the rent. I had been a sucker and he was using me for a soft touch. I am not sure that this man who now calls himself Chambers was George Crosley but it's possible. I would have to see him face-to-face.[17]

The next day, on August 17, in Room 1400 of the Commodore Hotel in New York City, a face-to-face confrontation was arranged between Chambers and Hiss. Members of the subcommittee were

17. The testimony of Alger Hiss before HUAC on August 16, 1948: Linder, "Famous American Trials," http://law2.umkc.edu/faculty/projects/ftrials/hiss/8-16testimony.html; Ruddy, *The Alger Hiss Espionage Case*, 58–59; *Hearings Regarding Communist Espionage in the United States Government, Before the House Committee on Un-American Activities*, 80th Cong., 2nd Sess. 940–41, 945–49, 952–53, 955–70 (1948).

present. Nixon said to Hiss, "The man standing here is Mr. Whittaker Chambers. I ask you now if you have ever known that man before." Hiss thought for moment, then began what seemed an elaborate, ritual interrogation directed at Chambers. He asked him to speak and then asked to look into Chambers's mouth, in order to examine his teeth. He asked Chambers whether he had dental work done. Chambers said yes. Hiss asked for the name of the dentist and a description of the dental work done. Still not satisfied, Hiss asked Chambers more questions. Had Chambers lived in his apartment? Was he George Crosley? At various times during this meeting, Hiss said, "I think he is George Crosley," but then issued a clarification: "I believe that I am not prepared without further checking to take an absolute oath that he must be George Crosley." Further pressed, Hiss indicated, "I will, on the basis of his answers, positively identify him as George Crosley."[18]

Hiss began to remember more details about Crosley. Not only had Hiss leased him his apartment and had him in his house, he had given him his old car. Hiss also remembered that Chambers had given him an Oriental rug. Hiss was now recalling what appeared to be a rather close relationship for several months, with a figure who had been an indistinct, unnamed shadow just a day or two earlier. When challenged by Stripling as to why it took so long for Hiss to recognize Chambers as Crosley, Hiss explained that he was not given, on important occasions, to snap judgments.

The next confrontation was a public ten-hour session when, for the first time in history, a congressional hearing was televised. Chambers identified Hiss as a dedicated member of the communist underground. Hiss identified Chambers as Crosley, denied he himself had ever been a communist, and was in all other respects extremely cautious. He qualified his answers with "To the best of my

---

18. The testimony of Alger Hiss before HUAC on August 17, 1948: Linder, "Famous American Trials," http://law2.umkc.edu/faculty/projects/ftrials/hiss/8-17testimony.html; Ruddy, *The Alger Hiss Espionage Case*, 70–80; *Hearings Regarding Communist Espionage in the United States Government, Before the House Committee on Un-American Activities*, 80th Cong., 2nd Sess. 975–9, 984–9, 991–2 (1948); Younger, *The Irving Younger Collection*, 526–33; for the entire transcript, see *In re Hiss*, 542 F. Supp. 973, 979–80 (S.D.N.Y. 1982).

recollection," "I have no present recollection," "I am unable to recall in terms of actual present memory," or "I don't have a positive definite recollection." According to the committee's count, he used these qualifiers a total of 198 times during his testimony. As lawyers know, these phrases make perjury convictions difficult. At one point, Hiss was asked to identify his notarized signature on a photostat of his automobile transfer of title. He answered, "I do not like the idea of swearing to a signature on a photostat. I would prefer to see the original." Hiss was also unable to come up with any witness who had ever known Chambers as Crosley or any evidence that a George Crosley, whom he had identified as a writer, had ever written anything.

The committee members now believed Chambers. That was made abundantly clear in HUAC's interim report, issued on August 27, 1948, part of which was titled "Hiss-Chambers: Testimony." It concluded that the testimony of Hiss was "vague and evasive" and characterized him as having a "strangely defective memory." On the other hand, it found Chambers's testimony "forthright and emphatic." The report concluded that the verifiable portions of Chambers's testimony had stood up strongly, while those of Hiss's testimony had been badly shaken.[19]

Nonetheless, there was not enough evidence to prove perjury beyond a reasonable doubt. Thus, there could be no criminal prosecution. The committee issued its report and Nixon went on a three-week cruise in the Caribbean. That would have been the end of it, except for one remarkable development.

Until now, in some ways, Hiss had acted like an innocent man. When Chambers made his charges, Hiss denied them forcefully and demanded the immediate right to respond. He insisted upon, and got, a face-to-face public confrontation with Chambers in public. But Hiss also did something else. At the meeting at the Commodore Hotel, he stood over Chambers, with his fists clenched, and said, "I would like to invite Mr. Whittaker Chambers to make those same

19. Ruddy, *The Alger Hiss Espionage Case*, 99–102; *Hearings Regarding Communist Espionage in the United States Government, Before the House Committee on Un-American Activities*, 80th Cong., 2nd Sess. 1348–9, 1352–4 (1948); Weinstein, *Perjury*, 68.

statements out of the presence of this committee without their being privileged for suit for libel. I challenge you to do it, and I hope you will do it damned quickly."[20] He issued the same challenge in the televised public hearing on August 25. "Be careful what you wish for," is the saying that comes to mind.

Five days after the public hearing, Whittaker Chambers appeared on the radio program *Meet the Press*. The reporter's first question was, "Mr. Chambers, are you willing to say now, when your statements are not privileged, that Alger Hiss is or was ever a communist?" Chambers answered, "Alger Hiss was a communist and he may be one now." Less than a month later, Hiss sued Chambers in a civil action in the Maryland state court, seeking $50,000 in damages for defamation. Hiss said that in addition to being false, Chambers's accusations had "damaged his professional reputation and office, and brought him into public odium and contempt and caused him great pain and mental anguish."[21] He added, "I am glad my case is now in the hands of the court." For Hiss, this turned out to be a fatal mistake.

Chambers welcomed "Mr. Hiss's daring suit," saying, "I do not minimize the audacity or the ferocity of the forces which work through him. But I do not believe that Mr. Hiss or anybody else can use the means of justice to defeat the ends of justice."[22] In response, Hiss asked for an additional $25,000.

A day after Hiss filed his suit, President Truman used a national radio broadcast to say that HUAC was fostering a climate where "an innocent man may easily find himself accused of terrible things." Truman had already twice before called the HUAC hearings "a red herring."[23]

Lawyers know that the process of civil litigation can often take on a life of its own, and the *Hiss* case was no exception. In the elaborate provisions for pretrial discovery, one never knows what surprising

20. Sam Tanenhaus, *Whittaker Chambers: A Biography* (Random House, New York, 1997); Ruddy, *The Alger Hiss Espionage Case*, 78.
21. Weinstein, *Perjury*, 173.
22. Ibid.
23. Ruddy, *The Alger Hiss Espionage Case*, 136–8; "Public Papers of the Presidents: Harry S. Truman, Address in Oklahoma City, September 28, 1948," Harry S Truman Library & Museum, http://trumanlibrary.org/publicpapers/index.php?pid=1965.

and substantive facts or evidence might turn up. In the American system of pretrial hearings, the parties are questioned under oath by each other's lawyers, and all documents relevant to the claim and defense must be produced on demand. This approach is designed to ensure that each side can prepare with all the information at hand.

At his deposition, Chambers was asked if he had ever obtained documents from Hiss for transmittal to the Soviet Union. As expected, Chambers said, "No, not to my knowledge." His answer was consistent with everything he had previously said. He had told Berle in 1939, the State Department security officer in 1945 and 1946, the House Committee, and the grand jury that Hiss was a communist, but that his purpose was not to commit espionage but only to infiltrate the government to influence policy.

The deposition of Chambers was adjourned. When Chambers reappeared two weeks later, he changed his answer and indicated that he did have documents showing that Hiss had engaged in espionage. Shocked silence descended on the room. Then came the obvious follow-up: "Where are these documents? Give us your proof." Chambers's attorney then delivered copies and summaries of secret State Department documents that Alger Hiss allegedly gave Chambers in 1938 to deliver to Soviet Russia.

According to Chambers's own testimony at trial, the following is a summary of what happened: In 1937, Chambers and Alger Hiss met secretly with a professional Soviet spy and a Russian army officer, one Colonel Bykov. Bykov asked Hiss to procure documents from the State Department that would help Russia in its fight against fascism. Hiss agreed and the plan was as follows: Chambers would notify Hiss in advance when he was coming to Hiss's house, only about every ten days or so, and on that day Hiss would bring home documents. Hiss could not keep the documents longer than overnight, so Chambers would arrive that night, take the documents, and drive to Baltimore to have them microfilmed by one Felix Inslerman, the official communist photographer. Chambers would then immediately take the originals back to Hiss, who returned them to the government files when he went to work the next morning; the microfilm would go to Colonel Bykov.

Chambers said that a decision was made to increase the flow of information. Hiss would bring home originals every night to copy, which could only be done by typewriter, as there were no copying machines at that time. So every night Alger Hiss, or more likely Priscilla Hiss, would type the documents, and the originals would be returned the next day. Then, when Chambers came, he would take not only that day's originals but also the typed copies of the previous days to Inslerman to microfilm. He would then give the originals back to Hiss to replace, the typed copies would be destroyed, and the microfilm would be delivered to Bykov to be sent on to Soviet Russia.[24]

In 1937, Chambers began to think about breaking with the Communist Party because he "sought to live an industrious and God fearing life."[25] Before doing so, Chambers felt he needed protection; an insurance policy to use against the party should they try to punish him for leaving. In 1938, Chambers decided to keep some of the typed copies, summaries, and microfilm:

> I then took these items in an envelope and gave them to my wife's nephew, Harold Levine, and said keep this envelope and hide it. After the first part of my deposition, after the adjournment, I went to Harold. He dug up the now 10-year-old envelope, which he had hidden in a shaft over the bathtub in his mother's house.[26]

Chambers testified that there were three items in the envelope:

(1) Typewritten copies of secret State Department documents that had been typed by Hiss or Mrs. Hiss on their typewriter.

---

24. Weinstein, *Perjury*, 260–1; Younger, *The Irving Younger Collection*, 550, 552.
25. Tanenhaus, *Whittaker Chambers*, 221.
26. Weinstein, *Perjury*, 185–7; Younger, *The Irving Younger Collection*, 535–6.

(2)   Notes in Hiss's own handwriting that were summaries of State Department documents, which, for one reason or another, Hiss could not or did not take home.

(3)   Microfilm of original government documents.

At the deposition, however, Chambers produced only the first two items, the typed copies and the handwritten summaries, but not the microfilm, which he kept hidden on his Baltimore property. The explanation he gave for withholding the microfilm was that he needed more time to examine it. Fearing that Hiss's investigators would break into his house, Chambers said he took the film to his farm and concealed it in a hollowed-out pumpkin. An enthusiastic press dubbed the microfilm, as well as the collection of notes and typewritten documents in the case, as "the pumpkin papers."

Word of these documents being delivered at the deposition was leaked to the House Committee, and Investigator Stripling fired off a telegram to the vacationing Nixon, suggesting that he return at once.

Pumpkin with microfilms at Whittaker Chambers's farm.
© Bettmann/CORBIS

Rep. Richard M. Nixon (R-Cal.) takes a close look at one of the
microfilm strips brought to light by Whittaker Chambers.
© Bettmann/CORBIS

The committee served a subpoena duces tecum on Chambers to
pressure him to identify and deliver any material in his possession.
On December 1, 1948, Nixon and Stripling drove to the Baltimore
farm and Chambers took them to the pumpkin patch and gave them
the microfilm.

This was, to put it mildly, bad news for Hiss. But the presence of
the previously withheld evidence also called into question Cham-

bers's integrity. If what Chambers was now saying was true, then he had deliberately withheld evidence of espionage from the FBI, from the House Committee, and from the grand jury, until the defamation action compelled him to reveal it. All these years, while Hiss rose in the ranks, was involved in the Yalta Conference, helped establish the United Nations, and became an advisor to presidents, Chambers had said nothing. Murphy knew Stryker would hit this issue hard, so he made sure Chambers explained himself on direct examination:

> Before the deposition when I handed over the documents, in all my prior testimony and statements, I had a twofold purpose. One purpose was to destroy the communist conspiracy within the country. The other purpose was to do as little injury as possible to the human beings involved in that conspiracy.
>
> In my own case, a kind of grace had been given to me to find the strength to break and time had been given me in which to work out a new life. In breaking with the communist party, time is the most essential factor. I wanted to give these people the same opportunity that had been given me.
>
> But I had been now forced into a position where I had no choice but to introduce these documents into evidence. I had previously testified to the House Committee and to the grand jury that I had no evidence of espionage and what I have just said was the reason why I so testified. Now after the introduction of the documents I went before the grand jury and I told them about the espionage activities and I added in my testimony to the grand jury that in disclosing this testimony some damage was inevitably to be done to the people involved—the people I mentioned.
>
> There was a distinction, at least in my mind, in disclosing the ultimate perfidy by which I mean espionage and merely disclosing the fact that these people were communists. In general, I think that there are two kinds of men. One kind believes that God is a God of justice and the other kind believes that

the god is a God of mercy. And I am so constituted that I will always range myself on the side of mercy.[27]

Much to the chagrin of members of the House Committee, the Justice Department investigation displaced them. Matters were now the subject of a criminal investigation, and Chambers testified again before the grand jury. Responding to evidence that the typed copies were created on a typewriter once owned by the Hisses, Hiss testified, "I never passed government documents to the man I now know to be Whittaker Chambers." And "I never saw Whittaker Chambers after January 1, 1937, until he surfaced in 1948 with his accusations."

For these two statements, Alger Hiss was indicted on two counts of perjury. Both indictments sprang from what the jury saw as a single act of deception. As the documents delivered to the grand jury were dated in the first months of 1938, the grand jury was telling Hiss, "When you say that you never saw Chambers after January 1937, you are lying because you passed documents to him in early 1938."

It is fair to treat both trials in the Southern District of New York as if they were one, since the evidence, save for a few differences, was essentially the same. In the second trial, for example, Murphy did not repeat his statement, "If you don't believe Whittaker Chambers, we have no case." Though this was just as true then as before, perhaps he didn't want to hear his words repeated time and again by the new defense counsel, Claude Cross. Murphy also made more of an effort in the second trial to portray Chambers as a man with a sense of duty and the courage to reveal his past and quit the Communist Party. The defense also adjusted its emphasis. In the first trial, Stryker gave a four-hour summation but spent only eleven minutes on the documents. Cross realized that the secret State Department documents needed much more attention.

Four areas of evidence at the trials merit comment, although only one was decisive: (1) the prosecution effort to corroborate Chambers's

27. Younger, "Was Alger Hiss Guilty?"; Weinstein, *Perjury*, 188; Ruddy, *The Alger Hiss Espionage Case*, 116–7.

Alger Hiss issues a statement less than two hours after
he was indicted by a grand jury.
© Bettmann/CORBIS

story, (2) the defense presentation of reputation witnesses, (3) the
psychiatric testimony of Dr. Carl Binger, and (4) the secret State
Department documents.

The initial thrust of the prosecution's evidence was to corroborate
the details of Chambers's description of the close relationship he had
with Hiss. Much of this proof was developed by and explored in the
HUAC hearings.

Perhaps the most damaging to Hiss was the mystery of the 1929
Ford that Hiss initially claimed he had given to Chambers around
1935 as part of the sublet of Hiss's 28th Street apartment. Hiss testified before HUAC that he gave the car to Chambers because he had
recently bought a Plymouth. Hiss indicated at first that he had no
knowledge of the Ford after that. Chambers did know what happened to the car. It had not been given to him but instead was kept by
Hiss until sometime in 1936. Chambers explained that Hiss had told

him that he wanted to have the Ford delivered to the Communist Party so that it would reach an operative in need of a car. Chambers communicated this wish to J. Peters, who ran the communist organization in the Washington, D.C., area. The FBI discovered the paperwork, which showed that Hiss had signed a notarized certificate of title in 1936 assigning the Ford to the Cherner Motor Co., a large Ford agency in Washington. When presented with his notarized signature, Hiss conceded that it was his handwriting. Another certificate was uncovered that was a transfer from Cherner to one William Rosen. The implication was that a communist at Cherner Motor had facilitated the transfer to Rosen. When asked about his connection to the Ford, how he got it, and if he was a member of the Communist Party, Rosen refused to answer on the grounds of his Fifth Amendment privilege against self-incrimination. The evidence also showed that Hiss did not purchase the Plymouth until the fall of 1935. Hiss testified that he had no "clear recollection" of the transfer. He mused that Chambers might have returned the Ford to him or that maybe someone contacted him to sign the certificate after he gave the car to Chambers.[28]

Another piece of damaging evidence involved the oriental rug that Hiss received from Chambers. Chambers testified that in late 1936 Colonel Bykov announced that the Soviets wanted to give gifts to Chambers's colleagues who were providing information to the Soviet Union. Money was sent to Meyer Schapiro, a Columbia University professor of art history, who was asked to buy four rugs and send them to one George Silverman. According to Chambers, the rugs were transported in Silverman's car and by prearrangement, Chambers picked up one of them and delivered it to Hiss. Invoices confirmed that Professor Schapiro made the purchases for about $900, a considerable sum in those days, and shipped them to Silverman in compliance with Chambers's request. Hiss admitted getting a rug from Chambers but insisted it was partial payment for the rental of his 28th Street apartment.[29]

---

28. Weinstein, *Perjury*, 63–64.
29. *In re* Hiss, 542 F. Supp. 973, 985 (S.D.N.Y. 1982).

Chambers also testified that in November 1937, in preparation for his break with the Communist Party, he borrowed $400 in cash from the Hisses to purchase an automobile. Records of the car dealer confirmed the sale of the car to Chambers at that time, and bank records revealed that the Hisses withdrew $400 in cash four days before the sale. The Hisses insisted that they used the cash to buy furniture for his family's forthcoming move to a new house. The new house, it turned out, had not been purchased or under contract to be purchased at the time of Hiss's cash withdrawal. Moreover, Mrs. Hiss had charge accounts at various department stores, making cash purchases unnecessary and contrary to past financial practices. If Chambers's version was true, it showed that a friendly relationship existed in late 1937 and contradicted Hiss's grand jury testimony of no contact after January 1937.[30]

There was further confirmation of Chambers's testimony that he had a close relationship with the Hisses. Chambers testified that he purchased a Westminster, Maryland, farm that Hiss formerly had under contract. According to Chambers, Hiss drove him out to see the farm in early 1935 when Hiss was still intending to buy it. When Hiss changed his mind and withdrew from the purchase, Chambers decided to buy the property himself. Hiss admitted that during April and May in 1936, he had indeed negotiated for the purchase of the farm, but he denied taking Chambers to see it. When asked if he had ever mentioned the negotiations to Chambers, he said, "I don't remember doing so. I certainly might have." The "coincidence" that Chambers, with whom Hiss denied any sort of close relationship, could independently have learned of the availability of this very farm for later purchase strongly supported Chambers's credibility.[31]

Each of these incidents, when taken together with Hiss's grudging and belated recognition of Chambers as George Crosley during the HUAC hearing, presented major problems for the Hiss defense.

---

30. *In re* Hiss, 542 F. Supp. 973, 985 (S.D.N.Y. 1982); Weinstein, *Perjury*, 504.
31. Weinstein, *Perjury*, 64–68; *In re* Hiss, 542 F. Supp. 973, 985–6 (S.D.N.Y. 1982).

One of the highlights of the trials was the extent to which the defense used character evidence to bolster its case. The general legal rule is that evidence of good character or bad character is not admissible. In a criminal case, however, the accused is allowed to show good character to bolster a claim that he or she is innocent. While the defense may not introduce evidence of specific acts, it is permitted to have witnesses testify to the defendant's "reputation." It's faster; a witness can be called and dismissed after a few questions, e.g., "Mr. Witness, are you familiar with the reputation of Mr. Defendant?" "I am." "What is his reputation for honesty or for peacefulness or for truthfulness (or for whatever trait is relevant)?" "It is excellent." Reputation evidence can be significant. The standard instruction given to the jury provides that "evidence of good character may, in itself, create a reasonable doubt where, without such evidence, no reasonable doubt would exist."

The Hiss defense took advantage of this opportunity. They called to the stand a phenomenal array of famous, highly placed witnesses to testify to Hiss's outstanding reputation for integrity, loyalty, and trustworthiness. No trial in American history before or since has ever seen such a parade of notables to defend a person accused of a felony.

Nineteen individuals testified as character witnesses, many of them after the first trial when the jury voted 8-4 to convict. That's how highly regarded Hiss was by his peers.

Hiss's character witnesses included two sitting justices of the United States Supreme Court, Felix Frankfurter and Stanley Reed. Their testimony was unprecedented because the case might have been appealed to the Supreme Court of the United States. Other character witnesses included John W. Davis, a presidential candidate in 1924; Adlai Stevenson, a future candidate for president; and John Foster Dulles, who became secretary of state under President Dwight Eisenhower.[32]

This procession of witnesses did Hiss little good. In fact, students of advocacy cite the *Hiss* case as a classic example of the limited effectiveness of character evidence. The witnesses were all men of

---

32. Weinstein, *Perjury*, 471–2.

the same class, cut from the same cloth, all men of privilege, influence, and power. They seemed to suggest to the jury that a man like Hiss, like them, would *never* do such a thing. But the jury was not composed of men like them. In his summation, Murphy gave the character witnesses the back of his hand:

> The defendant has called 19 character witnesses, more than one-third the total number of his witnesses. . . . they've told you what the gossip is that they've heard, the accumulation of gossip over the years that they heard about him and what it is. And all of them say his reputation is good . . . and I ask you, what kind of reputation does a good spy have?
>
> Well, of course, it must be good. The fox barks not when he goes to steal the lamb. No, the spy's reputation must be good. We're here on a search for truth, we're not concerned with reputations. Just think how many people could call good reputation witnesses. Benedict Arnold, a Major General in our army—he sold out West Point to the enemy and before they caught Major Andre right up there in Tarrytown, don't you believe that Major General Benedict Arnold could have called George Washington as a character witness? And Brutus, before he stabbed Caesar, don't you think he could have stood in front of the Roman Senate and called upon the great Augustus and said, "Tell them what kind of man I am"? And lastly, the devil himself. The devil was a fallen angel, and before he was thrown out of heaven, he was in the sight of God. He could have called upon the Almighty Himself as a character witness. Well, character witnesses belong to another era. This is the age of reason. This is the age of common people. We're here, you are here, Judge Goddard is here, to ascertain the facts. We don't want gossip.[33]

The Hiss defense next turned to the expert testimony phase of their case and was faced with an especially difficult challenge. The

---

33. Younger, *The Irving Younger Collection,* 560; Younger, "Was Alger Hiss Guilty?"

jury, with considerable help from Murphy, was certain to ask what motive Chambers could possibly have for lying about Hiss. Chambers had turned his life around in 1948 and had held a prestigious, well-paid position as a senior editor at *Time* magazine. But as a result of his own admission about his communist background, and his accusations about Hiss, he had had to resign from *Time*. Hiss's lawyers had not turned up a single credible reason for Chambers to embark on a self-incriminating lying spree. They could only conclude, for their purposes, that Chambers was mentally ill. Although he had never been diagnosed or treated for mental problems, the Hiss defense presented expert psychiatric testimony.

Dr. Carl Binger testified that Whittaker Chambers had a "psychopathic personality" disorder that made him prone to lying. In the first trial, Judge Kaufman had rejected the admissibility of this testimony on the ground that "the credibility of witnesses was strictly a question for the jury and not an appropriate subject for expert testimony." Judge Goddard, in the second trial, did allow Dr. Binger to testify. His decision was remarkable for several reasons. Never before in federal court had a psychiatrist, who had not met a witness, been allowed to give an opinion that impeached that witness's credibility. Dr. Binger had not examined Chambers. He knew nothing about his childhood nor had he spoken to any of his family, friends, or associates. Binger explained that his opinion was based on watching Chambers testify in both trials, on reading some of Chambers's writings, and his German to English translations. Binger was asked by Hiss's lawyer, Cross, to "assume the truth" of certain facts. Included in the so-called hypothetical question were facts that could be disputed or explained but were required to be accepted by Binger as accurate for purposes of giving his opinion. In other words, the hypothetical question was a one-sided presentation of Chambers's alleged bad behavior.

Legal scholars and trial lawyers have questioned the wisdom and propriety of admitting this testimony. Judge Goddard's decision to admit it did not survive as a precedent and has not been followed in future cases. This is understandable when one considers that many criminal cases involve conflicting testimony between accuser and accused. If the *Hiss* case precedent was applied, these cases might all involve a battle of expert psychiatric witnesses who had not examined either party.

Dr. Binger testified that he had formed an opinion based upon "reasonable medical certainty" and stated that:

> Mr. Chambers is suffering from a condition known as psychopathic personality, a disorder of character, the distinguishing features of which are amoral and asocial behavior. Some of the symptoms of this condition are chronic, persistent and repetitive lying, acts of deception and misrepresentation; alcoholism and drug addiction, abnormal sexuality, vagabondage, panhandling, inability to form stable relationships and a tendency to make false accusations.[34]

The cross-examination of Dr. Binger went on for five days. Murphy started by getting Binger to concede that nothing in his testimony explained how secret government documents, including some with Hiss's handwriting, came into Chambers's possession. Dr. Binger also admitted that although he had graduated from medical school thirty-five years earlier, he had been certified as a practicing psychiatrist for only three years.

Murphy then asked Binger to admit that "psychopathic personality" was a vague and almost meaningless "wastepaper basket classification" of alleged symptoms. When Binger disagreed with that characterization, Murphy read into the record the view of a well-known psychiatrist who wrote "the term 'psychopathic personality,' as commonly understood, is useless in psychiatric research. It is a diagnosis of convenience arrived at by a process of exclusion. It does not refer to a behavioral entity. It serves as a scrap basket to which is relegated a group of unclassified personality disorders and problems."

34. Weinstein, *Perjury,* 510; Cooke, *A Generation on Trial,* 304–5; Testimony of Carl A. Binger in second Hiss trial: Linder, "Famous American Trials," http://law2.umkc.edu/faculty/projects/ftrials/hiss/hisstrialtranscripts.html#Dr. Carl A.

When asked if he agreed with that assessment, Dr. Binger surprisingly replied, "Yes, with every word of it. I think that is excellent."[35]

Murphy noted that repetitive lying was part of the basis for Binger's opinion. But with careful questioning, Murphy got the doctor to admit that the number of lies by Chambers totaled about twenty over thirty-six years. "That's not bad, is it Doctor?" Binger then defied common sense by refusing to admit that the *reason* and *purpose* for a lie was important in assessing its medical value. He testified that Chambers's lie about his affiliation with communists in order to obtain a passport was relevant to a diagnosis of psychopathic personality. When Murphy asked about American prisoners of war who lie to the enemy, Binger finally conceded that the reasons for lies were important.[36] When pressed to admit that some aspects of the basis for his opinion were inadequate, the doctor acknowledged they were inadequate for treatment, but not for an in-court opinion. This dichotomy probably did not impress the jurors who were recipients of his in-court opinion.

One of the symptoms applicable to Chambers, according to Binger, was "insensitivity to the feelings of others." He cited as an example the fact that Chambers moved into his mother's house, bringing with him the woman with whom he was living. Did the doctor know that the move had been made at his mother's request and that she had said, "I have lost one son; I don't want to lose another." No, the doctor did not know that. Murphy then made the point that the doctor's opinion was based on "assumed facts," but that the doctor had no idea whether the facts he assumed were true or not.

Murphy went through Binger's list of Chambers's symptoms, one by one. "Panhandling": Binger conceded there was no evidence that Chambers ever begged on streets. "Unable to form stable relationships": Chambers had been married to the same woman for eighteen years and seemed dedicated to his family. He had worked at *Time* magazine for ten years. "Alcoholism": There was no evidence of Chambers having an issue with alcoholism, nor was there any evidence to

35. Author/Compiler Last Name, "transcript of testimony of Dr. Carl Binger," 2609–10.
36. Ibid., 2621–2, 2626, 2629.

support "drug addiction or abnormal sexuality."[37] In response to the doctor's emphasis on Chambers's "personal untidiness and bad teeth," Murphy asked, "How about Will Rogers and Bing Crosby? They were not fashion plates—were they psychopathic?" As to Chambers "hiding documents in a pumpkin," which the doctor had characterized as "bizarre behavior," Murphy asked, "Is that so bad, doctor? How about putting the Connecticut charter in the Hartford oak—were the early colonials "psychopathic"?

On direct examination, Dr. Binger actually expanded his list of Chambers's symptoms. He added that while on the stand, Chambers rarely answered questions directly by stating facts and constantly used the expressions, "it would have been" or "it might have been." Murphy later referred to the transcript of 770 pages of testimony that showed only ten such instances by Chambers. In fact, Murphy pointed out, Binger himself had used those phrases 158 times.[38]

Binger also stated that Chambers, on the stand, exhibited no relationship with his questioner because he repeatedly glanced up at the ceiling, as if trying to recall something he had previously said. On cross-examination, Murphy asked Dr. Binger, "You say that looking up at the ceiling is one of the symptoms that confirms your diagnosis?" "Yes," Dr. Binger replied. "Well, Doctor," Murphy shot back, "I kept a check on your own ceiling gazing. You looked up at the ceiling fifty-nine times in twenty minutes. Psychopathic, doctor?"[39] Murphy's approach was effective in amplifying the shakiness of Binger's opinion. As Alistair Cooke noted about the prosecutor's performance, "Mr. Murphy, for all his feigned archness and voluntary astonishment, had put just the questions that a jury would want to ask."[40]

So it went, for all five days of cross-examination. When it was over, the defense was likely very sorry they called Dr. Binger to testify. No doubt Binger was as well.

---

37. Ibid., 2619.
38. Ibid., 2729.
39. Ibid., 2664.
40. Cooke, *A Generation on Trial*, 312.

Before Hiss was indicted, he tried to get the grand jury to hear Dr. Binger. This is the substance of the colloquy between Hiss and the grand jurors:

Q: Mr. Hiss, is your psychiatrist in any position to offer any information . . . [w]ith reference to explaining to this grand jury how it came about that the documents, . . . [w]ere written on your typewriter?

A: No, he is not. He can only talk from the point of view of motive which has come up . . .

Q: . . . Motive on whose part?

A: Mr. Chambers.

Q: Has he examined Mr. Chambers?

A: No, he has examined his writings, letters, testimony and everything that we have been able to find out about him—his whole career.

The grand jury declined to hear Dr. Binger.

With his attitude of being no more than an interested layman, Alistair Cooke pointed out that Murphy "exposed the central risk of bringing psychiatrists to testify in cases where the suspect character is in obvious control of his senses and—if he is Whittaker Chambers—of his intelligence and his wit." When Murphy was finished with his cross-examination, Dr. Binger and the *Hiss* team must have realized that they blundered by including so much ordinary human behavior in their basket of symptoms. It's no wonder that Cross made scant reference to the psychiatric testimony in his summation.[41]

The essential problem for the defense was that neither their character witnesses nor the expert psychiatric testimony could make the

---

41. For a summary and analysis of Binger's testimony, see Weinstein, *Perjury*, 210–9.

documents disappear. And that brings us to the fourth and decisive category of evidence: the State Department documents, or the so-called pumpkin papers. Chambers alleged that they were provided to him by Hiss to be passed on to communist agents. One set of these documents would be enough to prove beyond a reasonable doubt that Hiss had committed perjury.

Three types of documents were in question. In reverse order of importance, there was the microfilm of the government documents that came through Assistant Secretary of State Sayre's office, where Hiss worked. Hiss's initials were on some of these papers. It was confirmed that the films in question were taken in Baltimore, by a camera used by Felix Inslerman.

Hiss denied that Chambers got these documents from him. This defense was plausible, as the documents also resided in government offices other than the one in which Hiss worked. Further, Chambers admitted that he received documents from others. In fact, one person, Julian Wadleigh, a former communist, actually testified that he knew nothing about Hiss, did not recognize the documents in question, but had given material to Chambers.

The second set of documents were summaries of government notes, in Hiss's handwriting, describing the content of secret government papers. Hiss explained that it was his job to make these notes for use in his briefing sessions with Assistant Secretary of State Sayre: when he finished the briefings, he threw them away and had no idea of what happened to them or how they ended up in Chambers's possession.

The implication was that the notes were stolen from his wastebasket or from his desk. But the notes were folded neatly in half and not crumpled as one would expect discarded material to be. In addition, Sayre testified that some of the handwritten notes were lengthy and sometimes complete copies of cables that were not what he remembered being briefed on.

The third pieces of evidence form the crux of the case. These were the forty-three typewritten copies, most of which were verbatim copies of secret government documents that were all dated between January and April 1938, and that Chambers maintained were typed by the Hisses. Hiss said it was not true, and further, he had no idea how they came into existence. The issue before the jury was both simple and critical. If Hiss or his wife, Priscilla, made the copies by typing those documents, then they were engaged in espionage and he had committed perjury. There was no other plausible explanation for the preparation of these papers. The microfilm Hiss could explain, as it may have come from somebody else. The handwritten notes he could explain by saying that he created them as briefing notes and then threw them away. But the typed pages were a different story. They were the only pieces of evidence that, by themselves could meet the standard for proof beyond a reasonable doubt. If they were typed on the Hiss typewriter by the Hisses, then Hiss is guilty of espionage and, therefore, perjury.[42]

The Hisses did, in fact, own a typewriter around the relevant time, a Woodstock as the evidence showed, and the government did everything they could to find it. The Hisses didn't remember what they did with it. They said they either junked it or gave it away and the government couldn't find the actual typewriter.

Every typewriter has a typeface, a kind of fingerprint, unique unto itself, that becomes more distinctive with use. The FBI found a series of letters that were typed by Mrs. Hiss around 1937. These were four items of personal correspondence; an alumni report she typed and sent to the Bryn Mawr Alumni Association in 1937, a letter she typed to her child's school, and two others.[43]

Using photographic enlargements, FBI laboratory expert Ramos C. Feehan, who had served as a Bureau document examiner for eleven years analyzing "questioned handwriting, hand printing, and typewriting," explained that he had compared the four letters from Mrs. Hiss with the typewritten copies of the secret government documents. He testified that all except one of the government documents had been typed on the same machine that had produced Mrs. Hiss's letters. Defense Attorney Cross conceded both in his opening statement and in his summation that the defense experts agreed with

42. Younger, *The Irving Younger Collection*, 570–6.
43. Ibid.

Feehan. To further buttress Feehan's testimony, *Time* magazine hired its own expert, who reached the same conclusion.[44]

As for the Woodstock typewriter itself, it was later found to have been given to the Hiss's maid, Mrs. Catlett, who in turn gave it to her sons, who then used it as a decoration in their apartment. The machine was obtained by the defense and put into evidence by Cross. But the typewriter itself was not important because the match was made without it.

If the defense admitted, as they did, that the typewriter that typed Mrs. Hiss's correspondence also typed the documents presented by Chambers, there was little left for the defense to argue. They had only the theory that somebody other than the Hisses typed the documents. And the only other likely party would be Chambers himself. Defense counsel Cross was thus reduced to arguing that maybe after the Woodstock was given away by the Hisses, Chambers himself or his stooge went out, found the Woodstock, and used it to type the documents. "Could it not have happened that way," asked Cross in summation; "Isn't it possible?"

Murphy, in response, ridiculed this for what it was—a theory born of desperation. He laid it out for the jury: Everyone knew the typewriter was not stolen, or ever missing, but found in the possession of the sons of the Hisses' maid. So Chambers could not have stolen it or taken it away. "Let's imagine what the defense is asking us to believe," he said. "Chambers goes to the sons' house. Maybe he pretends to be a Woodstock repairman. Can't you see him with his Woodstock repairman cap on? He says to the maid's boys, 'I need to fix the typewriter.' He doesn't steal it. He surreptitiously sits down before the typewriter, in the Catletts' home, with the secret documents in one hand while he types with the other." Murphy ended by saying, "Oh, Mr. Cross, you got to do better than that."[45] The match with the Hiss typewriter made the typed State Department docu-

---

44. *In re* Hiss, 542 F. Supp. 973, 984 (S.D.N.Y. 1982); Younger, *The Irving Younger Collection*, 574; Weinstein, *Perjury*, 498–9.
45. Cooke, *A Generation on Trial*, 323; Younger, *The Irving Younger Collection*, 575–6.

ments unexplainable. Although Hiss claimed "forgery by typewriter," he could not explain plausibly how it was done.

On January 21, 1950, less than twenty-four hours after receiving the case, the jury found Hiss guilty. His last words just before he was sentenced were: "I would like to thank your Honor for the opportunity to again deny the charges that have been made against me. I want only to add that in the future, the full facts of how Whittaker Chambers was able to carry out forgery by typewriter will be disclosed."[46] Hiss was sentenced to the maximum sentence of five years. There were appeals and motions for a new trial, but all were unsuccessful, and Alger Hiss went to prison. Although the decision remains controversial in some quarters, twenty out of the twenty-four jurors in the trials found Alger Hiss guilty. Nixon went on to win a U.S. Senate seat, and Chambers went home to write a memoir, *Witness,* which was published in 1952.

In the years following, Chambers showed no signs of regret and seemed eager to let the legacy of the trials carve out his role in history. In an oft-quoted passage from his autobiography, Chambers expressed his view of the partisan division that split the nation during the *Hiss* trials and thereafter. He wrote:

No feature of the Hiss Case is more obvious, or more troubling as history than the jagged fissure, which it did not so much open as reveal, between the plain men and women of the nation, and those who affected to act, think, and speak for them. It was, not invariably, but in general, the "best people" who were for Alger Hiss and who were prepared to go to almost any length to protect and defend him. It was the enlightened and the powerful, the clamorous proponents of the open mind and the common man, who snapped their minds shut in a pro-Hiss psychosis, of a kind which, in an individual patient, means the simple failure of the ability to distinguish between reality and unreality, and, in a nation, is a warning of the end. It was the great body of the nation,

---

46. Weinstein, *Perjury,* 522.

which not invariably, but in general kept open its mind in the Hiss Case, waiting for the returns to come in. It was they who suspected what forces disastrous to the nation were at work in the Hiss Case, and had suspected that they were at work long before there was a Hiss Case, while most of the forces of enlightenment were pooh-poohing the Communist danger and calling every allusion to it a witch hunt.[47]

Chambers's influence in conservative politics continued to be felt well after the trials. Ronald Reagan acknowledged Chambers's book, *Witness*, as an inspiration, and he frequently mentioned Chambers in his speeches, saying he "sparked the counterrevolution of the intellectuals" and that Chambers's story "represents a generation's disenchantment with statism and its return to eternal truths and fundamental values." In 1984, President Reagan posthumously awarded the Medal of Freedom to Whittaker Chambers.

Hiss served forty-four months at Lewisburg Federal Penitentiary in Pennsylvania before being released for good behavior in 1954. He staunchly maintained his innocence, as did his wife, Priscilla, up until his death in 1996.

In the years after his release from prison, Hiss maintained a favorable public profile among a segment of American society that continued to see him as an innocent victim of reactionary forces. In 1957, Hiss published a memoir titled *In the Court of Public Opinion*. His rejuvenation was aided by the excesses of the McCarthy era, the Watergate crisis, the Vietnam War, and the downfall of his nemesis, Richard Nixon. By the late 1970s, attitudes toward those in power grew more cynical. As the people who had led the prosecution of Hiss fell from grace, the possibility that Hiss had been a scapegoat seemed more credible and he regained public prominence. A new generation of Americans, unfamiliar with the facts or the evidence, responded sympathetically to Hiss's lectures, press conferences, and TV appearances.[48]

47. Whittaker Chambers, *Witness* (Random House, New York, 1952), 793–4.
48. Weinstein, *Perjury*, 586–7.

During this period of renewed influence, Hiss achieved some successes. Hiss's government pension was restored with the help of the American Civil Liberties Union. And, although the conviction for perjury required his disbarment, in 1975 the Massachusetts Supreme Court unanimously approved his readmission to the bar as well as his right to practice law. The court's decision may be the only time that a lawyer convicted of perjury based on acts of espionage, and who refused to admit wrongdoing, has ever been readmitted to the practice of law. Speaking for the court, Justice Tauro said, "Hiss comes before us as a convicted perjurer, whose crime is further tainted by the breach of confidence and trust which underlay his conviction." He added that "Nothing we have said here should be construed as detracting one iota from the fact that in considering Hiss's petition, we consider him to be guilty as charged." As for the argument that Hiss lacked "repentance," Tauro concluded that forcing Hiss to admit guilt as the price of readmission to the bar, when he believes himself to be innocent, "would force a man to forgo the last vestige of human dignity."[49]

> One of the major goals of Hiss's quest for vindication was to overturn his conviction in the courts. This goal was never accomplished in spite of repeated appeals. Following the jury verdict in 1950, Hiss moved for a new trial but Judge Goddard denied the motion. On December 7, 1950, his conviction was affirmed by the Court of Appeals, which rejected each point made in the defense brief. Hiss also sought relief from the United States Supreme Court, which denied certiorari and refused to hear the case.[50]

Then in 1952, shortly before Hiss was released from prison, his attorneys moved again for a new trial based on newly discovered evidence. The heart of this motion was to establish "forgery by typewriter." His defense team argued that the Woodstock typewriter that

49. Ibid., 587–9.
50. United States v. Hiss, 185 F.2d 822 (2d Cir. 1950), cert. denied, 340 U.S. 948 (1951).

they themselves had found and put into evidence at the second trial was not really the machine that had belonged to the Hisses.

Instead, the claim was that Chambers and his allies had manufactured a Woodstock look-alike, typed copies of the documents on the fake typewriter, and placed the fabricated machine in a location where the defense would find it. As evidence that this trickery was possible, the defense had hired an expert to craft a duplicate Woodstock. It took a year to do it and it was, even then, an imperfect match. Judge Goddard again denied the motion for a new trial. He stated that "there is not a trace of any evidence that Chambers had mechanical skill, tools, equipment or material for such a task." The judge went on to ask how Chambers, if he had constructed the phony Woodstock, would know where to place it so it would be found by the defense. And what would be the consequence if he had planted it in such a place and then the real machine was found? In Judge Goddard's view, the defense theory of "forgery by typewriter" made no sense. Again the Court of Appeals affirmed and the Supreme Court declined to review the matter.[51]

In 1995, some twenty years after he had been released from prison, Hiss applied for a writ of coram nobis in the United States District Court of New York where he had been tried and convicted. Coram nobis is a way to try to reopen old cases because of factual errors not apparent in the record. The affidavit in opposition to this motion by the United States Attorney labeled it as "a frivolous attempt to perpetuate in some quarters the myth of the defendant's innocence." Given the rough treatment it received in the courts, the judges must have agreed. The application again raised the fabricated typewriter argument that was dismissed thirty years earlier. The petition for coram nobis was denied without hearing testimony in a twenty-six-page opinion by District Court Judge Owen. He concluded:

Whether the [defense claims] are considered singly or together, they raise no real question whatsoever let alone a reasonable

---

51. United States v. Hiss, 107 F. Supp. 128 (S.D.N.Y. 1952), *aff'd* on opinion below; 201 F.2d 372 (2d Cir. 1953), cert. denied, 345 U.S. 942 (1953).

doubt as to Hiss's guilt. The trial was a fair one by any standard and I am presented with nothing requiring a hearing on any issue. The jury verdict rendered in 1950 was amply supported by the evidence—the most damaging aspects of which were admitted by Hiss—and nothing presented in these papers, extensive though they are, places that verdict under a cloud. Accordingly, the Hiss petition for a writ of error is dismissed.[52]

The Hiss defense appealed to the Court of Appeals, which responded curtly one day after hearing oral argument: "We find the appeal to be completely without merit and affirm the judgment substantially for the reasons stated in the thorough opinion of Judge Owen." Eight months later, in October of 1983, the United States Supreme Court denied Hiss's petition without comment. Thus, Judge Owen's opinion remains as the last legal word in one of the most celebrated cases in this nation's history.[53]

The historian Allen Weinstein set out to write an account sympathetic to Hiss, using the Freedom of Information Act to gain access to previously classified materials from the State Department and the FBI. In his authoritive and carefully researched book titled *Perjury: The Hiss-Chambers Case*, he concluded that Hiss was guilty.

In 1996, a series of decoded cables sent from the United States to Moscow known as the Venona Intercept Files were released by the Russians. Relevant to the *Hiss* case is a document dated 1945 that refers to a communist agent named "Ales," described as a State Department official who flew from the Yalta Conference to Moscow. As Hiss was one of only four men who flew from that conference to Moscow, "Ales" is believed by many intelligence experts to be Alger Hiss.[54]

---

52. *In re* Hiss, 542 F. Supp. 973, 999 (S.D.N.Y. 1982).
53. For a critical analysis of the opinion, see William A. Reuben, Footnote on an Historic Case: In Re Alger Hiss, No. 78 Civ. 3433 (Nation Institute, 1983).
54. The Venona Files and the Alger Hiss case: Linder, "Famous American Trials," http://law2.umkc.edu/faculty/projects/ftrials/hiss/hissvenona.html; Weinstein, *Perjury*, 386, 389, 598–602.

Today, some sixty-five years after Hiss's conviction, the number of historians and other interested observers who believe that Hiss was innocent has dwindled to just a few. The conspiracy theories attempting to explain how Hiss was framed have run their course.

One questions remains. If Hiss was guilty, as the evidence showed, why did he persist in a lifetime of lies? Thomas Powers, in *The Plot Thickens*, put it this way:

> Why did Hiss lie for 50 years about his service to a cause so important to him that he was willing to betray his country for it? The faith itself is no problem to explain. Hundreds shared it enough to do the same thing and thousands more shared it who were never put to the test by a demand for secrets. But why did Hiss persist in the lie personally? Why did he allow his friends and family to go on carrying the awful burden of the lie?[55]

These questions have not yet been satisfactorily answered.

---

55. Thomas Powers, "The Plot Thickens," *NY Review of Books*, May 11, 2000, 53–54; the same question has been asked by Fred Rodell, "Come Clean, Alger Hiss," *The Progressive*, June 1950; and by Leslie Fiedler, "Hiss, Chambers, and the Age of Innocence: Who Was Guilty—And of What?," *Commentary*, August 1951.

FIVE

The Sam Sheppard Trial: A Mockery of Justice[1]

THE OHIO SUPREME COURT DESCRIBED the Sam Sheppard case with this introduction:

> Murder and mystery, society, sex and suspense were combined in this story so as to captivate the public fancy to a degree unparalleled in recent annals. Throughout the pre-indictment

---

1. This chapter relies on trial transcripts, court decisions, and secondary sources, including especially the authoritative books that present diverse views of the Sheppard case, including in particular James Neff, *The Wrong Man: The Final Verdict on the Dr. Sam Sheppard Murder Case* (Random House, New York, 2001); F. Lee Bailey and Harvey Aronson, *The Defense Never Rests* (Stein and Day, New York, 1971); Cynthia L. Cooper and Sam Reese Sheppard, *Mockery of Justice: The True Story of the Sheppard Murder Case* (Northeastern University Press, 1995); Jack P. DeSario and William D. Mason, *Dr. Sam Sheppard on Trial: The Prosecutors and the Marilyn Sheppard Murder* (Kent State University Press, 2003); Dr. Sam Sheppard, *Endure and Conquer: My Twelve-Year Fight for Vindication* (World Publishing Company, 1966); Louis B. Seltzer, *The Years Were Good* (World Publishing Company, 1956). Also extensively used were newspaper articles and other forms of publicity from the Cleveland and national press as well as from Ohio state and federal courts, opinions on the Sheppard affair. Also helpful were law review articles and Internet sources such as Douglas Linder, "Famous American Trials: The Dr. Sam Sheppard Trial" transcripts, and accounts of the Sheppard trials at http://law2.umkc.edu/faculty/projects/ftrials/sheppard/sheppardaccount.html.

investigation, the legal skirmishes and the nine-week trial, circulation-conscious editors catered to the insatiable interest of the American public in the bizarre.

Special seating facilities for reporters and columnists representing local papers and all major news services were installed in the courtroom. Special rooms in the criminal courts building were equipped for broadcasters. In this atmosphere of a "Roman holiday" for the news media, Sam Sheppard stood trial for his life.[2]

The saga of Dr. Sam Sheppard, now more than six decades old, lives on. Its claim to fame is based on two factors.

First, it is a classic unsolved murder mystery. Did Dr. Sam beat his young and beautiful wife to death in the middle of the night with a never-identified blunt instrument? If he didn't do it, who did?

These questions were submitted for decision to three juries in three separate trials. Once in 1954, verdict "guilty"; again in 1966, verdict "not guilty"; lastly in the year 2000, verdict "not innocent."

The plot of this real-life whodunit has inspired eight books, a long-running TV series called *The Fugitive* with the fictional Dr. Richard Kimble as its hero, and a 1993 movie of the same name starring Harrison Ford.

Syndicated columnist Dorothy Kilgallen, who covered the first trial, declared that the question of Sheppard's guilt or innocence "ranked with . . . the classic puzzle of Lizzie Borden."[3] Following the daily court dispatches, Ernest Hemingway wrote from Havana, "A trial like this, with its elements of doubt, is the greatest human story of all . . . This trial has everything the public clamors for."[4] Indeed, the case's incredible appeal is what initially drew the media to cover it so heavily. And this coverage is what ultimately made this case so

---

2. State of Ohio v. Sheppard, 165 Ohio St. 293, 294, 135 N.E.2d 340, 343 (1956).
3. Linder, "Famous American Trials"; Brent Larkin, "Speaking up for Marilyn in the 60-year-old Sam Sheppard murder case," cleveland.com, July 3, 2014, http://www.cleveland.com/opinion/index.ssf/2014/07/speaking_up_for_marilyn_in_the.html.
4. Neff, *The Wrong Man*, 138; Larkin, "Speaking up for Marilyn in the 60-year-old Sam Sheppard murder case."

significant in terms of legal precedent. And that is the second reason that makes this case noteworthy.

The United States Constitution, of course, protects the right of the press to report on crimes and criminal proceedings and the right of the public to know about threats to its safety. A free press guards against miscarriages of justice by subjecting the police, prosecutors, and the judicial process to public scrutiny.

On the other hand, the constitutional guarantee of a fair trial implies that jury members have not been unduly influenced by pre-trial publicity, including media accounts that reveal inadmissible evidence and press statements that may not be true. It means that the jury's verdict must be based exclusively on evidence received in open court. It also means that guilt or innocence should be determined in an atmosphere of calm, free of courtroom disruption or confusion. These two goals, free press and fair trial, may be hard to reconcile in highly publicized trials.

In England, the balance is tilted toward ensuring a fair trial. The press is forbidden to publish any story that might compromise the fairness of a trial. It can report on the proceedings only after the trial is over. If the press violates these restrictions, the editors and journalists involved can be punished for contempt of court.

First Amendment jurisprudence in the United States largely eliminates this kind of press control; prior restraint is unconstitutional. This means that the court cannot issue orders forbidding publication of certain matters except in extremely unusual circumstances. Nor, as a rule, would a court be allowed to directly punish the press even after it published irresponsibly. To put it simply, United States courts cannot tell the media what they can communicate to the public.

What can American courts do to preserve a balance between a free press and a fair trial? That was the issue that made the *Sheppard* trial a landmark in the law. In 1966, the United States Supreme Court decision in *Sheppard v. Maxwell*[5] became the foundation for modern free press–fair trial practices.

---

5. 384 U.S. 333, 86 S. Ct. 1507 (1966).

This story of crime, punishment, and exoneration began in 1954 over the Fourth of July weekend in Bay Village, an affluent suburb of Cleveland, Ohio. For Dr. Sam Sheppard, it was the best of times.[6] The youngest son of an osteopathic surgeon, he had grown up on a tree-lined street in Cleveland Heights. As a high school senior, he was voted class president and outstanding athlete. He graduated from Western Reserve University as well as the Osteopathic School of Physicians and Surgeons in Los Angeles and did his residency at Los Angeles County Hospital. By the age of 30, he was making $30,000 a year—a handsome sum in 1954. He had his own office in Cleveland and also practiced with his father and two older brothers at the Sheppard Clinic in Fairview Park. In addition, he was in charge of neurosurgery at the family-owned Bay View Hospital that his father, Dr. Richard J. Sheppard, had founded in 1948. He was married to his high school sweetheart, Marilyn Reese, and they had a seven-year-old son, Chip. They lived in a four-bedroom house on a wooded lot that included a small beach on Lake Erie. He also had a Lincoln Continental and a fourteen-foot aluminum outboard boat, co-owned with his friend Spencer Houk, who was the Bay Village mayor.

Sam and Marilyn enjoyed waterskiing and playing tennis and golf, and they took an active part in community life. Marilyn was involved with the Bay Village Women's Club as well as church work; Sam served as the village police surgeon. They had a busy social life and were close friends with Spencer Houk and his wife, Esther, and with their neighbors, Doug and Nancy Ahern.

There was, however, a discordant note in their seemingly happy marriage. The painful birth of Chip had left Marilyn so fearful of another pregnancy that her sexual drive had been blunted. From 1951 to 1954, Sam had engaged in an on-and-off affair with Susan Hayes, a twenty-year-old medical technician at Bay View Hospital. He would later insist that his relationship with Susan was a "purely physical arrangement of convenience," that Marilyn was aware of the affair and that, although not happy about it, "she understood

---

6. The early life of Sam Sheppard is fully explored in Bailey and Aronson, *The Defense Never Rests*, 55–56.

and recognized why it had developed."[7]

By the summer of 1954, Sam and Marilyn had been married for nine years. About a month before her murder, Sam's parents hosted a family dinner for their sons, daughters-in-law, and their grandchildren. At this gathering, Marilyn announced that she was expecting a second child.

On July 3, 1954, Marilyn spent the afternoon at home preparing for the holiday weekend. The Sheppards had invited eighteen couples to their home for a Fourth of July picnic. Dr. Sam, as he was affectionately known among friends and neigh-

Marilyn Sheppard, wife of Dr. Samuel Sheppard, was found bludgeoned to death in the couple's lake shore home.
© Bettmann/CORBIS

bors, was working a few miles away at the hospital. That evening, Sam and Marilyn were entertaining their friends, the Aherns, for dinner. Afterwards, they all watched television, but Sam had fallen asleep on the couch in the living room. The Aherns would later testify that the Sheppards were affectionate toward each other and for part of the evening Marilyn had sat on Sam's lap. The Aherns left about 12:30 A.M. on July 4.

The rest of the story comes from the account Sam Sheppard gave to the police and the jury. He said he remembered that Marilyn tried to wake him from the couch and get him to come to bed, but that he was a very heavy sleeper, and she must have given up and gone upstairs alone. He then stated:

---

7. Ibid., 56–57.

The next thing I knew, Marilyn was screaming or moaning my name. It was not exactly a scream. I really can't explain it. I jumped off the couch and headed up the stairs. My subconscious reaction was that she was having a convulsive seizure similar to those she had during her first pregnancy. I rushed into the room and several things happened almost simultaneously. I thought I could see a white form—an individual. I heard Marilyn moaning loudly and then some other noises. Then I felt I was struck down from behind, but can't say for sure.

Sometime after that (I have no way of knowing how long), I came to in a sitting position, facing the doorway of the bedroom. I felt an excruciating pain in my neck and I knew I had been injured.

I was fearful for my wife. I got up from the floor, went over to the twin bed, where Marilyn was lying, looked at her and felt her pulse. Everything was hazy and it was difficult to see clearly, but I felt that she was dead. I believe I then rushed into my son Chip's room, adjacent to ours. I wanted to find out if anything had happened to him. I don't know how I determined it, but after seeing him I came to the conclusion he was not harmed.

As I came out of Chip's room, I thought I heard a noise downstairs and ran down the stairs as rapidly as I could. It seemed to me that the noise was coming from the front of the house—the part toward the lake. I turned down on the north section of the stairway and rounded the L-portion of the living room and went toward the dining room table. At that point, I spotted a figure between the front door of the house and the front door of the porch or slightly beyond that point, perhaps toward the yard.

I gave chase but lost sight of this intruder on the stairs heading down to the beach. By the time I got to the landing where the beach house was located, the figure was on the beach. I bolted down the remaining stairs and tackled this individual from behind. It seemed to me he had a rather large head. Then I felt as if I had been twisted or choked. That's all I remember.

The next thing I can remember with any clarity at all was returning to consciousness on the water's edge at the beach. My head was facing toward the shore and my feet were in the water. I had the impression I was being wallowed back and forth by the waves. I slowly dragged myself onto the beach and came to some sort of sensibility. Somehow, I made it up the stairs.

The time element is hard to estimate. I went back up the stairs to the bedroom where Marilyn was. I looked at her and felt for her pulse on her neck. When I touched her I thought she was gone. It's hard to explain my reaction. I guess I thought I would wake up and find out it was all a horrible, fantastic dream. I'm not sure what I did in the next few moments. I may have gone into other rooms. I may have walked around upstairs. I may have gone back into the room where Marilyn was and looked at her again.[8]

The rest of his story was confirmed by others. At around 6:00 A.M., Sam called Spencer Houk, who lived just two houses away. He said, "My God, Spence, get over here quick. I think they have killed Marilyn." Houk and his wife, Esther, arrived quickly and found Sam sitting in the den without a shirt. His face was bruised and he complained of neck pain. Desk drawers had been pulled out, his medical bag was turned upside down and the contents were strewn all over the floor. Esther went upstairs and found Marilyn Sheppard sprawled face up on her bed in a pool of blood. She had been beaten so badly she was unrecognizable. The coroner's examination would reveal thirty-five wounds, including fifteen blows to the head, a broken nose, and nine abrasions on the hands, arms, and fingers. There was blood on her face, on the bed, and on the walls and floor. Her

---

8. Sheppard, *Endure and Conquer*, 12–13; Bailey and Aronson, *The Defense Never Rests*, 57–58; Linder, "Famous American Trials," "Dr. Sam's Statements," http://law2.umkc.edu/faculty/projects/ftrials/sheppard/sheppardinterview1.html; Sheppard v. Maxwell, 231 F. Supp. 37, 39–40 (S.D. Ohio 1964) gives a brief summary of his story.

pajama tops were rolled up around her neck and the bottoms were down around her ankles. Her teeth appeared to be pulled forward as if she had bitten her assailant and she had a badly torn fingernail that suggested she may have scratched him as well.

Esther ran downstairs and shouted to her husband to call for help. Houk phoned the Bay Village police about an hour and a half after Marilyn's estimated time of death. Houk then called Sam's brother, Richard, who, as soon he arrived, raced upstairs to see if he could revive Marilyn but soon came back down and said, "She's gone, Sam." Houk would later claim that Richard said to Sam, "Did you have anything to do with this?" And that Sam had responded, "Hell, no." Richard and Sam denied that any such conversation ever took place.[9]

If there had been DNA technology in 1954, the crime might have been solved quickly and we would have no mystery; but perhaps not. The crime scene was very quickly contaminated. Police, press, and family members were walking throughout the house, touching and moving evidence, and taking photographs in the crime scene bedroom.

A neighbor boy found a green cloth bag in the bushes leading to the lake. It contained a man's watch, a class ring, other jewelry, and some keys on a chain. It seemed to suggest that a thief might have used the bag to carry stolen items but threw it away when being chased by Sheppard; or perhaps it was planted to make it look that way.

At 8:00 A.M. that Fourth of July morning, coroner Samuel Gerber arrived at the house. Gerber was a doctor, had a law degree and also had a national reputation as a forensic expert. It was reported by some that Gerber disliked Sheppard and was jealous of the success of the Bay View Hospital. A young resident there, Dr. H. Max Don, heard Gerber say about a month before the murder, that he intended someday "to get" the Sheppards.[10] After a look around the house,

---

9. Bailey and Aronson, *The Defense Never Rests*, 59.
10. Neff, *The Wrong Man*, 16.

Dr. Gerber told his men, "Well, it's obvious the doctor did this, so let's go get a confession out of him."[11]

Gerber then went to the hospital where Sheppard was resting under sedation, questioned him for about ten minutes and took away the clothes Sam had been wearing. Later that afternoon, Sheppard was questioned by Cleveland detectives Robert Schottke and Pat Gareau, who had been charged by Gerber to get a confession. They pushed Sheppard to take a lie detector test. At one point Schottke said to him point blank, "I don't know what my partner thinks, but I think you killed your wife."[12] After that, Gerber had a physician examine Sheppard to determine if his claimed injuries could have been self-inflicted. The fact that Sheppard was suspected was not surprising; a number of factors point toward guilt. There was no sign of a forced entry in the house. The only open window in the bedroom was screened and latched, and the dust on the windowsill was not disturbed. During the trial, however, many witnesses would testify that the Sheppards frequently left their doors unlocked. Moreover, Sam's corduroy jacket had been found neatly folded across a pillow at the head of the couch, but the Aherns said that Sam was wearing it when he fell asleep. The police thought that if Sam had really been awakened by Marilyn's screams, he would not have paused to fold his jacket. Sam's explanation was that he took it off in the middle of the night because he was hot.

Although there was blood all over the bedroom, there was none on any of the yanked-out drawers, the medical bag, or even on the knob of the door Sam had said the intruder used when he ran out. Drops of human blood were found leading from the second floor, down the stairs to the first floor, and then to the basement, where there was a sink. The police thought that this blood trail indicated that the killer knew the layout of the house and had gone to the basement to wash off the blood, a theory that contradicted Sam's version of the events.

---

11. Linder, "Famous American Trials"; Neff, *The Wrong Man*, 16; Sheppard v. Maxwell, 384 U.S. 333, 337 (1966).
12. Sheppard v. Maxwell 384 U.S. 333, 338 (1966); Neff, *The Wrong Man*, 20.

Gerber speculated that the bloodstains on a pillowcase on Marilyn's bed indicated that the murder weapon had rested on it. According to the coroner, the imprint showed two blades, each about three inches long and joined in the middle, which he suspected was from a surgical instrument. But the imprint was subject to other interpretations, including that it was caused by the bloody pillow merely being folded over.

Then there was the vagueness and bizarre nature of Sam's story. Marilyn was savagely beaten to death in a way that suggested a crime of passion that made it unlikely to be the act of a burglar. Nor is it likely that he would have done it after seeing Sam asleep on the couch and risk awakening him with such a violent action. And would he then go downstairs and ransack the house? There is also the delay in Sam's calling the police and his story of the vague shadowy form and of being knocked out not once but twice. In addition, while all this was supposedly going on, the normally alert Sheppard dog never barked. When confronted with these questions, Sam could only answer, "I don't know."

On the other hand, some of the evidence supported Sam. Marilyn's blood was everywhere, but there was not a drop on Sheppard, only a smudge on the left knee of his trousers and a drop on his wristwatch. Sam explained those by describing kneeling on the bed to take Marilyn's pulse.

The detectives claimed that Sam's injuries were self-inflicted and minor, but X-rays taken two days after the murder showed that Sam had suffered a fracture of a cervical vertebra and a bruise on the spinal cord. Two of his teeth were broken and his face was swollen. He could not have inflicted these injuries on himself.

Also, although statistics indicate the most men who kill their partners have a history of violence against the victim, Sam had no such reputation. None of his friends or coworkers could remember him ever becoming angry, let alone violent. Moreover, there was no explanation for the trail of blood that led from the bedroom to the downstairs area of the house. Sam had no scratches or cuts, so the blood could not have been his. The investigators assumed that the blood drops came from the murder weapon that Sam must have car-

ried with him throughout the house, but it was scientifically established that Marilyn's blood on the weapon would have congealed
quickly and could not have dripped for more than a foot or two. If
the blood trail was Marilyn's how did it get downstairs? The police
investigators were so confident that Sam was the murderer and that
the trail of blood had to be Marilyn's, that they never tested it even
for the most routine A, B, O, or AB classification that might have
indicated that the blood came from a wounded assailant.

Another instance of sloppy police work was that even though the
bloody bedroom closely resembled a sex crime scene, the coroner's
assistant never examined Marilyn's nearly nude body for the presence
of sperm. In addition, the blood from her wounds was washed away
instead of being microscopically examined for hair, fibers, or any
other foreign matter that might help to identify the killer and/or the
weapon. The attitude of the investigators seemed to be that of "why
bother with exacting tests when we have an open and shut case?"[13]

The Sheppards hired Bill Corrigan to be Sam's lawyer. Well
known for handling sensational cases, Corrigan had represented
two crime syndicate figures during the nationally televised Kefauver
organized crime hearings. He was a skilled trial lawyer and excep-
tionally good at handling the press.

From the day of the crime until after the trial ended, the media,
in particular Cleveland's three daily newspapers, conducted a relent-
less campaign to convict Sam Sheppard. Headlines and news articles emphasized the evidence against Sheppard and negative rumors
about his past life were reported as fact. Particularly irresponsible was
the then-powerful, but now defunct, *Cleveland Press*.

The editor and owner of the *Cleveland Press* was Louis B. Sel-
zer, one of Ohio's most influential citizens. Almost from the beginning, Seltzer seemed certain that Sheppard was guilty, and he and
his newspaper led the vigilante crusade against Sam. He admitted as
much in his autobiography, which included a full chapter in which
he boasted of his success in going after Sheppard. Complaining that
the police did not pursue Sam aggressively enough, Seltzer wrote:

13. Neff, *The Wrong Man*, 19.

It was a calculated risk—a hazard of the kind which I believed a newspaper sometimes, in the interest of law and order and the community's ultimate safety, should take. I was convinced that a conspiracy existed to defeat the ends of justice, and that it would affect adversely the whole law enforcement machinery of the county if it were permitted to succeed.[14]

He justified his editorials, saying:

Dr. Sam was fenced in by his family, his friends and the public authorities in Bay Village. The protective wall had been put up quickly. It was almost impossible to penetrate. . . . The purpose seemed obvious—to hold the wall secure around Dr. Sam until public interest subsided and investigating authorities turned their interest elsewhere. [15]

The undisputed prejudicial coverage of the investigation and trial of Sam Sheppard is contained in five binders of newspaper articles, television stories, and radio transcripts that later became part of the official appellate record.[16]

Prejudicial stories erroneously stressed Sheppard's lack of cooperation with the police when, in fact, during the entire month of July, Sheppard made himself available for frequent and extended questioning without the presence of an attorney. He was interrogated three times on the day of the murder and again on July 8 for three and a half hours at the Bay View Hospital. He also voluntarily appeared

---

14. Seltzer, *The Years Were Good*, 270.
15. Ibid., 269.
16. All the virulent prejudicial publicity contained in the three Cleveland newspapers was stipulated as authentic by both sides in litigation that occurred a decade later in federal court. Most of the publicity during the investigation and trial of Sam Sheppard, as described in the rest of the chapter, is from detailed accounts from the opinions by chief judge of the Federal District Court of the Southern District of Ohio, Carl A. Weinman, in Sheppard v. Maxwell, 231 F. Supp. 37 (S.D. Ohio 1964) and by Justice Tom Clark speaking for eight of the nine justices of the U.S. Supreme Court in Sheppard v. Maxwell, 384 U.S. 333 (1966).

at the Cuyahoga County sheriff's office where he was questioned by detectives for four and a half hours and gave a signed statement.[17]

The press played up Sheppard's refusal to take a lie detector test and his refusal to be injected with truth serum. The *Cleveland Press* opened fire with a front-page charge that somebody was "getting away with murder." The editors attributed the failure to "get Sheppard" to "friendships, relationships, hired lawyers, a husband who ought to have been subjected instantly to the same third degree to which any other person under similar circumstances is subjected."[18] The following day, another page-one editorial was headed: "Why No Inquest? Do It Now, Dr. Gerber."[19] The coroner called an inquest that same day and subpoenaed Sheppard to testify. It was staged in a school gymnasium with the coroner presiding, the county prosecutor acting as his advisor, and two detectives as bailiffs. The hearing was broadcast live; print, radio, and television reporters and photographers swarmed around the room. Sheppard was brought into the gym by policemen who searched him in full view of the several hundred spectators. The search could have and should have been conducted in the private room where Sam was being held, but that would not have been dramatic enough for Gerber and the press.

Sheppard's lawyer was present during the three-day inquest, but when he attempted to place some documents in the record, he was forcibly ejected from the room while the audience cheered.[20] Sam Sheppard was questioned for five-and-a-half hours about his actions on the night of the murder, his married life, and about an alleged affair with Susan Hayes. When Sheppard was asked whether he had been intimate with Miss Hayes, he denied it. The next day, Miss Hayes admitted that she and Dr. Sam had indeed slept together.

17. Linder, "Famous American Trials," supra note 8.
18. Sheppard v. Maxwell, 384 U.S. 333, 339 (1966); Sheppard v. Maxwell, 231 F. Supp. 37, 48 (S.D. Ohio 1964); Neff, *The Wrong Man*, 84–85.
19. Sheppard v. Maxwell, 384 U.S. 333, 339 (1966); Sheppard v. Maxwell, 231 F. Supp. 37, 49 (S.D. Ohio 1964); Neff, *The Wrong Man*, 85.
20. Sheppard v. Maxwell, 384 U.S. 333, 339–40 (1966); Sheppard v. Maxwell, 231 F. Supp. 37, 49 (S.D. Ohio 1964); Neff, *The Wrong Man*, 90–91.

When the inquest was over, Gerber was embraced and congratulated by members of the audience.[21]

Now the media really had a field day. Articles stressed his extramarital affair as a motive for the crime. The newspapers fully explored his relationship with Susan Hayes and, although no testimony regarding other women would be presented at his trial, named others who were allegedly involved with him.[22]

The papers also reported supposed comments from some detectives that scientific tests had established that the killer had washed off a trail of blood from the murder bedroom to the downstairs section of the house. But no such tests existed.

Next, an editorial, "Why Don't Police Quiz Top Suspect?" demanded that Sheppard be taken to police headquarters for questioning. They characterized him as:

> Now proved under oath to be a liar, still free to go about his business, shielded by his family, protected by a smart lawyer who has made monkeys of the police and authorities, left free to do whatever he pleases. . . .[23]

A front-page editorial the next day asked, "Why isn't Sam Sheppard in jail?" Another, titled "Quit Stalling—Bring Him In," claimed that "except for some superficial questioning during coroner Sam Gerber's inquest, he has been scot-free of any official grilling. . . . "

That night at ten o'clock, Sam Sheppard was arrested at his father's home on a charge of murder. He was taken to the Bay Village city hall where hundreds of onlookers, newscasters, photographers, and reporters were awaiting his arrival. He was immediately arraigned and bound over to the grand jury, having been denied a delay to secure the presence of counsel.

---

21. Sheppard v. Maxwell, 384 U.S. 333, 340–1 (1966); Sheppard v. Maxwell, 231 F. Supp. 37, 51 (S.D. Ohio 1964); Neff, *The Wrong Man*, 90–91.
22. Sheppard v. Maxwell, 384 U.S. 333, 340; Neff, *The Wrong Man*, 93–94.
23. Sheppard v. Maxwell, 384 U.S. 333, 341 (1966); Sheppard v. Maxwell, 231 F. Supp. 37, 53–54 (S.D. Ohio 1964); Neff, *The Wrong Man*, 101.

A poll showed that nearly everyone in Cleveland had read about the case and that nearly everyone thought Sheppard was guilty. Defense efforts to gather evidence of community prejudice to support their motions for a change of venue were denounced by the press as "mass jury tampering."[24]

Sam Sheppard was put on trial for murder on October 18, 1954. The trial began two weeks before the elections in which the chief prosecutor was running for a local judgeship and the presiding judge, Edward Blythin, was a candidate for reelection. A conscientious judge might have granted a continuance until after the election to avoid any suggestion of a conflict of interest. Instead, both judge and prosecutor realized that it benefited them to do everything to accommodate the press, and they did.

Judge Blythin set up, inside the bar, a long table that stretched the entire width of the small courtroom and extended about six inches from the jury box. It seated approximately twenty reporters and was located directly behind the counsel tables, making confidential conversation between Sam and his lawyers practically impossible. The judge had also reserved almost every row in the courtroom for the press, leaving only the very last row to be shared by Sam and Marilyn's families. Furthermore, the press was allowed to use every other room on that floor, and the judge had telephone and telegraph equipment installed for the convenience of the press. In addition, a radio station was allowed to set up broadcasting equipment on the third floor of the courthouse, right next to the room where the jurors rested during recesses and where they would deliberate. Newscasts were made from this area, while the jury was in the next room trying to reach a verdict.

In the hallway outside the courtroom, a large group of photographers and reporters took pictures of the judge, jury, witnesses, and counsel every time they entered or left. The Supreme Court would later refer to this activity as "running the gauntlet." Inside the courtroom, a rule prohibited the press from taking pictures during the trial, but not during recesses. Then they would often take pictures

---

24. Sheppard v. Maxwell, 384 U.S. 333, 345–6 (1966).

of whatever was lying on both the prosecution and defense table, including notes and exhibits. The intrusive news coverage was at its worst during the first few days of jury selection. "Flashbulbs were popping and lighting devices, backed by powerful reflectors, were sprouting from chairs, tables and the floor to near ceiling height, their cables twisting and coiling over the carpet."[25]

The jurors themselves were a prominent focus of media attention. They were not sequestered during the trial and were allowed to go home each night. The judge "suggested" but did not order them to avoid the press or television coverage of the trial. Since all three Cleveland papers had published the names and addresses of every member of the jury, they were bombarded with letters and telephone calls. During the trial, their pictures appeared almost daily. One newspaper ran pictures of them when they went to the Sheppard house to view the scene of the crime; another featured the home life of a juror. It is reasonable to assume that the jurors would look for the photos and read the accompanying articles about the trial. As a result, the jurors had unusual and unprecedented access to extraneous and prejudicial nonevidentiary data.

On the first day of jury selection, the editors of the *Cleveland Plain Dealer* and Seltzer's *Cleveland Press* debated the topic, "Which newspaper deserved the most credit for the indictment of Dr. Sheppard?" Each one claimed the prize, but the winner was clearly the *Press*. As the editor gloated, "The *Press's* handling of the Sheppard story produced the trial that we have got over there today because I don't think the officials were going to do anything about it."[26]

Misinformation continued to be reported for the duration of the trial. Headlines such as "But Who Will Speak for Marilyn?" with a story asking for justice for the victim and "Sam Called a Jekyll and

---

25. The manner in which the trial judge allocated the courtroom to members of the news media contributed to the bedlam that was described as "a carnival atmosphere." Sheppard v. Maxwell, 384 U.S. 333, 342–4 (1966); Sheppard v. Maxwell, 231 F. Supp. 37, 63 (S.D. Ohio 1964).
26. Neff, *The Wrong Man*, 126–7.

Hyde by Marilyn—Cousin to Testify" (though no such testimony was ever given) were common.[27]

The famous newsman Walter Winchell broadcast that a woman in New York had been Sheppard's mistress and had borne him a child, and two jurors admitted they had heard the report. When asked, they told the judge that it didn't affect their judgment and no further inquiry was made, nor did Winchell retract the story when it proved false.[28] Another well-regarded newsman, Robert Considine, in a broadcast heard in Cleveland, called Sheppard a perjurer, and in a radio discussion of the case, some reporters asserted that Sheppard had conceded his guilt early on by hiring a prominent criminal lawyer.[29]

After each one of these incidents, Sheppard's attorney moved for a change of venue, but his requests were denied. He also moved unsuccessfully for an adjournment until the gossip died down and later for a mistrial.

If Corrigan had known more about Blythin, he would have had excellent grounds for asking the judge to recuse himself. One of Blythin's sons, Arthur, was a Cleveland homicide detective who had worked with an assistant prosecutor interviewing possible witnesses in the case. In addition, it was learned later that three people heard the judge express, during the trial, his certainty that Sam was guilty.

One person who the heard the judge was Dorothy Kilgallen, the syndicated journalist and panelist on the TV program *What's My Line?* When the judge learned she was covering the trial, he asked to see her in his chambers. Here is her account as she related it years later in a court deposition:

> The judge was very affable. He shook hands with me and said, "I am very glad to see you, Miss Kilgallen. I watch you on television very frequently and enjoy the program." And he

---

27. Sheppard v. Maxwell, 231 F. Supp. 37, 54–56, 57, 60 (S.D. Ohio 1964); Sheppard v. Maxwell, 384 U.S. 333, 346–8 (1966).
28. Sheppard v. Maxwell, 384 U.S. 333, 348–9 (1966); Neff, *The Wrong Man*, 151–2.
29. Sheppard v. Maxwell, 384 U.S. 333, 346–7 (1966); Sheppard v. Maxwell, 231 F. Supp. 37, 61–62 (S.D. Ohio 1964).

said "What brings you to Cleveland?" and I said, "Well, your Honor, this trial," and he said, "But why come all the way from New York to Cleveland to cover this trial?" and I said, "Well, it has all the ingredients of what in the newspaper business we call a good murder. It has a very attractive victim, who was pregnant, and the accused is a very important member of the community, a respectable, very attractive man." And I said, "Then in addition to that, you have the fact that it is a mystery as to who did it." And Judge Blythin said, "Mystery? It's an open and shut case." And I said, "Well, what do you mean, Judge Blythin?" and he said, "Well, he's guilty as hell, no question about it."[30]

Two other individuals stated that they heard Judge Blythin express the same opinion: Edward Murray, an employee in the clerk's office, and Oliver Schroeder, a criminal law professor who assisted the coroner.[31]

The prosecution began by showing there were no signs of forcible entry and that there was a trail of blood leading to the basement. They also showed photographs of Marilyn's bloody head and face. Susan Hayes testified to having sex with Dr. Sam, and Sheppard's neighbor, Nancy Ahern, testified that Marilyn said she had been told by a friend that Sam was considering a divorce. Over a defense objection, the judge made an obvious error by allowing the testimony to stand. As any lawyer should know, it was not only hearsay, it was double hearsay. With reference to this ruling, Walter Winchell, who was not a lawyer, announced that "no matter the verdict, the defense counsel cannot be overly concerned . . . because legal experts are *sure* the case has at least one reversible error, which would require a new trial."[32]

---

30. Neff, *The Wrong Man*, 124–5, 128; Cooper and Sheppard, *Mockery of Justice*, 38; Sheppard v. Maxwell, 231 F. Supp. 37, 64–65 (S.D. Ohio 1964); Sheppard v. Maxwell, 384 U.S. 333, 337 (1966).

31. Neff, *The Wrong Man*, 127–8; Sheppard v. Maxwell, 231 F. Supp. 37, 64–65 (S.D. Ohio 1964).

32. Neff, *The Wrong Man*, 139, 164–5.

The star witness for the prosecution was Dr. Gerber. He said that when he examined the bloody pillow, he found that a fold in it had trapped some of Marilyn's blood, and in the bloodstain, he could see an imprint of a claw-like instrument. He theorized that this was an imprint of the murder weapon, which the murderer had laid down on the pillow. He described the impression as the imprint of a "surgical instrument." A Cleveland paper published a front page picture of the pillow after the photo had been "doctored" to show more clearly the imprint of the alleged surgical instrument.

Detective Robert Schottke testified that he asked the defendant if he would submit to a lie detector test, but that Sheppard refused. Carl Rossbach of the Cuyahoga County sheriff's office added that he asked the defendant at least ten or fifteen times to take the lie detector test, but Sheppard said, "I won't take it because my attorney advised me not to and members of my family asked me not to." Corrigan objected strenuously, arguing that the results of the test would be inadmissible at the trial because polygraph tests were considered, under the law, to be unreliable. Corrigan was correct. The testimony about Sheppard's refusal to take the test should have been excluded as misleading, prejudicial, and irrelevant. A juror might understandably think the test was reliable and that refusing to take it revealed a consciousness of guilt. But Judge Blythin allowed it and never told the jury that the tests, even if taken, would be inadmissible; another clear evidentiary error.[33]

The defense produced evidence of the state's sloppy investigation as well as evidence that Sam and Marilyn were a happy couple. There was expert medical testimony about Sam's condition after the murder. An X-ray technician, a radiologist, a dentist, and a neurologist testified that he was bruised and disoriented, that he had a fractured cervical vertebra, a swelling at the base of his skull as well as chipped teeth, and a spinal cord injury that affected his reflexes. The witnesses said these injuries could not have been simulated or self-inflicted. Sam himself took the stand and told his story.

---

33. Sheppard v. Maxwell, 231 F. Supp. 37, 66–69 (S.D. Ohio 1964); Neff, *The Wrong Man*, 140.

An objective lawyer watching this case unfold would probably have concluded that although there was enough circumstantial evidence to convict, room remained for jurors to have reasonable doubt.

The State left the scenario with Sam snoozing on the living room couch after a pleasant evening with friends who witnessed him affectionately sharing an armchair with Marilyn and reminding her not to smoke so much. They picked up his story after Marilyn was murdered and proclaimed that he did it. There was a great deal of plot for the jury to fill in.

The jury deliberated four days after discarding murder one almost immediately. The first ballot revealed six for guilty of murder in the second degree and six for acquittal. By the next day, the vote was unanimous for conviction with a few holdouts for conviction of manslaughter. It took two more days before jurors recorded a unanimous verdict of guilty of second-degree murder.

Dr. Sam Sheppard was sentenced to life imprisonment. Two weeks later, Sheppard's mother committed suicide. Eleven days after that, his father died of a hemorrhaging ulcer.

The deliberation of the jury was tainted by a violation of Ohio law. An Ohio statute mandates that once the case is submitted to the jurors, they must be kept together and are not allowed to communicate with anyone. While deliberating, however, jurors did use bailiffs' phones to make numerous telephone calls. No record was made of the number of calls, the identity of the jurors who used the phones, the identity of the recipients of the conversations, or of the content of the information transmitted or received.[34]

The guilty verdict came as a surprise to the media outside of Cleveland. Dorothy Kilgallen wrote: "I heard the same evidence the jury heard. I saw Dr. Sheppard on the stand. I listened to the summation by both sides. I could not have convicted him of anything except possible negligence in not locking his back door."[35]

An editorial in the *Toledo Blade* reported:

34. Ohio, "Section 13448-1" (Section 2943.33, revised code), in *Ohio General Code* (W.H. Anderson Company, 1910); Sheppard v. Maxwell, 231 F. Supp. 37, 69.
35. Neff, *The Wrong Man*, 168.

At this distance, some 100 miles from here, it looks to us as though the Sheppard murder case was sensationalized to the point at which the press must ask itself if freedom, carried to excess, doesn't interfere with the conduct of fair trials.[36]

John M. Harrison wrote in the *Saturday Review*:

The question of Dr. Sheppard's guilt or innocence is still before the courts. Those who have examined the trial record carefully are divided as to the propriety of the verdict. But almost everyone who watched the performance of the *Cleveland Press* agrees that a fair hearing for the defendant, in that area, would be a modern miracle.[37]

Defense Attorney Corrigan moved, before Judge Blythin, for a new trial. When that was denied, he appealed the conviction, without success, to Ohio's intermediate appellate court and then to the Ohio Supreme Court, which affirmed the conviction by a vote of 5 to 2. All the Ohio appellate courts agreed that the publicity surrounding the trial was excessive, but they concluded that there was no evidence that it affected the jurors' ability to reach a fair verdict. The United States Supreme Court denied certiorari and declined to review the case.[38]

Ten years passed while Dr. Sam worked in prison as a four-dollars-a-month surgeon. He also participated in a research program allowing doctors to inoculate him with live cancer cells to determine if a healthy person would reject the cells more quickly than a patient who already had cancer.

---

36. Sheppard v. Maxwell, 384 U.S. 333, 356 (1966); Editorial Board, "Free Press and Fair Trial," *Toledo Blade*, December 22, 1954.
37. Sheppard v. Maxwell, 384 U.S. 333, 356 (1966); Harrison, "The Press vs. the Courts," *The Saturday Review*, October 15, 1958.
38. Sheppard was convicted in 1954 in the Court of Common Pleas of Cuyahoga County, Ohio. His conviction was affirmed by the Court of Appeals of Cuyahoga County in State v. Sheppard, 100 Ohio App. 345, 128 N.E.2d 471 (1955) and the Ohio Supreme Court, 165 Ohio St. 293, 135 N.E.2d 340 (1956). The Supreme Court denied certiorari on the original application for review, 352 U.S. 910, 77 S. Ct. 118 (1956).

During this time, Corrigan died.

The Sheppard family thought about the possibility of parole and of trying to change Cleveland's perception of Sam; maybe he should take a lie detector test. Sheppard was put in contact with a Boston lawyer, just one year out of law school, named F. Lee Bailey.

At this time, no one realized that F. Lee Bailey was destined to become one of the nation's most famous criminal defense lawyers, representing, among many others, the Boston Strangler, Patty Hearst, and O. J. Simpson.

Bailey did not obtain a lie detector test because the warden of the Ohio penitentiary would not allow polygraph examiners into the prison, and the courts refused to overturn his decision.

Ohio State appeals had been exhausted years ago, but one remedy still remained in the Federal court system.

With the benefit of research by a team of Harvard law students, Bailey brought a petition for a writ of habeas corpus in the federal District Court for the Southern District of Ohio. The timing of this suit could not have been better. In the 1960s, the Supreme Court had expanded the constitutional rights of defendants charged with a crime and removed procedural impediments to the use of federal habeas corpus.[39]

Defendants who had exhausted their state remedies and appeals could now seek the same or similar relief from federal courts on issues arising under the United States Constitution. Thus, Bailey was able to argue in the federal district court that in 1954, Sheppard had been denied his right to a fair trial by an impartial jury.

In his petition, Bailey listed twenty-three errors and argued in particular that the defendant was prejudiced:

[b]y the action of the trial judge in contributing to the "atmosphere of a 'Roman holiday' for news media" by making certain special and unprecedented arrangements within the courthouse and the courtroom itself, whereby facilities

---

39. See Townsend v. Sain, 372 U.S. 293 (1963) and Fay v. Noia, 372 U.S. 391 (1963); Bailey and Aronson, *The Defense Never Rests*, 66.

Dr. Samuel Sheppard (left) listens as his attorney, F. Lee Bailey (right),
answers reporters' questions.
© Bettmann/CORBIS

thereof were set aside almost exclusively for newsmen, thereby
encouraging and approving a massive, sustained, prejudicial
and inflammatory wave of publicity to which the jurors were
constantly exposed.[40]

Carl A. Weinman, chief judge for the Southern District of Ohio,
was assigned to decide the habeas corpus petition. Judge Weinman
condensed Bailey's twenty-three grounds into five major areas: (1)
the failure of the trial judge (Blythin) to grant a change of venue or a
continuance in the face of massive publicity; (2) the publicity before
and during the trial and the latitude given to the press; (3) the trial
judge's failure to disqualify himself after making certain statements
regarding petitioner's guilt; (4) permitting police officers to testify
that petitioner had refused to take a lie detector test and permit-

40. Sam Sheppard and F. Lee Bailey, "Petition for a Writ of Habeas Corpus," *1963–1966
Federal Habeas Corpus, Paper 4,* April 10, 1963, http://engagedscholarship.csuohio.edu/
sheppard_habeas/4/.

ting a prosecution witness to testify that he had taken a lie detector test; and (5) the action of the bailiffs in allowing the jurors, during deliberations and without authority from the court, to hold telephone conversations with persons outside the jury room.

In a thirty-five-page opinion, the district judge found that every one of these five allegations constituted violations of Sheppard's constitutional rights and held that:

> Each . . . is by itself sufficient to require a determination that petitioner was not afforded a fair trial as required by the due process clause of the Fourteenth Amendment. And when these errors are cumulated, the trial can only be viewed as a mockery of justice.[41]

The conviction was vacated. Absent further action by the prosecution, Sheppard was free.

There was further action, however. The State appealed to the three-judge federal court of appeals which, by a vote of 2 to 1, reversed the district court.[42] Bailey then petitioned the United States Supreme Court for certiorari. The Supreme Court reversed the court of appeals, holding in the landmark decision in *Sheppard v. Maxwell* that "the massive, pervasive and prejudicial publicity attending petitioner's prosecution prevented him from receiving a fair trial."[43]

In previous cases, the Court had insisted upon a showing that the publicity had produced identifiable prejudice to the accused. Justice Tom Clark, writing for an 8 to 1 majority, held that in extreme cases such as this one, the prejudice need not be proven; it can be assumed. The Court conceded that "freedom of expression should be given the widest possible range but it must not be allowed to divert a trial from its purpose of adjudicating controversies according to legal procedures received only in open court."[44]

---

41. Sheppard v. Maxwell, 231 F. Supp. 37, 71 (S.D. Ohio 1964).
42. Sheppard v. Maxwell, 346 F.2d 707 (6th Cir. 1965).
43. Sheppard v. Maxwell, 384 U.S. 333, 335 (1966).
44. Ibid., 350–1.

The Court did note the excesses of the press, but its major criticism was of Judge Blythin for failure to invoke procedures that would have guaranteed the petitioner a fair trial, "such as adopting stricter rules for use of the courtroom by newsmen as Sheppard's counsel requested, limiting their number and more closely supervising their courtroom conduct."[45] The court also should have "insulated witnesses, controlled the release of leads, information or gossip to the press by police officers, witnesses and counsel; proscribed extrajudicial statements by any lawyer, witness, party or court official divulging prejudicial matters and requested the appropriate city and county officials to regulate the release of information by their employees."[46]

The opinion made clear that:

> Neither prosecutors, counsel for the defense, the accused, witnesses, court staff nor law enforcement officers coming under the jurisdiction of the court should be permitted to frustrate its function. Collaboration between counsel and the press as to information affecting the fairness of a criminal trial is not only subject to regulation but is highly censurable and worthy of disciplinary measures.[47]

Some of the national press were stunned by the scope of the criticism in Justice Clark's Supreme Court opinion. They were upset at language such as "virulent publicity" and "commotion within the bar," the reference to the "Roman holiday atmosphere" and how "bedlam reigned in the courtroom." Some prominent members of the national press corps sent a letter of protest to the Court saying it was the Cleveland reporters who had created the problem:

> We never believed that the American Press as a whole would be condemned 12 years later for local stories about revelations

---

45. Ibid., 358–62.
46. Ibid.
47. Ibid., 363.

made by police, defense and prosecution attorneys and the coroner in one city in the Middle West.[48]

For the first time in years Sam Sheppard was, at least temporarily, a free man. The question was whether the state of Ohio would retry him. The answer was yes, they would, but this time some things would be different.

To begin with, he would not be facing the death penalty. Double jeopardy meant that he could not be tried again on murder one, so the retrial charge was limited to murder in the second degree.

Cuyahoga Common Pleas Judge Francis Talty, who had been assigned to the retrial, ordered that there were to be no cameras or radio equipment in the courtroom or on the premises; he even refused to allow sketch artists in the courtroom. Nobody was allowed to enter or exit the courtroom during the proceedings and no one—not the lawyers, not their agents, and not witnesses—was to make any statement or comment to the press.

The prosecution case was essentially the same as the first trial except they did not try to show that Sam's injuries were self-inflicted. There was no mention of his affair with Susan Hayes, and there was no talk of divorce or other women in his life. Apparently, the State was not going to try to prove a motive for the murder. Instead, they presented a stripped-down, bare-bones case. They proved that Marilyn was killed, and they proved that Sam was in the house at the time.

But then they called Mary Cowan to the stand. A blood expert in the coroner's office, she testified to something that had been ignored in the first trial. There was a small trace of blood on Sam's wristwatch that had been explained at the time as having come from contact when Sam tried to take Marilyn's pulse.

The blood on Sam's watch, Cowan explained, was not from contact between the watch and a flowing wound or a pool of blood. Instead, it was blood that had flown through the air to reach the watch. Because of their shape, the droplets of blood on the face of

---

48. Neff, *The Wrong Man*, 244.

Prosecutor Thomas Parrino shows medical technologist
Mary E. Cowan the wristwatch belonging to
Dr. Samuel Sheppard, during a recess.
© Bettmann/CORBIS

the watch could only have been made by "blood in motion." Since
the only blood flying around the murder room was blood that was
spurting from Marilyn's wounds upon impact or being tossed from a
flailing weapon, Sam's watch must have been in the room at the time
of the murder. Cowan's testimony was a major source of concern for
the defense.

At this trial, F. Lee Bailey represented Sheppard. He was very
effective. Coroner Gerber had testified about the bloody imprint of a
surgical instrument on Marilyn's pillow during the first trial, but not
this time; Bailey's cross-examination was unrelenting.

Q: Well now, Dr. Gerber, just what kind of surgical instrument do you see here?

A: I am not sure.

Q: Would it perchance be an instrument that you yourself have handled?

A: I don't know if I have handled one or not.

Q: Of course, you have been a surgeon, have you not, doctor?

A: "No."

Q: Do you have such an instrument back at your office?

A: No.

Q: Have you ever seen such an instrument in any hospital or medical supply catalog or anywhere else, Dr. Gerber?

A: No, not that I can remember.

Q: Tell the jury, Doctor, where you have searched for his instrument during the past twelve years.

A: Oh, I have looked all over the United States.

Q: My goodness, then please, by all means tell us what you found.

A: I didn't find one.

Q: Now doctor, you know that Sam Sheppard was and is a surgeon, don't you?

A: [Gerber nods to indicate yes.]

Q: Now you didn't describe this phantom impression as a surgical instrument just to hurt Sam Sheppard's case, did you doctor? You wouldn't do that, would you?

A: Oh no, oh, no.[49]

Gerber ended up admitting the imprint could have been by pliers or a flashlight or almost any commonplace tool.

As in the first trial, Dr. Elkins, an osteopath, testified that his examination of Sam two days after the murder revealed a fracture of a cervical vertebra and a bruise on the spinal cord. Bailey asked if Sam could have inflicted the wound on himself. Elkins answered only if he had dived out of a second-story window.

The most effective defense witness in the retrial was Dr. Paul Kirk, the reputed father of criminology who taught at the University of California at Berkeley and provided, pro bono, crime scene analysis for police departments and prosecutors. He was a blood splatter expert and had written one of the most authoritative textbooks, *Crime Investigation: Physical Evidence and the Police Laboratory.*

In preparation for his testimony, Kirk had vacuumed Marilyn's bedroom with a filter to trap minute particles. He photographed every part of the room and measured the size and shape of all the blood drops. After weeks of analysis, he was able to determine that, as the killer was battering Marilyn, he would have been splattered with a great deal of blood, which Sam Sheppard was not. It was also clear from the direction of the splatters that the killer was left handed, which Sam was also not. Nor could the blood trail leading downstairs be Marilyn's blood dripping from the murder weapon. And Kirk determined that Marilyn's broken front teeth were likely caused by her biting down hard on the finger of the killer as he placed his hand over her mouth; Sam had no such wounds on his hands. And Kirk noted that the condition of Marilyn's mostly unclothed body indicated it was a sex crime.

Kirk found blood on the bedroom wall that belonged neither to Marilyn or Sam. He refuted Mary Cowan's testimony, claiming that flecks of blood had probably reached Sheppard's watch by contact. He theorized that from the shape of the wounds, the murder weapon was a cylindrical object such as a flashlight, which the killer had

49. Bailey and Aronson, *The Defense Never Rests*, 87–88; Neff, *The Wrong Man*, 259–62.

probably carried to the scene. In fact, a dented flashlight was found in the shallow water near the Sheppard house, turned over to the coroner (Gerber) and never heard about again.[50]

Kirk testified for a full day and when he was finished, Mary Cowan's testimony for the State was largely nullified as a factor in the case. More importantly, the jurors now had expert testimony before them that another person had been in the house on the night of the murder, just as Sam had always contended.

In his summation, Bailey used the persuasive power of analogies:

> The State of Ohio in this case is like the woman who was hunting around in a gutter underneath a street light. When a passerby asked her what she was doing, she said, "I'm looking for a dollar bill that I dropped in the gutter." "Where did you drop it?" inquired the gentleman, offering to help. "Over there," she said, pointing to a spot fifty feet down the street. "Then why aren't you looking over there?" he asked in astonishment. "Because," she said, "the light is better over here."[51]

The jury deliberated for little over half a day. On the first ballot it was seven for acquittal, four for conviction and one undecided. A few hours later, the unanimous verdict was not guilty. At age forty-two, Sam Sheppard was a free man.

Sam never testified at the second trial. Bailey later explained that he was heavily into alcohol and pills, at times unaware of what was going on around him, and therefore putting him on the stand was risky.[52]

In 1967, the Ohio Medical Board gave Sheppard back his license to practice medicine, but his medical skills had deteriorated. He was sued twice for malpractice that led to the death of both patients. He stopped practicing and divorced his second wife, whom he had married while in prison. In a pathetic effort to capitalize on his notoriety,

---

50. Neff, *The Wrong Man*, 179–86, 270–1.
51. Linder, "Famous American Trials," Dr. Sam Sheppard trial transcript excerpts at http://law2.umkc.edu/faculty/projects/ftrials/sheppard/sheppardexcerpts.html.
52. Bailey and Aronson, *The Defense Never Rests*, 84.

he became a professional wrestler under the name of Killer Sheppard. Sam was drinking a quart or more of vodka daily. On April 6, 1970, he died at the age of forty-six of liver disease.

There is a final chapter to this bizarre story. Sheppard's son, Sam Reese "Chip" Sheppard, began a campaign to establish the innocence of his father. People still thought, "If not Sam, then who?" and Reese Sheppard thought he had an answer to that question. It was a man named Richard Eberling, and by the late 1990s, Reese hoped that maybe DNA evidence could prove it.

Richard Eberling, who at the time of the murder was twenty-five years old, had operated a small company called Dick's Window Cleaning, and Marilyn and Sam Sheppard were among his clients. By his own account, Eberling barely knew Sam but had what he perceived as a fairly close relationship with Marilyn; he recalled having brownies and milk with her and Chip at the Sheppard house. His comments seemed to suggest a sexual attraction. He said, "Oh, she had that California look; tight little brief shorts and a very little blouse. She was immaculate, all in white."[53]

In 1959, Eberling was arrested for larceny. A search of his house turned up cash and jewelry, and among the items was a ring owned by Marilyn Sheppard. During questioning, a police officer on a hunch asked Eberling why his blood had been found in the Sheppard house after the murder. Eberling replied that two days before the murder, while washing windows at the Sheppard home, he had cut his finger while installing window screens.[54]

Throughout the next thirty years he committed a number of fraudulent and violent crimes. In the late 1970s, Eberling became a nurse's aide for Ethel Durkin, an elderly widow. In 1981, he announced to an associate that he was constructing a new will "for the old bat." On November 15, 1983, he found Durkin face down, comatose, and close to death. The nature of her injuries and the medical evidence suggested that Eberling had delayed calling for medical help and was

53. Linder, "Famous American Trials," "The Bushy Haired Man" at http://law2.umkc.edu/faculty/projects/ftrials/sheppard/eberlinginfo.html.
54. Ibid.

responsible for injuries that caused Durkin's death. In order to recover her insurance, Eberling falsely claimed that he was her nephew and sole heir. In July 1989, Eberling was convicted of forgery, theft, and aggravated murder and sentenced to life imprisonment.[55]

Adding to the suspicion that he killed Marilyn Sheppard was that fact that during his employment as a nurse's aide, Ethel Durkin's sister, Myrtle, was brutally beaten on the head and strangled in her bed in a murder very similar to the killing of Marilyn Sheppard. In addition, over the years, Eberling made a series of admissions or near admissions to involvement in Marilyn's murder. Most notably, Kathy Wagner Dyal, the former nurse for Ethel Durkin, told the Cleveland prosecutor, David Zimmerman, that she had the following conversation with Eberling:

> Eberling asked her if she had ever killed someone. She exclaimed, "No!" and he said, "Well, I did." And I just looked at him. And he said, "Did you ever hear of Marilyn Sheppard?" He said, "I did her and someone else paid the bill." And I said, "You mean you killed her?" And he said, "Yeah, and I knocked her husband out with a pail and . . . the bitch bit the hell out of me, but I got her ring." Dyal said she just looked at Eberling, stunned, and then he told her, "Now, you didn't hear that, Katie."[56]

Eberling died in prison on July 25, 1998.

Armed with this information about Eberling, Reese Sheppard and his attorney, Terry Gilbert, asked the Cleveland prosecutor to reopen the investigation and prove Dr. Sam's innocence. The prosecutor responded, in effect, "Your father is dead. Marilyn is dead. Eberling is dead. This 40-year-old case is dead. Go away."

But they did not go away; they went to court. An Ohio statute states that a person who has been wrongly imprisoned can bring a

---

55. Neff, *The Wrong Man*, 291–306; Linder, "Famous American Trials," supra note 53.
56. Neff, *The Wrong Man*, 327, 328; Linder, "Famous American Trials," supra note 53.

civil action for damages against the State. In order to win, the plaintiff must first establish innocence. A verdict of acquittal in a prior criminal case would not suffice, because an acquittal means only a failure to prove guilt beyond a reasonable doubt. Under the statute, the plaintiff would carry the burden of proving actual innocence.[57]

In this third trial, the evidence tracked that of the other two trials but added evidence that Richard Eberling was the real killer. In addition, Dr. Mohammad Tahir, the director of the DNA and Serology laboratories at the Indianapolis-Marion County Forensic Services Agency, gave expert testimony that the bloodstain from Dr. Sam's trousers did not contain DNA from either Sam or from Marilyn, leading to the assumption that the stain was put there by the killer when he attacked Sam. He added that a drop of blood outside the bedroom on one of the stairs contained no DNA from Sam or Marilyn. This finding destroyed the State's theory that Marilyn's blood had dripped from the murder weapon. Tahir's blockbuster finding was that a vaginal smear from the victim's autopsy contained sperm from someone other than Dr. Sheppard. Sam and Marilyn were excluded as DNA contributors to several of the items, but Richard Eberling, Tahir said with scientific caution, "could not be excluded."[58] Also testifying for the plaintiff was John E. Douglas, a retired FBI expert on criminal personality profiling. He asserted there are generally accepted rules about spousal killings, none of which fit the facts of this case. Examples he gave were that the case lacked any predictive behavior of violence. "Nearly all men who kill their wives have assaulted them at least once in the year before the murder." After reviewing hundreds of cases classified as domestic homicides, it was typical for a husband to build up rage over a number of days. The facts of the *Sheppard* case were the exact opposite. The evening before the murder, Marilyn and Sam seemed affectionate. She made Sam's favorite pie, sat in his lap in front of their friends and she turned

---

57. Ohio, "Section 2743.48: Wrongful Imprisonment Civil Action Against State," in *Ohio Revised Code* (April 9, 2003), http://codes.ohio.gov/orc/2743.48.
58. Neff, *The Wrong Man*, 364–6.

down his bedsheets later that night. Most revealing to Douglas was the unlikelihood that Sheppard would have exposed her nakedness in an amateurish attempt to suggest a sex killing. "He would not have left her spread-eagled. Husbands don't do that."[59]

The defendant, the State of Ohio, was represented by William D. Mason, who had successfully prosecuted the first trial. Again, he presented much of the same evidence with limited exceptions. Unlike the first trial, Mason did not present the murder weapon as a "surgical instrument." This time, it was a lamp like one that would be expected to be on the nightstand between the single beds of Sam and Marilyn. This lamp was never found and served as a metaphor of the Sheppard mystery. It left an imprint on her pillow of Dr. Gerber's imagined surgical instrument, or maybe of a dented flashlight, or now of a lamp without its shade, or maybe that was just a stain on a folded pillow. The State also presented its own FBI profiler who testified that this case was typical of spousal murder. The state's blood expert ruled out the contention that Eberling's blood was at the crime scene. Foregoing the more modern tests for the older, less reliable method, he said that Eberling's Type A blood had not been found.[60]

After ten weeks of trial, seventy-six witnesses and hundreds of exhibits, the eight-member civil jury deliberated for only three hours and on April 12, 2000, returned a unanimous verdict in favor of the State of Ohio. Samuel Reese Shepard had failed to prove that his father had been wrongfully imprisoned; the equivalent of a "not innocent" verdict.

In his closing statement, Mason had emphasized to the jury that the plaintiff would have the burden to prove that Sam Sheppard did not kill Marilyn. If they were not convinced of Sam's innocence or if they were "just not sure, you don't know what happened," he informed the jurors, "then you must find for the State."[61] And that is what the jury did.

---

59. Ibid., 332–3, 370–1.
60. Ibid.
61. DeSario and Mason, *Dr. Sam Sheppard on Trial*, 313.

As a final irony, on February 22, 2002, the Ohio Appellate Court nullified the entire proceeding by declaring that there should never have been a third trial because the statute of limitations had expired. Any claim of wrongful imprisonment abated with Sam Sheppard's death.[62]

What lives on is a landmark "Free Press and Fair Trial" Supreme Court precedent.

---

62. Murray v. State of Ohio, Cuyahoga App. No. 78374, 2002 Ohio 664 (Feb. 22, 2002), http://engagedscholarship.csuohio.edu/sheppard_court_filings_2000/2/.

SIX

When the Nazis Tried to March in the Village of Skokie[1]

THE VILLAGE OF SKOKIE V. *The National Socialist Party of America* tested our nation's commitment to freedom of expression when it generated anguish in the people targeted by that speech. The Skokie affair fractured the alliance between civil rights advocates and other liberals over the issue of what speech is protected and what speech is not—a philosophical divide like few others in American history.

---

1. This chapter relies heavily on descriptions of facts and law contained in state and federal opinions in the Skokie litigation. It also relies on the accounts of the Skokie affair contained in secondary sources, including in particular the outstanding work of Philippa Strum in her book, *When the Nazis Came to Skokie: Freedom for Speech We Hate* (University Press of Kansas, 1999). Also of particular help were the insights and descriptions provided in Aryeh Neier, *Defending My Enemy: American Nazis, the Skokie Case, and the Risks of Freedom* (International Debate Education Association, 1979); David Hamlin, *The Nazi/Skokie Conflict: A Civil Liberties Battle* (Beacon Press, 1980); Anthony Lewis, *Freedom for the Thought That We Hate: A Biography of the First Amendment* (Basic Books, 2007); Ronald K.L. Collins, Sam Chaltain, *We Must Not Be Afraid to Be Free: Stories of Free Expression in America* (Oxford University Press, 2011); Jeremy Waldron, *The Harm in Hate Speech* (Harvard University Press, 2012); Erwin Chemerinsky, *Constitutional Law: Principles and Policies, 4th Ed.* (Wolters Kluwer Law & Business, 2011); Floyd Abrams, *Friend of the Court: On the Front Lines with the First Amendment* (Yale University Press, 2013). Also useful were newspaper and Internet accounts of Skokie events.

TEN GREAT AMERICAN TRIALS

The debate it spawned in 1977 and 1978 remains with us today. David Goldberger, a lawyer for the American Civil Liberties Union, described it as "a classic First Amendment case . . . [that] "tests the very foundation of democracy."[2]

Skokie lacks the element of mystery. There is no unsolved crime, no charismatic lawyer or nationally famous defendant, no authoritative United States Supreme Court decision, no jury trial, and no disputed facts.

The First Amendment of the United States Constitution protects the individual's right to freedom of expression. It declares without qualification that the government "shall make no law . . . abridging the freedom of speech."

The clause reflects the founding fathers' belief that government cannot be trusted to make judgments about what constitutes legitimate speech and establishes freedom of expression as a cherished component of our constitutional rights.

Many Supreme Court opinions honor the right to express unpopular opinions. Oliver Wendell Holmes said, "If there is any principle of the Constitution that more imperatively calls for attachment than any other it is the principle of free thought—not free thought for those who agree with us, but freedom for the thought that we hate."[3]

Or as Justice Brennan put it when writing for a unanimous Supreme Court, we have a "profound national commitment to the principle that debate on public issues should be uninhibited, robust and wide open. . . . That commitment was made with the knowledge that erroneous statements are inevitable in free debate."[4]

Why is free speech so important—so fundamental that it is the first of the Bill of Rights? The traditional rationale comes in three parts.[5]

---

2. Hamlin, *The Nazi/Skokie Conflict*, 53.
3. United States v. Schwimmer, 279 U.S. 644, 654–5 (1929) (Holmes dissenting); Collin v. Smith, 447 F. Supp. 676, 702 (N.D. Ill. 1978).
4. New York Times v. Sullivan, 376 U.S. 254, 270–1 (1964).
5. Collin v. Smith, 447 F. Supp. 676, 687–8 (1978); Whitney v. California, 274 U.S. 357, 375–6 (1927); Chemerinsky, *Constitutional Law*, 954–9; Strum, *When the Nazis Came to Skokie*, 29–31; Neier, *Defending My Enemy*, 160–1; For a full elaboration of free speech theories, see Collins and Chaltain, *We Must Not Be Afraid to Be Free*, 39–58.

186

First is the theory that free expression, the free flow of ideas, some good, some bad, ultimately leads to the discovery of truth. In the so-called marketplace of ideas, good ideas will drive out bad or false ones. The cure for offensive or destructive speech is more speech, not repressed speech. Some might say that this rationale for free, unfettered speech is wishful thinking; bad ideas can be seductive but harmful. However, the alternative would be government censorship of ideas, a cure worse than the disease.

The second justification is the belief that unfettered speech fosters an informed public that is capable of self-government. A citizenry that is educated about public affairs and is tolerant of dissent results in an effective democracy.

A third theory is that protecting speech promotes individual self-fulfillment by allowing citizens to define themselves and their ideas. The speakers who shout unpopular slogans such as "Stop the War" or "Impeach the President" at public events may know they are not persuading any decision makers. But they take pride in this exercise of free speech; they are involved and have a voice.

But when we celebrate the First Amendment in this way, do we really mean it? Are there not some limits on freedom of expression? In particular, are some kinds of speech so odious, so out of bounds, so offensive, so full of hate, so racist, that they are not protected by the Constitution?

Answers to these questions have evolved through "quasi absolutist" court decisions that recognize a limited number of exceptions to free speech. These include obscenity, defamation of individuals, and an incitement to imminent violence or harm under circumstances that make it likely that imminent violence will occur, which involves the "clear and present danger test" and which covers the oft-cited prohibition of "falsely shouting fire in a crowded theater." But beyond these exceptions all speech is free and protected under the First Amendment even if it's offensive, racist, sexist, or irreligious. In this regard, the United States is unique among the world's advanced democracies. As Justice Brennan said in the decision that held that the prohibition on burning the American flag was unconstitutional:

If there is a bedrock principle underlying the First Amendment, it is that the government may not prohibit the expression of an idea simply because society finds the idea itself offensive or disagreeable.

To be sure, many respected constitutional scholars disagree and claim that the government has an obligation to the community to promote harmony and to protect against the harm that pernicious vilification does to minorities. Their rationale is that hate speech is repugnant to any concept of civilized society and is not entitled to entry into the "the marketplace of ideas."[6]

Professor Alexander Bickel of Yale Law School argued that to permit an idea to be advocated is to concede its legitimacy, and that there are some policies whose implementation is so incompatible with a democratic society that advocacy should not be permitted. More recently, NYU School of Law professor and Oxford University professor of social and political theory Jeremy Waldron has written:

Maybe we should admire some [ACLU] lawyer who says he hates what the racist says but defends to the death his right to say it, but . . . [t]he [real] question is about the direct target of their abuse. Can their lives be led, their children be brought up, can their hopes be maintained and their worst fears dispelled, in a social environment polluted by these materials? Those are the concerns that need to be answered when we defend the use of the First Amendment to strike down laws prohibiting the publication of racial hatred.[7]

Aryeh Neier, executive director of the American Civil Liberties Union during the Skokie litigation, concedes that there are great dangers in giving the enemies of freedom the freedom to speak.

---

6. Texas v. Johnson, 491 U.S. 397, 414 (1989).
7. Waldron, *The Harm of Hate Speech*, 10.

Nazi leader Frank Collin warns that because his group cannot
demonstrate in Chicago's Marquette Park, they will reschedule
their march in Skokie.
© Bettmann/CORBIS

But, he argues that history teaches us that it is more dangerous to
allow government to silence these enemies because "almost invariably
government confuses the enemies of its policies with the enemies of
freedom."[8] These contrasting viewpoints pose one of the fundamental
dilemmas of free speech, one that was in dramatic focus when the
American Nazis tried to march in the Village of Skokie.

The central character and instigator in this case was Frank Collin. He was an American, but self-identified as a Nazi. He believed
that Jews and blacks were biologically inferior and that the United
States should strip Jews of citizenship and send all black Americans
back to Africa. Although he claimed not to advocate the immediate

8. Neier, *Defending My Enemy*, 160.

death of Jews, his idol was Adolf Hitler.[9] At public events, Collin and his followers dressed in Nazi storm trooper uniforms with swastikas prominently displayed on their clothing and on the flags that they carried. Collin himself was not an imposing figure; nor was he a good speaker. David Hamlin, the head of the ACLU at the time, said that Collin left "the distinct impression that he was incapable of leading a parade through a tunnel without losing his way." However, he was street savvy, tenacious, and he understood his First Amendment rights.[10]

The official program of his organization—the National Socialist Party of America—called for (1) awarding U.S. citizenship only to those of Aryan descent; (2) a National Eugenics Commission to make recommendations for the elimination of all racial impurities; (3) the prosecution of all individuals guilty of race-mixing activities; and (4) the liquidation of all Zionist, pro-Zionist and, as they called them, other treasonous organizations.[11]

Ironically, Collin was half Jewish. He was born Frank Cohn and changed his name in 1946. Stranger still is the fact that his father, Max, was a Holocaust survivor who had been imprisoned in the concentration camp at Dachau, Germany, for three months.[12]

Another irony in the minds of many is that Collin's campaign to express his racist ideas was supported by the American Civil Liberties Union, whose membership was disproportionately Jewish, and that Collin's primary advocate would be a Jewish lawyer, David Goldberger, of the ACLU.

The third irony is that Collin was clamoring for the free expression of ideas that, if implemented, would destroy the free expression of others. Of course, success of his program was unlikely if for no other reason than the fact that the National Socialist Party of America had no more than about twenty-five other members.

---

9. Collin v. Smith, 447 F. Supp. 676, 680 (N.D. Ill. 1978) and 578 F.2d 1197, 1198–9 (7th Cir. 1978); Strum, *When the Nazis Came to Skokie*, 1.
10. Hamlin, *The Nazi/Skokie Conflict*, 1–3; Neier, *Defending My Enemy*, 23–24.
11. Strum, *When the Nazis Came to Skokie*, 13–14; Hamlin, *The Nazi/Skokie Conflict*, 1; Collin v. Smith, supra note 9.
12. Neier, *Defending My Enemy*, 23; Hamlin, *The Nazi/Skokie Conflict*, 5–6; Strum, *When the Nazis Came to Skokie*, 4.

Collin was the leader of a façade. The National Socialist Party of America was not "national." It seldom ventured beyond the confines of the Chicago area. Nor was the organization "socialist." It wasn't even a "party" in any true sense. Its financial resources were practically nonexistent, and the office telephone was often disconnected for failure to pay the bill.[13]

What these neo-Nazis wanted, what they had to have, was publicity. When confronted with violence, with insults, or with counterdemonstrations, and they attracted media coverage, they had a chance to prosper.

Collin and his two dozen uniformed followers chose to proclaim their Nazism in the Chicago suburb of Skokie. A large village with a population in 1977 of 70,000, Skokie was the home of 40,000 Jews, about 7,000 of whom had managed to escape death in Hitler's concentration camps. The psychological damage that the Nazis would inflict on them gave them a right, many of them thought, that outweighed Collin's right to parade his ideas in their village. And so they went to court.

When an organization wants to march or demonstrate anywhere, it usually must ask for permission and give advance notice. The organization must provide details about the number of marchers, where will they march, and how long it will last so that the municipality can provide the necessary services to control the crowds and traffic.

Permission to march can't be denied arbitrarily, but one of the well-established limitations on free speech is the "time, place, and manner" exception. While the government might not be able to censor the content of speech, it can exercise common sense in restricting where, when, and how you deliver that content. One has a right to talk, but not by using a loud sound truck near bedroom windows in the middle of the night.

Collin wanted to march on the south side of Chicago in Marquette Park. Many African-Americans lived in that area, so there was the likelihood of counterdemonstrations and even national media coverage. But the City of Chicago said, "You can march in

---

13. Hamlin, *The Nazi/Skokie Conflict*, 2–3.

the park, but you have to post a bond, $300,000 worth of insurance, to compensate for any damage that results from your parade." Collin could not comply with that requirement. Even if his group had the money to pay for insurance, no insurance company would provide it. Insurance companies are reluctant to post bonds for fringe groups of troublemakers. Collin sued the City of Chicago, claiming that the insurance requirement was a denial of his right to speak. When the litigation dragged on, Collin grew frustrated and turned his attention elsewhere.

He wrote to twelve suburban towns and villages near Chicago, asking for permission to march. He also sent thousands of circulars prominently displaying swastikas to these neighborhoods saying, "We are coming."[14]

He was ignored by all of them except the Village of Skokie. Skokie mandated a $350,000 bond, whereupon Collin said, "The bond requirement is a guise to deny us our right to free expression. We are coming to Skokie on May 1, 1977."[15]

Informed by his experience with Chicago, Collin's formal request to march appeared to be innocuous. He wrote, "This is a free speech demonstration. It will take place on the sidewalks outside the village hall rather than on the streets, and it will not interfere with pedestrian or automobile traffic. It will last no more than 30 minutes. We will abide by all town ordinances. We expect between 30 to 50 members of our group to be in attendance. There will be no speeches and no circulars will be distributed. There will be a few signs saying 'Free speech for the white man.'" That was it.[16]

Of course, the members of the NSPA would be dressed in full Nazi storm trooper regalia with swastikas on every uniform. When asked by reporters whether his presence in Skokie would offend Holocaust survivors, Collin said,

14. Neier, *Defending My Enemy*, 46–47; Strum, *When the Nazis Came to Skokie*, 15.
15. Neier, *Defending My Enemy*, 46–47; Strum, *When the Nazis Came to Skokie*, 16; Hamlin, *The Nazi/Skokie Conflict*, 31–32.
16. Collin v. Smith, 578 F.2d 1197, 1200 (7th Cir. 1978); Neier, *Defending My Enemy*, 46–47; Strum, *When the Nazis Came to Skokie*, 16–17; Hamlin, *The Nazi/Skokie Conflict*, 32.

I hope they are terrified. I hope they're shocked. Because we are coming to get them again. I don't care if someone's mother or father or brother died in the gas chambers. The unfortunate thing is not that there were 6 million Jews who died. The unfortunate thing is that there were so many Jewish survivors.[17]

A meeting was convened by the village's most prominent rabbi. The mayor, the village attorney and a representative of the Chicago branch of the Jewish Anti-Defamation League spoke to an audience of other rabbis and Jewish leaders of the community. They agreed to adopt a "quarantine" policy—that is, permit the demonstration, but just ignore it. In that way, the demonstrators would be denied the publicity they sought.

Each of the rabbis and Jewish leaders met with their congregations and their constituents to explain the "quarantine" policy. The theme was, "If you attempt to block the demonstrators, you give them the publicity they crave." Holocaust survivors expressed intense opposition. Meeting after meeting ended with resolutions calling for counterdemonstrations.[18]

Some survivors explained their reaction like this: "We used to live in safe, small communities before the Holocaust, and we are living in safe, small communities now. But this time, we've got to stop our community from being invaded." One writer described the survivor's reaction as stemming from guilt. They felt guilty because they had survived and perhaps because they felt that if they had resisted, others who died might well have survived. Now they had the chance to atone—to assuage a guilt that might be unrealistic, but was no less painful. And in Israel's Six-Day War of 1967 and the Yom Kippur War of 1973, they had "Never Again" models to emulate.[19]

The *Chicago Tribune* described a grandmother whose parents and brother had been killed in a Warsaw ghetto. She said, "Years ago in

17. Strum, *When the Nazis Came to Skokie*, 15.
18. Strum, *When the Nazis Came to Skokie*, 17–19; Neier, *Defending My Enemy*, 50–51; Hamlin, *The Nazi/Skokie Conflict*, 32–36.
19. Strum, *When the Nazis Came to Skokie*, 20–21.

Europe, when the Nazis marched, we stayed in our houses, afraid. I want to face them. What can they do to me now? This time they won't put us in gas chambers."[20]

The mayor bowed to the will of the people. He directed the village attorney to go to court and to ask for an injunction to keep the demonstration from taking place. Legal papers were filed in the Illinois State Circuit Court in what became *Village of Skokie v. The National Socialist Party of America*. Who would represent the Nazis in court? Who would undertake to litigate on behalf of the despised Frank Collin? It would be the American Civil Liberties Union.

Founded in 1920 in large part to prevent government abridgement of the free speech rights of pacifists who opposed American involvement in World War I, the ACLU grew to be a nationwide organization with hundreds of thousands of members and branches in every state. It extended its mandate to include all aspects of civil liberties. It developed a public relations component, employed volunteer lobbyists, and tried to educate the public about civil rights.[21]

It made sense for the ACLU to enter the fray. Its focus was on the principle of free speech. The village's attempt to silence Collin was the same as the efforts that had been used throughout the South to stop civil rights demonstrators. Acknowledging that there is a vast moral difference between the content of Collin's speech in Skokie and Martin Luther King's addresses in the South, the ACLU maintained: "Now, as in the McCarthy days, freedom of speech can be defended only by resisting every incursion on the right to speak. The only social order in which freedom of speech is secure is the one in which it is secure for everyone."[22]

The ACLU reasoned that if Frank Collin lost his case, it would establish a legal precedent that could be used later against Jews, blacks, antiwar activists, and other minorities whose expressions might not be popular with certain audiences. If the swastika is too offensive

---

20. Strum, *When the Nazis Came to Skokie*, 21.
21. Strum, *When the Nazis Came to Skokie*, 22; a longer history of the free speech battles fought by the ACLU on behalf of despicable clients are explored in Neier, *Defending My Enemy*, 79–116.
22. Neier, *Defending My Enemy*, 160.

for some to tolerate today, the Star of David could be claimed to be intolerable by others tomorrow.

For the ACLU and David Goldberger, the senior litigator for the Chicago ACLU office, this was simply a free speech case with a distasteful client. When Goldberger, however, failed to persuade any attorney to volunteer to take the case, he himself represented Collin and his Nazi party.

The ACLU and David Goldberger paid an enormous price for their involvement. Approximately 30,000 ACLU members resigned. The ACLU, which was funded entirely by donations, lost $500,000 in income in 1977; the Illinois branch alone lost thirty percent of its income.[23]

David Goldberger took the full fury of the public response. He was referred to in court and in public as the "neo-Nazi counsel" and a Nazi sympathizer or dupe. His father and mother heard their son denounced in their synagogue by their own rabbi. When he appeared at a synagogue in Gary, Indiana, several congregants tried to present him with a "Nazi of the Year" award.[24]

The very groups—Jews, the media, and the organized bar—that in the past had been the staunchest defenders of the First Amendment, the groups who had the most to lose by restrictions on free speech, free press, and freedom of religion, now vigorously assailed the ACLU involvement in the Skokie case.

The position of the bar was that the Nazis should hire their own lawyers. Even the criminal defense bar, which defended mafia hit men, pornographers, and terrorists, found the Nazis too noxious to deserve representation. This argument came despite the provision in the Code of Ethics for lawyers that representation should not be declined solely because a client or a cause is unpopular or because the community reaction is adverse.[25]

And so it was that the Skokie controversy became a test of the nation's commitment to the First Amendment.

---

23. Neier, *Defending My Enemy*, 90.
24. Strum, *When the Nazis Came to Skokie*, 66–67; Hamlin, *The Nazi/Skokie Conflict*, 103–4.
25. Strum, *When the Nazis Came to Skokie*, 68.

On April 28, just three days before the announced date of the Skokie march, the village petition for an injunction came up for a hearing before Cook County Circuit Court of Illinois Judge Joseph Wosik. A jury was not required or appropriate for an injunction hearing, and so Judge Wosik would be the sole decision maker. Harvey Swartz, the village attorney, made three points in his opening statement. He said that Skokie was different from other locales because of the large number of Holocaust survivors who lived there. Secondly, the presence of swastikas would cause serious psychological harm and lastly, if the Nazis marched on Skokie, there would be violence. Goldberger responded for Collin and the NSPA by saying,

> This is a classic First Amendment case, your Honor. It tests the very foundations of democracy. The Village of Skokie moves for an order enjoining speech before it has occurred even though that speech is to occur in an orderly fashion in front of the Village Hall for a period of between twenty and thirty minutes on a Sunday afternoon, this Sunday afternoon. Such an order, whatever we might feel about the content of the speech, violates the very essence of the First Amendment.[26]

The village called five witnesses to support their contention that a march would result in violence. Fred Richter of the Synagogue Council testified about an expected counterdemonstration of about 15,000 people that might well get out of hand. Asked about the mood of the people in Skokie, he answered, "It is rage, sir . . . it is not anger, it is rage."[27] Ronald Lanski said that he had seen "smash the Nazis" leaflets in Skokie. The third witness, Sol Goldstein, a concentration camp survivor who had fought in the Resistance and whose mother had been buried alive by the Nazis, described in brutal detail the ordeal of his survival. "The swastika," he said, "reminds me [of] my closest family who were sent to death by the swastika, and it

---

26. Hamlin, *The Nazi/Skokie Conflict*, 53.
27. Strum, *When the Nazis Came to Skokie*, 53–54; Neier, *Defending My Enemy*, 54.

reminds me [of] a threat that I am not safe with my life. It reminds me that my children are not safe with their lives."[28]

Goldstein also said that he had received abusive telephone calls from persons identifying themselves as Nazis, and he predicted that there would be bloodshed if the Nazis marched. When asked if he would attack Frank Collin if he appeared in Skokie, Goldstein said, "I may."

The village also called Frank Collin as a hostile and adverse witness. Collin was shown a copy of his own flyer and indicated that he agreed with its contents. The flyer stated that Jews were behind the "black invasion of southwest Chicago" and therefore would be targets of NSPA street demonstrations in the future. Collin indicated as well that the views of his party were similar to those of the Nazi Party of Germany. He admitted that he had read *Mein Kampf* several times and agreed with much of it.[29]

The final witness for the Village of Skokie was its mayor, Alfred J. Smith, who testified that the meetings with community and religious groups had convinced him that if the march were held, a violent and uncontrollable situation would develop.[30]

Goldberger made the same two objections throughout the testimony of the village witnesses. All the evidence about the possibility of violence was irrelevant because Collin's proposed march was designed to be peaceful. It was up to the police to prevent the violence of the observers. As for testimony about Collin's beliefs, that too was irrelevant because the First Amendment protects beliefs, however odious they might be. All of Goldberger's objections were overruled. He then called his only witness, Collin, back to the stand and emphasized the peaceful nature of the intended brief demonstration.

On April 29, 1977, Judge Wosik found for the Village of Skokie and granted the injunction.

---

28. Neier, *Defending My Enemy*, 54–55; Strum, *When the Nazis Came to Skokie*, 53; Hamlin, *The Nazi/Skokie Conflict*, 59–60.
29. Neier, *Defending My Enemy*, 35; Strum, *When the Nazis Came to Skokie*, 54; Hamlin, *The Nazi/Skokie Conflict*, 60–61.
30. Neier, *Defending My Enemy*, 55.

The Nazis were prohibited from "(1) marching, walking, or parading within the Village of Skokie in uniform, (2) from displaying the swastika on or off their person, (3) from displaying pamphlets or displaying any materials which incite or promote hatred against persons of Jewish faith or ancestry or hatred against persons of any faith or ancestry or race or religion."[31]

One might have predicted this result in the lower court. The judge was an elected official and eventually would have to face the voters. Still, was he right under the law? The ACLU didn't think he was, and so they appealed.

In the meantime, Frank Collin, noting that the injunction served on him forbade any demonstration in Skokie on May 1, 1977, announced that the NSPA would not march on that day because to do so would violate the injunction. Instead, he proclaimed, "We will march tomorrow, April 30."

This sent the village officials scurrying back to the judge to amend the injunction so that it would ban marching on any day until further notice. The judge signed the new emergency order without giving notice to Collin or his attorney. The next day, April 30, Collin and his supporters drove, in several vans, from Chicago to Skokie. When they got off the highway they were greeted by the village police who served the new order. Collin and his entourage went back to Chicago.[32]

Even though they had won that day, the village officials began to realize that they could lose on appeal. In addition, although they told Collin he could not march unless he posted bond for $350,000, Skokie had no such ordinance that required posting a bond. So they decided to pass not one but three new ordinances to keep the Nazis out of Skokie for all time.

Ordinance 994 required that public assemblies of more than a small number of people secure a permit and post a bond for liability and property damage insurance of $350,000. Exceptions for school-

---

31. Neier, *Defending My Enemy*, 56; Strum, *When the Nazis Came to Skokie*, 56.
32. Hamlin, *The Nazi/Skokie Conflict*, 74; Strum, *When the Nazis Came to Skokie*, 58–59; Neier, *Defending My Enemy*, 56–57.

or village-sponsored activities were granted, and the mayor and village council were given the power to waive the insurance requirement at their discretion. The ordinance did not specify standards for this exercise of discretion. A catchall provision of this ordinance required that a permit be denied to assemblies that would engage in activity prohibited by any of the ordinances or to assemblies organized for unlawful purposes.[33]

Ordinance 995 made it a criminal offense to display or disseminate any material "which promotes and incites hatred against persons by reason of their race, national origin or religion or to wear markings and clothing of symbolic significance that would have the same effect."[34]

Ordinance 996 provided that "no person shall engage in any march, walk or public demonstration as a member of, or on behalf of any political party while wearing a military style uniform." A political party was defined as "an organization existing primarily to influence or deal with the structure or affairs of government, politics or the state." This definition was so broad that, as a court later pointed out, "[i]t would prohibit members of the American Legion from marching in uniform to support Republican or Democratic Party candidates." And in fact, a group of Jewish war veterans discovered later that this ordinance prevented them from demonstrating against Frank Collin in their United States military uniforms.[35]

The ordinances generated another round of litigation, this time in federal court, where Collin, again represented by the ACLU, became a plaintiff alleging that the ordinances were unconstitutional.

An additional lawsuit was brought by the Chicago office of the Anti-Defamation League, acting on behalf of Sol Goldstein and other Holocaust survivors, based on the novel theory that Collin be

---

33. The ordinances are described in the litigation brought by Collin against the village to declare them as unconstitutional, see Collin v. Smith, 447 F. Supp. 676, 681 (N.D. Ill. 1978); Collin v. Smith, 578 F.2d 1197, 1199–1200 (7th Cir. 1978); Strum, *When the Nazis Came to Skokie*, 61–62; Neier, *Defending My Enemy*, 57–58.
34. Ibid.
35. Ibid.

permanently banned from marching in Skokie lest he inflict "ment-acide," a form of emotional harm, on the survivors.[36]

By the end of June 1977, three pieces of litigation were pending. The original injunction against Collin by Judge Wosik was on appeal in Illinois state appellate courts. It was proceeding at a very leisurely pace until the Illinois state courts were ordered by the United States Supreme Court to expedite the appeal.[37] The Collin lawsuit brought in the federal district court to declare the village ordinances unconstitutional was also pending, as was the Sol Goldstein "ment-acide" litigation. All these lawsuits dealt with the single question of whether the attempt to keep Collin out of Skokie violated the First Amendment.

In all these actions, the courts would have to recognize and apply certain basic First Amendment concepts that were derived from previous United States Supreme Court decisions. These constitute a half-dozen principles that include the concepts of symbolic speech, prior restraint, the so-called heckler's veto, and the "overreach" and "vagueness" doctrines. Courts would also have to decide whether exceptions to free speech such as "group libel," "fighting words," and "incitement to violence" applied to the Skokie situation.

One might ask if what the Nazis wanted to do was "speech." Isn't parading around with swastikas really conduct and therefore not within the protection of their First Amendment rights? No, it is speech, symbolic speech, and is as fully protected as words would be.

In *Cohen v. California*,[38] the United States Supreme Court had set aside the conviction of a young man for breach of the peace when he walked into a Los Angeles courthouse wearing a jacket decorated with the words, "Fuck the draft." It held that the jacket was symbolic speech protected by the First Amendment. Similarly, the

---

36. Goldstein v. Collin was an Illinois state court class action on behalf of Sol Goldstein and the holocaust survivors sponsored by the Jewish Anti-Defamation League. See Neier, *Defending My Enemy*, 58–59.
37. In National Socialist Party of America v. Village of Skokie, 432 U.S. 43 (1977), the Supreme Court ordered the Illinois state courts to expedite the appellate process because the case involved a prior restraint. Neier, *Defending My Enemy*, 58.
38. 403 U.S. 15 (1971).

Court twice held in *Texas v. Johnson*[39] and *United States v. Eichman*[40] that burning the American flag during a demonstration protesting government policies is protected expressive speech. Marching in Nazi uniforms with swastikas is a form of speech indicating that the marchers agree with the principles of the German Nazi Party and thus, it too is speech.

Goldberger was correct in declaring that the Village of Skokie injunction was "a classic case of prior restraint." One way to punish a speaker or writer for improper speech is to wait until he gives his speech or publishes his paper and then charge him or sue him under the criminal or civil law. Another way is to prevent him in advance from speaking or publishing. That is "prior restraint." The government is censoring speech before it takes place. The U.S. Supreme Court has said, "Any prior restraint on expression comes to this court with a heavy presumption against its constitutional validity."[41] The Village of Skokie injunction was a prior restraint. The village thus had a heavy burden to overcome the presumption that the injunction was unconstitutional. Guessing in advance that violence might result is not enough to justify prior restraint.[42]

There is strong legal support for Goldberger's argument that the burden of avoiding violence should be on the audience, not on the speaker. The law does not recognize the so-called heckler's veto, meaning that the mere fact that a hostile, angry audience threatens to disrupt speech is not enough to justify silencing a speaker. Skokie officials would have the responsibility to control the audience rather than trying to solve the problem by excluding the Nazis.[43]

In *Terminiello v. Chicago*,[44] a right-wing racist denounced "communistic Zionist Jews and blacks" to his followers in a Chicago

---

39. 491 U.S. 397 (1989); Chemerinsky, *Constitutional Law*, 1100.
40. 496 U.S. 310 (1990); Chemerinsky, *Constitutional Law*, 1101.
41. New York Times Co. v. United States, 403 U.S. 713 (1971).
42. Strum, *When the Nazis Came to Skokie*, 45–46; Chemerinsky, *Constitutional Law*, 978–89.
43. Neier, *Defending My Enemy*, 132–3; Strum, *When the Nazis Came to Skokie*, 42; Collins and Chaltain, *We Must Not Be Afraid To Be Free*, 181; Chemerinsky, *Constitutional Law*, 1041–2.
44. 337 U.S. 1 (1949).

building. Outside, a thousand counterdemonstrators rioted, throwing bricks and bottles, and the police were not able to control them. After his speech, Terminiello was arrested and charged with breach of the peace. Justice Douglas, speaking for the Supreme Court, said:

> A function of free speech under our system of government is to invite dispute. It may indeed best serve its high purpose when it induces a condition of unrest, creates dissatisfaction with conditions as they are, or even stirs people to anger. Speech is often provocative and challenging. It may strike at prejudice and preconceptions and have profound unsettling effects. . . . That is why freedom of speech is nevertheless protected against censorship or punishment, unless shown likely to produce a clear and present danger of a serious substantive evil that rises far above public inconvenience, annoyance, or unrest.[45]

The village approach of "we can't allow the demonstration because it will promote violence" was the most common argument Southern officials used during the civil rights movement.

The most powerful testimony at the injunction hearing was the survivors': testimony about the images invoked by the Nazi uniforms and the swastika. It was supported by the village claim that Nazis would cause deep and serious psychological harm to the vulnerable survivors. The village coined a word to describe it; playing off the word "genocide," they called it "mentacide."

It seems heartless to say it in this case, but the appropriate response is "stay away." The law recognizes harm that would be caused to a captive audience such as a school classroom, where the listeners are not free to leave. But, as Goldberger was sure to point out on appeal, this case was not about a captive audience. The right to hear involves the right not to hear, to shut out speech by not being present to hear it. The Nazi demonstration is not about swastikas invading the survivor's homes or their synagogues. They were to be displayed at the village hall at noon on Sunday, when the village offices would be

---

45. 337 U.S. 1, 4 (1949).

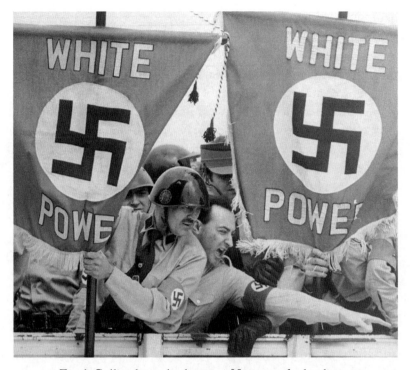

Frank Collin shouts back at anti-Nazi crowds that line a
parade route in St. Louis.
© Bettmann/CORBIS

closed. It would be perhaps the least populated place in Skokie on
that day. The answer to this situation is that if the sight of uniforms
and swastikas offends you, stay away.[46]

Attempts to legislate harmony and prohibit hate speech must
overcome problems of vagueness, or what is called the "overbreadth
doctrine." This doctrine has been defined by the U.S. Supreme Court

---

46. Collin v. Smith, 578 F.2d 1197, 1207 (7th Cir. 1978). This case does not involve intru-
sion into people's homes. There need be no captive audience as village residents may, if they
wish, simply avoid the village hall for 30 minutes on a Sunday afternoon. In rejecting the
analogy that swastikas in Skokie were like a man falsely shouting fire in a crowded theater,
Judge Harlington Wood, Jr. explained in Collin v. Smith, 578 F.2d 1197, 1210 that there
was ample warning of the proposed Skokie demonstration and that "recognition of the full
scope of freedom of speech does not compel anyone to listen, or if listening to believe." See
also Neier, *Defending My Enemy*, at 154–5.

as "a governmental purpose to control or prevent activities . . . by means which sweep unnecessarily broadly and thereby invade the area of protective freedoms." When that happens, the law is deemed unconstitutional "on its face," even if the law is applied properly to bar specific speech that should be prohibited. The theory here is that the very existence of such laws has a chilling effect on speech protected by the First Amendment that is not before the Court.[47]

Skokie Ordinance 995, for example, provided criminal penalties for the dissemination of materials that "promote and incite hatred against persons by reason of their race, national origin or religion." Under existing precedent, such a law could be found to be both overbroad and vague in the sense that it could be applied to debates over reverse discrimination or the busing of schoolchildren to achieve racial balance.[48] Skokie Ordinance 996 prohibited public demonstrations by members of political parties wearing military-style uniforms and forbade "assemblies organized for unlawful purposes." This ordinance is vague because it fails to give reasonable notice of the conduct that is prohibited, and because it provides for exceptions without specifying criteria it allows government personnel the opportunity to enforce it according to their personal prejudices. A court may also

47. Chemerinsky, *Constitutional Law*, 970–7; Collins and Chaltain, *We Must Not Be Afraid to Be Free*, 177–80. See discussion of vagueness and overbreadth and examples in Collin v. Smith, 447 F. Supp. 676, 691–2 (N.D. Ill. 1978).
48. Collin v. Smith, 447 F. Supp. 676, 692 (N.D. Ill. 1978); "The Skokie Ordinance [995] punishes language which intentionally incites hatred. This standard is subjective and impossible to clearly define . . . Ordinance 995 is unconstitutionally vague." "Even assuming . . . sufficient clarity, however, the Court also finds that the Ordinance is overbroad . . . it can also be applied to protected speech." The United States Court of Appeals for the Seventh Circuit agreed in Collin v. Smith, 578 F.2d 1197, 1207 (7th Cir. 1978), adding that ordinance 995 "could conceivably be applied to criminalize dissemination of The Merchant of Venice." Collin v. Smith, 447 F. Supp. 676, 692 (N.D. Ill. 1978) went on to say that . . . discussion of race and religion will often involve discussion of ideas and positions that are inherently offensive to many but which are nevertheless protected by the First Amendment . . . to choose an obvious example, discussion of the use of mandatory quotes in affirmative action programs cannot help but touch upon characteristics perceived to be shared by members of particular racial groups. The First Amendment does not permit the government to restrict discussion of such sensitive and emotionally charged public issues to the sanitary prose of legal and social sciences technical jargon."

consider it overbroad because, to the extent the language is specific, it could prohibit lawful symbols and expressions.[49]

So what was left for the Village of Skokie to argue? Even though the First Amendment reads as an absolute prohibition on government laws restricting speech, no court takes such an absolutist approach. Obscenity is not protected. Nor is defamation of individuals. If a speaker falsely calls another a thief before an audience and ruins his reputation, he can sue and get damages. A Supreme Court decision that expanded this concept into a doctrine of "group libel" could apply to hate speech.

In *Beauharnais v. Illinois*,[50] the Supreme Court in 1952 upheld the constitutionality of an Illinois criminal libel statute which made it unlawful "for any person to publish, present or exhibit in any public place . . . any publication . . . that "portrays depravity, criminality, unchastity or lack of virtue of a class of citizens of any race, color, creed or religion" or which "exposes the citizens of any race, color, creed or religion to contempt, derision or bigotry or which is productive of breach of peace or riots. . . ." Beauharnais was convicted of violating this statute on the basis of leaflets that called on the City of Chicago "to halt the further encroachment, harassment and invasion of white people, their property, neighborhoods and persons by the Negro." The leaflets added that "if persuasion and the need to prevent the white race from becoming mongrelized by the Negro will not unite us, then the aggressions . . . rapes, robberies, knives and guns and marijuana of the negro surely will." In a five-to-four decision, the Court held that this form of "group libel" was covered by the defamation exception to free speech and could be criminally prosecuted. The Village of Skokie relied heavily upon this decision. Indeed, its own ordinances were patterned in part on the very language that was upheld.

---

49. Collin v. Smith, 447 F. Supp. 676, 700 (N.D. Ill. 1978); "If Skokie really meant to enforce this ordinance [996-The Military Uniforms-Swastika ordinance] as written, it would prohibit, among other things, an appearance by members of the American Legion in support of the candidates of the Democratic or Republican Party." In the Seventh Circuit on appeal from the district court decision, the Village "conceded that 996 was unconstitutional." Collin v. Smith, 578 F.2d 1197, 1207 (7th Cir. 1978).
50. 343 U.S. 250 (1952).

In the twenty-five years leading up to the Skokie litigation, however, the *Beauharnais* decision was never again cited by the Supreme Court as precedent. Over time, lower courts concluded that Beauharnais and its "group libel" exception to free speech had become obsolete. Its obsolescence is supported by the fact that the Supreme Court has many times considered language that defames races or religions without giving any indication that a "group libel" exception to free speech still exists.[51]

Another village contention was that its ordinances and the proposed march of Collin and the NSPA fell under the "fighting words" exception to protected speech. This argument was derived from the 1942 Supreme Court case *Chaplinsky v. New Hampshire.*[52] *Chaplinsky* sustained the conviction of a Jehovah's Witness who caused a public disturbance by preaching that all religions were "rackets." After continuing his tirade in the midst of a hostile crowd, a city marshal warned him not to incite the crowd. In response, Chaplinsky called the marshal "a God-damned racketeer" and a "damned fascist." Chaplinsky was convicted under a statute prohibiting language "plainly tending to excite the addressee to a breach of the peace." On appeal, the Supreme Court upheld the conviction and referred to "insulting or fighting words," defining them as statements "which by their very utterance inflict injury or tend to excite an immediate breach of the peace; they are of such slight social value as a step to

---

51. Collin v. Smith, 447 F. Supp. 676, 693–7 (N.D. Ill. 1978) traces the long history of Beauharnais as an ignored precedent and concludes that "insofar as Beauharnais held that speech which defames racial and religious groups may be restricted in order to protect the reputation of individual members of the group, it has been overruled or at the very least so severely undermined that it should not be extended to new kinds of speech-inflicted damage to individuals where such an extension would pose a substantial danger of inhibiting free speech and debate"; 447 F. Supp. 697. See also the Seventh Circuit affirming opinion in Collin v. Smith where the court of appeals stated, "we agree with the district court" and added that it shows the doubts of other courts that "Beauharnais remains good law at all." 578 F.2d 1197 (1978). In Nuxoll v. Indian Prairie School District 204, 523 F.3d 668, 672 (7th Cir. 2008) the court stated that "Though Beauharnais . . . had never been overruled, no one thinks the First Amendment would today be interpreted to allow group defamation to be prohibited." Chemerinsky, *Constitutional Law*, 1043–5; Lewis, *Freedom for the Thought That We Hate*, 158–9; Neier, *Defending My Enemy*, 141–2, 152–3.
52. 315 U.S. 568 (1942).

truth that any benefit that may be derived from them is clearly out-weighed by the social interest in order and morality."[53]

But Chaplinsky turned out to be another precedent whose mean-ing had been limited by subsequent decisions. In fact in 1972, four years before the Skokie affair, the Court in *Gooding v. Wilson*[54] made clear that the "fighting words" exception to free speech could not be used to punish insults directed against groups of people. It restricted the "fighting words" exception to words "which have a direct tendency to cause violence by the person to whom *individually* the remark was directed." It was never applied to speech at a public assembly, and it was never applied in a case involving prior restraint.

Another exception denies free speech protection to speech that presents a "clear and present danger." Much of the public believed that the Nazi march in Skokie was covered by this exception, because it was similar to the prohibition against falsely shouting "fire" in a crowded theater. However, the analogy was flawed. The crowded theater involves a captive audience and imminent danger of physi-cal harm. Moreover, the "clear and present danger" test has been restricted to advocacy of the use of violence or violation of the law only where such advocacy is intentionally directed to producing imminent violent lawless action and is likely to produce such immi-nent action. The leading authority defining the "clear and present danger" is *Brandenburg v. Ohio*.[55] At a Ku Klux Klan rally, the leader, Brandenburg, exhorted his listeners to "send the Jews back to Israel" and "bury the niggers." If the government "continues to suppress the white Caucasian race," he added, "there might have to be some reven-geance taken." Brandenburg was prosecuted and convicted under an Ohio criminal syndicalism statute. The Supreme Court reversed the conviction, finding no "imminent danger" of harm in the actions or

53. 315 U.S. 572.
54. Gooding v. Wilson, 405 U.S. 518, 523 (1972); Chemerinsky, *Constitutional Law*, 1033, 1037; Collins and Chaltain, *We Must Not Be Afraid to Be Free*, 180–1; Strum, *When the Nazis Came to Skokie*, 42–43, 100; Neier, *Defending My Enemy*, 150–2.
55. 395 U.S. 444 (1969).

words spoken by the defendant. The racial and religious slurs were protected free speech.[56]

Not surprisingly, then, the Village of Skokie lost in both state and federal courts. The village injunction was dissolved and the three Skokie ordinances were declared unconstitutional. Sol Goldstein's "mentacide" class action was dismissed.

The string of losses for the village began on January 27, 1978. On that day, the Illinois Supreme Court in *Skokie v. NSPA* overturned the prohibition on the Nazi march and simultaneously dismissed the action of *Goldstein v. Collin*.[57] This was followed on February 23, 1978, by a United States District Court decision by federal Judge Bernard Decker, who wrote a detailed, twenty-six-page opinion that is regarded today as "one of the definitive statements about the theory and practice of speech under the American Constitution."[58]

Judge Decker found that each of the three ordinances enacted by the Village of Skokie unconstitutionally denied free speech. The ordinance requiring any applicant for a parade or public assembly permit to procure $350,000 of liability insurance violated the First Amendment, since this requirement was not shown to be necessary, some organizations could be exempted, and there were no principled standards for determining exemptions.[59] The opinion reasoned that the ordinance prohibiting the dissemination of materials "which promote and incite hatred against persons by reason of their race, national origin or religion was unconstitutionally vague," overbroad, and had an inhibiting effect on free debate.[60] The ordinances were also found defective as "prior restraints" on free speech.[61] The court

56. Chemerinsky, *Constitutional Law*, 1040–2; Neier, *Defending My Enemy*, 135–7, 154–5; Lewis, *Freedom for the Thought We Hate*, 124 explaining that the Brandenburg new test has transformed the clear and present danger test to require (1) advocacy directed to "inciting or producing imminent violence or lawless action," (2) and it is likely to produce such action and (3) was intended by the speaker to produce such imminent violence or lawless action.
57. Village of Skokie v. National Socialist Party of America, 69 Ill. 2d 605, 373 N.E.2d 21 (1978).
58. Collin v. Smith, 447 F. Supp. 676 (N.D. Ill. 1978).
59. Ibid., 684–6.
60. Ibid., 691–2.
61. Ibid., 699.

went on to explain why the doctrines of group libel,[62] fighting words, or incitement to imminent violence[63] were inapplicable to save the ordinances from nullification.

After summarizing the applicable First Amendment precedents and doctrines, Judge Decker concluded:

> The long list of cases reviewed in this opinion agrees that when a choice must be made, it is better to allow those who preach racial hatred to expend their venom in rhetoric rather than to be panicked into embarking on the dangerous course of permitting the government to decide what its citizens may say or hear. As Mr. Justice Harlan reminded us in *Cohen*, where a similar choice was made, "That the air may at times seem filled with verbal cacophony is . . . not a sign of weakness but of strength." The ability of American society to tolerate the advocacy even of hateful doctrines espoused by the plaintiffs without abandoning its commitment to freedom of speech and assembly is perhaps the best protection we have against the establishment of any Nazi-type regime in this country.[64]

The village and its employees were permanently enjoined from denying permits to plaintiffs Collin and the NSPA to hold a public assembly if the denials were based on expected violations of the now-discredited ordinances.

Following an appeal by the village, a panel of the Seventh Circuit Court of Appeals affirmed the decision.[65] The village then exhausted its appellate options when the United States Supreme Court denied its petition for certiorari.[66]

---

62. Ibid., 693–7.
63. Ibid., 689–93.
64. 447 F. Supp. 676, 702; A complete summary of the content of the decision can be found in Hamlin, *The Nazi/Skokie Conflict*, 146–9.
65. Collin v. Smith, 578 F.2d 1197 (1978).
66. Smith v. Collin, 439 U.S. 916 (1978). Justices Blackmun and White dissented from the certiorari, noting that the Seventh Circuit decision was in some tension with the Beauharnais group libel decision, which has never been overruled by the Supreme Court.

Collin and his band of American Nazis were now free to march in Skokie. Plans were made, but Collin vacillated. The hostile reaction to the court decisions guaranteed that if the Nazis showed up, there would be counterdemonstrators from across the country. Meir Kahane, founder of the Jewish Defense League, announced in Skokie that "we intend to bloody the Nazis should they try to come here." At a rally of supporters, Kahane added, "If I see a Nazi marching, I will break his head." Within the Skokie police force there were rumors that they might not be able to protect Collin and his supporters.[67]

There were also suggestions that the number of Collin's followers who were willing to march with him might be dwindling, and it would be humiliating if only a few showed up.[68] At first, Collin announced the demonstration for the Fourth of July, 1977. Sometime later, he declared that the NSPA would march on Hitler's birthday, April 20, 1978, only to reset the march for the first day of Passover on April 22. Finally, he secured a permit from the village to march on June 25. But on June 21, Collin announced that the City of Chicago had given him permission to demonstrate in both the Federal Plaza and in Marquette Park and stated in a press conference:

> The Skokie march is off . . . my overall goal was always Marquette Park speaking to my own white people rather than a howling mob of creatures in the streets of Skokie. . . . The Skokie demonstration had been pure agitation on our part in order to restore our free speech. The agitation has been successful. As it turns out, we now have permission to march in Chicago, which is what I wanted to do in the first place, so I have no intention to go to Skokie.[69]

---

67. Strum, *When the Nazis Came to Skokie*, 73–75; Neier, *Defending My Enemy*, 59; Hamlin, *The Nazi/Skokie Conflict*, 172.

68. Strum, *When the Nazis Came to Skokie*, 73–75; Neier, *Defending My Enemy*, 75; Hamlin, *The Nazi/Skokie Conflict*, 172.

69. Hamlin, *The Nazi/Skokie Conflict*, 161–4; Strum, *When the Nazis Came to Skokie*, 140–1; Bob Warden, "Nazi Wins May Cancel Skokie March," *Washington Post*, June 21, 1978, https://washingtonpost.com/archive/politics/1978/06/21nazi-wins-may-cancel-skokie-march/35819ae3-f542-449e-90be-619ea558f001/.

Planned counterdemonstrations in Skokie were cancelled and everyone declared victory. The village and the Holocaust survivors said, "This time we won. We kept the Nazis from coming to Skokie. In addition, the world was reminded of the Holocaust and what we went through. And this time we were not alone; the nation, and all segments of society were with us."

The Nazis said, "We won in court and we got the publicity we wanted." A spokesman for the Jewish Defense League disagreed and said, "What this does is give Collin a way to save face and cancel the Skokie march. We know he is afraid to go to Skokie and wants to get out of it any way he can."[70]

The American Civil Liberties Union lost members and money but also earned praise in some quarters for being an organization deeply committed to principle.

Frank Collin resurfaced two years later when he was arrested in Chicago for sexual activities with four boys, ages ten to fifteen. He was convicted and served three years in jail. After his release, he changed his name and told a Chicago reporter, "I am not into being a neo-Nazi anymore."[71]

The Skokie drama had built to a crescendo and then fizzled when the Nazis withdrew from the battle. However, the Skokie case lives on as a centerpiece of First Amendment jurisprudence.

The First Amendment position of the ACLU that tolerates most forms of hate speech is now supported by United States legal precedent. Still, the debate continues and some Americans support the criminalization of hate speech.

In the late 1980s and 1990s, in the wake of a series of incidents offensive to minorities on several college campuses, professors and administrators adopted controversial codes limiting hateful speech.[72] In 1990, University of Wisconsin students pledging a fraternity were required to dress in blackface and participate in a "slave auction." At George Mason University, a fraternity sponsored an "ugly woman"

70. Warden, "Nazi Wins May Cancel Skokie March."
71. Strum, *When the Nazis Came to Skokie*, 144; Hamlin, *The Nazi/Skokie Conflict*, 179.
72. Strum, *When the Nazis Came to Skokie*, 106–8; Lewis, *Freedom for the Thought We Hate*, 163–5; Collins and Chaltain, *We Must Not Be Afraid to Be Free*, 178–80.

contest, and at Stanford, two students turned a symphony poster into a Sambo caricature.[73] During the Gulf War, anti-Arab sentiments were expressed as well.

Critics claimed that the codes, which specified penalties for violations, duplicated the group libel provisions that had been abandoned by judicial decisions. Stanford's student code prohibited "personal vilification of students on the basis of their sex, race, color, handicap, religion, sexual orientation or national or ethnic origin when it was intended to stigmatize an individual or a small number of individuals."[74] Amherst College added "age, marital and veteran status" to the list of offensive speech areas. By 1990, over one hundred colleges and universities had enacted restrictive student speech codes.[75] The mood was such, in fact, that three ACLU affiliates in California adopted resolutions approving these codes.

However, law professor Nadine Strossen, then president of the ACLU, clarified the national organization's position by saying, "Now we have minorities and feminists and the left allied with fundamentalists who believe some communitarian values take precedence. To them, group rights are more important than individual rights. The First Amendment is being embattled from all sides."[76] *New York Times* columnist Anthony Lewis concluded that "the everything list of characteristics to be protected from harassing speech brought ridicule on the hate speech campaign."[77]

As expected, the courts made enforcement of these codes difficult. The University of Michigan hate speech code, under which a graduate student was disciplined for saying that Israel used the Holocaust to justify Israel's policies toward Palestinians, was invalidated in 1989 in *Doe v. Michigan*.[78] The federal district court noted

73. Strum, *When the Nazis Came to Skokie*, 107; Collins and Chaltain, *We Must Not Be Afraid to Be Free*, 187.
74. Lewis, *Freedom for the Thought We Hate*, 163.
75. Ibid.
76. Collins and Chaltain, *We Must Not Be Afraid to Be Free*, 186.
77. Lewis, *Freedom for the Thought We Hate*, 163.
78. 721 F. Supp. 852 (E.D. Mich. 1989); see David Hudson, First Amendment Center, Hate Speech and Campus Speech Codes at http://www.firstamendmentcenter.org/hate-speech-campus-speech-codes.

that "the Supreme Court has consistently held that statutes punishing speech or conduct solely on grounds that it is unseemly or
offensive is constitutionally overbroad."[79] Moreover, the court held
that the policy was "unconstitutionally vague" and it was "simply
impossible to discern any limitation of the policy's scope or reach."[80]
It concluded that "while the court is sympathetic to the University's obligation to insure equal educational opportunities for all its
students, such effort must not be at the expense of free speech."[81]
Courts in Wisconsin and Connecticut also struck down the speech
codes of their respective state universities as violations of the First
Amendment.[82] Judges referred to the Skokie precedent as indicating that even heinous speech was protected and that the laws specifically aimed at eliminating such expression could probably not be
constitutionally written. This view seemed confirmed by decisions
invalidating speech code enforcement attempts by George Mason
and Stanford universities.[83]

The approach to free speech that is embraced by the United
States does not prevail in Canada, the United Kingdom, or any of
the democracies in Western Europe. In these countries, civility and
community harmony trump commitments to the free speech rights
of individuals, and government has an affirmative duty to protect
the honor and dignity of citizens by prohibiting and punishing hate
speech.[84]

And in 1996, the United Nations adopted, with 168 signatory
nations, the International Covenant on Civil and Political Rights,
a multilateral treaty establishing universal standards for protecting
political and civil rights. It provides in part that "any advocacy of
national, racial or religious hatred that constitutes incitement to dis-
sention, hostility or violence shall be prohibited by law."[85]

---

79. 721 F. Supp. 852, 864 (1989).
80. 721 F. Supp. 852, 867 (1989).
81. 721 F. Supp. 852, 868 (1969).
82. Strum, *When the Nazis Came to Skokie*, 108.
83. Collins and Chaltain, *We Must Not Be Afraid to Be Free*, 199.
84. Strum, *When the Nazis Came to Skokie*, 123–35; Lewis, *Freedom for the Thought We Hate*,
160–2; Waldron, *The Harm in Hate Speech*, 12–14; Neier, *Defending My Enemy*, 169–73.
85. "International Covenant on Civil and Political Rights," Office of the United Nations High

In 2011, fashion designer John Galliano's anti-Semitic outburst in a bar was captured on videotape. He was subsequently found guilty of violating French law and fined 6,000 euros. In 1997, a Russian immigrant living in Israel put up hand-drawn posters mocking the prophet Muhammad as a pig and was sentenced to two years in prison. She was charged with "committing a racist act, harming religious sensitivities, supporting a terrorist group and endangering life."[86]

The latitude given to free speech rights in the United States is, of course, connected to our commitment to individualism and suspicion of government. We champion freedom *from* the state over the concept of freedom *through* the state. We believe that any government regulation of speech will likely cause more harm than good. And so, as long as the speaker does not threaten imminent violence or incite others to imminent violence, even the most detestable hate speech is allowed. As Anthony Lewis in *Freedom for the Thought We Hate* wrote, "Americans are freer to think what we will and say what we think than any other people."

The Skokie principle, that hateful racist speech is protected in the United States by the First Amendment, remains the law of the land. But it continues to be the subject of public and academic debate.

The Supreme Court revisited the Skokie precedent just a few years ago in *Snyder v. Phelps.*[87] The case involved the Westboro Church, whose members believe that disasters that befall our nation are divine punishment for our tolerance of homosexuality, particularly in the American military. The church seeks to spread its views by demonstrating at the funerals of dead soldiers.

Commissioner for Human Rights, http://www.ohchr.org/en/professionalinterest/pages/ccpr. aspx; The movement to circumscribe the bounds of free expression has its roots in three instruments of international law: The European Convention on Human Rights (ECHR), The International Convention on the Elimination of all Forms of Racial Discrimination (CERD), and the International Covenant on Civil and Political Rights (ICCPR). All three have language intending to protect the reputation of others. CERD obligates signatories to make "all decimations of ideas based on racial superiority or hatred" a punishable offense.

86. Serge Schmemann, "A Day in Court for Israeli Who Enraged Muslims," *New York Times*, July 19, 1997, http://www.nytimes.com/1997/07/19/world/a-day-in-court-for-israeli-who-enraged-muslims.html.

87. 562 U.S. 443 (2011).

After Marine Corporal Matthew Snyder was killed in the line of duty in Iraq, his grief-stricken father arranged for a church funeral in their hometown. Mr. Snyder said, "I just wanted to bury my son in peace and with dignity." But that did not happen. Members of the Westboro Church appeared during the funeral carrying signs that read, among other things, "Thank God for Dead Soldiers," "Thank God for IED's" (the improvised explosive devices that kill and wound American soldiers), "Thank God for 9/11," "God Hates Fags," "God Hates the USA," "God Hates You," and "You Are Going to Hell."

Mr. Snyder sued the demonstrators and their church in a civil action for the tort of intentional infliction of severe emotional distress. In order to prevail, the plaintiff had to prove that the defendants' conduct was "so outrageous in character and so extreme in degree as to go beyond all bounds of decency, and to be regarded as atrocious and utterly intolerable in a civilized community."[88] He also had to show that "the distress suffered by plaintiff was so severe that no reasonable person could be expected to endure it."[89] The jury found that both elements were established by the evidence. They returned a verdict for Mr. Snyder and ordered the payment of several million dollars in compensatory and punitive damages.

The defendants appealed. They did not dispute the elements of the tort nor did they question the jury's findings. Their basic argument was that even if the speech was "atrocious and intolerable in a civilized community" and even if it "caused distress so severe that no reasonable person could be expected to endure it," it was protected under the First Amendment.[90] The Supreme Court agreed by a vote of eight to one. The judgment was reversed, and the Skokie principle was reaffirmed. Speaking for the Court, Chief Justice Roberts explained:

Speech is powerful. It can stir people to action, move them to tears of both joy and sorrow—and as it did here—inflict

88. 562 U.S. 443, 464.
89. Ibid.
90. 562 U.S. 443, 465.

great pain. On the facts before us, we cannot react to that pain by punishing the speaker. As a nation we have chosen a different course—to protect even hurtful speech on public issues to ensure that we do not stifle public debate. That choice requires that we shield Westboro Church from tort liability for its picketing in this case.[91]

In his lone dissent, Justice Alito concluded simply, "In order to have a society in which public issues can be openly and vigorously debated, it is not necessary to allow the brutalization of innocent victims." [92]

In the Village of Skokie today, near the site where Collin and his group once sought to march, stands a Holocaust museum founded by one of the Jewish counterdemonstrators. And in 1990, Illinois became the first state in the country to require a Holocaust education. But even as the Skokie case endures as a defining moment in the dispute over free speech protection, people of good will continue to disagree about what limits, if any, should be placed on freedom of expression.

---

91. 562 U.S. 443, 460–1.
92. 562 U.S. 443, 475.

SEVEN

The Murder Trial
of Dan White:
The All-American
Assassin[1]

THE YEAR IS 1978. ON a cool morning in San Francisco, just after the Thanksgiving holiday, Dan White is dropped off by his aide in front of city hall. Until he resigned three weeks earlier, Dan was a member of the city Board of Supervisors, one of eleven, who, along with Mayor George Moscone, ran the city. As he later tells it, Dan had had a change of heart and asked the mayor to reappoint him to his former position. Moscone had agreed. A reporter, however, had just given Dan some unsettling news: the mayor had chosen another man, Don Horanzy, to fill the vacant position. Dan is now at city hall to confront Moscone. He has come with more than the force of

---

1. For this chapter we relied heavily on the authoritative work of Mike Weiss, *Double Play: The Hidden Passions Behind the Double Assassination of George Moscone and Harvey Milk* (San Francisco: Vince Emery Productions, 2010) and the lengthy article by John Geluardi, "Dan White's Motive More About Betrayal Than Homophobia," *San Francisco Weekly*, January 30, 2008, http://www.sfweekly.com/sanfrancisco/dan-whites-motive-more-about-betrayal-than-homophobia/Content?oid=2166110&showFullText=true. We also relied upon trial transcripts, legal authorities, newspaper articles, and other secondary sources.

his words. White is carrying a loaded Smith & Wesson .38-caliber revolver. The gun holds five bullets. He has ten rounds of ammunition in his jacket pocket.

White does not use the front entrance of city hall that day because he knows he would have to pass through a metal detector. Instead, he walks around the building, slips through an unguarded basement window and takes a staircase leading directly to the mayor's office. He asks the secretary to see Moscone and is told to wait until he finishes a meeting. Some twenty minutes later, White is ushered into the mayor's office. He asks Moscone to be reinstated. "Why aren't you gonna reappoint me?" Dan asks. Moscone tells him, "It's just a political decision, Dan, like we talked about and that's that. There's nothing more I can say."[2] The argument escalates. Dan draws his revolver and shoots the mayor twice, at point blank range, in the chest and shoulder. As the mayor lies on the floor, White stands over him, aims the two-inch barrel at his head and fires twice more, from six inches away. He empties the four spent cartridges from his gun and reloads it with hollow-point bullets.

White then leaves the mayor's office and walks to the other side of city hall. He is searching for supervisor Harvey Milk, the man who convinced Moscone not to reappoint him. At that moment, Milk is leaving a meeting with Board President Dianne Feinstein. White runs into Milk in the hallway and asks if they could talk for a few minutes in White's old office. Milk agrees. Fifteen seconds later, Feinstein hears gunfire coming from down the hall, three shots and then two more. She calls the police. Seconds later, Dan White emerges from his office, reholstering his gun, and walks away. Rushing into White's office, Dianne Feinstein finds Milk face down on the floor. He has suffered three shots to the body, and, like Moscone, two more from close range to the back of the head.

White goes to a diner and calls his wife from a pay phone. She meets him at nearby St. Mary's Cathedral, and from there, the two walk to the San Francisco police station where White once worked as

2. Weiss, *Double Play*, 27.

a police officer. Just one hour after the shooting, White turns himself in. He tearfully admits he shot Moscone and Milk. By coincidence, Dan's confession is taken by an old friend of his, Inspector Frank Falzon. The confession is videotaped.

Feinstein is tasked with identifying the bodies. Several hours later, she speaks to the press: "Today San Francisco has experienced a double tragedy of immense proportions. As president of the Board of Supervisors, it is my duty to inform you that both Mayor Moscone and Supervisor Harvey Milk have been shot and killed." The crowd of reporters erupts in

Dan White, the assassin of Harvey Milk and Mayor George Moscone.
© Bettmann/CORBIS

shock. Urging them to let her finish, she continues, "and the suspect is Supervisor Dan White."

So began one of the most emotionally devastating chapters in the history of San Francisco. Eight days earlier, the city had been shocked by news of the ambush assassination of California Congressman Leo Ryan and four others in Guyana. The Jonestown mass suicide led by Peoples Temple cult leader Jim Jones, who had been Mayor Moscone's housing commissioner, followed almost immediately: Over 900 Jonestown inhabitants including 303 children died from self-ingested cyanide poisoning. Many of the victims were from San Francisco. The city is reeling. And now this. Harvey Milk was gunned down at the age of forty-eight. Mayor Moscone was only forty-nine years old. For both crimes, thirty-two-year-old Dan

White is charged with murder in the first degree. In the words of reporter Duffy Jennings, who covered the trial for the *San Francisco Chronicle,* the case appears to be "a slam dunk" for a verdict of guilty of murder in the first degree, the sentence for which can be death.[3]

Harvey Milk was born in 1932 on Long Island to Jewish Lithuanian parents. As a young man, he was, by all accounts, witty, charismatic, and popular. He was comfortable with his homosexuality, but learned to keep it private. Milk played football in high school and graduated as a math major from what is now SUNY Albany, where he was also the sports editor on the school paper. After college, he enlisted in the navy and served as chief petty officer on board a submarine rescue ship during the Korean War. He later became a navy diving instructor. Following his discharge from military service in 1955, he drifted, holding a variety of jobs, including high school teacher, actuarial statistician for an insurance company, and financial analyst. Milk moved from Texas to Florida, then back to New York, dabbling in theater, traveling, hanging out with friends, seemingly focused only on the present moment. Finally, in 1972, he moved to San Francisco with his partner, Scott Smith, and there Milk's rootlessness ended. In one of the country's most vibrant centers of social transformation, he found a home and eventually a political career.

In the 1970s, the movement demanding equality for gays in the United States became more vocal and visible. As late as 1973, however, the American Psychiatric Association still categorized homosexuality as a disease. At the very time gay men and women were becoming more active in politics and civic life, a conservative backlash was growing as well.

Milk got an apartment on Castro Street in 1973 and opened a storefront camera shop. At the time, young families were moving out, following new jobs to the suburbs, abandoning the Castro Street neighborhood and leaving it to fall into economic decline. Young gay men began to claim the area as their own, one of America's first gay neighborhoods.

---

3. Geluardi, "Dan's White's Motive . . ."

Conflict did not take long to materialize. Violence occurred with some regularity in the early years of the 1970s, often with the police. Keeping their badges covered so as to avoid identification, the officers held nighttime raids on gay bars. By 1971, nearly 2,800 gay men had been arrested on public sex charges; some of them had been dragged into the streets and beaten. Sentences meted out for "gay offenses" were often higher than those for armed robbery, rape, and manslaughter.[4]

Seizing the moment, Milk called for increased participation of gay people in politics as the best solution to oppression. "We don't want sympathetic liberals," Milk told *The New York Times*, "We want gays to represent gays." His interest in politics was not limited to this single issue. Milk felt that the power brokers in San Francisco were also not responsive to the poor, to minorities, and to small businesses like his own. He began to garner support not only from the Castro community but from neighboring communities as well.

Milk founded and led the Castro Village Association, a coalition of gay and gay-friendly businesses. He organized the first Castro Street Fair and Gay Pride Parade, annual events that drew customers to the area and are celebrated to this day. Milk's political ambitions also grew. He helped defeat Proposition 6, an effort to bar gays from teaching in public schools. He ran for the Board of Supervisors twice and lost both elections, the final time in a close vote. Although he lacked funding for these campaigns and received little support from other gay leaders who deemed him too radical, Harvey was undaunted. He cut his hair, stopped smoking marijuana, and made a conscious effort to broaden his appeal throughout the city.[5] His campaign slogan, displaying his characteristic wit, was "Milk has something for everybody."

A change in the city's election procedure in 1976 proved fortuitous for Milk. The previous system selected the Board of Supervisors through at-large, citywide elections. This method allowed the

---

4. Randy Shilts, *The Mayor of Castro Street: The Life and Times of Harvey Milk* (New York: St. Martin's Griffin, 2008), 62–63.
5. Weiss, *Double Play*, 45.

Harvey Milk, a member of the Board of Supervisors.
© Bettmann/CORBIS

moneyed, downtown politicians to hold sway. Under the new rules, however, supervisor elections would be held in eleven newly created districts in the city. Supervisors would now be responsible to individual neighborhoods, making the board more diverse and elections far more representative. The Castro and its surrounding area were within the newly formed District Five.

In his third run for supervisor in 1977, Harvey won in a landslide. The "Mayor of Castro Street," as Harvey was called, was said to be the first openly homosexual man elected to public office in the United States. "This is not my victory," he told an ecstatic crowd, "it's yours and yours and yours. If a gay can win, then it means there is hope that the system can work for all minorities if we fight."[6]

Harvey Milk's increased stature as a city leader and national spokesman for gay rights was met with resistance from some conservatives in San Francisco. Often subjected to death threats, he

6. Shilts, *The Mayor of Castro Street*, 183.

prepared for the worst. A week after winning the district election, Harvey recorded his "political will" into a cassette tape recorder, listing his choice of successors were he to be assassinated. "If a bullet should enter my brain," he added, "let that bullet destroy every closet door."[7]

The same year that Harvey Milk was elected and joined the Board of Supervisors, Dan White became supervisor for District Eight. Were he to be defined by the killings alone, Dan White might be characterized as a vengeful, violent, and homophobic right-wing murderer. Indeed, this was how the gay community and some of the media later came to portray him. For Dan White's family and friends, however, this was simply not accurate. If one were to eliminate the events of that one day in November 1978, those closest to Dan would consider him an all-American hero.

Born in 1946, the second of nine children in an Irish Catholic working-class family, White spent his entire life in San Francisco. Affable and well liked, he was voted valedictorian of his class at Woodrow Wilson High School, where he was also a star athlete. He aspired to become a writer, like his boyhood literary hero, Jack London.

After graduation, Dan enlisted in the United States Army, serving in Vietnam before being honorably discharged in 1972. Rootless for a while, he traveled after the service and hitchhiked to New Orleans. Returning home, he joined the city police department.

One incident speaks to his sense of fairness. After he saw a fellow cop beating a handcuffed black suspect, Dan filed a report, naming the offending officer. When Dan's superior suggested he revise his account to protect his coworker, he refused.[8] As a result, many of Dan's fellow officers shunned him. Eventually, this lack of support led Dan to leave the police force.

White entered the fire academy in 1974, eventually graduating as class valedictorian. At the time, the fire department was under a federal mandate to increase minority hires. But it was common

7. Ibid., 184.
8. Geluardi, "Dan White's Motive . . ."

practice for the department to avoid this requirement by allowing African-Americans into the academy only to expel them, usually for failing written examinations. White went to bat for three black trainees who were about to be terminated, tutored the men after classes to help them pass their exams, and circulated a petition asking they be allowed to stay.[9] On the job, he risked his life to save a woman and her child from the seventh floor of a burning apartment building. The press called White's act "heroic."

Though he seemed to support noble causes, White was far from liberal. A working-class conservative, he regretted—and resented—the demographic changes his native city was undergoing.

In 1977, Dan ran for the Board of Supervisors. The change in the election procedure from at-large to district-by-district elections helped him as it had helped Harvey Milk. District Eight comprised mostly Irish working-class neighborhoods, with small, well-kept homes and family-run businesses. Lower-income neighborhoods could be found there too, nestled beside the Irish Catholic enclave. For decades, the district's residents had little influence with city hall.[10] In an early campaign speech, Dan proclaimed, "I am not going to be forced out of San Francisco by splinter groups of radicals, social deviants and incorrigibles. There are tens of thousands who are just as determined to legally fight to protect and defend our conservative values."

Dan's background and lack of experience marked him as a beginner in politics, but they also gave him distinct advantages. He had married Mary Ann Burns, the daughter of the lieutenant at the firehouse where he once worked, and the two were a wholesome and appealing couple. Being a former cop in a high-crime district helped as well. And then there was Ray Sloan, his campaign manager. A local, like Dan, Sloan was a shrewd organizer who knew how to get the most out of a cut-rate budget.[11]

---

9. Ibid.
10. Ibid.
11. Ibid.

One of Dan's closest friends, Sloan was openly homosexual. Years after the killings, Sloan spoke glowingly, in interviews, about Dan White: "Was Dan White bigoted against gays? I can't believe that. I am gay. He knew it but it was never a problem." To me," said Sloan, "Dan was a genuine hero . . . [O]f all the candidates who ran in all the city districts, he was the only one who campaigned in person in the public housing projects."[12] During his campaign, Dan White walked up and down the streets of the Eighth District; often greeted by Irish voters with shouts of "Hey Danny, Danny Boy," he won his election by a wide margin.

Hidden from the public picture of Dan White were less attractive aspects of his personality. Chief among these were his struggles with depression. Another was his naïveté. A hard-working novice, Dan had much to learn about the gritty city politics in San Francisco, where noble ideals and good intentions had less currency than favoritism, makeshift loyalties, and personal advantage. It was a culture foreign to Dan's view that a man's word was his bond and a broken promise was not easily forgotten or forgiven.[13] Mayor Moscone and Dianne Feinstein understood that political survival often required deception and cunning. Older and more mature than Dan, Harvey Milk was savvy enough to strike the requisite balance. Dan White was not prepared for the rough-and-tumble style of politics.

Nonetheless, White started out well. He cast the deciding vote that allowed Dianne Feinstein to become board president. He persuaded her to appoint Milk chairman of the Streets and Transportation Committee, a position Milk wanted. Feinstein was reluctant at first, but told Dan, "I'm going to give you what you want for Harvey so you'll learn who your friends are."[14] And White supported a number of gay rights issues. He voted with Milk to save a gathering spot for gay veterans and servicers, called the Pride Center. He voted for a resolution honoring a well-known lesbian couple on their twenty-fifth anniversary, and he voted, in committee, for Harvey's premier

---

12. Ibid.
13. Weiss, *Double Play*, 132.
14. Geluardi, "Dan White's Motive . . ."

piece of legislation, a gay rights ordinance protecting San Franciscans from losing their jobs simply for being gay. Dick Pabich, an aide to Milk, said of Dan, "He supported us on every position, and he goes out of his way to find out what gay people think about things."[15]

Dan White admired Harvey Milk. The two had a lot in common. As Sloan told the *San Francisco Weekly*, "They were both proud of their military service, they both hated big money interests and they both represented people on the political margins. And neither was afraid of a fight."[16] Dan even invited Harvey to his newborn son's baptism.

One of the key issues in facing the supervisors in 1978 was the placement of a youth center for wayward juveniles that mental health professionals had proposed be located near White's neighborhood in District Eight. Many residents were vehemently opposed. One organizer distributed leaflets describing residents that would live at the center as "youngsters whose behavior is so chronically destructive as to require long term treatment." Other critics said the behavior of these young people included "aggressive behavior with psychotic or borderline symptoms."[17] Dan promised his constituents he would oppose the location of the "Youth Campus" in District Eight. He asked for Harvey's vote and Milk, as Dan perceived it, agreed to oppose the placement of the Center. Perhaps Harvey was hedging or placating Dan. Perhaps Dan missed the nuances of this interaction. One thing was clear. Dan was confident that he now had six votes, just enough to stop the facility.

On the day of the vote, Dan was thrilled to see the chamber packed with his constituents from District Eight. Surely, he thought, they were about to witness an event that would renew their faith in city government. They would see that Dan White was a man who kept his promises. After lengthy debate, the voting began. Five votes were cast for the Youth Campus and five, including Dan, were cast against it. Harvey stood up to cast his vote. "There's no place in this

---

15. Ibid.
16. Ibid.
17. Weiss, *Double Play*, 113.

city where people want a mafia headquarters next door," he remarked flippantly. And then, turning sober, he said, "We have to put aside our fears and accept responsibility for the disturbed children."[18] Harvey Milk was voting for the Youth Campus.

Dan was stunned at this betrayal. Not only had Harvey broken his promise, he had not even told Dan in advance. Dan White felt humiliated in public before the very people who looked to him as their champion. The friendly relationship between Dan and Harvey ended abruptly.

A few weeks later, the gay rights ordinance came up for a vote before the full board. It was the same ordinance Dan had voted for in committee. But now, Dan voted against it. His was the only negative vote. Earlier that day, Harvey had sent his aide to encourage Dan to vote yes. A unanimous vote would send a stronger message. Dan refused, and responded coldly and bluntly saying, "I bent over backwards to help Harvey with his committee assignment, with the lesbian resolution, in committee on gay rights, and Harvey repays me how? By lying and stabbing me in the back. Never again will I feel my obligation to Harvey or anything he wants. I have learned who my friends are. From here on it's personal, personal between me and Harvey. Tit for tat."[19]

More pressures began to mount on Dan. The election race had tapped out his savings. Business and family concerns added to his problems. Because the pay for supervisor was only $9,600, Dan saw it as only a part-time job. Although he also made $18,000 as a fireman, the city attorney ruled he could not keep his job as a fireman and serve as supervisor. So Dan was forced to quit the fire department. To make ends meet, he secured a loan and bought a fast-food stand for his wife, Mary Ann, to run. After she became pregnant and had their first child, White felt obliged to take over the business and let Mary Ann be the homemaker that she wanted to be.

By November 1978, the stress of being a supervisor, the demands of his business, his family, and the brutal lessons of politics were

---

18. Ibid., 145.
19. Ibid., 146.

George Moscone, mayor of San Francisco.
© Bettmann/CORBIS

becoming too hard for White to handle. He was suffering bouts of depression. Something had to give. On November 10, he submitted his resignation from the Board of Supervisors to Mayor Moscone. He had consulted no one on the decision. The mayor was surprised. Although he and White were at opposite ends of the political spectrum, they had always been on good terms. Outgoing and eager to be liked, White brought an upbeat presence to the Board of Supervisors. The mayor suggested that Dan take a few more days to think about it. Dan assured him that it was not necessary. "Are you sure, absolutely certain, you've explored every avenue, every financial alternative?"

Moscone asked. Dan was calm and confident as he replied, "This is what I've got to do."[20] Moscone accepted White's resignation.

Eight days later, Dan had a change of heart. He felt that by quitting, he was letting down his district. With encouragement from his family and constituents, he asked George Moscone if he could take back his resignation. He was too late. In the preceding week, the board had voted to accept Dan's resignation. He had now officially resigned and legally could not take it back. Still, Moscone felt sorry for Dan. He promised to use his reappointment powers to return him to his now-vacant position as soon as possible, and he reiterated this promise the next day. Then politics intervened.

Harvey was ecstatic when he heard about Dan's resignation. He recognized that with a liberal in the seat, the liberal faction on the board, which included the mayor, would have a precious majority. "It's too good to believe," he told a friend, "Now I've got my sixth vote."[21] So, Harvey pressured Moscone to *not* reappoint Dan. And the mayor listened. He delayed Dan's reappointment and never told him that he was reconsidering. On the evening of Sunday, November 26, a reporter told Dan that at a press conference the next morning at 11:30, the mayor would announce the appointment of Don Horanzy. Dan White was stunned. Here was another broken promise. Another betrayal. Another public humiliation.

The next morning, Dan White went to confront the mayor about his decision. On the drive to city hall, Dan told his aide, Denise Apcar, "I just want George to tell me face to face. I want to see his face. I want to go tell Harvey, I went out on a limb for him, why is he doing this to me?"[22] Whatever his original intent was, Dan did more than talk. He executed Mayor George Moscone and Harvey Milk.

What's left to say about this tragedy? There is the trial, of course. Like any tragedy, there is no definitive end to the Daniel White story. Some good has arisen from the sorrow; some change has resulted. This is always the case with such tragedies. Part of this good, and

20. Ibid., 213.
21. Ibid.
22. Ibid., 264.

part of this change, came from the historic reckoning of Daniel White's highly significant American trial.

Dan White was charged with two counts of murder in the first degree. The California Penal Code defines Murder One as "the killing of another human being with malice aforethought." "Malice aforethought" may be considered legalese for "premeditation," or "deliberation," which itself is not easy to define, though it clearly means something more than "intent to kill." It implies deliberation, a weighing of the pros and cons, before making the decision to kill. Premeditation suggests the actor has some time to think, but it need not be a long time. A person can deliberate for only a few minutes, and that may be enough for a finding of premeditation.

There are three possibilities for a conviction based on an intentional killing. Murder in the first degree encompasses an intentional killing with premeditation. A conviction in this situation allows the death penalty. Murder in the second degree means an intentional killing without premeditation. In this instance, a person formed the intent to kill more or less on the spur of the moment, with little or no time for deliberation. A conviction here takes the death penalty off the table. And then there is voluntary manslaughter, which can mean a killing done in the "heat of passion," or "under extreme emotional distress," or, one might say, where the mind is so clouded that it overwhelms the actor's intent. The killing itself may still be "intentional," but the intent has been forged in the "heat of passion" or born of a period of "extreme emotional distress." The judge has the difficult task of explaining to the jury the meaning of these concepts.[23]

The State of California vs. Dan White is to be presided over by Judge Walter Calcagno and prosecuted by Tommy Norman, the chief homicide prosecutor in the San Francisco district attorney's office. An experienced attorney, Norman has one of the highest conviction rates in the state. After reviewing the facts of the case, Norman is confident that Dan White will be convicted of murder in the first

---

23. For an explanation of California homicide law, see Suzanne Mounts, "Premeditation and Deliberation in California," *University of San Francisco Law Review* 36 (2002): 261; People v. Berry, 18 Cal. 3d 509, 556 P.2d 777 (1976); People v. Logan, 175 Cal. 45, 164 P. 1121 (1917).

degree.[24] He has reputable witnesses who were present at the scene. He has the murder weapon. He has a full confession.

Still, Norman has to prove "malice aforethought." Could he prove "premeditation"? If one were to ask Norman this question before the trial, he might have said, "Of course I can." White came to city hall armed with a fully loaded weapon, carrying an additional ten bullets in his pocket so he could reload. Why did he do that, if not for the planned purpose of killing his intended targets? Dan White also avoided the security guards and the metal detector when he climbed in through a side window. What thinking motivated this seemingly stealthy behaviour? He shot Moscone not once, but twice, and then, while the mayor was lying wounded on the floor, he paused, and shot him twice more. Then he took the time to reload; to use the extra ammunition he brought with him. Why would he reload if not to kill again? White next walked across the hall, invited Harvey Milk to come into his office to talk and shot him three times. Again he paused, and shot him twice more. Only then did he leave the building.

Could any reasonable juror avoid finding premeditation in this case? Not a chance. That's what Tommy Norman would say and it was certainly the opinion of nearly everyone else. Dan White was going to die in the gas chamber or spend the rest of his life in prison.

Doug Schmidt was the defense attorney representing Dan White. He was the same age as Dan, clean-cut, self-effacing, and from a humble Midwestern background. Mary Anne White had chosen him, perhaps because she saw something of her husband in the young attorney.[25] Schmidt was not a famous lawyer, but he was competent, respected by his peers, with a reputation for hard work and careful preparation. He knew he faced a difficult task. There was no chance for an acquittal. Insanity was not an option, because it required that the defense prove that White was suffering from a mental disease or defect so powerful that he was unable to appreciate the consequences

24. Weiss, *Double Play*, 299.
25. Ibid., 303.

of his actions or did not know that he was doing was wrong.[26] It is unlikely that any psychiatrist would testify that White was insane under this test. Moreover, the insanity defense was not popular with juries at this time. In fact, less than two percent of such pleas succeeded, probably because they would result in an acquittal.[27]

Doug Schmidt decided to argue for manslaughter. California, by court decision, allowed mitigation of some homicides from first-degree murder to second-degree murder. Later rulings held that the mitigation process could reduce murder to manslaughter. This came to be called the mini-insanity defense or, more accurately, the "diminished capacity" or "partial responsibility" defense. The reasoning was that mentally impaired actors lacked the requisite mental state to be convicted of first- or second-degree murder, and deserved *less* punishment than a killer who acts with a normal state of mind.

A psychiatrist might be willing to testify as an expert that White had mental and emotional disabilities that grew worse and worse as external and internal circumstances rendered him unable to function on November 27, 1978. And this, Schmidt would argue, is why Dan White "lost it."

Schmidt had done his legal research. There were a number of California Supreme Court cases that supported the "diminished capacity" defense.[28] A defense lawyer's job is to paint his client in a sympathetic light. But that is not enough. He must also find a way to allow the jurors to implement that sympathy. The jury might, in the end, feel sorry for Dan, thinking that he really is a good man, but have no way to avoid finding him guilty of murder. Here was a way—the diminished capacity defense. Schmidt found the legal concept on which the jury could avoid a finding of murder one or

---

26. See, e.g., State v. Silvers, 323 N.C. 646, 655, 374 S.E.2d 858, 864 (1989).
27. Richard Kipling, "Dan White Trial: Insanity Plea at Issue," *Los Angeles Times*, April 30, 1979.
28. People v. Wells, 202 P.2d 53 (1949); People v. Gorshen, 336 P.2d 492 (1959); see, e.g., People v. Berry, 18 Cal. 3d 509, 556 P.2d 777 (1976), where defendant husband killed his wife by choking her to death. The court held that the continuous sexual taunting of the husband into jealous rages, alternating between arousing and then rejecting him, making repeated references to her love and sexual involvement with another man, were sufficient for the jury to find diminished capacity justifying manslaughter rather than murder.

even murder two. If it wanted to, a jury could in good conscience use it to find Dan White guilty only of manslaughter. That would be a victory for the defense.

To achieve this result, Doug Schmidt would not only have to be convincing, he would have to be lucky. Some of that luck arrived in the form of mistakes made by Prosecutor Norman.

Norman, it turned out, failed to prepare for two major developments in the trial. He did not anticipate how sympathetic the jury would be to Dan White. And he failed to understand the need to make clear to the jury not only what happened on that day in 1978, but *why* it happened. Norman did not emphasize for the jury Dan White's motive in killing Moscone and Milk. These two missteps presented no challenge to Schmidt's theory of the defense, and thus made it more effective.

In order to persuade a jury, a lawyer needs both a theory, meaning a strategy, and a compelling theme. Schmidt's defense strategy had two components. First, he had to show that Dan White was a good, sympathetic man, maybe even a hero, the kind of man anyone would want to have as a son or neighbor. And this was exactly who Dan White was—until the killings. Second, Schmidt had to explain Dan's unlikely, tragic behavior, and what made Dan "lose" it. This he would prove through evidence of Dan's severe and growing depression. He would tell the jury of the financial, family, and political pressures Dan suffered in the days leading up to that tragic Monday in November. Schmidt would then tie these narrative threads together with the expert testimony of psychiatrists.

Lawyers looking to persuade a jury know that it helps to have a compelling theme: a short and pithy sentence or two that harmonizes all the undisputed facts into one, brief, reasonable, and convincing statement that encapsulates the case strategy. The defense theme that Schmidt crafted, and repeated time and again throughout the trial was, *"Good people, fine people, with fine backgrounds, simply do not kill in cold blood. It just doesn't happen unless there is a mental problem."*

Schmidt's theme, however, was not immune to refutation. The prosecution could have blunted his strategy by humanizing the victims, with a counter-narrative of the exemplary lives of Moscone and

Milk. Norman could have spoken of Milk's courage in being the first openly gay elected official in the country. He could have made much of the fact that George Moscone, the son of a milk deliveryman, rose from a working-class Italian background to become the city's mayor. But Norman did not do so. In the opening statements, in summations, in the presentation of evidence, he did not portray either of the victims in any vivid or memorable way.

The prosecution team also failed to challenge the defense's depiction of Dan White's motive. Instead of ignoring the "why" question, they could have addressed it head-on, by pointing to anger and revenge, and the desire to punish. Dan didn't "lose it," Norman might have argued; he had felt disrespected and betrayed by Moscone and by Milk. White decided that he would make them pay for it, and he did, by taking their lives. But Norman largely ignored that argument, even though it was clear from several California judicial opinions that anger and revenge were *not* within the scope of the diminished capacity law.[29]

Most important of all, perhaps, was the opportunity Norman missed to select a jury more friendly to the prosecution.

As in all trials, the jury selection phase is critical. Prosecutor Norman and Defense Counsel Schmidt asked questions of a pool of prospective jurors. Each side had twenty-six peremptory challenges; that is, after asking a series of questions, each side could have challenged and removed as many as twenty-six jurors without giving any reason for doing so. During this process, Defense Counsel Schmidt used twenty-two challenges; Prosecutor Norman used four.

Norman employed his standard prosecutorial formula for jury selection. As in all his previous cases, he sought law-and-order types, stable members of the community, and conservative, older men and women who might not shy away from the death penalty. Liberals were out, of course, given the perception that they tended to favor defendants. Norman's formula is a good one in most cases and had

---

29. In People v. Logan, 175 Cal. 45, 48–49, 164 P. 1121, 1122–3 (1917), the court defined diminished capacity, saying "the inquiry is whether or not the defendant's reason was at the time of the act so disturbed or obscured by some passion—not necessarily fear, *and never, of course, the passion for revenge,* to such an extent as would render ordinary men of average disposition liable to act rashly or without due deliberation or reflection."

proved successful in his previous trials. But Dan White was not the usual murder defendant. He was not a loner, a radical, a long-time criminal, or a fringe member of society. Dan White was a conservative former police officer and fireman, a stable member of the community, and a traditionalist. In fact, Dan White, the accused, would normally be considered an ideal prosecution juror.

For this reason, Doug Schmidt wanted—and got—exactly the kind of jury that Norman did. As the evidence evolved, it proved to be a jury that related well to Dan White. It had no apparent gays or gay-friendly liberals on it. The jurors were all San Franciscans, living in working-class neighborhoods and holding traditional family values. Some of them were parents with children Dan's age. Some may well have been bothered by the influx of gays and immigrants to the city. Only two or three of these jurors, at most, it was estimated, had voted for the liberal Democrat, Mayor Moscone. None of them, it could be surmised, was likely to feel a fondness for Harvey Milk. This, as we have suggested, was a Dan White jury.

The trial began on May 1, 1979. In his opening statement, Prosecutor Norman emphasized the three elements that would secure him a first-degree murder conviction: premeditation, malice, and deliberation. He focused on the evidence and the timeline; Dan's entry through the side window, the extra bullets he carried, his reloading of the revolver, and the coup de grace shots to the head of the dying victims. Norman's account of what happened was too long—and he mentioned nothing about *why* it happened.

In his opening statement, Defense Counsel Schmidt rendered superfluous most of Norman's lengthy recitation of facts. Standing before the jury, with his client seated behind a bulletproof glass wall, Schmidt began: "It is not disputed that Dan White did, indeed, shoot and kill George Moscone, and I think the evidence is equally clear that Dan White did shoot and kill Harvey Milk . . . Daniel White gave a statement to that effect."[30]

---

30. Opening statement of the defense by Douglas Schmidt: Douglas Linder, "Famous American Trials," http://law2.umkc.edu/faculty/projects/ftrials/milk/openingstmts.html (citing Kenneth W. Salter, *The Trial of Dan White* (Market and Systems Interface, Inc., 1991).

Schmidt next outlined his trial strategy to the jury:

[Y]ou might ask, why is it necessary to have a trial, and the answer to that simply is . . . not so much as to what occurred on the twenty-seventh, but the facts as to why that occurred, and I think that when all the facts are out, the charge of first-degree murder simply will not be supported here, and it's simply not what happened. . . . The issue in this trial is properly to understand why that happened.[31]

Schmidt crafted an image of the kind of man Dan White was. He told the jury that Dan was a native of San Francisco, a good athlete, a soldier, a policeman, a fireman, a husband, a father, and working-class hero. He then delivered the theme of the case: *Good people, fine people with fine backgrounds, simply do not kill in cold blood. It just doesn't happen.*

Schmidt went on to articulate the legal standard that supported his contention that Dan White was not guilty of first-degree murder. He painted a compelling portrait of Dan White that explained that his actions on that fateful day were deeply out of character. He maintained that something was wrong with Dan that caused him to crack and act rashly. These mitigating factors, Schmidt argued, made Dan White guilty of voluntary manslaughter:

The part that perhaps went unrecognized, and certainly went unrecognized until it was too late, was the fact that Daniel White was suffering from a mental illness. He had been suffering from a mental illness since the time of early manhood, and it's a disease like any other disease, perhaps not as easily diagnosable as a broken leg or arm, but far more devastating to the person. . . . Daniel White was suffering from [a disease] called depression, sometimes referred to as manic depression. . . .[32]

---

31. Ibid.
32. Ibid.

Schmidt concluded with a description of the murderous act:

[S]hots rang out in the mayor's office, and Dan White, as it was quite apparent at that point, had cracked as to his underlying mental illness and stress factors . . . and the sudden emotional surge that he had in the mayor's office was simply too much for him, and he cracked. He shot the mayor, reloaded his gun, . . . on instinct, because of his police training, and was about to leave the building [when] he saw somebody that he believed to be an aide to Harvey Milk. . . . [I]n the same state of rage, emotional upheaval . . . having cracked, this man, ninety seconds from the time he shot the mayor, shot and killed Harvey Milk. . . .

Given those facts, I believe that the theory of the people as to first-degree murder simply is not supported. . . . I believe you will agree that mental illness and stress, and the emotion of that moment simply broke this man, and this was not a deliberate premeditated killing.[33]

Schmidt did not have to wait long to offer proof for these claims. Prosecutor Norman gave him several opportunities when he presented his own case.

Norman called Dianne Feinstein, who had replaced George Moscone as mayor. Feinstein testified to the events of November 27; how she ran into Dan leaving his office, how she heard the gunshots and saw Harvey Milk's dead body. On cross-examination, Schmidt asked her:

Q: Would it be fair to say Dan was politically inexperienced at the time he took his seat as Supervisor?

A: Yes, I felt that Dan was new to the process.

Q: Did you feel generally that he was somewhat idealistic?

___
33. Ibid.

A: Yes, I felt Dan had very strong ideals. He had always worked very hard and he took the process very seriously.

Q: Given that you knew Dan White quite well, would it be your opinion that the man you knew was the type of man that would have shot two people?

A: No, it would not be my opinion that Dan White was the type of man who would have killed two people.[34]

Schmidt had no further questions. Dianne Feinstein's words clearly supported the defense's theme, "Good people do not kill in cold blood."

As the trial continued, Doug Schmidt reinforced his theme again, this time with the prosecution witness, Inspector Frank Falzon. Falzon, the officer who took Dan's confession, had been Dan's friend and associate from his days on the police force. After the tape-recorded confession was played for the jury, Schmidt began his cross-examination:

Q: Can you tell me [Inspector], when you first saw [Dan] on November 27, how did he appear physically to you?

A: Destroyed. This was not the Dan White that I had known, not at all.

Q: Destroyed in what respect?

A: Totally unlike Dan White, the man I knew. . . . a man among men. . . . He was a . . . hustler . . . [h]e had tremendous drive. That day I saw a shattered individual.

---

34. Trial testimony of Dianne Feinstein: Linder, "Famous American Trials," http://law2. umkc.edu/faculty/projects/ftrials/milk/feinsteintestimony.html (citing Salter, *The Trial of Dan White*).

Q: Knowing, with regard to the shootings of Mayor Moscone and Harvey Milk, knowing Dan White as you did, is he the type of man that could have premeditatively and deliberately shot those people?[35]

At this, Norman leaped to his feet and objected. But Schmidt was prepared. He presented his memorandum of legal authorities. The judge read it and suggested that Schmidt first lay a foundation with some preliminary questions. Schmidt happily agreed.

Q: Inspector Falzon, again, you mentioned you were quite familiar with Dan White. Can you tell me something about the man's character . . . prior to November 27, 1978?

"Objection!" Norman shouted again. He was overruled.

A: The Dan White that I knew [before] . . . was a man who seemed to excel in pressure situations, and it seemed that the greater the pressure the more enjoyment Dan had.

Falzon then gave several examples of Dan's commendable actions under pressure.

Q: Given these things that you mentioned about Dan White, was there anything in his character that you knew of him, prior to these tragedies of the twenty-seventh of November, that would have led you to believe that he would ever kill somebody cold-bloodedly?

A: Absolutely not. Dan White was an exemplary individual; a man that I was proud to know and to be associated with.

---

35. Trial testimony of Inspector Frank J. Falzon: Linder, "Famous American Trials," http://law2.umkc.edu/faculty/projects/ftrials/milk/falzontestimony.html (citing Salter, *The Trial of Dan White*).

Aided by Norman and the court, Schmidt had turned the chief investigator of the case into a character witness for the defense.

Thus far in the trial, the prosecution had given the jury no insights into the character, personality, or accomplishments of the victims, Mayor Moscone and Harvey Milk. But the jury was getting a clear idea that Dan White was a good person and that something happened that led him to kill. Because after all, good people, people like them, do not kill.

Prosecutor Norman next played the audiotape of Dan's confession for the jury. Surely, he must have thought, this was his ace. He was following the prosecutor's dogma: if you have a confession, and it's on audiotape, you don't just offer a typed transcript, you play the tape. Let the jury hear the defendant's own words confessing guilt. But this decision proved to be a questionable decision.

In his taped statement to Inspector Falzon, Dan White is heard saying, in a halting, sobbing voice, "I, I, want to explain[36] . . . I shot them, I don't know what happened." He goes on, describing the events, the facts, in an apologetic tone: "Well, it's just that I've been under an awful lot of pressure lately, financial pressure, because of my job situation, family pressure because of ah . . . not being able to have the time with my family. . . ."[37]

Falzon asks, "Is there anything else you'd like to add at this time?" Dan answers, still crying: "Just that I've always been honest and worked hard, never cheated anybody, or, you know, I'm not a crook or anything. I wanted to do a good job. . . ."

Dan talked about why he wanted the job of supervisor and how he cared about the city: "I'm trying to do a good job, an' I saw this city as it's goin' kind of downhill an' I was always just a lonely vote on the Board and tryin' to be honest, an', an' I just couldn't take it anymore, an' that's it."

---

36. Weiss, *Double Play*, 284.
37. Transcript of Dan White's taped confession, November 27, 1978, People's Exhibit 54 in the Trial of Dan White: Linder, "Famous American Trials," http://law2.umkc.edu/faculty/projects/ftrials/milk/whiteconfession.html.

The confession ended with Dan White sobbing into the microphone. When Norman looked at the jury, he was shocked. Two of the female jurors were crying. Another was wiping away tears and others had wet eyes. The *Los Angeles Times* carried this headline: "Jurors weep as White tells of two slayings." The news story reported that half the jurors and some spectators were in tears after the twenty-five-minute tape was played.[38] An admission of two murders had been eclipsed by sympathy for the perpetrator.[39] And Schmidt had good reason to believe this approach would resonate with members of this jury.

Criticized by some for playing the tape, Norman may well have had no alternative. If he had offered only the transcript, Schmidt would almost certainly have played the tape as part of the defense case. Some jurors might have believed the prosecution was hiding evidence.

After three days, Norman rested his case. He had called nineteen witnesses. In all that testimony, not a single person talked about Mayor Moscone or Harvey Milk, about their accomplishments and legacy, or about what their deaths would mean to the community and their families. Only the coroner, speaking in medical terms about autopsies and dead bodies, seemed interested in the victims. And here again, Norman missed an opportunity. He could have questioned the coroner about the nature of the bullet wounds, to show a foundation for premeditation. He did not. He seemed to think, as he did throughout the trial, that a mere recitation of the facts of the killings would be enough. But Norman's greatest misstep was his failure to address the key question in the juror's minds: "*Why* would an apparently good person like Dan White kill?"

It was time for the defense's case. As Schmidt began, he was careful to provide exactly the answers the jury was waiting for. In questioning his witnesses, he had three goals in mind.

---

38. "Jurors Weep as White Tells of 2 Slayings: Ears Were Roaring, Head About to Burst, He Says on Police Tape," *Los Angeles Times*, March 4, 1979; *see also* Weiss, *Double Play* at 348 for a description of the reactions of the jurors to the playing of the tape.
39. Weiss, *Double Play*, 348.

First, the witnesses were to establish facts that weakened any unfavorable inferences from Dan's conduct on the day of the killing and which tended to explain away actions that suggested premeditation. For example, there was evidence that other supervisors, including Dianne Feinstein, carried guns when they went to city hall, just as Dan had. And the idea that White used the window to enter city hall instead of the main entrance was not nearly as unusual as it seemed. Other people were known to use the window to gain access to the building simply because it was faster. As for Dan reloading his gun, there was testimony that police officers are trained to reload after they fire guns, as well as carry additional ammunition so they can continue to reload. As a former police officer, reloading would be an instinctive act for Dan White.

The second point Schmidt hammered home for the jurors was that Dan was a heroic working-class figure. He called Dan's friends, family members, fellow police officers, and firemen to provide good character evidence. These witnesses also described Dan's episodes of depression, the pressures that caused the depression, and how they escalated. This was the testimony of Denise Apcar, Dan's legislative aide, who drove him to city hall on the morning of November 27.

Q: Now, you mentioned that he was hard-working [in his city supervisor position] initially. . . . Did there come a time when that seemed to change a bit?

A: Yes, . . . as early as March, 1978 . . . he became frustrated with the job quite early. He was having difficulty . . . adjusting to the political process . . . and, he became moody and withdrawn . . . started [showing up to work] less, started to cancel meetings, just basically depressed a lot. And, by November 1978, it was much worse.[40]

---

40. Trial testimony of Denise Apcar: Linder, "Famous American Trials," http://law2.umkc.edu/faculty/projects/ftrials/milk/apcartestimony.html (citing Salter, *The Trial of Dan White*).

A former councilman testified that the job was so stressful that it had caused him to have a heart attack. Dan's sister, Nancy, a nurse, testified Dan had had mood changes, and got severely depressed, spending hours in bed and not going near members of his family for days. Others followed, friends, policemen, and firefighters, all testifying to Dan's good qualities. They mentioned that he often carried a gun and that it was a trained and automatic response to reload it.

Mary Ann White, by now the mother of two, was in tears throughout her testimony. Her face ashen, she described how she met and fell in love with Dan, and how he always treated her well. She spoke of his idealism, his vitality and energy, and how he was able to "inspire in you something that made you want to do your best, like he always did. He made you feel good all the time. He was so thoughtful. He was always trying to do things for you, like arranging little surprises for you."[41]

Mary Ann also spoke of Dan's bouts of depression, and the difficult financial pressures he carried after being forced out of his job as a fireman. She talked about his guilt and worry at her needing to work long hours at the food stand. His work on the Board of Supervisors, she told the jury, only increased the frequency of his depressed moods and periods of withdrawal. By the fall of 1978, these periods of depression and isolation began to last as long as a week. There was no sex. Throughout all this, Dan reassured her, "Don't worry, I am ok, I'll get myself together."[42] When Mary Ann left the stand, the jury was shaken. Schmidt sensed that they were beginning to believe that he killed because he was sick.

The third and final goal of the defense was to tie all the testimony together into a cohesive narrative, bolstered by specific details about the nature of Dan's mental illness. And so Schmidt called five mental health experts (four psychiatrists and one psychologist) to the stand.

These experts were among the most prominent in California. Included in this group was Doctor Martin Blinder, whose testimony formed the basis for one of the leading California cases that approved

41. Weiss, *Double Play*, 400.
42. Ibid., 401.

and authorized the use of diminished capacity in homicide cases. Also testifying for the defense was Doctor Donald Lunde, one of California's most renowned forensic psychiatrists. Each of these witnesses had spent days examining Dan, speaking with his family, friends, and coworkers and going over his taped confession. By explaining all the research they had done to arrive at their opinions, they gave the jurors a scientific basis that would allow a finding of manslaughter.

Each of the five began with a recitation of qualifications. Each then recounted the elaborate work he had done in preparation for the testimony. Then, in one form or another, each was asked three key questions which were relevant to the only disputed issue in the case:

Q 1. Doctor, were you able to diagnose or detect any mental illness or disease in Mr. White, and if so, what would it be?

Q 2. Do you have an opinion based upon your reasonable psychiatric certainty as to how that condition affected Mr. White on November 27, 1978, at the time of the shootings?

Q 3. Explain, Doctor, how you arrived at that conclusion.

All five agreed, with slight variations, that Dan White's severe depression rendered him mentally unable to act with deliberation, premeditation, or malice.

Doctor Blinder stated that Dan White's depression circumvented the mental processes necessary for premeditation, malice, and intent. He elaborated: "I think any man, even one not carrying all the special burdens that Mr. White carried, even one for whom reappointment did not hold that very special significance that it did for Mr. White, would be aroused to tremendous emotions and tremendous passion, emotion and passion which might serve to short-circuit some of the mental processes necessary for premeditation, malice and intent."[43]

---

43. People v. White, 117 Cal. App. 3d 270, 277, 172 Cal. Rptr. 612 (1981); Weiss, *Double Play*, 378–9.

Doctor Lunde agreed that the "defendant was suffering from severe depression and that on November 27 he did not premeditate nor was he capable of mature meaningful reflection." Lunde concluded that at the time of the killings, White's "mental condition was such that even if he had tried, which he didn't, he would not have been capable of sitting down and maturely, meaningfully, reflecting upon the act, weighing the pros of doing it or not doing it . . . that sort of thing, all of which is part of premeditation and deliberation which is necessary for someone to commit first-degree murder." Nor did White show signs of malice, which is necessary even for a finding of murder in the second degree. "He was not capable of thinking about his obligations to society, what the laws were and how they might affect him."

Note that some of the expert testimony of Lunde and of several other experts involved more than psychiatric opinion. It also involved opinions on the law. When the doctors seek to define the meaning of legal terms such as "premeditation" and "malice," their views reflect what the law requires and what the law means. They are asserting that these elements are required under the law for a finding of murder and that they are missing in this case. It is one thing for the psychiatrist to opine on the mental condition of a defendant. It is acceptable to say Dan lacked the capacity to deliberate. But allowing testimony that "therefore defendant lacked the necessary mental state for a finding of murder" may well have encroached on the province of the judge and of the jury. Happily for the defense, however, there was no such objection in the Dan White case.

And so it went. Psychiatrist George Solmon concluded that White was suffering from recurrent bouts of unipolar depression and that, to a major degree, on November 27 the defendant lacked the mental ability to meaningfully premeditate and was in a dissociated state of mind that blocked out all awareness of his duty not to kill. Psychiatrist Jerry Jones agreed. Psychologist Richard Delman testified that he administered three scientifically recognized psychological tests to the defendant and concluded that at the time of the shooting, White's ability to deliberate and premeditate was impaired; that he lacked the capacity to weigh considerations and rationally decide on a course of action; and that he lacked the capacity to harbor malice and to appreciate his duty not to do wrong.[44]

The defense experts made a powerful case supporting diminished capacity. However, one snippet of testimony by Doctor Blinder led the public to misunderstand and mischaracterize the case. In court, Blinder described Dan White's depression. Among the many symptoms was the tendency of White, a one-time athlete and normally devoted to health and good nutrition, to gorge himself with sugary junk foods during periods of severe stress. Blinder spent two minutes of his day-long testimony on this point:

> During these spells he'd become quite withdrawn, quite lethargic. He would retreat to his room. Wouldn't come to the door. Wouldn't answer the phone. . . . And during these periods he found he could not cope with people. . . . [A]ny confrontations would cause him to become argumentative. . . . [W]henever he felt things were not going right, he would abandon his usual program of exercise and good nutrition and start gorging himself on junk foods, Twinkies, Coca Cola. . . . When something would go wrong, he'd hit the high sugar stuff. He'd hit the chocolate and the more he consumed the worse he'd feel.[45]

Some journalists seized on this testimony and a new (and derisive) term entered the American lexicon: "Twinkie Defense." Articles and headlines failed to indicate, however, that no one, including Blinder, had maintained that consumption of junk food caused White's depression,[46] that it wrought psychological or physiological changes

---

44. People v. White, 117 Cal. App. 3d 270, 277, 172 Cal. Rptr. 612 (1981).

45. Weiss, *Double Play*, 375–6.

46. Snopes.com presents this appropriate analogy: Blinder's testimony "was similar to offering evidence that the habitual wearing of torn and dirty clothes by someone who had previously always been a snappy dresser was a sign that the person was suffering from depression. Nobody who paid attention would claim that such testimony asserted that bad clothing caused the defendant's depression. There would be no discussion of a "sloppy clothing defense": David Mikkelson, "The Twinkie Defense," Snopes.com, October 30, 1999, http://www.snopes.com/legal/twinkie.asp. See also Philip Hager, "Twinkie defense proves successful," *Los Angeles Times*, May 23, 1979.

in White, or that it justified a finding of mental incapacity. The testimony was offered as one of many concrete behavioral changes that were symptoms of White's depression. In short, Schmidt never made a "Twinkie Defense."

To rebut Schmidt's five mental health experts, Prosecutor Norman called only one psychiatrist. On November 27, after White had formally confessed, Norman had decided that he would ensure a truly airtight case by closing off the mental defect escape hatch. So he arranged for White to be seen and interviewed by Doctor Roland Levy, a psychiatrist on the staff of the University of California Neuropsychiatric Institute. In court, Doctor Levy relied solely on his two-hour interview and the taped confession. He did not interview any of White's family members, coworkers, or friends. Levy, however, had an advantage over all the others. He saw Dan roughly eight hours after the killings and was thus able to diagnose Dan's condition at about the time of the event. The doctor testified that White was calm and that he found no evidence of mental illness that would affect Dan's ability to premeditate or deliberate. He disagreed with the testimony of the five mental health experts who testified for the defense. Schmidt had noticed, however, that Doctor Levy concluded his written report to Norman by saying: "If you (i.e., the prosecutor) have any questions, please get in touch with me. I am sure there are many aspects of this defendant's life that were not touched upon in the interview. And should these seem significant areas, I would be happy to talk to him further."

This, of course, was fertile ground for cross-examination:

Q: You didn't do a complete assessment, is that a fair conclusion?

A: Well, I would say it is not as complete as I would have done. . . .

Q: This was an important case, was it not?

A: Yes, it was.

Q: And you didn't do a complete assessment?

A: I was never asked to do a complete assessment.[47]

Schmidt then got Levy to specify what additional pertinent information he might have elicited had he done a complete assessment. Since Levy admitted he did not speak to White after their first meeting, nor did he speak to any members of Dan's family, friends, or coworkers, he had to concede that further information and interviews would have been helpful. The contrast between the limited basis for Levy's opinion and the extensive preparation supporting that of the defense experts was obvious.

In addition, Doctor Levy said that at the time of the interview Dan was "calm—just like he was at the time of his taped confession." Schmidt pounced:

Q: You think he was calm at the time of the confession?

A: Well, according to the tape he was.

Q: So, when you examined him, he was calm just like he was calm during his taped statement?

Doctor Levy replied, "Yes." [48] This must have weakened his credibility, as the jury had already heard Dan's taped confession, and no one could reasonably believe Dan sounded calm.

Both sides rested their cases and the summations began. Speaking for four hours, Norman left the jury numb. He reviewed every factual detail of the case and the testimony of his nineteen witnesses. George Moscone was absent from the case as Norman presented it, and all the jury heard of Harvey Milk was that he "smirked," as Dan

47. Trial transcript of Doctor Levy: Linder, "Famous American Trials," http://law2.umkc.edu/faculty/projects/ftrials/milk/levytestimony.html (citing Salter, *The Trial of Dan White*).
48. Ibid.

had said in his taped statement. Norman's summation, like the rest of his case, failed to provide any credible motive for the killings. He seemed satisfied with a strategy that said, "Sure, Dan White may be a good man, but he still murdered two people."

It was now the defense's turn. Schmidt's summation lasted only an hour. Through it all, he focused on his theme, "Dan White was a good man. And good men do not deliberately kill without reason." Schmidt argued that Dan White killed because he was suffering under tremendous pressure, a pressure that created a state of mental illness. Dan White had cracked. Throughout his summation, Schmidt carefully emphasized the words of the psychiatrists to support this theme.

Now that summations had ended, one vital part of the trial remained before submitting the case to the jury, the judge's charge. In this phase, the judge explains to the jury what, under the law, in the statute and cases, distinguishes murder from manslaughter. To define and to understandably communicate these legal concepts is not an easy task.

Trial lawyers know the importance of the court's instructions in this phase of the trial. They understand that the judge's charge provides the framework for their evidence, their legal strategy, and their theme. Careful lawyers prepare legal instructions that they intend to suggest to the judge at the beginning of the case; instructions that will best serve their particular strategy. So, Schmidt got Judge Calcagno to instruct the jury about diminished capacity. Calcagno did so, in these exact words, taken from the leading California case, *People v. Logan:*

> The law does not undertake to limit or define the kinds of passion which may cause a person to act rashly. Such passions as desperation, humiliation, resentment, anger, fear, or rage, or any other high wrought emotion . . . can be sufficient to reduce the killings to manslaughter so long as they are sufficient to obscure the reason and render the average man likely to act rashly.[49]

---

49. Weiss, *Double Play,* 432.

This language proved helpful for the defense. But that was only part of what the *Logan* opinion said. Later in the opinion, the court imposed a limitation: "The inquiry is whether or not the defendant's reason was, at the time of his act, so disturbed or obscured by some passion—*but, never, of course, the passion for revenge.*"[50]

One might say that "a passion for revenge" is exactly what Dan White had.

But Norman may not have read the case. Had he done so, he could have used the words "passion for revenge" in his opening, in his summation and throughout the trial, as a powerful counter to Schmidt's contention that Dan killed because he was mentally impaired. But he did not. Worse yet, Norman failed to raise this "revenge exception" when the judge charged the part favorable to the defense.

Other opinions discussed the effect of a "cooling-off period" prior to the act. In these instances, the opinions stated that if murder is to be reduced to manslaughter, "the killing must be upon a sudden quarrel or heat of passion, i.e., suddenly as a response to the provocation and *not belatedly as revenge or punishment.*"[51] That is to say, the diminished capacity defense does not apply if the actor has had time to cool off. But the jury never heard these words.

After about thirty-eight hours over six days of deliberation, the jury reached its verdict. On May 21, 1979, the clerk read it to a tense, packed courthouse: "We the jury find the defendant guilty of the crime of voluntary manslaughter in the death of George Moscone and Harvey Milk."[52] Some of the jurors were in tears. Dan looked at his wife, Mary Ann. She was crying too. Dan White had escaped the death penalty.

As many saw it, as the gay community certainly saw it, Dan White had gotten away with cold-blooded murder. His sentence for manslaughter was seven years. He served five years and was released on parole. The truth behind this controversial outcome lies in the strength of Schmidt's defense strategy and Prosecutor Norman's fail-

50. People v. Logan, 175 Cal. 45, 49, 164 P. 1121, 1123 (1917).
51. Weiss, *Double Play*, 432.
52. Ibid., 436.

Demonstrators gather to mourn the deaths of
Harvey Milk and George Moscone.
© Roger Ressmeyer/CORBIS

ure to successfully combat it, due in part, perhaps, to overconfidence. "There was no question that Dan White was guilty," Darlene Benton, a former juror on the case said, but "the prosecution thought it was such a clear-cut case they didn't do their job."[53]

When the gay community heard that Harvey Milk had been killed, it responded with sorrowful restraint. Thousands of people joined a peaceful, candlelight parade in the streets of San Francisco. But when the verdict of manslaughter was announced and the leniency of Dan White's sentence revealed, the public outcry known as the "White Riots" erupted. With chants of "Avenge Harvey Milk" and "Kill Dan White," nearly 5,000 protestors set fire to parked cars and smashed windows at city hall. That same night, the police raided the Castro, beating and arresting people. By the next morning, over

53. Carol Pogash, "Myth of the 'Twinkie defense' / The verdict in the Dan White case wasn't based on his ingestion of junk food," *San Francisco Chronicle*, November 23, 2003, http://www.sfgate.com/health/article/Myth-of-the-Twinkie-defense-The-verdict-in-2511152.php.

sixty police officers and a hundred gay men and women were hospitalized. Total damages were in excess of a million dollars.

Many believed that had Dan White shot and killed only Mayor Moscone, he would have been found guilty of murder. They saw the verdict as a message that "Gays were fair game. Kill them and you only get a slap on the wrist."

The verdict was a shock to the prosecutor's team, to the people of San Francisco, and to the media. Many, including Tommy Norman, blamed the jurors, suggesting that they disregarded the facts and the law and reacted out of undue sympathy for Dan White. We think that conclusion is unfair. This was not a "jury nullification case," where the jurors improperly ignored the evidence or the law in order to reach a result that suited their own sense of justice. The jury verdict was not a travesty. The verdict was supported by the evidence that was presented in court and by the law as it then existed. In that sense it was reasonable. Different findings of murder one or of murder two would also have been reasonable and supported by the evidence. No appellate court would reverse any of those three findings.

From tragedy, some good and some change often result. The author Mike Weiss, who wrote the most authoritative and detailed account of the trial, put it well when he wrote that "[t]he biggest change Dan White wrought was unintended: the acceptance of gay people here and in many other places across the country was inspired in part by the martyrdom of Harvey Milk. In death, Harvey's influence grew far greater than he had any reason to expect it would be, had he lived."[54] President Carter released a statement lauding Milk as "a hard-working and dedicated supervisor, a leader in San Francisco's gay community, who kept his promise to represent all constituents."[55] Milk's life and death became the subject of an opera, an Academy Award-winning documentary, a Broadway play and the 2008 film *Milk,* which earned Sean Penn an Oscar for his portrayal of Harvey.

Neither the diminished capacity defense nor Dan White fared well in the years that followed the jury verdict. In 1981, roughly a

---

54. Weiss, *Double Play,* 467.
55. Shilts, *The Mayor of Castro Street,* 274.

year after the Dan White verdict, the State of California abolished the diminished capacity defense. Senate Bill 54 provided: "There shall be no defense of diminished capacity, diminished responsibility or irresistible impulse in a criminal action." The new statute stipulated that any expert testifying in the guilt phase of a criminal action "shall not testify as to whether the defendant had or did not have the required mental states, which include intent, knowledge or malice aforethought, for the crimes charged." Six months later, the California electorate approved Proposition 8, the "Victims' Bill of Rights," "which, as part of a package that has been called the Prosecutor's wish list," also abolished the defense of diminished capacity.[56]

Dan White served less than five years in prison. Two years after his release, he killed again; this time he took his own life. On October 21, 1985, he sat in his car in his garage with a hose attached to his exhaust pipe and took his own life. He left behind a wife and three small children. A final journal entry in his notebook read:[57]

Dearest Mary Ann,

My last journal entry is written to express my ever-faithful love for you and our children.

Your devoted husband

Danny

---

56. For an exposition of the effect of the legislative action and the enactment of Proposition 8, see Miguel A. Mendez, "Diminished Capacity in California: Premature Reports of Its Demise," *Stanford Law & Policy Review* 3 (January 1991): 216.
57. Weiss, *Double Play*, 471.

EIGHT

The von Bülow
Case[1]

IN THE 1980S, THE TRIALS of Claus von Bülow for the attempted murder of his wife Sunny fascinated the nation. The case resulted in Alan Dershowitz's book called *Reversal of Fortune*, which became a film that received several Academy Award nominations. As Prosecutor Stephen Famiglietti said, "This case has everything. It has money, sex, drugs; it has Newport, New York and Europe; it has nobility; it has maids, butlers, a gardener . . . this case is where the little man has the chance to glimpse inside and see how the rich live."[2]

It had all the elements one expects from great courtroom dramas; wealthy, fascinating and mysterious players; an alleged insidious crime, motivated by lust and greed; a fearless maid testifying against her rich and powerful employer; two of the earliest fully televised

---

1. This chapter relies most heavily on Professor Alan M. Dershowitz's description of the appellate process and of the new evidence unearthed by him and his team in *Reversal of Fortune: Inside the von Bulow Case* (Random House, 1986). Also relied upon were court transcripts, decisions, and a variety of secondary sources, including William Wright's book on the first von Bulow trial and the events leading up to it: *The von Bulow Affair* (Delacorte Press, 1983). In addition, magazine and newspaper articles were consulted, along with Internet accounts of the trials contained in Douglas Linder's "Famous American Trials" and user dg1952's post on April 17, 2008, "Claus von Bulow."
2. Dershowitz, *Reversal of Fortune*, xvii.

trials resulting in constant media coverage; a verdict of guilty on a strong circumstantial case; and newly discovered evidence which led to a second trial with a different result. The case was, above all, a mystery story in which the question was not just "who did it?" but "if a crime had been committed at all."[3]

The alleged victim was Sunny von Bülow, the beautiful, sensitive, shy, incredibly rich woman. Born Martha Sharp Crawford in Manassas, Virginia, in 1932, Sunny was the daughter of George Crawford, a utilities magnate who founded Columbia Gas, Lone Star Gas, and Northern Natural Gas.[4] He died when she was four years old, leaving Sunny and her mother with $700 million. Sunny went to the Chapin School in Manhattan and St. Timothy's prep in Maryland, but opted not to attend college. *Vogue* magazine listed her among the World's Ten Best-Dressed Women.[5] Her friend Truman Capote once described her as "very pretty, but a psychological wallflower."[6]

In 1957, when she was 24, Sunny married Prince Alfred von Auersperg, a handsome, impoverished German aristocrat. She became Princess von Auersperg and built a life in Germany. During their eight years of marriage, the couple had two children, Ala, the daughter, and Alexander, the son. Prince Alfred adapted poorly to married life and continued to be the same philanderer he had been before meeting Sunny. During a dinner party, Sunny met a handsome and charming bachelor of Danish and German ancestry named Claus von Bülow. They carried on a two-year secret affair. Eventually, Sunny divorced Prince Alfred, moved back to the United States, and married Claus in 1966. Her net worth was over $75 million.[7]

Claus von Bülow was born in Denmark in 1926. His given name was Claus Cecil Borberg. His father was a playwright and a suspected Nazi collaborator; his mother, Jonna von Bülow, came from a German Danish noble family. In order to associate himself with his

3. Ibid., xxiv.
4. Douglas Linder and Cynthia Ernst, "Famous American Trials," http://law2.umkc.edu/faculty/projects/ftrials/vonbulowlinks.html.
5. Obituary, "Sunny von Bülow," *The Telegraph*, December 7, 2008, http://telegraph.co.uk/news/obituaries/3660291/Sunny-von-Bulow.html.
6. Ibid.
7. Linder and Ernst, "Famous American Trials."

Sunny von Bülow at home with her pet dog.
© Condé Nast Archive/CORBIS

mother's more distinguished heritage—her father served as minister
of justice and as a member of the Danish parliament—Claus chose
her surname as his own. Claus graduated from Cambridge University
with a law degree at age nineteen and apprenticed in England as a
barrister. Before he met Sunny, he worked in London as an assistant
to oil tycoon J. Paul Getty. In his autobiography, Getty called von
Bülow "my right arm" and a "man with a razor sharp mind."[8] Tall,
well-mannered and debonair, Claus seldom showed any emotion. His
reputation in London was of a man of modest means who maneu-
vered himself into the highest social echelons.[9] A person who knew
him well once said of Claus, "He's a fake. He's always been a fake.
His name is a fake. His life is a fake. He has created a character that
he plays. Claus is *trompe l'oeil*."[10]

---

8. Obituary, "Sunny von Bülow."
9. Susan J. Drucker and Janice Platt Hunold, "The Claus von Bulow Retrial; Lights, Camera, Genre?" in *Popular Trials: Rhetoric, Mass Media, and the Law*, ed. Robert Hariman (The
University of Alabama Press, 1993), 133.
10. Dominick Dunne, "Fatal Charm: The Social Web of Claus von Bülow," *Vanity Fair*,
August 1985, http://www.vanityfair.com/magazine/1985/08/vonbulow198508.

Claus and Sunny had a daughter, Cosima, and the family lived in Newport, Rhode Island, at Clarendon Court, a twenty-room mansion overlooking Narragansett Bay. The couple also maintained a palatial, fourteen-room apartment on Fifth Avenue in New York City.

According to Claus, Sunny lost interest in sex but agreed to allow Claus to satisfy his needs elsewhere, as long as he was discreet. For Claus, this usually meant assignations with call girls. But in 1978, Claus began an affair with Alexandra Isles, a beautiful soap opera actress with a Danish aristocratic background. By mid-1979, Alexandra insisted that he get a divorce and marry her. When Claus hesitated, Alexandra gave him several ultimatums.

During this time, bad things started happening to Sunny. At Christmastime 1979, she suffered her first coma. Blood tests taken at the hospital indicated very low blood sugar. She was diagnosed with reactive hypoglycemia and advised by her doctors to follow a strict diet, which involved limiting her sugar intake and avoiding alcohol.

One year later, on the night of December 21, 1980, Sunny was found on her bathroom floor, having suffered her final, irreversible coma. Tests taken at the hospital again revealed very low blood sugar and very high levels of insulin. Sunny remained in a vegetative state for twenty-eight years, until her death in 2008. As it emerged later, the prosecution theory was simple. Claus was trapped in an unhappy marriage. He remained in love, however, with her money and the lifestyle it provided. Because he also loved Alexandra Isles, Claus faced a dilemma. If he divorced Sunny and married Alexandra, he would have to give up Sunny's money and abandon the luxurious lifestyle to which he was accustomed. If he remained with Sunny, he would have to give up Alexandra. Claus had to choose.

According to the prosecution, he did not choose. He wanted both Sunny's money and Alexandra's love. The only way to have them would be if Sunny died, so Claus secretly injected her with insulin, a hormone secreted naturally in the body. The source of insulin's presence in the body, by secretion or from an externally administered overdose, is almost impossible to detect. Claus's first murder attempt failed when Sunny recovered from her 1979 coma. But the plot seemed to succeed one year later.

Claus maintained that this theory was nonsense. Over the years, he claimed Sunny had turned to all manner of pills, drugs, and alcohol, stemming largely from depression and feelings of insecurity. Claus didn't know how Sunny became comatose, but the most likely explanation was that Sunny had caused her own coma deliberately or accidentally by injecting herself or by swallowing either insulin or barbiturates.

How did the police uncover the evidence to support their theory? They didn't. The evidence was procured and presented to them by a private investigator hired by Claus's stepchildren, Ala and Alex. While performing her routine duties, sometime after the first coma, Sunny's personal maid, Maria Schrallhammer, found a black bag that apparently belonged to Claus. In it, according to Maria, were various prescription drugs, barbiturates, and a vial marked "insulin." Maria reported what she found to Ala and to Alex. After Sunny's second coma, Ala and Alex hired a private investigator named Richard Kuh, a lawyer and former district attorney for New York County, who was recommended by Sunny's banker. Kuh conducted an investigation to determine whether Sunny's comas had been induced by criminal means.

Kuh interviewed all the crucial witnesses he could without alerting Claus to the family's suspicions. He talked with Maria Schrallhammer, the maid, as well as Ala and Alex and Sunny's banker, Morris Gurley. Then, while Claus was away, Kuh sent Alex with a private detective and a locksmith to Clarendon Court to search Claus's rooms. The black bag was found in a locked closet used by both Sunny and Claus. In the bag was a used syringe with some form of liquid encrusted on the point of the needle. Alex and the detective took other medicines from the house and brought everything to Kuh, who called the police and turned the materials over to them.

The combination of the laboratory tests done at the hospital on Sunny and on the black bag's contents as well as the testimony of Maria, the maid, and of Alex, Ala, and Sunny's banker led to the

Claus von Bülow (right) is led into Newport Superior Court to appear
at a pretrial hearing on charges of attempted murder.
© Bettmann/CORBIS

indictment of Claus von Bülow on July 6, 1981, on two counts of
assault with intent to murder, one for each of Sunny's two comas.

The first trial began on February 1, 1982, in Newport. Rhode
Island had just adopted a one-year experiment to allow television
and cameras in the courtroom. The von Bülow case became a media
spectacle.

More than sixty witnesses testified in a trial that would continue
for forty-seven days. Each day, the courtroom was packed with more
than one hundred spectators and thirty-eight reporters from the
print, radio, and television media. Another one hundred reporters
were housed in a building across the street. For four months, virtually
every local newspaper and television evening news program carried
a daily story on the von Bülow case. CNN broadcast the trial live to
a national audience, while the three major network affiliates reached
300,000 homes in Rhode Island with local in-depth reporting.

In January 1982, at the suggestion of Rhode Island Senator Clai-
borne Pell, Claus hired two high-profile attorneys, John Sheehan and

Herald Fahringer. The quiet, hardworking Sheehan was well-versed in the Rhode Island legal landscape, and the flamboyant Fahringer was best known for representing Jean Harris in the appeal of her murder conviction of Herman Tarnower, the "Scarsdale Diet" doctor. Sheehan was the main architect of the defense. According to the *Providence Journal*, it was Sheehan who "found and interviewed most of the defense witnesses, and who prepared most of the pretrial motions."[11] The flashier and more press-savvy Fahringer would take the lead in trying the case.

The defense made two important pretrial motions. First, they moved to have the black bag and its contents excluded as evidence on the ground that they were obtained by an unreasonable search and seizure under the Fourth Amendment as incorporated in the Fourteenth Amendment Due Process Clause. There is no question that if the police or any state law enforcement officers had gone to Clarendon Court without a warrant and taken the bag, it would have been an illegal search. There was also, at that point, no probable cause to obtain a warrant. But the search was done by private individuals, and not by the police or the State.

The Bill of Rights acts as a limit on state power and protects the public from government abuse. Kuh, Alex, and the private detective who accompanied Alex on the search were private actors. Could someone pay another party to break and enter, obtain evidence or information, and then deliver it to the police as a way of circumventing limitations on police conduct? The Rhode Island trial court said that yes, there was no Fourth Amendment violation, as long as the police were not part of the scheme. The defense's motion to suppress evidence was denied.

The second pretrial defense motion was to compel the disclosure of any notes made by Richard Kuh. Kuh claimed they were covered by the attorney-client privilege that protects from disclosure confidential communications between attorney and client. The Rhode Island court agreed and refused to compel production of the notes.

---

11. "The Defender," *Brown Alumni Magazine,* January/February 2003, http://www.brownalumnimagazine.com/content/view/1057/40/.

Were von Bülow to be convicted, these two legal issues would likely be the only grounds for reversal on an appeal.

During the opening arguments, Famiglietti, the prosecutor, portrayed Sunny's death as the result of "a clandestine and ingenious attempt by her husband, Claus von Bülow, to secretly murder her," with a drug that, "up until a few years ago, was undetectable in the human body."[12]

Fahringer, for the defense, countered with a portrayal of Claus as a patient and loving spouse who endured for years his wife's refusal to have sexual relations with him. "If there's one thing we really resent in this case," Fahringer told the jury, "it is the suggestion, the innuendo, that he was acting in an unhusbandly fashion."[13] Fahringer then described Sunny von Bülow as a woman who consumed "sweets and alcohol and daily . . . four to five packs of cigarettes, 20 aspirin, 24 laxative tablets and a variety of tranquilizers and other drugs including Valium, Seconal and barbiturates." Fahringer's explanation for Sunny's coma was a self-administered overdose of the barbiturate amobarbital. "What happened to her," he said, "was not anyone's fault but her own."[14]

In presenting its case, the prosecution essentially told the maid's story. In fact, they made Maria Schrallhammer their star witness. As Lieutenant John Reise, the Rhode Island state trooper who conducted the investigation, said, "If you believe her story, how could you think the guy was innocent?"[15]

She had been trained to be a "lady's maid" at a convent outside of Munich in Germany. She had performed domestic service for the family of Alfred von Krupp, the armaments manufacturer who used slave labor during the Nazi regime and was convicted of war crimes at Nuremberg. She then became Sunny's maid during Sunny's first marriage. From that moment on, Maria devoted her entire existence

12. Dudley Clendinen, "Prosecution and Defense Outline von Bulow Cases," *New York Times*, February 3, 1982, http://nytimes.com/1982/02/03/us/prosecution-and-defense-outline-von -bulow-cases.html.
13. Ibid.
14. Ibid.
15. Wright, *The von Bulow Affair*, 2.

to Sunny. She dressed her, listened to her, and watched over her. Husbands may come and go, children grow up and leave, but Maria was the constant in Sunny's life.

Maria described for the jury the first coma that occurred during the 1979 Christmas holidays. At about 8:00 P.M., Sunny retired for the night to the bedroom she shared with Claus. The next morning, Maria was on her way to the master bedroom when Claus told her that Sunny had a sore throat and that Maria should let her sleep. Five minutes later, Maria heard Sunny moaning, so she entered the bedroom. By this time, Claus was back in bed lying next to Sunny, who appeared to be unconscious. "Call the doctor," Maria told Claus. "Call her mother, she is not sleeping. I can't wake her up." Claus was unperturbed: "No, let her sleep." Maria left and then returned a half hour later. She saw no improvement and again implored Claus to call the doctor. Maria's entreaties and Claus's refusals continued throughout the day. At about 6:00 P.M., Maria came back and found that Sunny, still unconscious, was having difficulty breathing. Finally, Claus called a local Newport physician, Dr. Gailitis, who came, declared, "She's stopped breathing—call the fire department," and started cardiopulmonary resuscitation. He cleared her throat of vomit, administered mouth-to-mouth resuscitation, and saved her life. Sunny was rushed to the hospital, where she regained consciousness the next day. Despite her suspicions, Maria never told Sunny how her husband had acted. "I didn't want to go between married people," she explained. "I was only employee."[16]

It was this chilling account of those critical hours and how Claus refused to call a doctor that formed the basis for what the media, picking up on Fahringer's term, called von Bülow's "unhusbandly behavior."

During the year before the final coma, Maria had shared her suspicions with Alexander and with Sunny's mother, Mrs. Aitken. At one point, Mrs. Aitken confronted Claus about why he had waited so long to get help for Sunny. In response, Claus wrote a letter to Dr. Gailitis, who, it should be noted, was not Sunny's regular doctor

16. Dershowitz, *Reversal of Fortune*, 7.

and had seen her only twice,[17] asking him to vouch for his behavior. Claus's letter began:

Dear Dr. Gailitis,

My wife is making excellent progress and has fully recovered her physical strength. We are both most grateful to you. Now I need your professional opinion, preferably in writing.

My mother in law feels that I was remiss in not getting medical aide [sic] earlier in the day. In hindsight, it is naturally a question I asked myself repeatedly in the days following the crisis. The facts, as I have given them to you, can be recapitulated as follows. . . .

Von Bülow went on to describe how he had tended to his wife and kept "vigils" over her following her various ailments. Then Claus gave a timeline for the events of the day leading up to her coma. He spoke of how she had finally fallen asleep after days without sleep on the twenty-seventh. He mentioned that he had observed her breathing was regular and let her sleep through lunch. He indicated that he had called Dr. Gailitis at 6:00 P.M., immediately after hearing Sunny's breathing change to a "rattle." He closed the letter by asking the doctor:

Have I stated everything fairly? Was I to blame? By lunchtime on the 27th I had myself gone without sleep for 50 hours and my judgment may have been poor. I already have cause to be grateful to you, and I now need your opinion on this question, even if it turns out to be frank and unpalatable.

Sincerely yours,

Claus Bülow[18]

---

17. Wright, *The von Bulow Affair*, 85.
18. Ibid., 86.

Dr. Gailitis's reply was exactly what von Bülow wanted to hear:

The events leading to the catastrophic deterioration of Mrs. von Bülow's condition vomiting aspiration of gastric contents and cardio respiratory arrest were unpredictable.

There is no doubt in my mind that by recognizing the change in Mrs. von Bülow's condition and by alarming me you saved her life.[19]

The request for a written response from Dr. Gailitis suggests von Bülow wanted to create evidence that he could use to exonerate himself. It also allowed him to establish his own timeline of events. And finally, in Claus's mind, the letter pitted the word of Dr. Gailitis and himself against that of a mere servant such as Maria.[20] The letter would indeed play a significant role for Claus in the trial. But it would be a damaging one.

About two months later, Maria testified, she made another discovery. She was cleaning a walk-in closet off Claus von Bülow's bedroom in the New York City apartment, a closet that was shared by Claus and Sunny. She came across a traveling case that Claus used each week in traveling back and forth to Newport. The suitcase was open and, as she moved it, she noticed a small black vinyl zippered bag. She unzipped it. Inside were Valium, pills, a kind of paste and powder and a vial with liquid. The Valium had a prescription label made out to "Leslie Baxter," a name that was unfamiliar to Maria.

A few days later Maria brought the bag to Ala's apartment. They inspected the contents, took note of the labels, and removed samples from the paste and powder. They then put the vials back in the bag and returned it to Claus's closet. The samples were taken to the von Bülows' New York family doctor, Richard Stock, for analysis. The paste turned out to be Valium and the white powder was secobarbital, a barbiturate. Dr. Stock knew that Sunny took both these drugs because he had often prescribed them for her. But the form they

19. Ibid., 88.
20. Ibid., 88–89.

were in was strange. These drugs came in pill form. Why were they in a paste and powder, a form that was not generally available from pharmacies? And who was Leslie Baxter, the name on the Valium prescription? No one knew.

Dr. Stock now tried to discover the cause of Sunny's prior coma. He put her in the hospital and ran a battery of tests. The diagnosis was that she had a rather common condition called reactive hypoglycemia—a problem in the mechanisms that control the relationship between the body's natural insulin and its blood sugar. For diabetics, eating carbohydrates raises the blood sugar level. But in a patient with hypoglycemia, blood sugar is reduced after carbohydrates are consumed. So for Sunny, the recommendation was to keep to a common-sense diet and avoid large intakes of carbohydrates such as sweets, ice cream, and liquor. Since reactive hypoglycemia is not life-threatening, Maria recalled, everyone appeared to be relieved.

However, Maria kept her eye out for the mysterious black bag. Around Thanksgiving, she spotted it again while she was cleaning Claus von Bülow's room in the New York apartment. This time it was in a small white canvas sack that Claus had packed for family excursions to Newport. When Maria unzipped the black bag, she found something different and more ominous. In addition to the vials, she saw a small bottle marked "insulin" along with several needles and a syringe. She immediately called Alex and showed him the new bottle and the implements for injecting its contents. "Insulin, for what insulin?" she asked. "Mrs. von Bülow is not a diabetic. She doesn't need insulin."[21]

Maria went on to testify that this was not the first time she had seen syringes and needles. She remembered that many years earlier, in 1969, she saw Claus use these kinds of implements when he gave himself vitamin shots. She had never seen her lady in possession of syringes or needles.

Maria then testified about the events of Sunny's second coma. As Christmas approached, the family made arrangements to travel to Newport. Maria helped the family pack, and she got her third

21. Dershowitz, *Reversal of Fortune*, 13.

look at the black bag. As she was carrying the suitcase down in the elevator, she looked in the bag and again saw the "insulin" vial and the syringes. Two days later, Maria learned that Mrs. von Bülow had been hospitalized and was again unconscious. Maria traveled immediately to Newport. The doctors told Maria "there is no hope."

The defense tried to discredit Maria in cross-examination, but she held firm to her testimony. As one of the assistant prosecutors said, "Fahringer is a good lawyer, but he couldn't make a dent in Maria."[22] The maid's loyalty to her "lady" made her an even more appealing figure for the jury, and the media made the most of it, calling her "the iron maid" and "the maid of the century."

Claus's stepson, twenty-two-year-old Alexander, then took the stand. The young man testified for two days, and spent most of that time staring ahead to avoid looking at his stepfather.[23] He said that he was six at the time his mother met von Bülow and that he had always gotten along with "Uncle Claus." But as he grew older, he became suspicious. He told the court that he had never seen his mother on drugs, drunk, or disoriented, save for her two comas. He testified that Claus had once told him that he felt like a kept man, and that Sunny had prevented him from realizing his full potential in the business world. Alexander also provided a time line of the events leading up to his mother's coma. Famiglietti asked him, "Did your mother ever talk to you about her relationship with the defendant?" He said that she had spoken of divorcing him, but the reasons, according to her, were "too horrible to tell."[24] The conversation occurred, Alexander said, in November 1980, shortly after Thanksgiving. Famiglietti reminded the jury that this was about a month before Sunny's final coma.

Under cross-examination, Alexander stuck to his version of the events. When a frustrated Fahringer asked, "If you thought somebody was trying to murder your mother, wouldn't you have told her?" Alexander replied, "It seems to me that's not a very nice thing to accuse somebody of, unless you're absolutely sure."[25]

22. Ibid., 17.
23. Lally Weymouth, "The Case Against Claus," *New York Magazine*, March 8, 1982.
24. Wright, *The von Bulow Affair*, 218.
25. Ibid., 223.

Alex's time line of Sunny's second coma was as follows: After arriving in Newport, Sunny spent Saturday decorating the Christmas tree. The family had an early dinner. Sunny insisted on having a large ice cream sundae with caramel sauce for dessert. Throughout the evening, Alex noticed that his mother's speech was slurred. When she grew visibly weaker, Alex picked her up and carried her to her bedroom. The next morning, Claus went for an early morning walk and afterwards mingled with the family. When Sunny was still not up at 11:00 A.M., Claus and Alex went to her bedroom and found Sunny lying unconscious on the marble bathroom floor. She was rushed to the Newport hospital. Her temperature was eighty-one degrees and her pulse was a very slow thirty-six beats per minute. She suffered cardiac arrest. Two doctors tried to resuscitate her, but she never regained consciousness.

A few weeks later, Alex and Ala met in the New York apartment of Sunny's mother. Also present was Sunny's banker and family confidante, Morris Gurley. This was a secret meeting to vent suspicions about Claus. Should they leave bad enough alone or risk an investigation? No one wanted a scandal. It was decided they would move slowly. The first step was to retain an experienced criminal lawyer to conduct a discreet but thorough inquiry.

Alex described for the jury how they hired Richard Kuh, and how Alex and a private detective found the black bag in a locked closet at the Newport mansion. Inside the bag, they did not find the vial labeled "insulin" which Maria claimed to have seen earlier. There were three hypodermic needles in the bag. Two were sealed in their original containers. One was loose and appeared to have been used. Maybe this was the attempted murder weapon, they thought. Inside the bag they also found a vial of Dalmane bearing a prescription label in the name of Claus von Bülow. That label, the equivalent of Claus's fingerprints, seemed to establish that the bag belonged to Claus. Alexander told the court that he told his brother and sister what the investigators had found this time. Before leaving, they gathered together all the items they had found in several other rooms in the house, including vials found in Sunny's medicine cabinet and night table and in Claus's coat pockets and bathroom. For convenience, and this detail is important, they placed everything they had gathered into the black bag. They then took the bag and its contents back to New York.

A few days later, the contents of the bag were given to the family doctor, Richard Stock, who sent them to a laboratory. When the test results came back they provided the last important piece of the puzzle. The loose needle had in fact been used. The residue that was left on the tip of the needle contained a high concentration of insulin along with traces of Valium and amobarbital. By the time these results came in, Dr. Stock had also learned that the tests done on Sunny at the Newport hospital right after she was admitted had shown unusually high levels of insulin in her blood.

The family concluded they had the smoking gun; the insulin-encrusted needle. They had Claus's fingerprints on the gun because his name was on the Dalmane prescription in the black bag. And they had the "bullet wound," so to speak, in the high level of insulin found in Sunny's blood. "Leslie Baxter," it was discovered, was a prostitute that Claus had frequented. Although the black bag was found in a closet used by both Sunny and Claus, the only reasonable assumption was that the bag belonged to Claus.

With the evidence contained in the black bag, along with Claus's pattern of "unhusbandly" behavior during Sunny's first coma, the prosecution's strong case was nearly complete. All that remained was the medical testimony. For this to be effective, there needed to be expert testimony that Sunny's two comas were caused by insulin injections as well as evidence that Claus had a clear motive to kill Sunny.

The most important expert witness to testify for the prosecution was Dr. George Cahill, a professor of medicine at Harvard Medical School. Cahill was the director of a world-renowned center that specialized in blood sugar disorders, and had written the leading books and articles on the subject. He was considered the world's most respected expert on blood sugar; the prosecution described him as "the expert's expert—the guy that endocrinologists go to when they're baffled."[26]

26. Dershowitz, *Reversal of Fortune*, 25.

With Cahill, the prosecution had a witness who could explain to the jury in laymen's terms why the laboratory tests showed conclusive medical proof that Mrs. von Bülow's comas could only have been caused by an injection of insulin.[27] These laboratory tests showed that when Sunny was admitted to the hospital for her first coma, her blood sugar was down to forty-one milligrams. Even after she was then given glucose "pushes" (intravenous sugar), her blood sugar continued to go down. Just under four hours after her admission, her blood sugar had gone from forty-one to twenty milligrams.

Dr. Cahill was asked whether he had "an opinion within a reasonable degree of medical certainty as to the cause of this woman's coma." He said that his opinion was that the first coma was caused by "exogenous insulin," that is, insulin from outside the body. In other words, an injection of insulin. Dr. Cahill explained that the continued lowering of the patient's blood sugar even after administration of substantial amounts of glucose "can only be due to insulin or an insulin-like factor telling the tissues in her body to consume glucose at a rapid rate." Cahill excluded "all the other possible causes, with the exception of exogenous insulin."[28]

He testified as well that the laboratory evidence concerning the second coma was even more compelling than the evidence concerning the first. Mrs. von Bülow's blood sugar upon admission was again low; twenty-nine milligrams. But there was also a serum insulin level that the prosecution claimed was taken from the same blood sample that produced the sugar level. That insulin level was extraordinarily high; 216 micro-units per milliliter, the normal range being under 15. The combination of low blood sugar and high insulin level supported the prosecutor's theory that her low blood sugar was *caused* by high insulin—an amount far higher than her body would produce naturally. Dr. Cahill emphasized again that only exogenous insulin could explain the simultaneous low blood sugar and high insulin levels.

---

27. Ibid.
28. Ibid., 26.

The defense could not shake this testimony. A defense expert did testify later that factors other than insulin had probably caused the comas, but he had to admit that he could not exclude exogenous insulin as the cause of one or both comas.

When the prosecution's expert—indeed the expert's expert—is certain of the cause and the defense expert cannot exclude that cause, then it is most likely that the jury will be persuaded by the prosecution's witness. But a question remained. If the cause of the comas was insulin injections, who did it? Was it Claus or was it Sunny herself? The prosecution's answer was provided by evidence of motive.

Sunny's banker, Morris Gurley, told the court that he did for Sunny financially what Maria the maid did for her personally. He estimated Sunny's fortune at approximately $75 million, $45 million of which was held in trust. As the officer at Chemical Bank in charge of trust management, he handled this money for Sunny and Sunny's mother. Gurley testified that if Sunny died, Claus would get $14 million, the Clarendon Court mansion, the New York apartment, all the lavish furnishings, plus control over charitable trusts and a fixed income from other trusts. A widowed Claus von Bülow would live very well.

Gurley also testified that Claus had exhibited an acute interest in Sunny's will and trusts, especially in the years leading up to her comas. Gurley also told the jury that Claus had brought little income into the marriage and had not earned much during his fourteen years with Sunny.[29]

If there were a divorce, Clause would get about $120,000 a year in income from an irrevocable trust that Sunny had set up for him. Not bad, but a mere pittance compared to what he would inherit if Sunny died. And if there were a divorce, he would lose Clarendon Court and the New York apartment.

Gurley also implied that Ala, Alexander, and Cosima could be eliminated from suspicion of complicity. Complicated tax schemes involving the strategic use of charitable donations, he explained, allowed fortunes to skip generations, so that when a wealthy par-

29. Ibid., 28–29; Wright, *The von Bulow Affair*, 272–4.

ent died, a fortune can be passed on to their descendants without being taxed by the government. The way this system was set up, Sunny's children were in line to inherit money from another relative and would not inherit their mother's fortune until twenty-one years after her death.[30] It was Claus, and Claus alone, who stood to gain in the event of Sunny's death.

The prosecution next called Claus's former mistress to the stand. Alexandra Isles, the soap opera actress, testified that by March 1979, before the first coma, she and Claus were talking about marriage and the necessity for Claus to get a divorce. She indicated that she had said to him several times: "Get a divorce or I'm out of here." At a critical point in her testimony Isles was asked these questions:

Q: Do you still love the defendant?

A: [Sadly, after a long pause] I don't know.

Q: At one time you thought the charges against Claus were, as you put it then, "a pack of nonsense." Do you still think the attempted murder charges are a pack of nonsense?

A: I don't know.[31]

For the jury to hear the defendant's lover express uncertainty about her belief in his innocence was a devastating blow to von Bülow. [32]

That was the prosecution's case. It was strong, and everything fit together.

The defense was unable to dismantle the prosecution's evidence. They tried to portray von Bülow as a caring, independently wealthy husband who loved his wife and had no reason to kill her. Among their first witnesses was Robert Biastre, the couple's Newport butler, who said that Claus was always concerned for his wife's welfare. The

30. Dershowitz, *Reversal of Fortune*, 28–29; Wright, *The von Bulow Affair*, 273.
31. Dershowitz, *Reversal of Fortune*, 32.
32. Ibid.

family chauffeur testified that he drove Mrs. von Bülow to two doctors on Central Park South in New York, in addition to her regular doctor, and sometimes to drug stores to get prescriptions filled.[33] But under cross-examination, the chauffeur could not remember the names of the doctors or their addresses.

The defense tried to get the jury to believe that Claus had no interest in Sunny's fortune because he had a lucrative career as a businessman.[34] Fahringer called Mark Millard, a New York investment banker for whom von Bülow acted as a consultant. Millard testified that von Bülow could earn an annual salary of up to $200,000 as an upper-management executive. But on cross-examination, Millard admitted that the financial services company for which Claus sometimes consulted paid him only $17,600 in 1980 and 1981, for reimbursement of travel expenses.[35]

Fahringer's most difficult task was to convince the jury that Sunny had injected herself with insulin. The most convincing witness for this would have been Claus himself. But the defense team decided not to have him testify. Fahringer feared that his client might come across to the jury as haughty and condescending. "Claus von Bülow did not take the witness stand because we didn't think the prosecution had made a sufficient case against him," Fahringer said, "But it's no secret that his personality was another problem."[36]

Opting against having the defendant testify can be a good strategy. But in this case, it was not. One school of thought is that if you are not going to put a defendant on the stand, then no other witnesses should be called. A defense case with witnesses but no appearance by the defendant, Alan Dershowitz has written, "serves to underline to the jury the fact that the defendant must have something to hide."[37]

33. Dudley Clendinen, "After 11 Weeks of Trial, von Bulow Opens Defense," *New York Times*, March 3, 1982, http://www.nytimes.com/1982/03/03/us/after-11-weeks-of-trial-von-bulow-opens-defense.html.
34. Scott Patrick Johnson, *Trials of the Century: An Encyclopedia of Popular Culture and the Law* Volume I (ABC-CLIO, 2010), 528–9.
35. "Witness Says Mrs. von Bulow Talked of Shots," *New York Times*, March 4, 1982, http://www.nytimes.com/1982/03/04/us/witness-says-mrs-von-bulow-talked-of-shots.html.
36. Dershowitz, *Reversal of Fortune*, 35–36.
37. Ibid., 36.

The von Bülow defense did call other witnesses. Around the testimony of Joy O'Neill, Sunny's private exercise trainer, they based their contention that Sunny could have injected herself with the insulin that caused her comas. O'Neill testified that after instructing Sunny over a four-year period "on the average of five days a week," she and Sunny had become "like sisters."[38] During one conversation she had with Mrs. von Bülow at the end of 1978 at the exercise studio, Miss O'Neill indicated that after she had confessed concern about gaining weight, Sunny had said, "What you probably need is a shot of insulin or vitamin B. At least then you could eat everything you want, including sweets." O'Neill added that Sunny also told her, "It's easy to inject yourself."[39]

O'Neill's credibility was decimated during cross-examination. There were no witnesses to O'Neill's alleged conversations with Sunny. What's more, the prosecution proved that the exercise studio had no record of Sunny being trained by O'Neill "five times a week" for four years, as she had claimed. In fact, the records showed O'Neill had only taught Sunny a handful of times, and never once during 1978. And the proprietor of the exercise studio, Manya Kahn, said Miss O'Neill had been dismissed, was not qualified to teach private classes, and was allowed to do so only on an emergency basis.[40] O'Neill denied these allegations, but the damage was done.

During summation, the defense tried to emphasize that there were other likely contributing factors for Sunny's coma, such as a hypoglycemic reaction to sweets. And Fahringer asked the jury, "Is there any question in anyone's mind in this courtroom that Martha von Bülow had a drinking problem?" Unfortunately, the defense had not called a single witness to confirm that Sunny had such a problem.[41]

In his summation, Famiglietti pointed out to the jury how the defense had altered its theories throughout the trial whenever the evidence refuted their claims. He described the contention that Sunny's

---

38. "Witness Says Mrs. von Bulow Talked of Shots."
39. Ibid.
40. Ibid.
41. Wright, *The von Bulow Affair*, 320.

coma could have been induced by means other than an injection by Claus as a "multiple choice" defense; if the jury didn't care for the idea that Sunny induced the coma herself, then maybe she had a hypoglycemic reaction to eggnog. If not that, then maybe, as Joy O'Neill had suggested, Sunny's coma was a result of her trying to lose weight. "Or perhaps," Famiglietti said, "it was none of the above. Perhaps she was hit by a meteorite from outer space."[42]

Addressing the defense's portrayal of von Bülow as sophisticated and smart, Famiglietti said, "So are his crimes. He was ingenious enough to paint himself as a loving husband while he was having an affair with Alexandra Isles and to try to establish that his wife was an abuser of alcohol and drugs."[43]

As the first trial neared its end, the media fervor surrounding von Bülow intensified. While the jury deliberated, and public opinion seemed decidedly against him, vendors sold "Free Claus" T-shirts for ten dollars apiece outside the courtroom.[44] On the marquee of a movie theater facing the courthouse, someone had replaced the name of the current movie with the words "Free Claus."[45] Of these displays, Kuh remarked that he "smelled the fine hand of a public relations firm."[46] Nonetheless, unlike the average anonymous criminal, von Bülow became "familiar"—and something of a celebrity. Some admired the refined, patrician figure Claus cut on camera. They concluded he was incapable of committing such a heinous crime. It was a view some members of the jury may have shared. As one of them later admitted in an interview, "When you walk by the man every day, this isn't just a figure, this is someone you start to get to know."[47]

The jury took six days to reach their verdict. They pored over the medical evidence and all the testimony of the doctors. They eliminated, one by one, all the people besides Claus they thought *could* have injected Sunny. One juror said, "The only ones we didn't suspect

42. Ibid., 323.
43. Ibid., 324.
44. Ibid., 333.
45. Ibid.
46. Ibid.
47. Ibid., 343.

were the dogs."[48] They discounted the testimony of defense witnesses who suggested that Sunny may have injected herself. Noting the discrepancies between von Bülow's recounting of the timeline and events of the first coma, and Maria's description, they asked to hear Maria's testimony again. They also gave great weight to von Bülow's letter to Dr. Gailitis, concluding that it was an attempt to get the doctor on record to absolve him of guilt. The jurors voted until they reached unanimity. The last juror to find von Bülow guilty later said in an interview, "I kept thinking Cosima has no mother; if we find him guilty, she'll have no father."[49]

On March 16, as a motionless von Bülow looked on, the jury pronounced him guilty of two counts of attempted murder.

Claus von Bülow was sentenced on May 7, 1982. TV cameras, reporters and pro-Claus groupies, called "Clausettes," were gathered outside the courthouse. Inside the courtroom was a new face: Cosima von Bülow. Not quite fifteen years old, she was making her first public appearance, shedding her anonymity in support for her father.[50] The prosecutor, Famiglietti, attacked her appearance as Claus's "blatant attempt to evoke compassion and pity for himself."[51]

Judge Thomas H. Needham sentenced von Bülow to thirty years in prison: ten years on the first count and twenty years on the second. Claus was freed on one million dollars bail, which he raised through his assets and with the help of friends.[52]

At this point, Alan Dershowitz entered this drama. First in his class at Yale Law School and editor-in-chief of the *Yale Law Journal*, Dershowitz was later appointed to the Harvard Law faculty, where at age twenty-eight he became a full professor, the youngest in the school's history. Although a full-time teacher at Harvard, Dershowitz occasionally took criminal defense appeals. He was known as a dedicated defender of civil rights and had a reputation for being aggressive and very, very smart. At their first meeting, von Bülow

---

48. Ibid., 338.
49. Ibid., 339.
50. Ibid., 352.
51. Ibid., 352–3.
52. Ibid., 358.

told Dershowitz, "I need the best lawyer I can get. I am absolutely innocent and my civil liberties have been egregiously violated."[53]

Dershowitz agreed to handle von Bülow's appeal to the Rhode Island Supreme Court. An excellent appellate lawyer himself, Dershowitz assembled a staff comprised of about twenty of his brightest Harvard law students. He divided them up into teams—the "insulin team," the "black bag team," the "needle team," the "self-injection versus other person-injection team," the "illegal search team," and the "Kuh notes team."

With Dershowitz now leading the defense, Fahringer withdrew from the case. Von Bülow retained Sheehan for his expertise with the Rhode Island judicial system.

In order to overturn von Bülow's conviction, Dershowitz faced two legal challenges. First, he had to show that the search of von Bülow's closet and belongings and the finding of the black bag and its contents constituted an illegal search and seizure. He had to get around the lower court finding that the search was done by private persons and not by officers of the state.

The second challenge Dershowitz faced involved obtaining access to private investigator Kuh's interview notes, which were never disclosed, either to the defense or to the prosecution. Dershowitz knew they could be vitally important in discovering the truth. Suppose, for example, Kuh's notes showed that when he interviewed Maria, she never mentioned seeing a bottle that said "insulin" on the label. Contemporaneous notes would tend to show that her later testimony of seeing insulin was concocted *after* she learned about the results of Sunny's hospital tests showing high levels of insulin. The lower court held that the notes were not discoverable because of the attorney-client privilege. After reviewing the trial record, Dershowitz realized that he had an additional argument, one that had not been made by Fahringer.

At the trial, the defense had called to the stand a family chauffeur who testified that he had driven Sunny to various doctors and pharmacies for prescription drugs. In rebuttal, the prosecution called

53. Dershowitz, *Reversal of Fortune*, 51.

Richard Kuh, who referred to his notes to testify that the chauffeur made statements that contradicted the chauffeur's trial testimony. In essence, then, Kuh was allowed to use the privilege as a "shield" to prevent disclosures that might have helped the defense, while at the same time using the allegedly privileged information as a sword to help the prosecution. Dershowitz argued that if there is a privilege, it was waived when Kuh used his notes during his testimony.

There were difficulties with both these points. The search and seizure issue was a guilty man's argument ("You got the goods on me but you did it wrong."). And as for Kuh's notes, even though Dershowitz might be successful in procuring them, they might not produce anything worthwhile.

Dershowitz would, nevertheless, press these arguments. But he wanted to do more. Research into decisions of the Rhode Island Supreme Court showed that it tended to reverse convictions when there were indications that the defendant might really be innocent. If the defendant appeared guilty, the court often ignored technical legal arguments.

So, as Dershowitz explained, he wanted to let the court know that Claus might really be innocent. With this goal in mind, Dershowitz and his staff embarked on a root-and-branch reexamination of the prosecution's case. They examined every piece of medical evidence and every bit of testimony.[54]

They uncovered evidence that Sunny had for many years used all manner of drugs and that she had taken them by mouth and by injection. One of the witnesses who provided an affidavit to that effect after the verdict in the first trial was the celebrated author, Truman Capote. He told Dershowitz's investigators that he had known Sunny for many years and they often had lunch together. Capote stated that he had once complained to Sunny that his every-other-day visits to the doctor for vitamin B-12 injections were disrupting his writing. "Why don't you inject yourself?" said Sunny. "Once you do it,

---

54. What follows is taken from Professor Dershowitz's account of the steps that he and his team followed and the discoveries that ultimately secured von Bülow's acquittal at his retrial. See Dershowitz, *Reversal of Fortune*, 72–80.

there's nothing to it." Capote hesitated, but Sunny persisted. She said, "I'll teach you,"[55] . . . and she did. They went to Capote's apartment where Sunny took a small black zippered bag out of her purse. Sunny opened it and inside were three disposable needles. She took out a syringe and injected herself in the arm with distilled water. Capote and Sunny continued to have lunch together from time to time, and on some occasions they injected drugs together. Sunny told him, "I have been giving myself amphetamines for a long time." She told him she had found a new concoction that was very relaxing. "You mix Demerol and amphetamines together as an injection." Capote's story was confirmed by others; some of whom said that Capote had discussed Sunny's drug habit long before either of her two comas.

Capote's revelations, of course, suggested that the black bag belonged to, or was regularly used by, Sunny, and not Claus. But he still needed an explanation for the so-called fingerprints, the Dalmane pills found in the bag that had Claus's name on the prescription label. To get it, Dershowitz went back to the trial testimony. Both Alexander and the detective who accompanied him testified to finding and seizing the black bag. Alex testified that the Dalmane bottle of pills with Claus's name was in the bag. But the detective testified that only he had handled any of the materials found in the black bag, and that Alex did not touch anything at all. The detective remembered finding "two containers, one containing a liquid and one a dry substance, a powder." But he did not recall seeing "any containers with pills inside the black bag." Nor did he see a vial "in the black bag with a prescription on it."

Since the detective's primary task was to find evidence linking Claus von Bülow to Sunny's coma, it would be quite surprising if the detective had actually found the most incriminating piece of evidence, the telltale vial with the prescription for Claus von Bülow, and then proceeded to forget that singularly significant piece of evidence.

---

55. Gioia Diliberto, "Truman Capote's Most Startling Story: He Says Claus von Bulow is Innocent," *People Magazine*, May 31, 1982, http://www.people.com/people/archive/article/0,,20082283,00.html.

What is more likely is that the Dalmane bottle of pills with Claus's name on was found elsewhere in the rooms or clothing or cabinets. The search, it should be emphasized, was conducted in an extremely haphazard manner. No inventory was made. No photographs were taken. No fingerprints were preserved. And most important, *all* the items found during the entire search, which included items found outside the black bag in various rooms, were "all mixed together" and placed in the black bag for "convenience." No record was made of which items had been found *in* the bag and which had been *outside it* before they were comingled.

All this strengthened the likelihood that the bag was being used by Sunny, not Claus. At the very least, it removed Claus's "fingerprints," the Dalmane bottle, from the smoking gun.

If that part of the prosecution case was weak, perhaps the rest of it was weak. The assumption that the insulin-encrusted needle, the "murder weapon," was injected into Sunny, also received careful scrutiny.

The evidence describing the insulin-encrusted needle found in the black bag was shown to several of the world's leading forensic experts. They all came to the same conclusion, citing four reasons why the needle was not and could not have been injected into Sunny.

First, if the needle had been injected, any routine examination of it would have disclosed traces of human tissue and blood elements in addition to insulin. But no such material was found on this needle.

Second, amobarbital was found on the needle, but that highly corrosive drug could not have been injected under anyone's skin without leaving enormous and easily visible welts, called barbiturate burns, at the site of the injection. These welts produce oozing and sloughing and could not possibly have escaped even superficial examination. Mrs. von Bülow's body had been searched for injection marks when she was admitted to the hospital. None were found.

Third, Valium was found on the needle in the black bag, but no traces of Valium turned up on the drug tests performed on Mrs. von Bülow.

Finally, the fact that "crystalline encrustations" were found on the outside of the needle near the tip is "inconsistent with injection." They could only have been produced by the needle having been "dipped into a solution." That conclusion, the experts pointed out, could be confirmed by a simple experiment. When a needle is injected, "withdrawal of the needle from under the skin serves to cleanse its surface of drug encrustations." In simple language, the skin surrounding the needle would act like a cotton swab; it would wipe the needle clean—and push all the residue up to the top. "Thus there would be no residue where the needle went in and came out of the skin." The only drug residue that might be visible after injection would be located "at the lever fitting of the needle, that is, the point of attachment of the needle to the syringe." The encrustations at the tip of the needle meant that the needle was "dipped" into a solution, and was not injected.

Dershowitz had what he needed; proof that the used needle was not and could not possibly be the so-called murder weapon. The "smoking gun" shot only blanks.

For a thorough reexamination of the prosecution's case, however, it must be shown that the encrustation on the needle was really insulin. The laboratory that tested the needle, BioScience Labs, found that the encrustation contained insulin, amobarbital, and Valium. The BioScience laboratory worksheets, data, and findings were shown to several experts and again the experts were unanimous. The test results on the needle showed no presence of insulin.

How was that possible? It turns out that when needle washings containing amobarbital and Valium, but not insulin, are placed in saline solution, they often produce a false positive result for insulin; that is, they falsely show the presence of insulin when none is there.

To prove this hypothesis, a doctor prepared five different needle washings and sent them to BioScience just as the washing from the "murder weapon" had been sent. Two of the experimental washings contained insulin, amobarbital, Valium, and saline solution; one contained only saline solution; the remaining two contained amobarbital, Valium, and saline solution but no insulin.

When the BioScience report came back, it confirmed the hypothesis: the two washings that contained amobarbital, Valium, and saline solution—*but absolutely no insulin*—both came back with *false positive readings for insulin*.

So what was left of the prosecution's case? There was still the so-called bullet wound. If there was no insulin, why did the hospital tests done on Sunny immediately after her second coma show high insulin levels? In fact, levels so high that the prosecution experts testified that the coma could only have been caused by an insulin injection. For this, Dershowitz and his team rechecked the hospital tests.

Again, tests were done by BioScience Labs. Again, the conclusions were unanimous. Dr. Arthur Rubenstein, chairman of the Department of Medicine at the prestigious University of Chicago Medical School, concluded that the high insulin level found in Sunny's blood "may not be a valid result." And Dr. Harold Lebovitz, professor of medicine and head of endocrinology and diabetes at Downstate Medical Center in New York, concluded that the insulin reading reported by BioScience "is not a valid result." These doctors relied on insulin readings every day in their practice and research. They accepted certain scientific safeguards. One such safeguard, widely employed in the profession, is that before an insulin level can readily be relied on, the blood sample must be tested several times and the insulin levels obtained must correspond to each other within acceptable limits (plus or minus ten percent). In the test performed by BioScience, there were four different readings, but no two of them even came close to corresponding within the required percentages. One reading was 216 serum insulin level; another was 0.8; a third was 350 measure; and the fourth was recorded as "NSC," meaning "non-significant counts." Citing these widely diverse results, the experts indicated that "it is impossible scientifically to determine which of the discrepant values is 'correct.'"

On a retrial, not much would be left of the prosecution's case. Now the problem was to win the appeal in order to get a retrial.

An appeal is based on the record. The material indicating that Claus may have been innocent was not on the record but was, in part, new evidence that likely should have been discovered before the first trial. According to the rules, such evidence can't be put before the appellate court. So Dershowitz had to go back to the trial court, that is, the Circuit Court, and move to vacate the conviction on the ground of newly discovered evidence.

But that was not what Dershowitz wanted. He wanted the Rhode Island Supreme Court to realize that Claus von Bülow might well be innocent. So he bent the rules a bit.

First, he drafted a motion to vacate the petition based on newly discovered evidence. It included all the discoveries just catalogued and affidavits from witnesses and experts supporting the new developments. He sent it to the Rhode Island Supreme Court and asked that body to decide when to send it to the trial court. He told the Supreme Court, in effect: Look, we've obtained all this new evidence showing innocence. We could file it in the trial court, but we shouldn't have two actions in two separate courts at the same time. So we'll wait and file the new trial motion after the appeal is decided. But there is a time limit on motions to vacate, and by the time the appeal is decided, it might be too late. So why don't you hang on to this motion and send it down to the trial court when you think it's appropriate. Of course, if you want to take a peek at our new stuff, that would be okay, too.

Second, Dershowitz framed a legal argument that made the new evidence relevant on the appeal. His legal argument was that pure circumstantial evidence was not sufficient to convict, if another equally persuasive alternative theory supported by the facts suggests innocence. There was some limited Rhode Island precedent that could be cited to support this proposition. Dershowitz also attached much of the new evidence to his brief and talked about it in his appellate argument.

On March 15, 1983, one year after von Bülow had hired him, Dershowitz filed the brief. "This was the longest, most complex brief I had ever written," Dershowitz wrote. "But then again, this was the longest criminal trial in Rhode Island history."[56]

The brief pulled no punches. It described Sunny as "a self-destructive, deeply depressed and addictive woman who experimented with drugs not prescribed for her, and who continued to engage in

---

56. Dershowitz, *Reversal of Fortune*, 128.

life-threatening behavior after experiencing life-threatening emergencies and after being warned by doctors to desist."[57]

It laid out the newly discovered evidence and argued that use of Kuh's notes at the trial was a waiver of the attorney-client privilege and that the notes should be made available to the defense. As for the claim of an illegal search and seizure, Dershowitz claimed that although the initial search may have been valid, the use of the objects of the search by the police and the prosecution constituted State action that required a warrant.

Then came the oral arguments. Dershowitz alone stood before the court to make his case for von Bülow and answer the judges' questions. It was the first time the Supreme Court of Rhode Island had allowed television cameras in its courtrooms. As von Bülow watched from a hotel room, Dershowitz presented his arguments before the five judges. He ended by asking the court to "grant Claus von Bülow the tools necessary to establish the whole truth—a new trial with full access to all available information at which the whole truth and not a version edited by interested parties can be heard."[58]

The Supreme Court of Rhode Island reversed the conviction. The court ruled that although the search that turned up the black bag was valid because it was done by private parties, the fact that the police sent the bag and its contents out for testing was State action and therefore a violation of the search-and-seizure provisions of both the federal and the Rhode Island State Constitution. Before sending out the pills for testing, the state police should have obtained a search warrant.[59]

The court also ruled that Kuh's notes should have been given to the defense. It concluded that use of the notes to benefit the prosecution constituted a waiver and that the trial judge was wrong in finding that the Kuh documents were protected from disclosure by the attorney-client privilege.[60]

57. Ibid., 129.
58. dg1952, post on *Watching True Crime Stories: Sleeping With The Enemy*, "Claus von Bulow."
59. State v. von Bulow, 475 A.2d 995 (R.F. 1984); http://law.justia.com/cases/rhode-island/supreme-court/1984/475-a-2d-995.html.
60. Ibid.

Claus von Bülow (center) is flanked by attorneys (left to right)
Alan Dershowitz, John Sheehan, and Thomas Puccio as he leaves
Providence Superior Court during his retrial.
© Bettmann/CORBIS

Kuh's notes were delivered to the Dershowitz staff. They
turned out to be very helpful for the defense. Maria Schrallhammer described to Kuh in detail what she had found in the black bag
when she opened it after the first coma. Kuh's notes say she saw
"Valium, several bottles but no labels—all scraped off." But she had
made no mention of insulin and no mention of syringes or needles.
The notes also revealed that Alex told the family banker within days
of his mother's coma that Alex was "ready to provoke a fight with
Claus"; that Alex was "eager not to lose Clarendon Court—which
was willed to Claus—under any circumstances"; that Ala "has never
gotten along with Claus"; and most importantly, that before the family decided to prosecute Claus, they discussed buying him off and
getting him to renounce all interest in his wife's will.

The State retried Claus von Bülow. At the second trial, von Bülow
was represented by Thomas Puccio, a tough, Brooklyn-born attorney

and former federal prosecutor with a reputation for winning verdicts for high-profile clients. Puccio used the Kuh notes to effectively cross-examine Maria and Alex and then presented the new evidence that Dershowitz and his team had unearthed. On June 10, 1985, von Bülow was acquitted on all charges.

In a review of Dershowitz's book *Reversal of Fortune*, the *New York Times* would later call Claus's acquittal, "Pulling Victory Out of the Black Bag."[61]

After the acquittal, the court battles and family turmoil continued. Ala and Alexander filed a $56 million lawsuit to bar Claus from inheriting Sunny's fortune. For supporting her father in his retrial, Cosima von Bülow was disinherited by her grandmother and stood to lose $30 million. In return for Cosima being reinstated into her grandmother's will, Claus dropped his claim against Sunny's estate.[62]

Claus von Bülow currently lives in London. Alex, Ala, and Cosima each inherited $45 million from Sunny's mother and their grandmother.

Martha "Sunny" von Bülow died in a New York nursing home on December 6, 2008. She lived for twenty-eight years in an irreversible coma, unaware of the pivotal but silent role she played in both trials.

61. Nora Ephron, "Pulling Victory Out of the Black Bag," *New York Times,* June 15, 1986, http://www.nytimes.com/1986/06/15/books/pulling-victory-out-of-the-black-bag.html.
62. dg1952, post on *Watching True Crime Stories: Sleeping with the Enemy,* "Claus von Bulow."

NINE

The McMartin Preschool Child Sex Abuse Case: A National Disgrace[1]

LOCATED IN MANHATTAN BEACH, AN affluent suburb of Los Angeles, the McMartin Preschool had cared for the children of the community's most respected families and had a stellar reputation. Parent after parent indicated that their children never wanted to come home.[2] And so, couples whose children had not yet been born made

---

1. This chapter relies heavily on the authoritative accounts of the McMartin Preschool sexual abuse trials contained in Paul and Shirley Eberle, *The Abuse of Innocence: The McMartin Preschool Trial* (Prometheus Books, 1993); Richard Beck, *We Believe the Children: A Moral Panic in the 1980s* (PublicAffairs, 2015); Debbie Nathan and Michael Snedeker, *Satan's Silence: Ritual Abuse and the Making of a Modern American Witch Hunt* (Author's Choice Press, 2001). It also draws from trial court transcripts, judicial opinions, and scholarly articles on coercive and suggestive interviewing of alleged child victims. Also relied upon were a variety of secondary sources including media accounts of McMartin and other daycare child abuse cases as well as Internet descriptions such as those contained in Douglas Linder, "Famous American Trials," http://law2.umkc.edu/faculty/projects/ftrials/mcmartin/mcmartin.html; and Douglas Linder, "The McMartin Preschool Abuse Trial: A Commentary," (2003), http://law2.umkc.edu/faculty/projects/ftrials/mcmartin/mcmartinaccount.html.
2. David Shaw, "Where Was Skepticism in Media?: Pack journalism and hysteria marked early coverage of the McMartin case. Few journalists stopped to question the believability of the prosecution's charges," *Los Angeles Times*, January 19, 1990, http://articles.latimes.com/1990-01-19/news/mn-226_1_media-coverage; quoting *Herald Examiner* story of April 1, 1984.

sure to put their names on its long waiting list.[3] The members of the McMartin family were highly regarded. Virginia McMartin, the founder of the school, was given the Rose and Scroll award by the Chamber of Commerce, commending her as Citizen of the Year. Virginia and her sixty-year-old daughter, Peggy McMartin Buckey, who belonged to many of the community's most prestigious clubs, had been honored with other civic awards. Peggy and her twenty-five-year-old son, Ray Buckey, worked at the McMartin school. On March 22, 1984, Virginia McMartin, Peggy, Ray, his sister, Peggy Anne, and three teachers at the school, were arrested, jailed, and charged with 397 counts of child abuse.[4]

KABC Los Angeles reporter Wayne Satz broke the story of allegations of horrific cases of child abuse.[5] "More than 60 children," he said, "some of them as young as two years of age, who were enrolled in the McMartin Preschool in Manhattan Beach, have now each told authorities that he or she had been keeping a grotesque secret of being sexually abused and made to appear in pornographic films while in the preschool's care, and of having been forced to witness the mutilation and killing of animals to scare the kids into staying silent."[6]

Shortly thereafter, the district attorney of Los Angeles County, Robert Philibosian, announced, "We have just cracked the biggest case of organized crime and child pornography in American history."[7] The lurid and shocking accusations sent the national media into overdrive. Nearly all the coverage accepted the prosecution's view of the events. On ABC-TV's *20/20*, Tom Jarriel referred to the McMartin Preschool as "a sexual house of horrors." The children might have remained quiet for so many years, Jarriel suggested, because their abusers used mind-control methods akin to "the brainwashing techniques used on prisoners of war." *People Magazine* called

---

3. Eberle and Eberle, *The Abuse of Innocence*, 17.
4. Linder, "The McMartin Preschool Abuse Trial." Initially, the grand jury indictment charged the seven accused with 115 counts of child abuse. Two months later, an additional ninety-three were added. By August 1994, the number of counts reached 397 sexual crimes.
5. Shaw, "Where Was Skepticism in Media?"
6. Ibid.
7. Eberle and Eberle, *The Abuse of Innocence*, 21.

the preschool "California's nightmare nursery."[8] KABC-TV bought a full-page ad in the *Los Angeles Herald Examiner* showing a ravaged, ripped teddy bear. The ad told of the "McMartin Preschool horror," and concluded: "this is a sick, sick story." An anchor on ABC News *Nightline* declared, "all of those accused have pleaded not guilty but there is no question in the minds of the investigators that children were abused over a period of many years." The *Los Angeles Times* proclaimed, "They have told their secrets, the little ones and the adolescents, of rape and sodomy, oral copulation and fondling, slaughtering of animals to scare them into silence, and threats against them and their parents." A reporter in a local South Bay paper asserted, "The truth must be faced that beyond any reasonable doubt, the molestation did occur."[9]

The *McMartin* ritual day care sex abuse case resulted in what was, and still is, the longest, most expensive criminal trial in American history. It lasted six years and cost nearly $16 million, adjudicating crimes for which there were never any convictions and that most people now believe the Buckeys never committed.

Representing a massive failure of the criminal justice system at all levels, *McMartin* had more than its share of incompetence, zealotry, and misconduct. And everyone, including the detectives, the therapists, the prosecutors, the judges, the media, and many of the parents, was at fault. The police investigation was shoddy. The decision to arrest and charge the defendants was hasty and wrong. The accused were denied bail and imprisoned for years. The preliminary hearing and trial were too lengthy. The decision to retry Ray Buckey was unwise.

McMartin is important for another reason; it added substantial momentum to nationwide hysteria over a so-called day care ritual sexual abuse epidemic and to trials across the country, including prosecutions of Violet and Gerald Amirault in Malden, Massachusetts, Betsy Kelly in Edenton, North Carolina, and Kelly Michaels in New Jersey. The wave of hysteria began to subside in the 1990s after

---

8. Ibid.; Shaw, "Where Was Skepticism in Media?"
9. Eberle and Eberle, *The Abuse of Innocence*, 21; Shaw, "Where Was Skepticism in Media?"

researchers discredited the now self-evidently defective techniques used by therapists and police who interrogated the supposed child victims and shed new light on the suggestibility of children and on the reliability of child testimony.

Cases with accusations of child sexual abuse must balance fair presentation and prosecution of the alleged offenses, while protecting the defendant from unreliable and unsubstantiated accusations. The *McMartin* case was more difficult than most in this regard because it had multiple alleged victims and multiple alleged offenders (MVMO).

And MVMOs are, inevitably, high-profile cases with political considerations. In communities where they play out, reputations are made, and prosecutors, in particular, know it. Because he was facing a difficult bid for reelection, then-District Attorney Philibosian had every motivation to bring charges against the Buckeys and to court the media. What's more, political and publicity considerations also made it difficult to drop the charges.

The media attention that MVMO cases breed favors the prosecution. After the *McMartin* trials ended, the *Los Angeles Times* conducted an extensive evaluation of media coverage. It concluded that the media had been "major players in the story, influencing events as well as chronicling them, both by the stories they have published and broadcast and by the stories they haven't."[10] With precious few exceptions, reporters believed that all the charges, including the ritual killing of animals, the forced drinking of blood, and the presence of secret tunnels under the school, were true. "More than most big stories," the *Times* concluded, "*McMartin* at times exposed basic flaws in the way the contemporary news organizations function. Pack journalism. Laziness. Superficiality. Cozy relationships with prosecutors."[11]

Defense attorneys did not counter or correct the narratives and analysis in the media because they did not have the facts. After all, the prosecution had been investigating the charges for months before

---

10. Shaw, "Where Was Skepticism in Media?"
11. Ibid.

the arrests were made. When defense counsel came on board, there was not much more they could say, for quite some time, beyond, "My client says he is not guilty." Sin and sexual innuendo sell, while mere denials of wrongdoing do not. Reporters often take direction from their editors, but in the *McMartin* case, they took their cues from the prosecutors, who were delighted to pass along sensational stories.

Multi-victim child abuse cases stoke parental anxiety. Parents speak with other parents. They have meetings and speculate about what "might have happened." Overwrought parents may ask leading questions of their children: "Johnny down the street says Ray did this to him. Did Ray do it to you, too?" They may not take "no" for an answer—and a kind of cross-fertilization of stories can result. The danger of contaminating the memories of children in a MVMO case is greater than in a single victim one. In addition, therapists have more weapons, such as peer pressure, to extract tales of real or imagined incidents of abuse.

The laws regarding child abuse began to change in the 1970s. Prior to 1970, child abuse, which tended to be committed by family members, went largely unrecognized and unreported. To be sure, all states had statutes requiring doctors to report signs of child abuse. In 1974, in response to concerns about the transformation of nuclear American families, out-of-wedlock births, the migration of moms into the workplace, and "latchkey" children, the United States Congress passed the "Child Abuse Prevention and Treatment Act" which offered money to states to expand and improve the reporting of child abuse. The states passed laws requiring therapists, teachers, school officials, and caseworkers, as well as doctors, to report incidents of abuse. By the mid-1980s allegations of child abuse had increased substantially.

Also relevant was the growing popularity of child therapy. In this new age, therapists, in effect, told parents "You'd be surprised what you don't know about your child." And parents were increasingly willing to listen to experts.

In the courtroom, child therapy and child therapists came to play a bigger and more authoritative role. Expert psychologists or psychiatrists were still not permitted to testify that a particular witness was or was not telling the truth because it was the function of the jury to determine the credibility of witnesses. But courts began to allow child psychologists or qualified therapists to explain to juries why children might delay reporting abuse; why some of them might deny, at first, the fact that they were violated; why they might recant; or why they might want to continue living with the person who abused them. Although an adult witness who makes inconsistent accusations or recants might well be viewed skeptically, therapists were now allowed to explain to juries that this logic does not apply to child victims of abuse. If a child testified on direct examination that "the defendant molested me" and the defense, in cross, got the child to say, "You're right, it never happened," a therapist might insist, "That doesn't mean a thing." In essence, therapists instructed juries and judges that inconsistency should not affect the credibility of the child's current testimony for the prosecution.

The slogan of the parents and the prosecution—"Believe the Children"—generates a no-win situation for the defense. In effect, that slogan meant: believe them when they say they were abused, not when they deny or recant.

The rules of evidence in the legal approach to child abuse cases changed around this time as well. The classic rule in American litigation is the "rule against hearsay." For example, the victim of a crime must come to court, testify in person and say, "That's him, Mr. Defendant, he's the man who did it." The prosecution could not call a policeman to the stand and have him say, "Well, the victim can't come to court today, but let me tell you that the victim told me, that Mr. Defendant did it." But in many states in the 1970s and 1980s, a new exception to the rule against hearsay was created. The "tender years exception" provided that in a sex abuse case, a child under the age of twelve does not have to testify. Instead, a therapist or anybody who may have heard the victim's prior out-of-court accusation of abuse, can testify about what the child said, provided the court thinks the statement is reliable. This exception to the hearsay rule is a potent weapon for the prosecution.[12]

---

12. California Evidence Code, Section 1360 is an example of one of the statutes.

As a result of these changes in the law, skepticism about children's statements gave way to acceptance of the idea they could and should be believed on serious matters such as sexual abuse. These trends provided the legal context for *McMartin*, the first big multi-victim, multi-offender case.

The case originated with Judy Johnson, the mother of a two-and-a-half-year-old boy who attended the McMartin Preschool on ten occasions in 1983. Alarmed that her son had begun to play doctor (a game he learned at McMartin Preschool), that he wandered into her room while she was partially undressed and said, "Matthew wear bra," and that his anus was itchy and red, Johnson had him examined by physicians at Kaiser Hospital in Harbor City and at Marion Davies Children's Clinic at UCLA. These doctors filed suspected child abuse reports. Mrs. Johnson then told Detective Jane Hoag that Ray Buckey, an aide at the school, had molested her son. Johnson followed up her accusations with a letter to District Attorney Robert Philibosian. She and her son were interviewed. Johnson continued to call and write authorities over the next several months to make further, increasingly bizarre, allegations of abuse. She said that her ex-husband had sodomized their son and the family dog, that her son had been injured by an elephant and a lion during a school field trip, that her son had been tortured by teachers who had dressed as witches, put staples in his ears, nipples, and tongue, and poked his eye with scissors, that Matthew had been flown to Palm Springs, that he had been buried in a coffin, and that he had been made to drink a baby's blood. Mrs. Johnson produced no physical evidence of any of these traumas and some of the detectives and prosecutors suspected that she had severe emotional problems. Some years later, she was diagnosed as suffering from acute paranoid schizophrenia.

Nonetheless, Detective Jane Hoag took the complaint seriously. However, when she interviewed Johnson's son, the boy could not identify Ray Buckey from photographs. A medical exam was given and the boy showed no signs of sexual abuse. Detective Hoag called the parents of twelve other children to inquire about any incidents of abuse they may have suffered. There was no positive response from these now-anxious parents. The police conducted a search of Buckey's home and confiscated, as "evidence," a rubber duck, a graduation robe, a teddy bear, and *Playboy* magazines.[13] The officers also seized a box of 3" × 5" cards with the names and addresses of every child that had attended the McMartin preschool.

Based on the complaints of Judy Johnson and her son, Detective Hoag arrested Ray Buckey on September 7, 1983. Buckey was released when the district attorney said there was insufficient evidence to hold him. However, the police redoubled their efforts to get more evidence. From the addresses on the 3" × 5" cards taken from Buckey's home, Police Chief Harry Kuhlmeyer sent a letter to over 200 families, whose children were attending, or had attended, the McMartin Preschool. The letter read as follows:

September 8, 1983

Dear Parent:

This Department is conducting a criminal investigation involving child molestation (288 P.C.). Ray Buckey, an employee of Virginia McMartin's Pre-School, was arrested September 7, 1983 by this Department.

The following procedure is obviously an unpleasant one, but to protect the rights of your children as well as the rights of the accused, this inquiry is necessary for a complete investigation.

Records indicate that your child has been or is currently a student at the pre-school. We are asking your assistance in this continuing investigation. Please question your child to see if he or she has been a witness to any crime or if he or she has been a victim. Our investigation indicates that possible criminal acts include: oral sex, fondling of the genitals, buttock or chest area, and sodomy, possibly committed under the pretense of "taking the child's temperature." Also photos may have been taken of the children without their clothing. Any information from your child regarding having ever observed

---

13. Linder, "The McMartin Preschool Abuse Trial."

Ray Buckey to leave a classroom alone with a child during any nap period, or if they have ever observed Ray Buckey tie up a child, is important.

Please complete the enclosed information form and return it to this Department in the enclosed stamped return envelope as soon as possible. We will contact you if circumstances dictate same.

We ask you to keep this information strictly confidential because of the nature of the charges and the highly emotional effect it could have on our community. Please do not discuss this investigation with anyone outside your immediate family. Do not contact or discuss the investigation with Raymond Buckey, any member of the accused defendant's family, or employees connected with the McMartin Pre-School.

THERE IS NO EVIDENCE TO INDICATE THAT THE MANAGEMENT OF VIRGINIA MCMARTIN'S PRE-SCHOOL HAD ANY KNOWLEDGE OF THIS SITUATION AND NO DETRIMENTAL INFORMATION CONCERNING THE OPERATION OF THE SCHOOL HAS BEEN DISCOVERED DURING THIS INVESTIGATION. ALSO, NO OTHER EMPLOYEE IN THE SCHOOL IS UNDER INVESTIGATION FOR ANY CRIMINAL ACT.

Your prompt attention to this matter and reply no later than September 16, 1983 will be appreciated.

HARRY L. KUHMEYER, JR.
Chief of Police

JOHN WEHNER, Captain[14]

---

14. Letter to McMartin Preschool parents from Police Chief Kuhlmeyer, Jr: Linder, "Famous American Trials," http://law2.umkc.edu/faculty/projects/ftrials/mcmartin/letter-toparents.html; Eberle and Eberle, *The Abuse of Innocence*, 18–19.

Word spread instantly throughout the community. Parents called each other, questioned their children, and compared notes. They demanded a full investigation of the McMartin Preschool. The preschool was shut down. The words "Ray Must Die" were spray painted on the building wall. Local residents patrolled the streets of Manhattan Beach looking for child molesters. More charges surfaced. Dr. Cheryl Kent, a psychologist, announced that one hundred children at a neighboring preschool had been molested. Daniel Lewis, an attorney for the Department of Social Services, claimed that children had been sent back and forth between McMartin and other preschools to be molested. Seven preschools in the South Bay were subsequently closed.[15]

In the next step, or misstep, in the investigation, the district attorney's office asked Kee MacFarlane of the Los Angeles-based sexual abuse clinic, Children's Institute International, or CII, to handle a large part of the investigation. The CII is a nonprofit organization founded in 1906 by a female probation officer to help young, at-risk women. By the time the *McMartin* case appeared, the organization had expanded its services to offer trauma support to youth affected by sexual abuse, neglect, and violence.

Appointed director of the "Child Abuse Diagnostic Center," Kee MacFarlane was tasked with building a sex abuse program at CII. MacFarlane held a masters degree in social work and called herself a psychotherapist, but she was not licensed as a therapist in California.

Initially, many parents were unwilling to meet with her. But at the behest of the district attorney, they sent their children to CII for two-hour interviews. As a result, 400 children were interviewed on videotape. Following these conversations, MacFarland and the CII determined that 369 children had been sexually abused. One hundred fifty of the children also underwent medical examinations at the CII, performed by Dr. Astrid Heger. She reported that eighty percent of the children had been molested. Her findings were not based primarily on physical evidence, she said, but on the children's

---

15. Eberle and Eberle, *The Abuse of Innocence*, 20.

Mary Emmons (left), former director of the Children's Institute
International, and Kee MacFarlane (right).
Mike Meadows, © 1990 Los Angeles Times. Reprinted with permission.

medical histories and her feeling that "any conclusion should validate
the child's history."[16]

According to CII, the children revealed they had been forced to
participate in numerous horrific acts at McMartin. They included "The
Naked Movie Star Game," where children were told to take off their
clothes and pose while the McMartins photographed them. Though
the prosecution would claim these alleged pictures were part of a child
pornography business run by the Buckeys, no photographs of naked
McMartin students were ever found. Moreover, as the defense would
later point out, the preschool was always open and parents were free
to drop in anytime. So it is difficult to imagine photo sessions freely
and frequently taking place. Visitors were kept at bay, the prosecution
would counter, because of "The Lookout Game," where a child was
stationed at a window at the school while Ray was inside, naked, with

16. Linder, "The McMartin Preschool Abuse Trial."

naked children. If the "lookout" saw a parent coming, he or she would run inside and tell Ray, who would, presumably, stop molesting the children, get dressed, have all of the children get dressed, go outside, and greet the visitor. It was later pointed out by the defense that, as anyone familiar with toddlers would attest, Ray couldn't possibly have had enough time to complete these tasks. And there was an allegation that at least one child was taken to a cemetery and forced to dig up dead bodies. CII claimed the children reported satanic rituals, where Ray killed turtles, cats, and horses with baseball bats. Many of these acts, the children said, were designed to scare them into remaining silent. One child said that a rabbit was killed on an altar and he had to drink its blood. Another child claimed that a human baby was sacrificed. There were allegations of underground tunnels beneath the school, where Ray took children to be molested. Some said that Ray took them to a car wash and molested them in the bathroom and to a grocery store where he assaulted them in the stock room. The children also said that Ray flew them, sometimes by airplane, sometimes by hot air balloon, to other locations to be molested by other people working at other schools. And that Ray had a secret room, where he kept a roaring lion.

Based on the children's accusations, a grand jury indicted Ray Buckey, his mother Peggy McMartin Buckey, Peggy Ann Buckey (Ray's sister), and his grandmother and school founder, Virginia McMartin (Peggy's mother). Also indicted were three other teachers at the school: Mary Ann Jackson, Betty Raidor, and Babette Spitler. These individuals, dubbed "The McMartin Seven," faced a collective 115 counts of child sexual abuse. Two months later, 93 indictment counts were added. When a reporter asked Virginia, "You're seventy-nine years old. Do you think you'll survive this?" Virginia replied, "I'll survive it. I'm tougher than they are."[17] When Betty Raidor was asked, "Do you feel this is unfair to you?" she said, "Well, my home is gone. All the things I put away for my old age are gone. And I didn't

---

17. Eberle and Eberle, *The Abuse of Innocence*, 29.

do anything."[18] Peggy Buckey's bail was set at one million dollars. Ray Buckey was held without bail.

If these allegations were untrue, why would so many children make them? The answer lies in the common point of contact or, more accurately, "contamination" of the children. Before the intervention by the CII, there were no specific complaints from parents or children, except Mrs. Johnson. However, after the CII videotaped interviews, nearly all parents claimed their children had been abused.

Although psychologists continue to debate the reliability of "recovered memory," the CII interrogation techniques are now regarded as an encyclopedia of flawed interviewing, as textbook examples of what therapists should *not* do.

Since *McMartin*, numerous studies have assessed the accuracy of children's memory, the suggestibility of children, and the effect of interviewer bias on children's reports. In one study, conducted by Clarke-Stewart, Thompson, and Lepore (1989), five- and six-year-olds witnessed a live, staged event in which one group of children interacted with a man, who played a janitor, as he cleaned dolls and toys in a playroom. Another group of children watched him handle the same dolls, rather roughly. In each of the two scenarios, the janitor spoke in a way that reflected his behavior: e.g., if he was cleaning the dolls "This doll is dirty, I had better clean it," or playing roughly e.g., "I like to play with dolls. I like to spray them in the face with water." The children were later questioned about these events, several times, on the same day, by different interviewers, who offered different interpretations of the event. They were either: (1) accusatory (suggesting that the janitor's behavior was not appropriate, in that he was playing with the dolls instead of working), (2) exculpatory (suggesting that the janitor was just cleaning the toys and not playing), or (3) neutral and non-suggestive.[19]

The study found that children were much more likely than those who were not questioned to incorporate the interviewers' suggestions

---

18. Ibid., 26.
19. Child suggestibility studies: Linder, "Famous American Trials," http://law2.umkc.edu/faculty/projects/ftrials/mcmartin/suggestibility.html.

into free recalls and responses to direct questions about the event. Even when subsequently questioned by their own parents, the study showed, the children's answers were consistent with the interviewers' biases.[20]

In a landmark study, Professor Stephen Ceci of Cornell University[21] delineated a number of techniques employed by therapists that might "lead the witness": "question repetition within the same interview," "stereotype inducement," "guided imagery," "peer pressure," and "selective reinforcement." In the first technique, an interviewer asks a question over and over, or doesn't take "no" for an answer if the child's initial response does not fit the hypothesis. For example: "Did he touch you?" "No." "No? Are you sure? So where did he touch you?" This technique exploits a child's natural desire to please. In "stereotype inducement," an interviewer creates expectations in his or her subjects that will be consistent with the interviewer's bias. For example, the interviewer introduces a villainous character during the interview, and then says: "Ray does yucky things. What yucky thing did Ray do to you?" In the "guided imagery" technique, a therapist engages in fantasy play with a child subject. In the CII interviews, Kee MacFarlane selected an ugly naked doll, presented it to the children and said, "Let's call this Ray." With "peer pressure," Professor Ceci explains that the interviewer may tell the child "what others said" and ask for confirmation: "Johnny said Ray played the photo game. Do you remember the game?" With "selective reinforcement," positive signals are given to the child when he or she gives

---

20. Ibid.
21. Stephen J. Ceci and Richard D. Friedman, "The Suggestibility of Children: Scientific Research and Legal Implications," *Cornell Law Review* 86 (2000): 33; See also Nadja Schreiber, "Suggestive interviewing in the McMartin Preschool and Kelly Michaels daycare abuse cases: A case study," *Social Influence* 1 (2006): 16–47;

"Confirming the impression of prior commentators, systemic analyses showed that interviews from the two daycare cases were highly suggestive. Compared with CPS interviews, the McMartin and/or Michaels interviewers were significantly more likely to (a) introduce new suggestive information into the interview, (b) provide praise, promises, and positive reinforcement, (c) express disapproval, disbelief, or disagreement with children, (d) exert conformity pressure, and (e) Invite children to pretend or speculate about supposed events."

answers consistent with the questioner's view and negative signals if inconsistent.

Here are examples from the CII videotapes illustrating some of these techniques:

BOY: Like, like somehow I can't remember. I'm not sure about. Ah, there was a room I wasn't supposed to go in or something.

KEE: There was a room you weren't supposed to go in?

BOY: Yeah, I guess. I can't—I'm making this up. I'm not sure. Yeah, I can see it, I think.

And later in the interview:

KEE: Boy, you are, you're really something. You're amazing, your memory is just amazing. It's incredible. Are you surprising yourself?

BOY: Yeah. I, ah, I, my dad talked to me and my ma, and my mom and I couldn't remember anything. Guess it's coming back to me.

KEE: Oh boy, your memory is just incredible.

BOY: I'm not sure about all these things.

A year after this interview was conducted, the boy testified at the preliminary hearing that his parents designed "fill in the blank" questions for him about the *McMartin* case. He said he would use his imagination to answer the questions after watching television news reports that included stories of children being transported to cemeteries. The boy also said he remembered playing "naked movie star" with Ray and the other teachers in the "secret room" five times a week. It turned out he had attended the McMartin school only twice a week and Ray Buckey did not start working at the school until long after the boy had graduated.

Convinced that denials masked their pain, MacFarlane encouraged children to tell secrets to a microphone, from where it would travel down a wire, into a box, into the TV, and then be gone. She used puppets that asked, "Are you smart or are you dumb?" and made fun of younger children who were "too little to tell us because they're babies." And when one child indicated he had not seen Ray Buckey play "the naked game," MacFarlane said, "You're just a scaredy cat. How come you won't tell me?"[22]

CII used all these techniques. For most of the two-hour long interviews, the children would often deny any act of abuse, or claim they couldn't remember. But near the end they would say, "Yes, it happened." MacFarlane showed parents only the moments in the videos when accusations had been made or affirmed.

Many parents believed the CII reports, especially when they were supplemented by the testimony of Dr. Astrid Heger, the young medical consultant at CII. Heger relied heavily on the theories of Dr. Bruce Woodling, who specialized in finding subtle signs of child abuse. If a physician applied a swab to touch a spot near a child's anus and it opened, Woodling concluded that the child had been sodomized. The wider it opened, the more frequent the abuse had been. In addition to this "wink response test," Woodling used a magnifying instrument he called a colposcope to identify "microtraumas" (wounds only the device could detect) and "synechiae" (scar tissue). And he endorsed the idea that any opening of the hymen greater than four millimeters constituted evidence of sexual trauma. After acquiring a colposcope, Dr. Heger conducted physical examinations on almost one hundred children and concluded that eighty percent of them had been abused.[23]

Once they were told by MacFarlane and Heger that their children had been abused, the parents began to see, or imagined they saw, symptoms of that alleged abuse. If a child did not want to go

22. Beck, *We Believe the Children*, 46–47, 54–55.
23. Ibid., 58–59.

to school or had had a nightmare, in a kind of self-fulfilling prophecy, the parents interpreted these events as evidence or symptoms of abuse.

In many ways Ray Buckey was an ideal target for the suspicious parents. Twenty-five years old in 1983 and unmarried, he was soft-spoken and not emotionally expressive. He also enjoyed working with children. Ray often seemed calm and unaffected by the hysteria surrounding him, but in his own way, he stood up for himself. At his 1986 bail hearing, and in his first statement to the court, he told the judge:

> I have never in my life harmed a child, nor can I comprehend how anyone would, or could, harm a child. . . . This case is my life. My future is this case. There is one thing I do not fear, and that is the truth, the truth of my innocence and my mother's innocence . . . the truth will set me free. . . . I have never in my life threatened a child or harmed an animal.[24]

The denial of bail for Buckey, according to the judge, was based on the testimony of the children who said that Ray threatened to kill them or their parents if they revealed he was molesting them. The judge's decision to keep Ray off the streets was made in the "interest of public safety."[25]

In California, the first step in the judicial process is a preliminary hearing, where a judge decides if there is enough evidence to hold a defendant. In a typical case, a preliminary hearing can last a day or up to two weeks. The McMartin preliminary hearing, which began in August 1984, lasted eighteen months. Each of the seven defendants had his or her own attorney, and 40,000 pages of testimony were recorded. The cost of the proceedings was $2.5 million.

Kee MacFarlane testified that the abuse continued undetected for years because the children suffered from "denial syndrome" or were afraid for their own lives. She explained that her method of get-

---

24. Eberle and Eberle, *The Abuse of Innocence,* 32.
25. Ibid.

ting the children to reveal their secrets was through the use of hand puppets named Mr. Alligator, Mr. Snake, Detective Dog, and Mr. Sparky. Tapes of some of these interviews were shown and on one a therapist could be heard telling a child that 183 kids had already revealed "yucky secrets," and that all the teachers at McMartin were "sick in the head" and deserved to be beaten up.[26]

Then it was the children's turn. The prosecution had selected the twenty-five most convincing children, and from this group, 13 were chosen to testify. One child was on the stand for sixteen days. The children told stories of sexual assaults that took place on farms and at circuses and the naked game of cowboys and Indians. One said he saw Ray Buckey kill a horse with a baseball bat. Another child said he was forced to go to a cemetery, dig up coffins, and watch as Ray dismembered the bodies. When shown a selection of photographs and asked to pick out who molested him, one child picked out Chuck Norris and the mayor of Manhattan Beach. On cross-examination, some of the children recanted.

During this time, searches of the McMartin Preschool and the Buckey homes were conducted but yielded nothing. In March 1985, a group of nearly fifty McMartin parents, determined to find secret tunnels, began digging in a lot next to the school. An archeological firm, hired by the district attorney's office, joined them in the excavation but turned up nothing but soil and rocks.[27]

At this point, some members of the prosecution's team expressed reservations about MacFarlane's interview techniques. One of them said, "Kee MacFarland could make a sixth [sic] month old baby say he was molested." Thus far, the case had cost Los Angeles County four million dollars and the trial had not yet begun.[28]

After the preliminary hearing, the judge ruled there was enough evidence to go to trial. Before the trial began, however, a new district attorney, Ira Reiner, was elected. Rainer dropped the charges against

26. Linder, "The McMartin Preschool Abuse Trial."
27. Chronology of the McMartin Preschool abuse trial: Linder, "Famous American Trials," http://law2.umkc.edu/faculty/projects/ftrials/mcmartin/mcmartinchrono.html.
28. Linder, "The McMartin Preschool Abuse Trial."

all the defendants except Ray Buckey and his mother. Also around this time, Judy Johnson died of alcohol poisoning.

By 1986, Ray had been in custody for three years. He was being held without bail and faced seventy-one counts of child molestation and one count of conspiracy. Peggy was being held on $500,000 bail and faced twenty counts of child molestation and one count of conspiracy. Ray and Peggy were ordered to return to court for a pretrial hearing on February 20.

The Buckeys received court-appointed lawyers. Daniel Davis represented Ray and Dean Gits represented Peggy. At thirty-eight years old, they were the youngest of all the lawyers participating in the trial. Davis was outspoken, verbose, and often at odds with judges, while Gits was subdued and spoke barely above a whisper.[29] Both worked tirelessly for their clients.

Deputy District Attorney Lael Rubin was chief of the prosecution team that included a co-prosecutor, Roger Gunson. Rubin was age forty-seven, new to her position, and had a reputation for taking on and winning tough cases.[30] She was in charge from the beginning. She chose to bring all charges. She was responsible for denying bail to the Buckeys. She insisted that the parents send their children to CII. She also withheld evidence.

The law requires that the prosecution turn over to the defense any evidence it has that would tend or might tend to help the defendants.[31] Rubin withheld all the reports made by the original complainant, Judy Johnson. She subsequently claimed that she forgot and overlooked these documents. When one of them, a police report containing allegations by Judy Johnson, was turned over to the defense, however, it bore a notation that said, "Confidential information. Not to be relayed to defense in McMartin Seven trial, per D.A. Lael Rubin."[32]

---

29. Eberle and Eberle, *The Abuse of Innocence*, 24.
30. Ibid.
31. Brady v Maryland, 373 U.S. 83 (1963) established the requirement that the prosecution must turn over to the defense any exculpatory information in its possession that would tend to exonerate the accused. This includes information that would reflect negatively on the credibility of government witnesses.
32. Eberle and Eberle, *The Abuse of Innocence*, 32–33.

How do these revelations come to light? Just before the trial began, a taped interview with Glenn Stevens, a former member of the *McMartin* prosecution team, surfaced. Abby and Myra Mann, who were working on a documentary about the *McMartin* trial, recorded the interview. Believing the tapes relevant to the case, the filmmakers gave them to the defense attorneys and the California attorney general's office. On the tapes, Stevens maintains that the children began "embellishing" their sexual abuse stories. He also says "we had no business being in court."[33] Most important of all, Stevens revealed that prosecutors withheld exculpatory information from defense attorneys, including evidence about the mental stability of Judy Johnson and the inability of Johnson's son to identify Ray Buckey in a police lineup.[34]

As a result of the revelations, the defense moved to dismiss charges against Ray and Peggy on the grounds of prosecutorial misconduct. Judge William Pounders denied the motion. "Why should I dismiss a case," he asked, "and bury the truth forever, rather than seek the truth in a trial?"[35] Instead, Judge Pounders ordered an evidentiary hearing to determine if the prosecution had engaged in discriminatory practices by dismissing the charges against five of the Buckey defendants and proceeding only against Ray and Peggy.

At the hearing, Glenn Stevens accused Rubin and the prosecution of withholding information that might exonerate the defendants, overfiling charges to assure the Buckeys would be denied bail, and lying to the court during the preliminary hearing. Of the veracity of Judy Johnson's abuse claims, Stevens said, "It was pretty much believed by both of us (he and Rubin) that the woman (Johnson) was crazy."[36] Stevens ended his six weeks of testimony by declaring Ray and Peggy innocent. Angry Manhattan Beach parents present at the

33. Linder, "The McMartin Preschool Abuse Trial."
34. Ibid.
35. Marcia Chambers, "Judge Declines Request to Halt Sex Abuse Case," *New York Times*, December 10, 1986, http://www.nytimes.com/1986/12/10/us/judge-declines-request-to-halt-sex-abuse-case.html.
36. Eberle and Eberle, *The Abuse of Innocence*, 33.

Peggy McMartin Buckey listens to the opening statements in the
McMartin Preschool trial.
© Bettmann/CORBI

hearing were unmoved by Stevens's testimony. Lael Rubin called it
"lies."

The judge rejected the defense's claim that the prosecution had
engaged in discriminatory practices against Ray and Peggy. "The
defendants are in a distinctly different position," he proclaimed. "I
am saying there is credible evidence."[37] The trial would move forward.

A jury of seven men and five women was selected. They ranged in
age from the twenties to seventy-three. Seven were Caucasian, three
were black, one was Asian, and one was Filipino. The trial began on
July 14, 1987. It lasted almost five years, so long that, toward the end,
the judge and jury had to be shown photographs of witnesses who
had testified years earlier so they could remember who they were.

During her opening statement, Lael Rubin told the court, "Your
Honor, ladies and gentlemen, this is a case about trust and betrayal
of trust . . . trust you placed in the hands of Peggy Buckey and Ray

---

37. Ibid., 34.

Buckey."[38] Rubin reasserted the claims of CII and the children. She told the jury of the sexual games the Buckeys played, of children being transported away from the McMartin school to be molested in other locations, and of the parents' own claims that their sons and daughters had been abused.

Dean Gits began his opening by reframing the narrative of the case: "Ladies and gentlemen . . . Miss Rubin told you this is a case about trust. . . . This is not a case about trust. It's case about victims. It's your job to decide who are the victims, and what I call the enemy." Gits characterized the children, parents, and McMartin teachers as the victims, and Rubin and the district attorney's office as the perpetrators.[39] He reminded jurors that the McMartin Preschool had been in business for over twenty years without complaints of any kind. He told them that the prosecution had searched twenty-one residences, seven businesses, thirty-seven cars, three motorcycles, four churches, two food markets, two airports, one exercise club, one national park, and one farm, seized twenty blankets, twelve items of clothing, nine rags, four towels, sheets, underpants, sponge mops, spiral notebooks, and soil samples; reviewed customs records, real estate filings, bank and utility records; interviewed at least 450 children and 150 adults; used forty-nine photo lineups, and found no relevant physical evidence to corroborate any of the prosecution's claims; no secret tunnels, no pornographic photographs, no dead animals, and no evidence of sexual molestation.[40]

Danny Davis offered a "common sense defense." He made a passionate plea for Ray Buckey, portraying him as a good-hearted, dedicated teacher who had become the target of a witch hunt. He hammered home the idea that his client was a victim of CII's manipulative interviewing techniques: "We were told they were experts, that they had expert credentials," but "Kee MacFarlane's only credentials were a driver's license and a welder's license."[41] Of Dr. Astrid Heger's report, Davis told the jury that there is "no medical knowl-

38. Ibid., 39.
39. Ibid., 41.
40. Beck, *We Believe the Children*, 153–4.
41. Eberle and Eberle, *The Abuse of Innocence*, 46.

Private investigator Ted Gunderson shows hole dug by parents searching
for secret room used for molestations.
Larry Davis, © 1990 Los Angeles Times. Reprinted with permission.

edge that enables a physician to determine whether a five year old
blemish on the tissue of a child's genitals is proof of molestation."[42]

Over the course of the trial, the prosecution produced a parade of
witnesses. First, there were the parents, who described their fears and

---

42. Ibid.

suspicion of the Buckeys. Then the children repeated the stories of abuse they told at the preliminary hearing; the bizarre sexual games, the sexual abuse, and the killing of animals. Kee MacFarlane then testified for five weeks. She described her interview techniques with puppets and she defended her method of telling children during an interview what accusations other children had already made. The more she went on, the less believable she seemed. Even Judge Pounders was heard to remark, "In my view, her credibility is becoming more of an issue as she testifies here."[43]

Among the expert witnesses the defense called was Dr. Michael Maloney, a professor of psychiatry at the University of Southern California. He testified for two weeks, steadily dismantling the credibility of MacFarlane. Before the jury was brought into the courtroom, Maloney told the judge he had viewed the CII tapes and found them "definitely invalid." He said the children were "so contaminated by the process itself, that no matter what they said . . . you'd have a hard time saying where it came from."[44] On direct examination before the jury, Maloney testified that MacFarlane's interview techniques, her use of dolls, her suggestive questioning, her use of social and peer pressure, and her positive reinforcement methods invalidated her conclusions and the claims of the children. "In a way these kids were all machined right through the same process," Maloney indicated; "toward the end of that process they were being asked very direct and almost coercive questions about sexual behavior."[45]

Dr. Astrid Heger also testified for the prosecution. She reported finding numerous scars on the children that were "consistent with rape." But the defense's medical expert, Dr. David Paul, would later testify that he saw no medical evidence of molestation. In fact, he found that the body parts in nine of the eleven children were "perfectly normal."[46] The defense attacked Heger's credibility by pointing out that her expertise in the field of child sexual abuse was minimal

43. Linder, "The McMartin Preschool Abuse Trial."
44. Eberle and Eberle, *The Abuse of Innocence*, 241.
45. Lois Timnick, "Videotaped Interviews in McMartin Case Hit," *Los Angeles Times*, March 15, 1989, http://articles.latimes.com/1989-03-15/local/me-625_1_peggy-mcmartin-buckey.
46. Linder, "The McMartin Preschool Abuse Trial."

and that medical diagnosis of past sexual abuse was not an exact science. The defense explained that by the time Heger conducted these examinations, in some cases years after the children had left the McMartin school, any physical injuries resulting from sexual abuse would have healed. And Heger's conclusions, they said, often contradicted testimony from the children's parents, information on the forms parents filled out at CII, and on medical records from the pediatricians who cared for them while they attended McMartin.

Perhaps the most devastating moments in Dr. Heger's cross-examination involved quotations from her writings. In a book coauthored by Kee MacFarlane and another doctor in 1986, Heger had written, "Any conclusion should validate the child's story and state clearly that the presence, or absence, of physical findings is consistent with a history of sexual abuse."[47] Referring to this passage, Gits asked Heger, "How could 'absence' of physical finding indicate abuse?" When Heger replied, "The absence of evidence does not mean a child was not molested." Gits shot back, "Then what good is a medical exam?"[48]

It was established that at the time Heger examined the children, her experience in the diagnosing sexual abuse was minimal; prior to this case, she had examined fewer than a dozen children. She acknowledged that she had received her training regarding childhood sexual abuse from Dr. Bruce Woodling and had worked under his supervision when she performed the examinations for the *McMartin* case in 1984. A perennial prosecution witness, Woodling, at a conference, had given the following advice, "It is imperative that an examiner of children never make a diagnosis of 'no evidence of sexual abuse,' which is probably the single worst thing a medical examiner can do, because if you make that conclusion, the case will never go forward."[49]

When Peggy McMartin took the stand, Gits asked her, "Did you ever molest any of those children?" She replied, "Never."[50] Neither

47. Eberle and Eberle, *The Abuse of Innocence*, 142.
48. Eberle and Eberle, *The Abuse of Innocence*, 142–3.
49. Eberle and Eberle, *The Abuse of Innocence*, 142.
50. Peggy Buckey testimony: Linder, "Famous American Trials," http://law2.umkc.edu/faculty/projects/ftrials/mcmartin/peggybuckeytestimony.html.

Ray Buckey on the witness stand.
Joe Kennedy, © 1990 Los Angeles Times. Reprinted with permission.

had she ever seen her son act in a sexually inappropriate way with the children.

When Ray Buckey testified, he stated that he was not teaching at McMartin when he was accused by some of the children of molesting them. During cross-examination, Lael Rubin focused on allegations about whether Buckey did or did not wear underwear and if he owned sexually explicit magazines. Ray maintained, "I have never had any sexual desire for children. Never had and never will. . . ."[51]

---

51. Ray Buckey testimony: Linder, "Famous American Trials," http://law2.umkc.edu/faculty/projects/ftrials/mcmartin/raybuckeytestimony.html.

In the middle of the trial, two assistant prosecutors resigned. They later testified that Lael Rubin told them to withhold documents from the defense; one of them asserted that he believed that all the defendants were innocent.

During closing arguments, Gunson tried to do damage control on the children's contradictory statements and the prosecution's lack of medical evidence. He relied on recapping hearsay testimony of the parents. As he showed photographs of the children's genitals, he recited their testimony. He claimed that Ray Buckey fit the profile of a perpetrator and alluded to allegations of his drug and alcohol use.[52]

In his closing, Danny Davis angrily attacked the prosecution's case. Of the role of CII in the investigation, he said, "The truth never had a chance" and "The doctors did not know what they were doing."[53] He called claims from the child witnesses "impossible, unreal occurrences."[54] He argued that the prosecution failed to prove "beyond a reasonable doubt" that the alleged crimes occurred or, if they did, that Ray Buckey committed them. He concluded that "The standard of integrity and the requirement that there be a consistent proof beyond a reasonable doubt" requires an acquittal.

In her final argument, Lael Rubin had the difficult task of explaining away the implausible and often fantastical stories of the children and how it was possible that hundreds of children could have been molested at the preschool without any of them telling anyone. Rubin urged the jurors not to disbelieve the children because their statements seemed unbelievable. She maintained that "these stories were simply less painful ways of dealing with the truth." Rubin asserted that the children had repressed memories of their sexual abuse until they were evaluated at CII and that "many of these kids tried to talk in their own way and nobody listened."

After two-and-a-half months of deliberation, the jury announced their verdict on January 18, 1990. Peggy McMartin Buckey was acquitted on all counts. Ray Buckey was acquitted on thirty-nine

---

52. Eberle and Eberle, *The Abuse of Innocence*, 327.
53. Ibid., 335.
54. Ibid., 336.

of fifty-two counts. On the remaining thirteen counts, the jury was divided, with seven of twelve in favor of acquittal. There were no convictions.

Immediately following the verdict, an angry crowd gathered in Manhattan Beach before the amassed television cameras. *Geraldo* ran a segment on the verdict with a banner on the screen that read, "The *McMartin* Outrage: What Went Wrong."[55] When court adjourned, reporters were allowed to interview jurors. One young female juror said, "I'm sorry if the world isn't happy with the verdict, but they weren't there. That was me in there for two and a half years, and I can live with it."[56]

The parents and the community lobbied for a retrial on the remaining thirteen counts. Large crowds marched through the streets of Manhattan Beach with signs that said, "We Believe the Children." So Buckey was retried on eight of the thirteen charges. The trial lasted two months. Lael Rubin was removed as lead prosecutor. Once again, the verdict was a hung jury on all counts; the vote, though not unanimous, favored acquittal. The case was over. There would be no more trials.

In both trials, jurors found the children's stories too fantastic and the CII interviews fatally flawed. Mark Bassett thought "some of the expert testimony about the children told you more about the expert than the child. I mean, if the expert says children are always 100 percent believable and then you have a child who is not believable, either the expert is extremely biased or they've never seen anything like that child before." Brenda Williams realized "how easily something can be said and misinterpreted and blown out of proportion."[57]

Due in no small measure to the *McMartin* debacle, public opinion about child care and ritual abuse cases was changing. Glenn Stevens's skepticism about the case was reported in the *Los Angeles Times* and other newspapers. In November 1986, before the first trial began, *60*

---

55. Ibid., 355.
56. Ibid., 354.
57. Linder, "The McMartin Preschool Abuse Trial."

Minutes, the most prestigious news program on television, provided sympathetic portraits of the defendants and a critical evaluation of the "embattled" prosecutors and therapists. In the next few years, convictions in Kern County, California, and El Paso, Texas, were overturned.

But fears about the perils of protecting children and predictions of moral decay, social breakdown, and social license did not go away. Although the abduction of children from public places is a rare occurrence, a poll revealed that sixty-eight percent of Americans believed that parents should be prohibited from allowing children under ten from playing in public parks without adult supervision. And stories of abuse in preschools, another rare occurrence, continued to command media attention.[58] The *McMartin* trial was over, but the damage lingered. Not least of all, for the children. Many of them remained convinced they had been molested, and justice had not been served. K.C. Watts, who was eleven years old at the time of the trial, was "mad at the verdict. The jurors believed we were molested, so why didn't they let their conscience be their guide? I'm angry they let those guys off and angry at the Buckeys for what they did. They are perverts and they are back on the street."[59] Kyle Daniels, who was fourteen, and one of nine children who testified at the trial, noted that there was "a little scream of terror in the room when the verdicts were read . . . I had never considered a not guilty verdict."[60]

In a CBS interview, Ray Buckey acknowledged that "those poor children went through hell," but reiterated that "I'm not the cause of their hell and neither is my mother. The cause of their hell is the . . . adults who took this case and made it what it was."[61]

Since *McMartin*, some of the children have recanted their stories. In 2005, one of them, now an adult, announced, albeit anonymously, "Never did anyone do anything to me, and I never saw them doing anything. I said a lot of things that didn't happen. I lied. . . . Anytime

58. Beck, *We Believe the Children*, 264.
59. Susan Schindehette, "The McMartin Nightmare," *People Magazine*, February 5, 1990, http://www.people.com/people/archive/article/0,,20116681,00.html.
60. Ibid.
61. Linder, "The McMartin Preschool Abuse Trial."

I would give them an answer that they didn't like, they would ask again and encourage me to give them the answer they were looking for. . . . I felt uncomfortable and a little ashamed that I was being dishonest. But at the same time, being the type of person I was, whatever my parents wanted me to do, I would do."[62] Another former McMartin student, Kyle Zirpolo, reflected, "The thing I remember about the case was how it took over the whole city and consumed our whole family. My parents would ask questions: "Did the teachers ever do things to you?" They talked about Ray Buckey, whom I had never met. I don't even have any recollection of him attending the school when I was going there." Of his experiences at CII, Zirpolo said, "The first time I went to CII . . . I remember waiting . . . for hours while my brothers and sisters were being interviewed. It was an ordeal. I remember thinking to myself, 'I'm not going to get out of here unless I tell them what they want to hear.'"[63]

Since *McMartin*, a number of judicial decisions concerning child testimony have been rendered. Some of them were meant to protect child witnesses in sexual abuse cases; others added protections for defendants charged as abusers.

In 1990, the United States Supreme Court in *Maryland v. Craig*[64] upheld as constitutional under the Sixth Amendment confrontation clause the right of child witnesses to testify on closed circuit video out of the presence of the defendant. Justice Sandra Day O'Connor said, "The State's interest in the physical and psychological well-being of child abuse victims may be sufficiently important to outweigh . . . a defendant's right to face his or her accusers in court."[65]

In another hearing, the so-called taint hearing was born. After the *McMartin* case, a young twenty-six year-old nursery school teacher, Kelly Michaels, was accused of sexually abusing children at

62. Kyle Zirpolo and Debbie Nathan, "I'm Sorry: A long delayed apology from one of the accusers in the notorious McMartin Preschool molestation case," *Los Angeles Times Magazine*, October 30, 2005, http://articles.latimes.com/2005/oct/30/magazine/tm-mcmartin44.
63. Ibid.
64. 497 U.S. 836 (1990).
65. 497 U.S. 836, 855–6 (1990).

the Wee Care Nursery School in New Jersey. She was said to have licked peanut butter off children's genitals; played the piano while nude; made children drink her urine and eat her feces; and raped and assaulted them with knives, forks, spoons, and Lego blocks. She was accused of performing these acts during school hours over a period of seven months. No alleged act was noticed by staff or reported by children to their parents. No parent reported signs of strange behavior or genital soreness in their children or smelled urine or feces on them. Michaels was convicted and sentenced to forty-seven years in prison. She served five years until the New Jersey Supreme Court reversed her conviction. The New Jersey Supreme Court stated:

> The interrogations undertaken in the course of this case utilized most, if not all, of the practices that are disfavored or condemned by experts, law enforcement authorities and government agencies. . . . The record of the investigative interviews discloses the use of mild threats, cajoling, and bribing. Positive reinforcement was given when children made inculpatory statements, whereas negative reinforcement was expressed when children denied being abused or made exculpatory statements.
>
> Throughout the record, the element of "vilification" appears. Fifteen of the thirty-four children were told, at one time or another, that Kelly was in jail because she had done bad things to children; the children were encouraged to keep "Kelly" in jail. For example, they were told that the investigators "needed their help" and that they could be "little detectives." Children were also introduced to the police officer who had arrested the defendant and were shown the handcuffs used during her arrest; mock police badges were given to children who cooperated.
>
> In addition, no effort was made to avoid outside information that could influence and affect the recollection of the children. As noted by the Appellate Division, the children

were in contact with each other and, more likely than not, exchanged information about the alleged abuses.[66]

The court then devised a new protection for defendants, holding that from now on in a child sexual abuse case, the defendant is entitled to a separate hearing before the judge, not the jury. At this hearing the defendant can challenge the interview techniques. If the judge finds that they tainted the testimony of the children, then he or she might deem any reports of what they said to be inadmissible at trial. In almost all cases, this would mean a dismissal of the criminal proceeding. In other words, the case would not be left exclusively in the hands of the jury. The judge has the responsibility of first approval of the fairness of the therapist interviews.

Had the New Jersey "taint rule" been applicable in California, there may well have been no *McMartin* trials. The heart of the prosecution case in *McMartin* was the expert testimony of Kee MacFarlane and Astrid Heger. These samples of their videotaped interrogations of the children reveal the defects in their methodology, their use of suggestiveness, coercion, peer pressure, refusal to take "no" for an answer, rewarding compliance with praise, criticizing resistance, and of external sources to persuade. They were advocates for the prosecution and the source of contamination.

Here is interview #1 (an eight-year-old boy):

Kee MacFarlane: Mr. Monkey is a little bit chicken, and he can't remember any of the naked games, but we think that you can, 'cause we know a naked game that you were around for, 'cause the other kids told us, and it's called Naked Movie Star. Do you remember that game, Mr. Alligator, or is your memory too bad?

Boy: Um, I don't remember that game.

---

66. State v Michaels, 136 N.J. 299, 314–5 (1994); Linder, "Famous American Trials," http://law2.umkc.edu/faculty/projects/ftrials/mcmartin/michaelsdecision.HTM.

MacFarlane: Oh, Mr. Alligator.

Boy: Umm, well, it's umm, a little song that me and [a friend] heard of.

MacFarlane: Oh.

Boy: Well, I heard out loud someone singing, "Naked Movie Star, Naked Movie Star."

MacFarlane: You know that, Mr. Alligator? That means you're smart, 'cause that's the same song the other kids knew and that's how we really know you're smarter than you look. So you better not play dumb, Mr. Alligator.

Boy: Well, I didn't really hear a whole lot. I just heard someone yell it from out in the . . . someone yelled it.

MacFarlane: Maybe. Mr. Alligator, you peeked in the window one day and saw them playing it, and maybe you could remember and help us.

Boy: Well, no, I haven't seen anyone playing Naked Movie Star. I've only heard the song.

MacFarlane: What good are you? You must be dumb.

Boy: Well, I don't know really, umm, remember seeing anyone play that, 'cause I wasn't there, when—I—when people were playing it.

MacFarlane: You weren't? You weren't? That's why we're hoping maybe you saw, see, a lot of these puppets weren't there, but they got to see what happened.

Boy: Well, I saw a lot of fighting.

MacFarlane: I bet you can help us a lot, though, 'cause, like Naked Movie Star is a simple game, because we know about that game, 'cause we just have had twenty kids told us about that game. Just this morning, a little girl came in and played it for us and sang it just like that. Do you think if I asked you a question, you could put your thinking cap on and you might remember, Mr. Alligator?

Boy: Maybe.

MacFarlane: You could nod your head yes or no. Can you remember who took the pictures for the naked-movie-star game? That would be a great thing to feed into the secret machine [the video camera], and then it would be all gone, just like all the other kids did. You can just nod whether you remember or not, see how good your memory is.

Boy: [Nods puppet's head.]

MacFarlane: You do? Well, that's remarkable. I wonder if you could hold a pointer in your mouth, and then you wouldn't have to say a word and [boy] wouldn't have to say a word. And you could just point.

Boy: [Places pretend camera on adult male nude doll using alligator puppet] Sometimes he did.

MacFarlane: Can I pat you on the head for that? Look what a big help you can be. You're going to help all these little children, because you're so smart . . . OK, did they ever pose in funny poses for the pictures?

Boy: Well, it wasn't a real camera. We just played. . . .

MacFarlane: Mr. Alligator, I'm going to . . . going to ask you something here. Now, we already found out from the other kids that it was a real camera, so you don't have to pretend, OK? Is that a deal?

Boy: Yes, it was a play camera that we played with.

MacFarlane: Oh, and it went flash?

Boy: Well, it didn't exactly go flash.

MacFarlane: It didn't exactly go flash. Went click? Did little pictures go zip, come out of it?

Boy: I don't remember that.

MacFarlane: Oh, you don't remember that. Well, you're doing pretty good, Mr. Alligator. I got to shake your hand.

And here is interview #2 (a six-year-old girl)

Dr. Astrid Heger: Maybe you could show me with this, with this doll [puts hand on two dolls, one naked, one dressed] how the kids danced for the Naked Movie Star.

Girl: They didn't really dance. It was just, like, a song.

Heger: Well, what did they do when they sang the song?

Girl: [Nods her head]

Heger: I heard that, I heard from several different kids that they took their clothes off. I think that [first classmate] told me that, I know that [second classmate] told me that, I know that [third classmate] told me. [Fourth classmate] and [fifth classmate] all told me that. That's kind of a hard secret, it's kind of a yucky secret to talk of—but maybe, we could see if we could find—

Girl: Not that I remember.

Heger: This is my favorite puppet right here. [Picks up a bird puppet.] You wanna be this puppet? OK? Then I get to be the Detective Dog. . . . We're gonna just figure it all out. OK, when that tricky part about touching the kids was going on, could you take a pointer in your mouth and point on the, on the doll over here, on either one of these dolls, where, where the kids were touched? Could you do that?

Girl: I don't know.

Heger: I know that the kids were touched. Let's see if we can figure that out.

Girl: I don't know.

Heger: You don't know where they were touched?

Girl: Uh-uh. [Shakes her head]

Heger: Well, some of the kids told me that they were touched sometimes. They said that it was, it kinda, sometimes it kinda hurt. And some the times, it felt pretty good. Do you remember that touching game that went on?

Girl: No.

Heger: OK. Let me see if we can try something else and—

Girl: Wheeee! [Spins the puppet above her head.]

Heger: Come on, bird, get down here and help us out here.

Girl: No.

Heger: Bird is having a hard time talking. I don't wanna hear any more no's. No no, Detective dog we're goinna figure this out.[67]

So what have we learned from *McMartin?* Mary A. Fischer, a free-lance writer who worked closely with the defense, has concluded:

This case was simply invented, transmogrified into a national cause célèbre by the intersecting ambitions and misplaced zeal of six people: Judy Johnson, the mother who suffered from mental illness and later died of the effects of alcoholism; Jane Hoag, the detective who originally investigated the complaints; Kee MacFarlane, the CII therapist; Robert Philibosian, the district attorney at the time who was engaged in a losing political battle for re-election; the media who reported on the case; and Ms. Rubin, the prosecutor. They were all operating out of zealousness for reasons of ambition or vested interest. Not that they were bad people, just very mistaken.[68]

Another lesson of the *McMartin* case is the influence of the media. A Duke University study showed that the *Los Angeles Times* favored the prosecution's point of view by a 14 to 1 ratio. The researchers also disclosed that David Rosenzweig, who had been metropolitan editor of the *Los Angeles Times*, was engaged to marry chief prosecutor Lael Rubin.[69] As the aforementioned *Los Angeles Times* investigation in 1990 put it, "From the day the McMartin Preschool molestation story broke on KABC-TV . . . the media have been major players

67. Sample interviews by investigators with former students of the McMartin Preschool: Linder, "Famous American Trials," http://law2.umkc.edu/faculty/projects/ftrials/mcmartin/victiminterviews.html.
68. Robert Reinhold, "The Longest Trial - A Post Mortem; Collapse of Child-Abuse Case: So Much Agony for So Little," *New York Times*, January 24, 1990, http://www.nytimes.com/1990/01/24/us/longest-trial-post-mortem-collapse-child-abuse-case-so-much-agony-for-so-little.html?pagewanted=2.
69. David Shaw, "Times McMartin Coverage Was Biased, Critics Charge," *Los Angeles Times*, January 22, 1990, http://articles.latimes.com/1990-01-22/news/mn-466_1_mcmartin-case/5.

in the story, influencing events as well as chronicling them, both by the stories they have published and broadcast and by the stories they haven't."[70]

Nor was it an accident that Wayne Satz broke the story at the beginning of "sweeps" month, the period during which networks broadcast their most sensational programing in order to attract high ratings and advertising dollars. Satz, moreover, was having a romantic relationship at the time of the trial with Kee MacFarlane.[71]

For the McMartin defendants, the abuse case remained a painful ordeal. Ray Buckey is alive, but his whereabouts are unknown. Virginia McMartin died in 1990 and Peggy Buckey passed away in 2000. "[Peggy] lost everything," Danny Davis said, "Now that she has passed away, [I] would say, that's one we should be ashamed of . . . Buckey derived much of her self-esteem and identity from her job as a teacher and administrator. When that was stripped from her, she never fully recovered."[72] As for CII, it is still in business. CII provides services to children and families in the Los Angeles area, but no longer conducts interviews, medical diagnoses, or makes determinations of abuse.

In 2014 interviews, some of the key players in the case reflected on the trial. Lael Rubin is still convinced that "the strongest evidence, the physical evidence, the medical evidence, I think was very significant." Rubin noted, however, that since *McMartin*, child abuse cases are handled with more care: "The criminal justice system, interviewers and police, law enforcement are much more concerned about eliciting information from children, as opposed to giving them clues."[73] Ray Buckey could not be found for an interview. But Danny Davis said of him, "He was singly the most heroic client I've ever

---

70. Shaw, "Where Was Skepticism in Media?"

71. David Shaw, "Reporter's Early Exclusives Triggered a Media Frenzy," *Los Angeles Times*, January 20, 1990, http://articles.latimes.com/1990-01-20/news/mn-230_1_news-analysis/4.

72. Mitchell Landsberg, "McMartin Defendant Who 'Lost Everything' in Abuse Case Dies at 74," *Los Angeles Times*, December 17, 2000, http://articles.latimes.com/2000/dec/17/local/me-1254.

73. "30 Years Later, Key Figures Reflect On McMartin Preschool Case," CBS News Los Angeles, August 4, 2014, http://losangeles.cbslocal.com/2014/08/04/30-years-later-key-figures-reflect-on-mcmartin-child-abuse-case/.

defended, not only because he was innocent, but he endured it with a quiet wisdom."[74]

In a 2001 article for the *New Times*, "Devil in the Nursery," Margaret Talbot characterized the *McMartin* disaster with these words:

> When you once believed something that now strikes you as absurd, even unhinged, it can be almost impossible to summon that feeling of credulity again. Maybe that is why it is easier for most of us to forget, rather than try and explain, the Satanic-abuse scare that gripped this country in the early 80's—the myth that devil-worshipers had set up shop in our day care centers, where their clever adepts were raping and sodomizing children, practicing ritual sacrifice, shedding their clothes, drinking blood and eating feces, all unnoticed by parents, neighbors and the authorities.[75]

In the 1980s—and more recently—journalists and commentators compared the day care abuse trial of *McMartin* with the Salem Witch Trials of 1692. The parallels they point to include the reliance on the testimony of children, accusations that multiplied over time, and questionable investigation methods. Also similar in both sets of trials was the unwillingness of people to come forward and say "this is crazy" for fear of losing standing or incurring wrath in their communities.[76]

On the question of how cases such as *McMartin* could contribute to the spread of hysteria to communities across the nation, Dorothy Rabinowitz declared in 1990:

> We are a society that, every fifty years or so, is afflicted by some paroxysm of virtue—an orgy of self-cleansing through which evil of one kind of another is cast out. From the witch

---

74. Ibid.
75. Margaret Talbot, "The Devil in The Nursery," *New York Times Magazine*, January 7, 2001, partners.nytimes.com/library/magazine/home/20010107mag-buckey.html.
76. Modern day Salem witchcraft trials: Linder, "Famous American Trials," http://law2.umkc.edu/faculty/projects/ftrials/mcmartin/salemparallels.htm.

hunts of Salem to communist hunts of the McCarthy era to the current shrill fixation on child abuse, there runs a common thread of moral hysteria. After the McCarthy era, people would ask; but how could it have happened? How could the presumption of innocence have been abandoned wholesale? How did large and powerful institutions acquiesce as congressional investigators ran roughshod over civil liberties—all in the name of a war on communists? How was it possible to believe that subversives lurked behind every library door, in every radio station, that every two-bit actor who had belonged to the wrong political organization posed a threat to the nation's security?

Years from now people will doubtless ask the same questions about our present era—a time when the most improbable charges of abuse find believers; when it is enough only to be accused by anonymous sources to be hauled off by investigators; a time when the hunt for child abusers has become a national pathology.[77]

How could so many people, prosecutors, therapists, and parents and most important, the media, lose their common sense? The McMartin Preschool had enjoyed an impeccable reputation for almost thirty years. Perhaps a lone molester might have joined the staff and started preying on children, but "was it reasonable that virtually the entire staff suddenly went from running a model school, the most prestigious in South Bay, to running a den of molestation and terror involving virtually every child?"[78] In each of the abuse cases across the country, including *McMartin*, it was alleged that hundreds of children were molested over a number of years. Is it possible that these hundreds of victims never told anyone about their ordeal; "that they were taken on airplane rides, forced to drink blood and watch animal mutilations, without one of them ever saying a

---

77. Dorothy Rabinowitz, "From the mouths of babes to a jail cell," *Harper's Magazine*, May 1990, http://harpers.org/archive/1990/05/from-the-mouths-of-babes-to-a-jail-cell/; Linder, "Famous American Trials," supra note 76.
78. Shaw, "Where Was Skepticism in Media?"

word to any parent, friend, classmate, doctor, neighbor—anyone—
and without one ever betraying symptoms far more severe than those
parents subsequently recalled?"[79]

We know, of course, that the sexual abuse of children does occur
and that, for a variety of reasons, victims often do not come forward. That said, statistics show that ninety-seven percent of all child
molesters are men.[80] Molesting is also almost always an individual
act. "How could the seven original *McMartin* defendants, six of them
women, have learned of each other's alleged perversions and kept it
all quiet for so long?"[81] And finally, we must wonder and worry about
why so many of our institutions—the judiciary, the media, and government prosecutors—failed to see all the red flags.

79. Ibid.
80. Ibid.
81. Ibid.

TEN

O. J. Simpson: The Criminal Justice System on Trial[1]

1. This chapter relies heavily on transcripts of trial and preliminary hearing testimony and on a wide variety of secondary sources including especially the superlative account of lawyer and author Jeffrey Toobin who sat through the entire trial and interviewed more than 200 people and who had access to the full documentary record of the case including internal memoranda of both the prosecution and the defense as well as the advice given by jury consultants, along with written summaries of police and defense interviews with witnesses. This more than two years of research produced the most authoritative work; Jeffrey Toobin, *The Run of His Life: The People v. O. J. Simpson* (Random House, 1996). The chapter also draws from the well-reasoned critique of the prosecution by Vincent Bugliosi, a former star prosecutor with the LAPD, which appears in Vincent Bugliosi, *Outrage: The Five Reasons Why O. J. Simpson Got Away with Murder* (W.W. Norton & Company, 1996). Other reliable secondary sources include Alan M. Dershowitz, *Reasonable Doubts: The Criminal Justice System and the O. J. Simpson Case* (Simon and Schuster, 1996); Marcia Clark, *Without a Doubt* (Viking Adult, 1997); Christopher Darden, *In Contempt* (HarperCollins, 1996); Mark Fuhrman, *Murder in Brentwood* (Zebra Books, 1997); Lawrence Schiller, James Willwerth, *American Tragedy: The Uncensored Story of the Simpson Defense* (Random House, 1996); Armanda Cooley, Carrie Bess, Marsha Rubin-Jackson, *Madam Foreman: A Rush to Judgment?* (Dove Books, 1995); Gilbert Geis and Leigh B. Bienen, *Crimes of the Century: From Leopold and Loeb to O. J. Simpson* (Northeastern University Press, 1998); Linda Deutsch and Michael Fleeman, *Verdict: The Chronicle of the O. J. Simpson Trial* (Andrews Mcmeel Pub., 1995). Among the secondary sources used to inform this chapter are law review articles, many of which were part of a symposium on the O. J. Simpson case in volume 67 of the *University of Colorado Law Review*, as well as Internet sources such as the impressive website of Professor Douglas Linder, "Famous American Trials," on "The O. J. Simpson Trial" at http://law2.umkc.edu/faculty/projects/ftrials/Simpson/Simpson.htm, and also Internet accounts of interviews of prosecution and defense attorneys.

The People of the State of California v. Orenthal James Simpson was the most publicized trial in history and O. J. Simpson, the football hero, actor, and media star was the most famous American ever tried for murder. This case may not have been the trial of the century, but it certainly was the media mother of all trials. Never before had a national network broadcast live a preliminary hearing, gavel to gavel, as they all did in the *Simpson* case. CNN, E! and Court TV aired the entire trial live from opening statements to closing arguments.[2] Because of the extensive media coverage, this case was an inescapable presence in the public's consciousness. It was an irresistible combination of a charismatic celebrity defendant accused of a brutal double murder linked with issues of race, gender, and domestic violence. It was set in Los Angeles, the media capital of the world. And most importantly, it brought to the courtroom the newly recognized science of DNA.

At the end of each day, many stations carried analyses of testimony by experts who opined about who won and who lost and what would happen next. In-depth accounts were provided by *Time, Newsweek,* the daily papers, and weekly television shows. *Nightline* alone had fifty-nine specials on the case. Larry King said that "if we had God booked and O. J. was available, we'd move God."[3]

Almost everyone connected to the case—witnesses, lawyers, jurors, detectives and commentators, and, of course, the judge— became famous or infamous. Interest in the case was not confined to the United States. When Russian President Boris Yeltsin visited the United States, his first question to Bill Clinton, as he stepped off the plane was, "Do you think O. J. did it?"[4]

2. Erwin Chemerinsky, "Silence Is Not Golden: Protecting Lawyer Speech Under the First Amendment," *Emory Law Journal* 47 (1998): 859–60; Robert A. Pugsley, "This Courtroom is Not a Television Studio: Why Judge Fujisaki Made the Correct Call in Gagging the Lawyers and Parties, and Banning the Cameras from the O. J. Simpson Civil Case," *Loyola of Los Angeles Entertainment Law Review* 17 (1997): 369–70; Dershowitz, *Reasonable Doubts,* 15–16.
3. Bugliosi, *Outrage,* 346–7.
4. Linder, "Famous American Trials," http://law2.umkc.edu/faculty/projects/ftrials/Simpson/Simpsonaccount.htm.

The trial of O. J. Simpson for the murder of his ex-wife Nicole Brown Simpson and her friend Ron Goldman began on July 22, 1994, when O. J. pleaded "absolutely 100 percent not guilty" to the court presided over by Judge Lance Ito. More than one year and two months later, a sequestered jury composed of eight African American women, one African American male, one Hispanic woman, and two white women reached a verdict. Sequestration is a drastic and seldom used arrangement to isolate jurors from outside influences. It means that the jurors are housed in hotel rooms away from family and friends except for weekly conjugal visits. All newspapers and television programs are censored to prevent access to media. One juror described sequestration as "being in a high priced jail."

On October 2, 1995, after the testimony of 150 witnesses, 857 exhibits, more than 50,000 pages of transcripts and three days of final arguments followed by the judge's instructions, the case went to the jury. The swift announcement that it had reached a verdict four hours later shocked everyone. Judge Ito decided to withhold announcing the verdict until 10 A.M. the next day so that the lawyers, media, and police could prepare for the result of the racially charged criminal case. When that time came, 142 million people worldwide watched or listened to the jury's decision. The United States came to a standstill. Long-distance telephone calls dropped by fifty-eight percent. Trading volume fell forty-one percent on the New York Stock Exchange. Almost everyone who could, stopped working; it was the most unproductive half hour in our nation's history.[5]

The verdict was "not guilty." O. J. Simpson was acquitted of the murders of Nicole Brown Simpson and Ronald Goldman.

Upon leaving the courtroom, the lone black male juror, Lionel Cryer, turned toward the defense lawyers and raised his fist in a 1960s black power salute.[6] Resting in a courtroom lounge, Carrie Bess, one of the female African Americans on the panel, said, "We've got to protect our own."[7] Lionel Knox, who was dismissed from the

---

5. Dershowitz, *Reasonable Doubts*, 11–12; Geis and Bienen, *Crimes of the Century*, 184–5.
6. Toobin, *The Run of His Life*, 431.
7. Ibid.

jury, agreed: For black jurors, he said, "Simpson was one of our own. He was a brother and he was in trouble."[8]

Television and print media stories revealed African Americans cheering the verdict in a variety of venues from college campuses to Times Square. Blacks shouted, "We won, we won," while whites greeted the verdict with silence and then anger. A prominent African American academic stated, "I was stunned by how much middle of the road to liberal people seemed to be very upset at the outcome."[9]

At the beginning of the trial in July 1994, a *USA Today*-CNN-Gallup poll showed that sixty percent of African Americans believed that the charges against O. J. Simpson were not true; only fifteen percent of whites agreed. An ABC poll, taken shortly before the verdict, emphasized the stark nature of the racial divide; seventy-seven percent of whites believed that O. J. was guilty while seventy-five percent of blacks thought he was innocent.[10] African Americans could not understand why whites would begrudge them a rare victory over racist police and an often unresponsive criminal justice system. A majority of white Americans could not understand how the jury could reach a verdict so at odds with the conclusion of intelligent and decent people conversant with the evidence. Four years after the verdict, the racial division persisted. In a 1999 Gallup poll, seventy-four percent of whites believed that Simpson either definitely or probably committed the murders. Only twenty-one percent of black people agreed.[11]

The events that led to the trial began on Sunday, June 12, 1994, around 10:15 P.M. in Brentwood, a prestigious area of West Los Angeles.[12] Neighbors of Nicole Simpson heard a dog barking and wailing

8. Darden, *In Contempt*, 309; quoting Michael Knox, *The Private Diary of an O. J. Juror: Behind the Scenes of the Trial of the Century* (Dove Books, 1995).
9. "Interview with Kimberlé Williams Crenshaw," Frontline, http://www.pbs.org/wgbh/pages/frontline/oj/interviews/crenshaw.html.
10. Geis and Bienen, *Crimes of the Century*, 186.
11. Ibid.; Opinion polls: Linder, "Famous American Trials,"; "Interview with Kimberlé Williams Crenshaw."
12. For a detailed account of the events of the discovery of the murders and the police investigation that followed, see Toobin, *The Run of His Life*, 19–67, 80–111; Fuhrman, *Murder in Brentwood*, 3–86; Geis and Bienen, *Crimes of the Century*, 168–74.

O. J. Simpson and Nicole Brown Simpson at the home of
Anna and Lee Strasberg. Brentwood, CA, July 4, 1981.
© Jim Demetropoulos/Retna Ltd./CORBIS

plaintively in an alley behind her house. Upon investigation, a white
Akita was found with bloody paws. Unfortunately, the dog had no ID
tag and because Nicole had only recently moved into the neighborhood, no one knew to whom he belonged. The people who found him
took the Akita home with them and then another couple agreed to
keep him for the night, but the dog was so restless and agitated, they
decided to take it for a walk. The distressed dog clearly had a destina-

tion in mind and pulled and when they reached the gate at 875 Bundy Drive, the neighbors saw, on the pathway at the bottom of the front steps, the body of Nicole Brown Simpson lying face down in a pool of blood. The murderer had slashed her throat, almost severing her head from her body. Lying next to Nicole was Ronald Goldman, a waiter at the restaurant, who had returned eyeglasses Nicole's mother had dropped there earlier that evening. He had been stabbed approximately thirty times. The coroner's office speculated that the killer had attacked Nicole first, rendering her unconscious, then killed Goldman and finally returned to Nicole. He then placed his foot in her back, pulled her head back by her hair and slashed her throat.

The first officer to arrive was Robert Riske. He found the front door open and, carefully avoiding the blood, entered the condominium. In his preliminary search, Riske discovered a letter written by O. J. Simpson as well as his picture. Upstairs, he found sound asleep Sydney and Justin Simpson, the young children of Nicole and O. J.

Returning to the crime scene itself, Detective Riske saw near Ron Goldman's feet a black knitted cap, a bloodstained white envelope containing eyeglasses, and one left-hand leather glove. Near Nicole's body was a fresh bloody footprint. Despite all the blood, there were no footprints coming from the front gate onto the sidewalk on Bundy Drive. However, along the 120-foot pathway leading to the back gate, Riske discovered a single set of bloody footprints indicating that the killer had escaped into the back alley where Nicole's dog had been found. On closer inspection, he noticed fresh drops of blood to the left of the shoe prints and surmised that the killer may have been bleeding from his left hand as he fled the scene. At this point, Riske notified his supervisor, Sgt. David Rossi, who was in charge of the West Los Angeles station. Rossi then notified the Los Angeles Police Department (LAPD) chain of command. He made many more than the usual calls because of "the possible notoriety of this particular incident."

A steady stream of officers began to arrive at the Bundy Drive murder scene. Officer Joan Vasquez was assigned to take the children out the back of the house through the garage so they would not see the crime scene. Riske showed Sgt. Monty Coon and Supervisor Rossi everything he had seen; the bloody footprints and dripped blood spots, the envelope, the black cap, and the single leather glove. Ron Phillips, the chief of the West Los Angeles Detective Homicide Unit was, for the time being, in charge of the investigation. His next on-call detective was Mark Fuhrman, who was the seventeeth officer to arrive at Bundy Drive. He was later joined by his partner, Brad Roberts.

At about 2:15 in the morning, Riske took Phillips and Fuhrman on a tour of the crime scene. Rossi was waiting for them in the back alley where he and Riske pointed out some blood on the rear gate and handle. Fuhrman made contemporaneous notes of everything he was shown, listing some seventeen items for follow up.

Soon afterward, the case was taken from the West Los Angeles division and given to Los Angeles Robbery-Homicide, which handles high-profile cases. At 4:05 A.M., Detective Philip Vannatter and his partner, Detective Tom Lange, neither of whom had ever met Fuhrman or Phillips, arrived to take over the case and tour the crime scene. Lieutenant Frank Spangler, who was in charge of all detectives in West Los Angeles, ordered Phillips to arrange to notify O. J. Simpson in person of the death of his ex-wife in order to protect him from the distress of learning about it from the media. Vannatter and Lange were also so informed, but no one seemed to know where O. J. lived. Fuhrman then remembered answering a domestic violence call in 1985 at Simpson's Rockingham Avenue estate in Brentwood, about two miles away. At about 5:00 A.M., Fuhrman, Phillips, Vannatter, and Lange arrived at 360 Rockingham Avenue at the corner of Ashford Street. Directly in front of the house, they saw a white Ford Bronco, slightly askew to the curb as though it had been parked hurriedly. The property was surrounded by a high wall with a locked gate. Two lights were on in the house, but there was no answer when Vannatter rang the gate buzzer. They rang again and again but to no avail. A medallion posted nearby announced that the house was protected by Westec, a Los Angeles security firm that the detectives called to obtain Simpson's home telephone number. Phillips called from his cell, but got "This is O. J., leave a message." Westec also had told the officers that a full-time housekeeper was usually on the premises. While the other officers were trying to get a response from the house, Fuhrman went to the Bronco, shined his flashlight into the back seat and saw some papers addressed to O. J. Simpson. He also noticed a small red stain just above the handle of the driver's door. Near the bottom of the door, on the exposed sill, he saw several thin red stripes. He called Vannatter over and the two agreed that the stains looked like blood.

When they ran the license plate number, they learned that the car was owned by the Hertz Corporation, for whom O. J. had long been a spokesman. Based on all the information thus far, Vannatter and Lange decided they had enough reason to enter the enclosure. The intent of the detectives was important. If they entered in the hope of finding evidence against O. J. Simpson because they thought he was a prime suspect, then entering without a warrant and probable cause would be a violation of the search and seizure clause of the Fourth Amendment. In that event, any evidence found on the premises would not be admissible in a prosecution. But a forced entry for "exigent circumstances," that is, to render assistance or to prevent injury to others, would not be a violation. When later challenged on this point by the defense, Lange testified that "I felt that someone inside that house may be the victim of a crime, maybe bleeding or worse."[13] Responding to two separate motions, two judges did not find the entry illegal.

Mark Fuhrman climbed over the wall, opened the gate, and admitted the other detectives to the property. They knocked on the door of the house several times but received no answer. Then with their flashlights on, they went to the rear of the house and saw three small connected guest houses, each with its own separate entrance. Phillips knocked on one and the door was opened by a just-awakened, disheveled young man with a mane of long blond hair. It was Kato Kaelin. When asked if O. J. was home, Kaelin said he didn't know but suggested they knock at the adjacent guest house where Arnelle, Simpson's daughter by his first wife, was living. Phillips, Vannatter,

---

13. Toobin, *The Run of His Life*, 36–37; Fuhrman, *Murder in Brentwood*, 95–97; explains the law and Vannatter's reasoning.

and Lange moved to the next door, but Fuhrman stayed behind. Fuhrman thought that Kaelin was more disoriented and confused than he should be if merely awakened. The detective gave him a test for intoxication, having him follow a pen with his eyes as Fuhrman passed it in front of his face. After asking for permission, Fuhrman looked around the small suite, checking Kaelin's shoes for blood and looking for any incriminating matter. He asked Kato if anything unusual had happened the previous night, and he replied that about 10:45 P.M., while he was on the phone, there were some loud thumps on his bedroom wall, near the air conditioner. The thumps were strong enough that a picture on the wall almost fell and he thought there was going to be an earthquake.

Fuhrman then walked around the house to the area opposite Kaelin's air conditioner and spotted a glove on the ground. It looked wet and sticky, and, most importantly, it appeared to be a match to the left glove found at the Bundy crime scene. Fuhrman did not touch it and went to notify the other three detectives.

In the meantime, Arnelle Simpson was told that there was an emergency and that they had to speak to her father. She used her key to the main house to let them in. She called O. J.'s secretary and was told that he had taken the red-eye flight to Chicago the previous night and was staying at the Chicago-O'Hare hotel. Phillips called the hotel at 6:05 A.M. and told Simpson, "I have some bad news for you. Your ex-wife, Nicole Simpson, has been killed." Simpson sounded distraught. "Oh my God, Nicole is killed? Oh my God, she is dead?" O. J. said he would take the first available flight back to Los Angeles. After the call, Phillips reflected on what O. J. did not say during the brief conversation. He never once asked how Nicole had been killed.[14]

At some point that morning, the detectives concluded that the left glove found at the Bundy Drive crime scene and the right one that Fuhrman found behind Kato Kaelin's house were a matched pair. The detectives speculated that the killer had dropped a left glove in the struggle at Bundy and had suffered a cut on his exposed left

14. Toobin, *The Run of His Life*, 39.

hand. Bleeding, the killer then walked to the rear, opened the gate, leaving blood on it and in the back alley, got into a car, possibly O. J.'s Bronco, drove to Rockingham, where he probably tried to find a place to hide his clothes and the weapon, went to the rear of Kaelin's cottage, bumped into the air conditioner, and dropped the right-handed glove.

As the sun began to rise, more drops of blood were discovered by Vannatter at O. J.'s property with a trail leading from the front gate where the Bronco was parked right up to the front door. On closer examination, he could now see more blood on the Bronco's console between the two front seats and on the inside of the driver's door. On returning to the house, he found additional blood drops in the foyer just beyond the front door.

The criminologist, Dennis Fung, arrived at Rockingham at 7:10 A.M. and concluded, though not definitively, that the stains were human blood. Vannatter contacted Deputy District Attorney Marcia Clark to determine whether there was sufficient probable cause to obtain a search warrant. When he warned her that O. J. Simpson would be involved, she responded, "Never heard of him." She concluded that not only was there sufficient evidence to obtain a warrant, there was enough for an arrest.

Vannatter made out the affidavit for the warrant but omitted the fact that the detectives had gotten some of the evidence by a forced entry. He also stated that criminologists had confirmed, not suggested, the presence of blood on the outside of the Bronco. The affidavit also said that "O. J. had left on an *unexpected* flight to Chicago during the early morning hours of June 13, 1994." In fact, his trip to Chicago had been arranged by Hertz. These errors, which Lance Ito later characterized as "reckless," were unknown to the judge at the time, and he granted the request for the warrant. The warranted search of Rockingham turned up another dramatic piece of evidence. On O. J.'s bedroom floor, the detectives found a pair of dark socks that were later discovered to have Nicole's and O. J.'s blood on them.

At 1:35 P.M. on the day of O. J.'s return from Chicago, Detectives Vannatter and Lange were allowed by his then-attorney, Howard Weitzman, to question Simpson without an attorney present.

Weitzman's decision on the matter was heavily criticized by the media and the criminal defense bar. His gift to the prosecution, however, was badly handled by Vannatter and Lange. Marcia Clark describes the police interview with O. J. as "one of the worst bits of police work I'd ever seen."[15] O. J. was not questioned as an ordinary suspect. Instead, he was treated by the detectives like a celebrity. They accepted his answers by saying, "I understand" or "Okay" and then moving on. Discussing his activity on the night of the murders, O. J. was asked, "When did you last park the Bronco?" He answered, "Eight something . . . maybe seven, eight o'clock. Eight, nine o'clock. I don't know, right in that area." The interrogators failed to follow up. Asked if he would take a lie detector test, Simpson replied, "I'm sure I'll eventually do it . . . but it's like hey, I've got some weird thoughts—you know, when you've been with a person for seventeen years you think everything. And I don't . . . " He stopped himself. The next question should have been "What kind of weird thoughts?" but Vannatter or Lange didn't ask it. At the time of the interview, O. J. had a bandage on his left hand covering a deep cut on his knuckle. When he was asked how he injured himself, he replied, "I have no idea, man," and the detectives did not challenge that nonanswer. Kaelin had told them that he last saw O. J. around 9:30 the night of the murders, standing outside the Rockingham house. What was needed was a rigorous step-by-step accounting of O. J.'s time from 9:30 P.M. until 11:05 P.M. when he left for Chicago, but that didn't happen. An interrogation that should have lasted several hours was terminated by Vannatter and Lange after thirty-two minutes.[16] When the interview ended, O. J. was sent to the lab at the Parker Center Police Station to give a sample of his blood for comparison with the samples taken at Bundy Drive and Rockingham.

The next day, the prosecutor, Marcia Clark, was shocked to learn that O. J. had not yet been arrested. She was concerned that he was free to destroy evidence or influence possible witnesses. Given the

15. Clark, *Without a Doubt*, 71–75; Fuhrman more than agrees with Marcia's assessment and devotes an entire chapter to laying out how the interrogation should have proceeded in Fuhrman, *Murder in Brentwood*, 59–76.
16. Ibid. The interrogation transcript appears as Appendix A in both Fuhrman, *Murder in Brentwood*, 361–85; and in Bugliosi, *Outrage*, 371–89.

available evidence, any other suspect probably would have been arrested. But O. J. was no ordinary citizen, and the police were being extraordinarily cautious.

Robert Shapiro replaced Howard Weitzman as the lead attorney for O. J. Simpson. Although not known primarily as a trial lawyer, Shapiro had excellent media skills, had represented celebrities, and had negotiated lighter sentences with district attorneys. In this case, he devised the defense strategy and selected the other defense team members.

The failure to arrest Simpson gave Shapiro several days to arrange for O. J. to undergo physical and psychiatric examinations. He also had him take a lie detector test administered by a top polygraph examiner. Such tests are not admissible in court, but criminal defense lawyers use them, if favorable, to influence prosecutors during sentencing negotiations. If unfavorable, they can be used to induce clients to agree to a plea bargain.

Simpson's polygraph was administered by Dennis Nellany and it measured, on a sliding scale, his physiological responses to the questions by his heart rate, breathing, and the electrical sensitivity of his skin. Nellany explained that any score higher than +6 meant that O. J. was telling the truth while any number lower than −6 would mean he was lying. O. J. Simpson scored a −24; a total failure! Although O. J. claimed that the questions about Nicole and the murders were emotionally distressing, Nellany informed Shapiro that he regarded the test results as conclusive.[17]

On Friday, June 17, Detective Lange notified Robert Shapiro at 8:30 A.M. that the police had an arrest warrant charging O. J. Simpson with double homicide "with special circumstances," which under California law meant he was eligible for the death penalty and would not be allowed bail. The detective gave Shapiro two and a half hours to bring Simpson in and avoid a public arrest.

Shapiro went to the home of Robert Kardashian, Simpson's friend, in the San Fernando Valley area of Encino, where O. J. was staying, to deliver the bad news. Shapiro arranged for a doctor and a

---

17. Toobin, *The Run of His Life*, 85–86; Schiller and Willwerth, *American Tragedy*, 31–33.

psychiatrist to be there as well, and they were joined by O. J.'s girl-friend, Paula Barbieri, and his football buddy, A. C. Cowlings. With all this activity, it was clear that the eleven o'clock deadline would be missed. Around noon, the police department called Shapiro and said they were coming for O. J. At 1:10 P.M., a police car arrived with a helicopter hovering overhead. But O. J. had vanished.[18]

The police department had scheduled a press conference to announce O. J.'s arrest. Instead, they had to announce that "Mr. Simpson is out there somewhere, and we will find him." With A. C. Cowlings at the wheel and O. J. Simpson in the back seat, the great "white Bronco chase" began.

Los Angeles District Attorney Gil Garcetti declared that Simpson was a fugitive from justice. At 2:00 P.M., an all-points bulletin was put out for a 1993 white Ford Bronco, which belonged to A. C. Cowlings; O. J.'s Bronco had been impounded by the police days ago. Because the police had not seized his passport, the U.S. Border Patrol, U.S. Customs Service, and the Mexican Judicial Police had to be alerted. Around 6:45 P.M., a couple notified the police that they had spotted the car heading north on Interstate 5, back towards Los Angeles.

When the police cars closed in, Cowlings shouted, "Put away your guns. He's in the back seat, and he's got a gun to his head." The dozen police cars fell in behind the Bronco as it drove about sixty miles per hour on the Los Angeles freeways. Every second of this bizarre parade was filmed by news helicopters and reported on by TV and radio stations all around the country, interrupting their regular programming. Media accounts labeled the event "the most famous ride on American shores since Paul Revere's." As many as ninety-five million people tuned in at some point to watch the chase.

Cowlings notified the police at about 7:00 P.M. that they were heading back to O. J.'s Rockingham estate. An hour later, O. J. emerged from the Bronco and surrendered. He said, "I'm sorry, guys. The only person who deserves to be hurt is me."[19]

---

18. Toobin, *The Run of His Life*, 89–90.
19. For more details of the Bronco chase see Toobin, *The Run of His Life*, 110; Geis and Bienen, *Crimes of the Century*, 174.

The "white Bronco chase" was watched by 95 million
television viewers nationwide.
© Branimir Kvartuc/ZUMA Press/CORBIS

A SWAT team examined the Bronco, and in O. J.'s travel bag
they found his passport, a fake goatee and mustache, three receipts
from Cinema Secrets Beauty Supply dated May 27, 1994, and a
fully loaded Smith & Wesson handgun. In the bag also were clean
underwear and socks. Cowlings had in his possession $8,750 in cash,
which he told the police belonged to O. J.[20]

The outlandish nature of these events was enhanced when, during
the car chase, Kardashian held a news conference and read a note
Simpson had written two days earlier. In the note, he insists on his
innocence, thanks his friends and says that sometimes he considered
"himself a battered husband." He expressed gratitude that God had

---

20. Toobin, *The Run of His Life*, 110–1; Bugliosi, *Outrage*, 121–2.

brought his girlfriend, Paula Barbieri, to him, and he expressed sorrow that they will not have their chance. "Don't feel sorry for me," he concludes. "I've had a great life, great friends. Please think of the real O. J. and not this lost person. Thanks for making my life special. I hope I helped yours."[21]

With Simpson in jail, the prosecutors and police began their preparations for trial. The lead attorney would be Marcia Clark, an experienced prosecutor with a success rate of nineteen out of twenty murder cases. Cocounsel would be William Hodgman as well as Christopher Darden, who was added after jury selection. An African-American lawyer, Darden had spent most of his fifteen years as a prosecutor with the Special Investigations Division of the LAPD that dealt with errant police officers and had less trial experience than either Clark or Hodgman.

Los Angeles District Attorney Gil Garcetti had suffered a number of high-profile losses in recent years, including the *McMartin* Preschool child abuse case; the first trial of the Menendez brothers, who were accused of murdering their parents; the Michael Jackson child abuse trial; and, most notoriously, the case against the police officers who had beaten Rodney King and their acquittals that led to the race riots in 1992. With the *Simpson* case, Garcetti and his team were so certain of victory that they violated the cardinal rule of prosecutors: "Let the evidence do the talking." Marcia Clark categorically stated two days after O. J.'s arrest that "it was premeditated murder. It was done with deliberation and premeditation. That is precisely what he was charged with because that is what we will prove." When asked whether O. J. could have had accomplices, she stated, "Mr. Simpson is charged alone because he was the sole murderer."[22]

The state faced some challenges. There were no eyewitnesses, no confession, and no murder weapon. However, the major hurdle would be the cult status of the defendant. He was a legendary American football hero, a 1968 Heisman Trophy winner, 1969 top NFL

21. Toobin, *The Run of His Life*, 97–102; the "suicide" or "farewell" letter is set forth in its entirety as Appendix B in Bugliosi, *Outrage*, 391–93.
22. Toobin, *The Run of His Life*, 114.

draft pick, NFL Hall of Famer. In his first year with the Buffalo Bills, he had a book deal, a broadcasting commitment with ABC, and endorsement contracts with Chevrolet and Royal Crown Cola. His good looks and easygoing manner made him a natural in front of the camera, and he cultivated his image. After he retired, the Hertz commercial of him running through airports, toting a briefcase, as a voice-over chanted, "Go, O. J., Go," kept him in the public eye along with roles in a string of movies.[23]

There is an adage in legal circles that says that if the accused is the type of person with whom jurors would be thrilled to share an elevator ride, then the prosecution is at a decided disadvantage.[24] D.A. Garcetti acknowledged that "there is no doubt the persona, the hero is something that most people don't want to let go of."[25]

Simpson married his high school sweetheart, Marguerite Whitley, in 1968, and they had two children, Arnelle and Jason. Before they divorced eleven years later, O. J. had begun a relationship with eighteen-year-old waitress Nicole Brown, a blonde beauty whom he met at a Beverly Hills nightclub. Nicole had moved into his Rockingham estate before his divorce was final, but O. J. did not marry her until she became pregnant with their first child, Sydney, who was born in 1985. A second child, Justin, was born in 1988, and O. J. and Nicole were divorced four years later. She left with the children and eventually moved with them to the Bundy Drive condominium where she was murdered.

During and after their marriage, the relationship between Nicole and O. J. was tempestuous. Between 1985 and 1988, the police were called on eight separate occasions to Rockingham, but no public record was ever filed. Once, Mark Fuhrman, then a patrol officer, arrived to find Nicole crying in a car with a broken front window that O. J. had bashed in with a baseball bat. Simpson told Fuhrman

23. Toobin, *The Run of His Life*, 44–51, presents a detailed description of Simpson's background and celebrity status. See also Deutsch and Fleeman, *Verdict*, 94–97; Bugliosi, *Outrage*, 52–53.
24. Stephen D. Easton, "Lessons Learned the Hard Way from O. J. and the 'Dream Team,'" *Tulsa Law Review* 32 (1997): 707, 733.
25. Deutsch and Fleeman, *Verdict*, 97.

it was his car, and he could do what he wanted to it. As on the other occasions, Nicole declined to press charges.

However, things went differently in the early morning of New Year's Day, 1989, when a 911 call was received and police officers were sent to 360 Rockingham Drive. The housekeeper told them, "There is no problem here." Minutes later, Nicole staggered out from some bushes, yelling, "He's going to kill me! He's going to kill me!" Officer Edwards asked who was going to kill her, and she replied, "O. J., O. J. Simpson, the football player." Edwards could see that her lips were cut and bleeding, her left eye was black and blue, and there was the clear imprint of a hand on her neck. When Edwards put her in the squad car, she said, "You guys never do anything. . . . You come out. You have been here eight times and you never do anything about him." O. J. then emerged from the house shouting, "I've got two other women. I don't want that woman in my bed." When Edwards informed Simpson that he was going to be arrested, O. J. responded, "I didn't hit her, I just pushed her." He continued to argue, insisting "This is a family matter." Edwards again said he was taking him to the station and to get dressed. O. J. returned, but when Edwards turned to brief the other officers who had arrived at the scene, Simpson jumped into his blue Bentley and roared out of the gate with Edwards and four police cars in a hot but unsuccessful pursuit.[26] This time, Nicole did sign a police report but was already beginning to show signs of becoming a reluctant witness. When the lead investigator asked officers in the West Los Angeles division if any of them had knowledge of prior incidents involving the Simpsons, only one of them, Mark Fuhrman, volunteered information. Ultimately, O. J. pleaded "no contest" to misdemeanor spousal abuse, was sentenced to community service, and placed on probation.[27]

There was, however, another 911 call made four-and-a-half years later. On October 25, 1993, less than eight months before she was murdered, the 911 operator heard Nicole crying, "He's back. Please . . . He's O. J. Simpson. I think you know his record. Could

---

26. Toobin, *The Run of His Life*, 51–56.
27. Ibid.

you please send somebody over here?" For thirteen minutes, Nicole pleaded with O. J. to leave her house while also answering the operator's questions. In the background, O. J. could be heard saying, "I'm leaving with my two fists is when I'm leaving." He had apparently broken down the door to get in. The prosecution also showed evidence of spousal abuse, or what the defense euphemistically called "marital discord," with the testimony of Nicole's sister as well as others about various acts of stalking and violence by O. J.[28]

This was all news to the public as well as to the jurors who knew little or nothing about Simpson's less-engaging personality until after his arrest. Nor did they know that on June 7, 1994, just five days before she was killed, Nicole, apparently giving up on getting help from the police, had called the Sojourn Battered Women's Shelter in Santa Monica, claiming that she was afraid and didn't know what to do because she was being stalked by O. J. Simpson. This out-of-court statement was ruled inadmissible hearsay and was never heard by the jury.

Even without it, the prosecution had a mountain of evidence against O. J. Simpson.[29] Every single drop of blood tested taken from every single crime scene venue and surface, whether on the grounds and gates and driveways of the Bundy and Rockingham residences as well the interior of O. J.'s estate, the two bloody gloves and his socks, as well as the Bronco, belonged to either Nicole Simpson, Ron Goldman, O. J. Simpson, or a combination of all three. This evidence came from two types of DNA tests; the PCR and the RFLP. The PCR test is less precise than the RFLP but can be conducted on much smaller blood samples as well as on samples that have been degraded because of bacteria or exposure to the elements. PCR tests

---

28. Ibid., 272–3.

29. See the list of what Marcia Clark in her final argument called irrefutable prosecution evidence at Clark, *Without a Doubt*, 472–3. An even more complete summary of the guilt factors appears in Bugliosi, *Outrage*, 276–80; where the author lists the number of coincidences that would have to be believed to find Simpson innocent. Also useful is the description of all the prosecution evidence in Fuhrman, *Murder in Brentwood*, 155–67; and in Easton, "Lessons Learned the Hard Way from O. J. and the 'Dream Team,'" 707, 710–1; The incriminating evidence: Linder, "Famous American Trials," http://law2.umkc.edu/faculty/projects/ftrials/Simpson/evidence.html.

were conducted on four of the five blood drops found to the left of the footprints on the Bundy driveway. Three drops showed that only one out of 240,000 people had DNA with genetic markers found in the sample, and Simpson was one of those people. The fourth sample showed that 5,200 people could have the same genetic markers, and Simpson was one of them. The fifth drop of blood had sufficient markers for an RFLP test and that showed only one in 170 million had the same DNA, and again, Simpson was one of them. The RFLP test on the blood that was found on the rear gate of Nicole's house on Bundy Drive indicated that its DNA could only belong to one out of fifty-seven billion people. And this blood was a match for O. J. Simpson. The countless other tests on every crime surface had less dramatic odds, but all were conclusively proved to be the blood of either Simpson, the two victims, or a mixture of two or three. The mixture of O. J.'s, Nicole's, and Goldman's blood that was found on the console and the carpet of the Bronco parked in front of the Rockingham gate was especially important, because Simpson had stated that only he had driven the car the day before and had probably bled in the car getting his cell phone, after he had cut his hand in the house.

All these statistics came from two different laboratories, using two different techniques: Cell Works Diagnostics in Maryland, the preeminent DNA lab in the country, and the laboratory at the California Department of Justice.[30]

In addition, the prosecution had hair and fiber evidence to add to their apparently devastating case. FBI expert Douglas Deedrick revealed that hair samples taken from the black knit cap found at Ron Goldman's feet as well as hair from his shirt, which was made by "direct contact," matched the hair samples taken from O. J. Simpson. Torn hair taken from the bloody right-hand glove found behind Kato Kaelin's cottage was a match with Nicole Simpson's hair. Blue-black fibers, consistent with the color of the shirt O. J. was wearing the night of the murders, were found on that same glove as well as on the socks in O. J.'s bedroom and on Goldman's shirt. Rare synthetic

---

30. Bugliosi, *Outrage*, 24–25; Clark, *Without a Doubt*, 395–6.

carpet fibers taken from Simpson's Ford Bronco were a match with those found on the knit hat and the Rockingham glove.[31]

Beyond the physical evidence, the prosecution had abundant circumstantial evidence. The bloody gloves each had a label with the brand name "Aris" and a style number. The detectives found that this particular style was only sold in the United States at Bloomingdale's department store chain. Upon further investigation, they discovered that Nicole had purchased two pairs of Aris Light leather gloves on December 18, 1990, at the Bloomingdale's in New York City. Only about 200 of these gloves, size extra-large, had ever been sold.

The bloody footprints of the killer were from size twelve Bruno Magli shoes, a size that only nine percent of the population, including O. J., wore. Experts also determined that the person leaving these footprints weighed about 200 pounds and was between 6 feet and 6 feet 4 inches tall. Guess who weighed 200 pounds and was 6 feet 2 inches tall?

The prosecutors would also be able to show that Simpson could not explain how he had cut his hand on the night of the murder and could not account for his time between 9:30 P.M. and 10:53 P.M. It was known that he tried to call Paula Barbieri from his cell phone in the Bronco at 10:03 P.M. The airport limo driver, Alan Park, said there was no Bronco parked at Rockingham when he arrived at 10:15 P.M. to pick up O. J. He rang the intercom there at 10:40, 10:43, and again at 10:49, but there was no answer. At about 10:51, approximately when Kato Kaelin heard thumps on his wall, Park saw a large person in dark clothes walk across the driveway and into the house. The lights of the house then turned on, and Park left the limo at 10:55, buzzed the house again, and this time O. J. Simpson answered, saying he had overslept and would be right out.

Finally, prosecutors felt that the pattern of repeated physical or emotional abuse of Nicole Simpson inflicted by O. J. Simpson, evidenced by a list of fifty-nine separate incidents, provided intent and motive for the murders.[32]

---

31. Clark, *Without a Doubt*, 413–7; Toobin, *The Run of His Life*, 373–4.
32. Defense attorney and law professor Alan Dershowitz called the domestic abuse evidence

GLENN C. ALTSCHULER AND FAUST F. ROSSI

Given the abundance of scientific, physical, and circumstantial evidence, how would it be possible for the jury to acquit O. J. Simpson? First, it would require a skillful defense team; second, a jury that was extremely sympathetic to the defendant; and third, there needed to be a bundle of mistakes by the police and prosecutors. All three of these requirements turned out to be present.

Robert Shapiro was able to put together an extremely effective defense team of attorneys, experts, and investigators. He recruited F. Lee Bailey, who had become nationally known for successfully defending accused wife-killer Dr. Sam Sheppard. His latest case had been the defense of Patty Hearst, of the Hearst newspaper family, who had been kidnapped by the Symbionese Liberation Army and then was accused of being their accomplice in an armed bank robbery. Shapiro hired two New York lawyers, Barry Scheck and Peter Neufeld, who were experts on DNA evidence. Soon after, Professor Alan Dershowitz, one of the nation's best appellate lawyers, and Professor Gerald Uelmen, former dean of the Santa Clara Law School, were added to the team. Finally, Shapiro turned to Johnnie Cochran, the best-known African-American lawyer in Los Angeles who had sued the LAPD in personal injury actions on behalf of black victims of police misconduct. Also hired were the country's top forensic experts: Henry Lee, the chief police scientist for the state of Connecticut, and Michael Baden, the former chief medical examiner of New York City. The media quickly dubbed this group, "The Dream Team," the best that money could buy.

Almost all the team assumed that O. J. was guilty. Before they were hired, Cochran and Dershowitz, in speaking to friends, had conceded as much. The defense made little effort to conduct their own blood tests, and only they knew that O. J. had failed his lie detector test. They decided to claim that their client was the victim

---

"massively irrelevant" because less than 1 percent of batterers actually kill their victims. Roger Park calls this argument "highly misleading." See Roger C. Park, "Proving the Case: Character and Prior Acts: Character Evidence Issues in the O. J. Simpson Case—or, Rationales of the Character Evidence Ban, with Illustrations from the Simpson Case," *University of Colorado Law Review* 67 (1996): 747, 751; Steven Strogatz, "Chances Are," *New York Times*, April 25, 2010, opinionator.blogs.nytimes.com/2010/04/25/chances-are/?-r=o.

Johnnie Cochran (left), Robert Shapiro (center) O. J. Simpson (right).
© Ted Soqui/Sygma/CORBIS

of a wide-ranging conspiracy of racist law enforcement officials who planted fabricated evidence to frame him for a crime he did not commit. With Cochran as the lead attorney, they would exploit the long history of racism in the LAPD and the understandable mistrust of the police in the black community. As *Time* magazine would indicate in an effort to explain the acquittal verdict:

> Jurors did not require too much coaching from Cochran to believe that Simpson may have been a victim of the Los Angeles Police Department. All they had to do was replay in their minds the videotape of the savage beating administered four years earlier to an unemployed black construction worker named Rodney King.[33]

---

33. Elizabeth Gleick, "Headliners: Johnnie Cochran Jr.," *Time,* December 25, 1995; Bugliosi, *Outrage,* 329.

The defense would combine their race-based theory with evidence of a police conspiracy and police incompetence in the process of collecting and processing the blood evidence.

In order for their strategy to succeed, the defense also needed a receptive audience, which they had in the African-American-dominated jury pool of downtown Los Angeles. Cochran reportedly said, "Give me one black juror, and I'll give you a hung jury."[34] He got nine.

The defense team also exploited the personal weaknesses of the prosecution team. Johnnie Cochran wrote: "Marcia Clark, I could see, was simply wearing down under the strain of an unsettled personal life. Chris Darden—his temper was wearing thinner—we began to look for ways to exploit that."[35] Robert Shapiro felt that Marcia Clark's "style and obvious personal antagonism towards me would be favorable to us and off-putting to the jury and I did what I could to elicit those responses from her at every opportunity."[36]

The defense also employed some techniques that may well have skirted ethical standards, or crossed the line.[37] Cochran's opening statement was extremely important because it was the jury's first impression of the defense evidence in the case. Lawyers are warned that they should not make promises they cannot keep or statements that can be proven false, but Cochran did exactly that. He said that O. J.'s arthritis was so severe that he couldn't deal a deck of cards, much less kill anyone. This statement would be repudiated by a thorough physical exam performed four days after the crime in which the doctor concluded that O. J. had no disability that hampered his movements, nor had he had any episodes of acute arthritis. Cochran also listed witnesses that he would call to testify on O. J.'s behalf. He said Mary Anne Gerchas, a Bundy Drive neighbor, would testify that she saw two Hispanic and two Caucasian men leave the murder scene

---

34. Darden, *In Contempt,* 166.
35. Johnnie Cochran, Jr. and Tim Rutten, *Journey to Justice* (Ballantine Books, 1996), 3.
36. Robert Shapiro and Larkin Warren, *The Search for Justice: A Defense Attorney's Brief on the O. J. Simpson Case* (Warner Books, 1996), 156.
37. Catherine Behan, "Alschuler: Dirty tricks a key element in O. J. victory," *University of Chicago Chronicle* 17 (1998).

in a speeding car. He said he would call Rosa Lopez, a neighbor's maid, who would testify that she had seen Simpson's Bronco parked in front of his home at the time of the murders. And he said the jury would hear from Doctor Lenore Walker, a Denver psychologist and the foremost authority on battered-woman syndrome, who would testify that Simpson did not fit the profile of a batterer.

Not one of these witnesses were ever produced by the defense.[38] The defense also disregarded the California Reciprocal Discovery Law that requires each side to give the other advance notice of all their witnesses and their statements.

The prosecution had given the defense thousands of pages of investigatory material and had repeatedly asked for the same disclosures from them. The defense said that it had nothing to give and then, at the beginning of the trial, deliberately blindsided the prosecution by unloading a huge list of new witnesses.

The willfulness of these discovery abuses was exposed in *American Tragedy* by Laurence Schiller, a friend of Robert Kardashian, who was allowed into some defense team strategy sessions. Schiller describes a debate among Barry Scheck, Johnnie Cochran, and Carl Douglas, the attorney in charge of assembling and disclosing all exhibits. Douglas was shocked when Scheck said, 'Stall them. They've been stalling us.' When Scheck considered leaving out the defense contention that there was blood missing from the Simpson's reference sample, Douglas protested, 'We're sandbagging them. I'll catch hell for this!' Cochran then weighed in: 'It's about the client. You'll have to fall on your sword. Go and do it.' They agreed to hold the material until the last moment."[39] Judge Ito ultimately advised the jury that the defense conduct "was deliberate and an illegal violation of law." But instead of imposing severe penalties, he advised Marcia Clark to make an additional opening argument after the disclosures were made.[40]

---

38. Bugliosi, *Outrage*, 300–2; Fuhrman, *Murder in Brentwood*, 265–6.
39. Schiller and Willwerth, *American Tragedy*, 332–3; Clark, *Without a Doubt*, 271–3.
40. Schiller and Willwerth, *American Tragedy*, 347; Clark, *Without a Doubt*, 278; Toobin, *The Run of His Life*, 249–52.

Schiller describes another defense gambit. After the jury was selected, the defense moved to exclude the DNA evidence on the grounds that it was unreliable and had not yet achieved general acceptance in the scientific community. The defense knew there was no real prospect of winning this motion, but it forced the prosecution to spend a lot of time preparing for a complex hearing while the defense could prepare for trial. On the day of the hearing, the defense team withdrew its motion. Since the jury was ready, the prosecution's request for delay was denied.[41]

The defense team's tactics were on display as well when the jurors visited the Bundy and Rockingham crime venues. These tours were a form of evidence to allow the jurors to visualize and better understand witness testimony. In anticipation of the tour, Shapiro, Cochran, and Douglas undertook to "redecorate" O. J.'s home in part to emphasize his African-American identity. Cochran said, "We've got to have pictures of his family, his black family up there" so a photograph of his mother was placed at his bedside and a Norman Rockwell poster of a little black girl being escorted to school by a federal marshal was removed from Cochran's office and hung at the top of the stairs where the jurors could not miss it. A nude portrait of Simpson's white girlfriend, Paula Barbieri, was removed, as well as pictures of other white women and his white golfing buddies.[42]

Another gambit was to encourage misinterpretations of the concept of reasonable doubt. At times, Scheck and Cochran appeared to suggest that if the jury had reasonable doubt on any single fact or piece of evidence, then they had to acquit. Scheck specifically stated that the prosecution had to prove beyond a reasonable doubt that the blood evidence wasn't tampered with.[43] Surprisingly, his misinterpretation of the law was ignored by both the judge and the prosecution but did prove persuasive to some jurors. Foreperson Armanda Cooley wrote that the jury could not explain away the presence of O. J.'s blood at the

41. This was Barry Scheck's idea as described in Schiller and Willwerth, *American Tragedy*, 286; Clark, *Without a Doubt*, 243.
42. Schiller and Willwerth, *American Tragedy*, 371–2; Behan, "Alschuler"; Clark, *Without a Doubt*, 303–5.
43. Schiller and Willwerth, *American Tragedy*, 663; Bugliosi, *Outrage*, 270–1.

Bundy murder scene; but then added, "Me personally, I have not tried to explain it away at all. . . . That was not one of the issues . . . that was definitely not the reasonable doubt we based our decision on." She also said that "if Fuhrman was a liar, you've got reasonable doubt right there."[44] "The great genius of the defense," Jeffrey Toobin concluded in *The Run of His Life*, "was that they would fixate on particular parts of the evidence and question it. But what about all the evidence together? Who had the motive to kill these people? Who had size 12 shoes? Whose time was unaccounted for? Whose blood was on the glove left at the Bundy crime scene? Who had a cut on his hand the next day?"[45]

Legal tradition dictates that lawyers avoid making objections that interrupt an opponent's summation unless absolutely necessary. However, during Marcia Clark's closing argument the defense ignored this tradition. Under California Procedure, the order of final arguments is first prosecution, then defense, and finally prosecution again with a rebuttal summation. After the first and second rounds, Marcia Clark gave her final argument. At that point, when there was no fear of retaliation, the defense team lodged more than fifty objections, of which all but two were deemed frivolous and overruled by Judge Ito. According to Laurence Schiller, Alan Dershowitz proposed this tactic at a defense team conference:

[T]hen Dershowitz offers Johnnie a suggestion: "Don't make any objections to the first part of Marcia's closing argument" he says, "Be very polite" . . . "but when Marcia comes back for the last word, then I save all my impoliteness for the very end of her closing argument. Stand up and object. The worst Ito can do is shut you up. It's important to keep interrupting her final summation because she is going to throw everything in the book at us when we can't respond any longer."[46]

44. Cooley, Bess, and Rubin-Jackson, *Madam Foreman*, 201–2; where juror responds to Geraldo Rivera question, "How can you explain away O. J.'s blood at the murder scene, found hours before his blood sample was taken?"; Bugliosi, *Outrage*, 270–2.
45. "Jeffrey Toobin interview," Frontline, http://www.pbs.org/wgbh/pages/frontline/oj/interviews/toobin.html.
46. Schiller and Willwerth, *American Tragedy*, 640, 665–6; Fuhrman, *Murder in Brentwood*, 299.

If race was prominently featured in the trial, it reached its zenith in Cochran's closing argument. Dominated by themes of police racism and misconduct, his summation suggested that the jurors should use their verdict to send a message that these behaviors would no longer be tolerated. He concluded:

> Your verdict goes far beyond the doors of the courtroom. . . . Stop this cover-up. Stop this cover-up. If you don't stop it, then who? Do you think the police department is going to stop it? Do you think the D.A.'s office is going to stop it? Do you think we can stop it by ourselves? It has to be stopped by you. Who then polices the police? You police the police. You are the ones to send the message. Maybe this is one of the reasons we are all gathered together this day. Maybe this is why you were selected. There is something in your background . . . that helps you understand that this is wrong. Maybe you are the right people, at the right time, at the right place to say "No more—we are not going to have this!"[47]

Cochran's rhetoric was an invitation to jury nullification; that is, to ignore the evidence and the judge's instructions and to instead render a verdict to send a message of racial solidarity against police misconduct.[48]

The defense strategy had two built-in ironies. The first was that O. J. himself never identified as being black. In a 1968 interview with

47. Toobin, *The Run of His Life*, 419–21; Schiller and Willwerth, *American Tragedy*, 661; Clark, *Without a Doubt*, 465–6; Darden, *In Contempt*, 369.
48. There is a substantial amount of academic literature on juror nullification in connection with the O. J. Simpson case. W. William Hodes, "Lord Brougham, The Dream Team, and the Jury Nullification of the Third Kind," *University of Colorado Law Review* 67 (1996):1075 (jury nullification is the only rational explanation for the Simpson verdict); compare Rebecca Love Kourlis, "Not Jury Nullification; Not a Call for Ethical Reform; But Rather a Case for Judicial Control," *University of Colorado Law Review* 67 (1996): 1109 (Cochran flirted with jury nullification, but the verdict was not the result of nullification); Paul Butler, "Racially Based Jury Nullification: Black Power in the Criminal Justice System," *Yale Law Journal* 105 (1995): 677 (approving of jury nullification by black jurors of black defendants in certain cases.).

Robert Lipsyte of the *New York Times*, he said, "I'm not black; I'm O. J."[49] Unlike other sports figures, such as Jim Brown or Muhammad Ali, O. J. was far removed from black political causes. In 1992, he proclaimed that Hertz "told me in all their surveys, I was colorless."[50] And yet, African-Americans still saw O. J. as one of them; a black man who had made it in the white man's world and deserved their support.

The second irony was that O. J. Simpson was, in fact, coddled and protected by many in the police department. Between 1985 and 1993, Nicole Simpson had called the police at least ten times begging for help. The police would come, listen to his excuses, talk Nicole into dropping the charges, and then let him off.[51]

To be sure, the prosecution made many, many critical miscalculations, none more serious than the decision of where the case should be tried. The trial should have been held in the Santa Monica District of Los Angeles County, where the murders were committed and where the jury would more likely be white, somewhat better educated, and sympathetic to the victims. Instead, the district attorney chose to file in the South Central District of downtown Los Angeles, which insured that the jury pool would be comprised predominantly of African-Americans sympathetic to Simpson. Heavily criticized for what was considered a blunder, Garcetti gave a series of reasons for the decision: the Santa Monica courthouse was too small for the expected (and desired) media, the courthouse had suffered earthquake damage (it had already been repaired), and the decision had been made by the court (not true). Later, prosecutors claimed that cases projected to last more than two months had to be tried in the large downtown Los Angeles courthouse (also untrue).[52]

The district attorney's office was confident to the point of arrogance that a conviction would be gotten wherever the case was tried.

---

49. Toobin, *The Run of His Life*, 49.
50. Bob Levin, "The real America, in black and white," *Maclean's*, October 16, 1995.
51. Toobin, *The Run of His Life*, 264, 267; Easton, "Lessons Learned the Hard Way from O. J. and the 'Dream Team,'" 707, 726.
52. Bugliosi, *Outrage*, 67–78 (author calls this "the biggest error" made by the prosecution in the case); Geis and Bienen, *Crimes of the Century*, 174–5.

And so, with an eye to reelection in 1996, District Attorney Garcetti thought it would be a plus if the guilty verdict came from a predominantly black jury in the South Central District. The large venue able to accommodate hordes of reporters and cameras wouldn't hurt either. In addition, the prosecutors would have the benefit of being near their downtown offices.

The reasons the prosecution team used to suggest they had no choice in having the trial filed in South Central Los Angeles were rebutted by one of their own team members. Years later, in a ten-year retrospective interview, William Hodgman conceded:

> Well, we had a choice. We could have very well filed the case in Santa Monica. And if we could have done something differently to avoid all the grief that flowed thereafter, it would have been smarter for our office to have filed the case in Santa Monica.[53]

When asked if he would have handled things differently, Hodgman went on to say:

> If it were up to me, if I were the elected D.A. or had that sort of horsepower, I would have filed the case in Santa Monica . . . since the O. J. case, that is precisely what is done. The cases are filed in the appropriate venue, and it's something that the courts now recognize and insist upon.[54]

Marcia Clark had been warned of the dangers of holding the trial in Los Angeles by Donald Vinson, one of country's most respected jury consultants. Vinson offered his services to Garcetti free of charge, and a mock trial was organized with a jury panel of six whites and four blacks. When they voted, the racial divide was stark; all whites for conviction and all blacks for acquittal. Vinson asked the black jurors

---

53. "William Hodgman interview," Frontline, http://www.pbs.org/wgbh/pages/frontline/oj/interviews/hodgman.html.
54. Ibid.

to assume that the blood and skin cells from the Bundy crime scene were proven one hundred percent to be from O. J. Three of the four black jurors still voted not guilty. When the black women were asked to assume that Nicole had been threatened and stalked, their reaction was that "in every relationship there is always a little trouble." "People get slapped around." "It doesn't mean he killed her." The next day's session with different jurors yielded the same results.[55] The African-Americans' characterizations of Marcia Clark were "shifty," "strident," and "bitch, bitch."[56] Clark, who believed she had a special relationship with black women jurors and had assumed they would be sympathetic to Nicole, was "stung" by their race-trumps-gender reaction:

> I figured I could talk to women. In cases past, I'd always been able to reach them somehow. . . . White, Hispanic, Asian, black. It didn't matter. Even when they failed to convict, I didn't feel they had it in for me personally. But *these* gals were ready to eat their own.[57]

Clark should have learned three things from this process. First, a predominantly black jury would be great for the defense and bad for the prosecution. Second, black women would be worse for the prosecution than black males, and third, African-Americans had little sympathy for Nicole and would consider the domestic violence insignificant. Instead, Clark viewed herself as an experienced trial lawyer and would "trust her gut," not this jury consultant's "mumbo jumbo."

She was particularly enraged about the criticism that she should have filed the case in Santa Monica. She wrote that filing the case there for a tactical advantage would be a "shameless and inexcusable display of racism."[58] She described Vinson and others as unethical

---

55. Toobin, *The Run of His Life*, 190–1; Bugliosi, *Outrage*, 115–7.
56. Toobin, *The Run of His Life*, 192–3.
57. Clark, *Without a Doubt*, 145. For the black women mock jurors, "one of their own" apparently included O. J. but not Nicole and not Marcia Clark.
58. Ibid., 184.

slick operators who work the angles. Christopher Darden agreed and said he would not have joined the team had the case been filed in Santa Monica.[59] Some might wonder why filing the case in the district where the crime was committed and where the defendant and both victims reside is unethical or racist.

For their righteousness, Clark, Darden, and the prosecution paid a high price. Ten pages after excoriating her critics, Clark then described her disgust with the jury and asked, "Why, on this of all cases, did we wind up with this [expletive] jury pool from hell?"[60] After weeks of reading the questionnaires the jurors had filled out, "I dragged myself home each night in a stupor of fatigue bowed under the weight that I'd have to go in there and fight every day in a battle that might already be lost."[61] During jury selection in front of the television cameras, she told Judge Ito that "the jurors are lying to the detriment of the people because they are sitting there as fans of this defendant saying, 'we want to get on this jury . . . so we can acquit this man, no matter what.'"[62]

Darden joined the prosecution team after the jury of twelve had been picked. He described his reaction:

I could tell it was one of the worst juries—from a prosecution standpoint—that I had ever seen. They were simply not happy-looking people. From the first day I sensed that many of them were angry at the system for various insults and injuries—twelve people lined up at the grinder with big axes.[63]

Two weeks after the verdict, *Newsweek* reported that "it is accepted wisdom now that the prosecutors lost the criminal trial virtually the day the predominantly African-American jury was sworn in."[64]

---

59. Darden, *In Contempt*, 192.
60. Clark, *Without a Doubt*, 192.
61. Ibid.
62. Ibid., 209.
63. Darden, *In Contempt*, 165.
64. Mark Whitaker, "Whites v. Blacks," *Newsweek*, October 16, 1995.

TEN GREAT AMERICAN TRIALS

Advocates must reach the hearts and minds of the jurors, and the very composition of this jury meant the defense task was half done before they'd even started. All the jury needed now were plausible reasons to back their predisposition to acquit, and those were provided by a series of errors by the prosecutors, detectives, and the LAPD criminologists.

Another prosecution misstep was the decision not to present to the jury four incriminating pieces of evidence; the thirty-two-minute tape of Detectives Vannatter and Lange interviewing Simpson on the day after the murders, his farewell and possibly suicidal note left with Kardashian, the details of the infamous Bronco chase, and finally, the testimony of a key witness, Jill Shively.

Although the detectives clearly botched the interview by not asking pertinent questions and by letting O. J. get away with vague answers, O. J. did make incriminating statements. He stated that his Bronco was parked in front of his house, when the limo driver clearly remembered that the car was not there when he arrived at 10:15 P.M. He could not explain how he had received the cut on his hand that bled all over the Rockingham house, the driveway, and his car. Who wouldn't remember that? O. J. also had stated in the interview that his car had been parked in front of his house from about eight or nine o'clock in the evening, and he only went to retrieve his cell phone from it at 11:05 before the Chicago flight. However, the phone records show that he used his cell phone to call Paula Barbieri at 10:03 P.M. when he said he was asleep in the house and where he had access to a land line. He said the last time he had visited the children at Bundy was five days to a week before, and he had not cut himself then or at any other time. That would surely have answered the possibility that his blood found at the crime scene had come from a prior innocent visit. In addition, the taped interview would have highlighted for the jury O. J.'s evasive and hesitant manner in answering the questions.[65]

Marcia Clark did not want the jury to hear the proclamation of innocence by an apparently grief-stricken Simpson without being

65. Bugliosi, *Outrage*, 129–32.

able to cross-examine him. But surely his statement, "I didn't do it," would not sway a jury; few murderers admit their guilt to police. Moreover, the jury was aware that the tape existed from previous testimony but never heard it, leaving them to imagine that it showed O. J.'s innocence . . . and Cochran used that in his summation.

There is no reasonable explanation for the prosecution's neglecting to provide any evidence pertaining to O. J.'s flight in A. C. Cowling's Bronco. Here was a murder suspect trying to escape with his passport, $8,750 in cash, a fake goatee and mustache, a change of clothing, and a Smith & Wesson .357 magnum. Also found were three receipts for the disguise items, dated May 27, 1994, just over two weeks before the murders and a few days after Nicole had returned to him earrings and a bracelet he had given her for her birthday. At that time she had told him, or maybe they agreed, that their relationship was over. How could Cochran and his cohorts have explained all that away? We never found out because they never had to.

Inexplicably, O. J.'s farewell note was never submitted into evidence. In it, he denies his guilt, proclaims his love for Nicole . . . and later for Barbieri, says that at times he felt like a battered husband, and concludes, "Don't feel sorry for me. I've had a great life, great friends. Please think of the real O. J. and not this lost person." Is this the letter from someone who believes he is being framed by the police?

Marcia Clark did not make use of Jill Shively, a woman who was in the vicinity of Nicole's home at the time of the murders. As Shively approached the intersection of San Vincente Blvd. and Bundy Drive, a large white car heading north on Bundy cut her off while a third car stopped suddenly to avoid a collision. The driver of the white car began shouting at the driver of the third car, "Move your damn car! Move it! Move it!" Shively recognized the shouter as O. J. Simpson and remembered his license number. After Shively learned of the murder, she gave her name to the police, and she later testified effectively before the grand jury, the only eyewitness placing Simpson near the scene at the time of the murder. However, she had sold her story to the tabloid TV show *Hard Copy* for $5,000, and in a fit of pique, Marcia Clark, who had instructed her not to talk to the media, denounced Shively "in terms that made her personally useless to the government." And so the jury never heard Jill Shively testify.[66]

The biggest miscalculation, of course, was the presence of Detective Mark Fuhrman on the witness stand. Although he had been promoted three times and was reputed to be an effective police officer, Fuhrman had a long history of racism that Marcia Clark was aware of. He had applied for a stress disability pension some thirteen years earlier and had disclosed to psychologists his antipathy toward minorities. When he was in the Marines, he said, he "got tired of having a bunch of Mexicans and niggers that should be in prison, telling me that they weren't going to do something."[67] In an article published in the *New Yorker* in July 1994, Jeffrey Toobin wrote that Simpson's lawyers would attempt to portray the detective as a racist who had planted the bloody right-hand glove at O. J.'s estate. The article encouraged a real estate agent, Kathleen Bell, to write a letter to Johnnie Cochran describing an encounter she had with Fuhrman, during which he said that "whenever he saw a nigger, as he put it, driving in a car with a white woman, he would find a reason to pull them over. Officer Fuhrman went on to say that he would like nothing more than to see all niggers gathered together and killed. He said something about burning them or bombing them, I was too shaken to remember the exact words he used."[68] As required by law, the defense team provided a copy of her letter to the prosecution. Marcia Clark did not believe her uncorroborated story and thought that Bell was seeking publicity.

The prosecution made a preliminary motion to exclude any reference to or evidence of racial animus as determined by the California Evidence Code section 352, which provides that the court has the discretion to "exclude evidence if its probative value (relevance) is substantially outweighed by the probability that its admission will (a) necessitate undue consumption of time or (b) create substantial

66. Toobin, *The Run of His Life*, 123–8; describes this as an example of Clark's self-defeating sanctimony; Clark, *Without a Doubt*, 62–65 responds that it was a matter of principle.
67. Bugliosi, *Outrage*, 162.
68. Toobin, *The Run of His Life*, 314–5.

danger of undue prejudice [to the opposing party], of confusing the issues or of misleading the jury." Clark assumed the law was on her side: in the absence of any evidence that Fuhrman had planted anything and in the light of testimony that no second glove was found at the crime scene, racist comments made by Fuhrman were irrelevant. Chris Darden, the African-American prosecution counsel, added passion to this argument:

> The word "nigger" is the filthiest, dirtiest, nastiest word in the English language. It has no place in this case or in this courtroom. It will do nothing to further this court's attempt at seeking the truth. . . . It will do one thing. It will upset black jurors. It will give them a test, and this test will be, whose side are you on; the side of the white prosecutors or on the side of the black defendant and his very prominent and capable black lawyer? That's what it's going to do. Either you are with the man or with the brothers. . . . [I]f you allow Mr. Cochran to use this word and play this race card, . . . the entire complexion of the case changes. It's a race case then. It's white versus black, African American versus Caucasian, . . . us versus the system. . . . [I]t becomes an issue of color. Who's the blackest man up here? Who are the real brothers?[69]

Judge Ito initially ruled that the defense would not be allowed to introduce evidence of racial animus unless the defense offered proof showing how Fuhrman could have planted the glove. Three days later, however, F. Lee Bailey insisted that the defense had the right to cross-examine Fuhrman on racial bias to impeach his credibility. "We are not arguing that he planted anything." Judge Ito reversed himself and held that the defense could cross-examine Fuhrman on whether he had used the N-word in the prior ten years.[70]

---

69. Bugliosi, *Outrage*, 80–1; Clark, *Without a Doubt*, 261.
70. Clark, *Without a Doubt*, 263; Bugliosi, *Outrage*, 81–83.

Judge Lance Ito presided over the O. J. Simpson murder trial.
© 2005 Phil Ramey/RameyPix/CORBIS

With this decision, race became a major issue in the case. Trial lawyer Vincent Bugliosi called Ito's decision contrary to law and lacking in common sense. He noted:

Every day in America, literally thousands of white police officers officially arrest or investigate black suspects. Does anyone really believe that when these thousands upon thousands of cases go to trial, it's proper to ask every one of these officers if he has ever used that racial slur and if he denies it and there is evidence he did, to have a satellite trial within a trial on that issue (which is what in effect happened in the Simpson case). That's crazy. Ito couldn't have been more off-base here, and the prosecution had to pay dearly for Ito's sins.[71]

---

71. Bugliosi, *Outrage,* 83–84.

At this point, the prosecution had a number of options, though none without risk. They could have immediately appealed Ito's ruling as is allowed under California law. However, Marcia Clark thought that if she did try to get his decision reversed, Ito would be infuriated and take it out on the prosecution for the rest of the case. To her credit, she later acknowledged having a failure of nerve and concluded that his decision should have been appealed.[72]

Having bypassed the appeal, the district attorney's office had another possible solution that might have avoided dire consequences. They could have had Fuhrman undergo days of rigorous mock cross-examination. Marcia Clark knew he had used the N-word thirteen years earlier in his disability process and she was aware of Kathleen Bell's accusations, even though she chose not to believe her. It was naïve to believe that a tough LAPD detective, who had worked for years in dangerous high-crime areas with other tough officers, had never used that word. But Marcia desperately wanted to believe his denials. So instead of subjecting Fuhrman to a real grilling, she simply had Chris Darden ask him if he ever used the N-word in the last ten years. Fuhrman said no, and although Darden didn't believe him, he inexplicably didn't question him any further. Darden or Clark should have told him that they knew he had used that language in the past, that it was one of his favorite words, and that he had to tell the truth because otherwise he ran the risk of a perjury charge when the defense proved his statements were false. He should have been told that, by lying under oath, he would jeopardize the prosecution's case against Simpson, but if he admitted the truth, then the judge would have no reason to allow the testimony of Bell or any other witnesses the defense claims that they had. Clark knew that none of this aggressive preparation had been done, yet she chose to ignore it.[73]

Clark and Darden were heavily criticized for putting Fuhrman on the stand at all and for embracing him as an excellent, hardworking detective. She showed him the Kathleen Bell letter, and he said he

72. Clark, *Without a Doubt*, 263–4.
73. Bugliosi, *Outrage*, 161–3.

did not remember meeting her and denied making any racist statements. He then testified to finding the bloody glove at the Rockingham estate, as well as seeing the blood in the Bronco and the bloody socks in O. J.'s bedroom.

And then came F. Lee Bailey's cross-examination:

Q: Do you use the word nigger in describing people?

A. No sir.

Q: Have you used that word in the past 10 years?

A. Not that I recall.

Q: You mean that if you called someone a nigger you have forgotten it?

A. I'm not sure I can answer the question the way you phrased it, sir.

Q: Are you therefore saying that you have not used that word in the past ten years, Detective Fuhrman?

A. Yes, that is what I'm saying.

Q: And you say under oath that you have not addressed any black person as a nigger or spoken about black people as niggers in the past ten years?

A. Yes, that is what I'm saying.

Q: So that anyone who comes to this court and quotes you as using that word in dealing with African-Americans would be a liar, would they not, Detective Fuhrman?

A. Yes, they would.

Q: All of them, correct?

A. All of them.[74]

Following this testimony, media pundits credited Fuhrman with a superb performance and concluded that Bailey "did not lay a glove on him." They were mistaken. In seven short questions, as later events would demonstrate, Bailey closed off any avenue of escape.

Around 1988, a novice writer named Laura Hart McKinney enlisted Fuhrman's help with her screenplay about the sexism women police officers confronted in the LAPD. They had twelve taped sessions and she agreed to give him $10,000 if the screenplay was sold; it wasn't, and they had no contact after 1988. The Fuhrman interviews somehow fell into the hands of the defense and were quickly leaked to the press. The tapes contained every racial slur imaginable; the N-word alone was used forty-one times. Although it's possible that Fuhrman was just playing a part for the screenplay, it was clear that he had lied under oath in responding to Bailey.

The defense selected sixty-one excerpts from these tapes for the jury to hear, but Judge Ito ruled that only two brief sentences could be played for them: "We have no niggers where I grew up" and "That's where niggers live." He would also allow McKinney to testify that Fuhrman had used the N-word forty-one times, but ruled that the remaining fifty-nine instances of racism were either irrelevant or unduly prejudicial to the prosecution.[75] Johnnie Cochran immediately called a press conference and denounced Ito's ruling: "[P]erhaps one of the cruelest, unjust decisions ever rendered in a criminal court . . . the cover-up continues. . . . This inexplicable, indefensible ruling lends credence to all those who say the criminal justice system is corrupt."[76]

Judge Ito let these contemptuous statements pass without a finding of contempt or a fine or a report of Cochran's conduct to the California Bar Association.

74. Toobin, *The Run of His Life*, 325–6; Schiller and Willwerth, *American Tragedy*, 589.
75. Ibid., 406; Bugliosi, *Outrage*, 87; Toobin, *The Run of His Life*, 406.
76. Schiller and Willwerth, *American Tragedy*, 590; Toobin, *The Run of His Life*, 406–7.

Even more difficult to understand is the ruling Ito made on August 29, 1995. Over strenuous prosecution objection, Ito decided to play, in open court but with the jury excused, all sixty-one excerpts that had been requested by the defense, including the fifty-nine that he had previously deemed irrelevant and potentially prejudicial. The TV audience, including millions of African-Americans, and, because of conjugal visits, members of the jury as well, were thus treated to an avalanche of racial slurs from Detective Fuhrman. Judge Ito's justification for his ruling, which had no known legal basis, was "I don't want this court to ever be in a position where there is any indication that this court would participate in suppressing information that is of vital public interest."[77]

After the McKinney tapes surfaced, the prosecution team treated Fuhrman like a pariah. Clark cut off all contact; she wanted him "out of her life."[78] The defense recalled him to finish its cross-examination, but because he had no assurance that the prosecution would allow him on redirect to explain his apparent racial slurs, he advised the court that he would plead his Fifth Amendment rights. That meant he would have to take the Fifth to all questions, leaving the defense free to ask him anything they wanted. Knowing this, the defense, outside of the jury's presence, asked Fuhrman whether he had planted any evidence in the case. Marcia Clark wrote that his taking the Fifth was a disaster, but if she had only responded to his phone calls, the situation might have been avoided, and she might have been able to at least partially rehabilitate him.

Indeed, there were black police officers, including his former African-American partner, who were willing to testify that whatever his private beliefs were, he had never displayed a trace of racism on the job. He had, on at least one occasion, helped to clear a black defendant who had been wrongly arrested for murder. Of course he shouldn't have lied, but if the prosecution had done its homework, this testimony could have been used to show that Detective Fuhrman

---

77. Bugliosi, *Outrage*, 87–88; describes Ito's decision as "inexcusable and for which there wasn't any possible legal argument in support of it."
78. Clark, *Without a Doubt*, 451–3.

was a good, fair-minded cop. In the months that followed the verdict, Fuhrman's police career was investigated by four different state and federal agencies, including the U.S. Department of Justice, and not one of these investigations uncovered a single incident of racial bias or illegal activity such as the planting of evidence.[79]

Still another of the prosecution's self-inflicted disasters, attributed to Darden's inexperience and impulsiveness, was the famous bloody glove demonstration. In five minutes, Darden undermined substantial elements of the prosecution's case by theatrically demanding that Simpson try on the gloves that were found at Bundy and Rockingham and that were in evidence. Darden did not consider that these gloves had been wet with blood and that leather tends to shrink and stiffen when damp. Or that in order to protect the gloves as evidence, they would have to be tried on over a protective latex glove. A more sensible experiment would have been to obtain an identical pair of new Aris gloves and use them in the demonstration. In addition, every trial lawyer knows that you never do a demonstration unless you are absolutely sure of the outcome. But Darden turned control of the demonstration, in full view of the jury and television audience, over to the defendant, an experienced actor, O. J. Simpson.

Walking toward the jurors, and grimacing dramatically, Simpson appeared to tug and struggle, muttering "too tight," as he tried to pull the glove on over the latex. He kept his thumb bent at a right angle to his wrist to make it virtually impossible for the glove to go on properly. Marcia Clark said to herself, "That's it, we just lost the case." In his summation, Cochran coined the now famous slogan, "If it doesn't fit, you must acquit," . . . and they did.[80]

The defense tried to minimize the damage. Robert Rubin, former vice president of Aris, measured Simpson's hand and testified that a size large or extra-large would fit him. He went on to explain that the evidence gloves could have shrunk, and the protective latex gloves

---

79. Bugliosi, *Outrage*, 165–70; describes an article in the November 8, 1995, *Los Angeles Times* by Greg Krikorian suggesting that Fuhrman was not the rogue cop as portrayed at the trial.
80. Geis and Bienen, *Crimes of the Century*, 180; Bugliosi, *Outrage*, 143–4; Clark, *Without a Doubt*, 404–8.

O. J. Simpson pulls the glove over the latex on his hand.
© CORBIS/Sygma

would make for a tighter fit. But jury members may already have made up their minds.[81]

The realization that the jury was disposed to favor Simpson also affected the tone and content of the prosecutors' arguments. For example, during jury selection, Marcia tried to identify herself with O. J.'s fans:

> He's such a famous guy. He's such a popular guy, . . . a good looking man. . . . This is not a fun place for me to be. . . . Do you feel a loyalty to the defendant? The defendant is such a famous guy. . . . You may not like me for bringing this case. I'm not winning any popularity contest for doing so.[82]

The implication is that she would rather not be prosecuting Simpson, but was assigned to the case.

---

81. Darden, *In Contempt*, 323–6.
82. Bugliosi, *Outrage*, 180.

And Darden, in his final argument to the jury, said: "Nobody wants to do anything to this man. We don't. . . . There is nothing personal about this. . . ." And then he added these final words: "Whatever you do, the decision is yours. I'm glad it's not mine."[83] Instead of communicating a strong sense of conviction, Darden seemed to be implying that this is a close, tough case, and he comes close to conceding there is reasonable doubt. The contrast between the aggressiveness of the defense and the weakness of the prosecution is striking.

One has to sympathize with the prosecution lawyers who, in addition to their own miscalculations, were saddled by the incompetence of the Robbery-Homicide detectives and criminologists of the LAPD. The defense attack on this part of the case was led by Barry Scheck, who insisted that the blood evidence was contaminated, that it had been sloppily gathered and examined; and when neither of these theories seemed likely, he argued that the blood could have been planted by the detectives in order to incriminate O. J. There actually was enough incompetent and suspicious conduct by the detectives to justify the defense speculation. All the points made by the defense were rebutted by the prosecution, but the explanations were complicated and undermined by admissions that mistakes had been made. For example, Dennis Fung had collected blood from the crime scene on Bundy Drive as well as from the back of the property on June 12, the morning after the murders were committed, but he missed the blood on the back gate until he collected it on July 3, three weeks later. Scheck showed Fung a photograph taken on June 13 that showed no blood on the gate, suggesting that the sample had been planted later, but the prosecution demonstrated that not only was the first photo taken from a problematic angle, but many of the officers had seen the blood on the gate the morning after the murders. Scheck also submitted reports that the blood collected the morning after the crimes was degraded, while the blood collected three weeks

83. Ibid., 197–8; Schiller and Willwerth, *American Tragedy*, 256. In his book, Darden reveals his own feelings when asked to join the prosecution team. He writes that, "I was torn. My responsibilities as a prosecutor clearly told me to take this case. But I had other responsibilities as a black man and they were difficult to sort out." Darden, *In Contempt*, 163.

afterwards was in good condition. Did that not indicate that the blood on the gate was put there later? Now Fung had to admit that the blood collected on June 13 had been improperly stored in plastic bags and then put in a truck that was not air-conditioned for several hours; since heat and humidity degrade DNA, another careless error had been made. But because the blood on the gate was on a clean, painted surface, in cool air, it was not degraded.

But Scheck had more. The police nurse, Thano Peratis, who took a blood sample from O. J. the day after the murders, had testified at the preliminary hearing that he had taken about 7.9 to 8.1 cubic centimeters of blood from Simpson's arm. Using this information, Scheck had looked at the laboratory records to see how much of the blood had been used in the prosecution's testing and found that only 6.5 cc were accounted for. This discrepancy allowed the defense to claim that the "missing blood" was the source of the Simpson blood that had been planted on the Bundy gate, in the Bronco, and on the socks in O. J.'s bedroom. To rebut this claim, the prosecution was forced to have Peratis admit that he had made a mistake at his preliminary hearing and now estimated that the blood he withdrew from Simpson was more like 6 cc.

Scheck also emphasized that after Nurse Peratis had taken the blood sample from Simpson at the Parker Center on June 13, Vannatter took the vial at 2:30 P.M. and placed it in a large blood collection envelope. But instead of booking it at the Center, he took it with him and drove twenty miles back to Simpson's Rockingham estate. A video shows Vannatter giving the envelope to Fung at the estate and Fung testified that he received it at 5:20 P.M., when it was put into the LAPD evidence truck. In their summations, Scheck and Cochran asked, "Why did Vannatter not book the blood where it was taken? Why take it all the way to Brentwood? The implication was that he or Fung wanted to plant it at O. J.'s house. But Vannatter had a reasonable explanation. He knew that Fung was still collecting evidence, and since each piece of evidence is sequentially assigned a property item number as it is collected, it made sense to deliver the vial to him and to keep the evidence all together. Nonetheless, at least three jurors commented after the verdict that they found Vannatter's account "suspicious."[84]

Scheck also argued that Mark Fuhrman had planted Ron Goldman's blood in O. J.'s Bronco by swiping the second glove like a paintbrush or by some other unspecified method; an unlikely event, since the Bronco was locked. Equally unlikely was the claim of the defense that Fuhrman discovered a second glove at Bundy that no one had seen, carried it to Rockingham, and planted it on the pathway behind Kato Kaelin's bungalow. The Rockingham glove, it is worth noting, had both O. J.'s blood and his hair on it. How could Fuhrman have gotten Simpson's hair? The glove also had fibers that matched the color of the clothes Simpson wore on the evening of the murders. At the time that Fuhrman is supposed to have picked up the glove at Bundy and planted it at Rockingham, he had no idea whether Simpson had an alibi or whether there were witnesses to the crime.[85] It would have been foolish, given what he did not know, to have risked planting the glove.

A major problem for the defense was the five blood spots along the Bundy pathway to the left of the bloody footprints made by the killer as he left the scene. It was established by both DNA tests that the blood came from Simpson, but at the time of its collection, Simpson was in Chicago and had not yet given a sample of his blood. The defense speculated that the blood could have been left at some earlier time at Bundy when O. J. was visiting his children. But that was a very weak argument because O. J. had stated that he had not bled at Bundy, and Fung had testified that the blood was fresh. If he had bled earlier at Bundy, how likely is it that he bled exactly along the left side of the killer's footprints?[86] To prove his point, Scheck seized upon the testimony of Fung's associate, Collin Yamauchi, that

---

84. Bugliosi, *Outrage*, 404–9; Fuhrman, *Murder in Brentwood*, 51.
85. Fuhrman's ignorance about these details was revealed in Clark's redirect of Fuhrman at the trial. Toobin, *The Run of His Life*, 325.
86. Some jurors discounted the Bundy blood drops, saying they were contaminated and degraded by their exposure to the dirt and weather. But contamination or degradation of the blood would have yielded no result. It cannot produce a false positive. Cooley, Bess, and Rubin-Jackson, *Madam Foreman*, 202–3.

a drop of the blood got on his gloves when he opened the Simpson vial. However, he also said that he promptly discarded the gloves and put on new ones. Scheck tried to make this "spillage," as he called it, proof of cross-contamination with other evidence samples, an unlikely result since each sample was sealed inside secure envelopes.

Many observers would agree with Jeffrey Toobin that notwithstanding the prosecution's errors, the catalogue of evidence against Simpson remained overwhelming. He wrote:

> Simpson had a violent relationship with his ex-wife, and tensions between them were growing in the weeks leading up to the murders. Simpson had no alibi for the time of the murders, nor was his Bronco parked at his home during that time. Simpson had a cut on his left hand on the day after the murders, and DNA tests showed conclusively that it was Simpson's blood to the left of the shoe prints leaving the scene. Nicole's blood was found on a sock in his bedroom, and Goldman's blood—as well as Simpson's—was found in the Bronco. Hair consistent with Simpson's was found on the killer's cap and on Goldman's shirt. The gloves that Nicole bought for Simpson in 1990 were almost certainly the ones used by her killer.[87]

It was possible that Simpson was the killer and that the police also planted evidence against him, though Toobin found that possibility unlikely. It would have required planting Nicole's and Goldman's blood, hair, and fibers in too many places. The cover-up would have had to involve many police officers and others, all acting under intense media scrutiny.[88]

If Toobin and the many knowledgeable Americans—mostly white—who agree with him are correct, then what accounts for the result? Although the jurors denied that race played any part in their

---

87. Jeffrey Toobin was assigned to cover the O. J. story for the *New Yorker Magazine*. He attended the entire trial, interviewed hundreds of people, and had access to the full documentary record including internal memoranda of both prosecution and defense. His conclusions are the result of two years of research and reporting. Toobin, *The Run of His Life*, 11.
88. Ibid., 435–6.

decision, Toobin concluded that "the perfunctory review of nine months' worth of evidence, the focus on tangential if not actually irrelevant parts of the evidence, the simply incorrect view of other evidence, and the constant focus on racial issues both inside and out-side the courtroom; all these factors lead me to conclude that race played a far larger role in the verdict than the jurors conceded."[89]

In the years following the *Simpson* decision, dozens of law review authors, prosecutors, and defense attorneys have analyzed the jury's not-guilty verdict. As one might expect, Marcia Clark condemned the verdict in her blame-everybody-but-me book prologue:

By virtue of his celebrity, he would be coddled by worship-ful cops, pumped up by star-[expletive] attorneys, indulged by a spineless judge and adored by jurors every bit as addled by racial hatred as their counterparts on the Rodney King jury. O. J. Simpson slaughtered two innocent people, and he walked free—right past the most massive and compelling body of physical evidence ever assembled against a criminal defendant.[90]

Darden no doubt agreed with her, but spoke of the jury with more restraint:

If they had just gone over the case and tried to answer their doubts with testimony from the trial, then they still could have come back with a not guilty verdict, and I would have accepted their decision. But that didn't happen. Twelve people could not make an honest assessment of nine months of testi-mony in just four hours.[91]

Alan Dershowitz spoke for the defense in his account of the cir-cumstances that led the jury to distrust the police and the prosecution:

89. Ibid., 437.
90. Clark, *Without a Doubt*, 2.
91. Darden, *In Contempt*, 381.

These circumstances included the resources available to the defense, which enabled it to challenge aspects of the prosecution case that usually go unchallenged; the decision by the prosecution to try this case in a location where a jury could be selected that was more receptive to the defense challenges; the combination of incompetence, perjury and suspicious actions by several police officers; recent events in Los Angeles, which created a climate of suspicion against the Los Angeles police and prosecutors; the luck of the Fuhrman tapes surfacing, coupled with the resources of the defense, which enabled it to obtain these tapes through litigation, and some very bad mistakes by Marcia and some of her colleagues.[92]

Perhaps the most thought-provoking analysis was given by Professor William Hodes.[93] He claimed that the jury knew Simpson was guilty and knew that he was proven guilty beyond a reasonable doubt, but that they had engaged in what he called "jury nullification of the third kind."

This phrase encompasses a situation in which the jury disregards the evidence not because they dislike the particular law or because they dislike the application of the law to a particular set of circumstances. This third kind of jury nullification may be precipitated by a perception of police misconduct. These jurors acquitted because they wanted to do what Cochran told them to do, "Send a message." Some might be saying, "Stop engaging in police misconduct"; others might be influenced by a desire to "stop prosecuting black celebrities." Still others, including the two white jurors, might believe that "racists like Fuhrman, whether he planted the glove or not, have no place in the police force." Hodes goes further than most by suggesting that jury nullification of this kind can have long-term benefits. What if the jury believes that the police tried to frame a guilty O. J. Simpson? Hodes writes:

---

92. Dershowitz, *Reasonable Doubts*, 97–98.
93. Hodes, "Lord Brougham, The Dream Team, and Jury Nullification of the Third Kind," 1075.

According to a strict interpretation of the law and of the instructions of the court, the proper response under those circumstances would be to convict O. J. Simpson of the homicides, but then perhaps to join with other citizens in pressing for the arrest and conviction of the guilty police officers. Under jury nullification of the third kind, however, it would be quite appropriate for some of the jurors to vote for acquittal in order to send a more direct message that police misconduct of this kind is not only intolerable, but is ineffective since the intended purpose of more surely convicting the guilty will be frustrated.[94]

Unlike Dershowitz, Hodes finds no reasonable doubt. Insisting that jury members in the *Simpson* case had "reasonable doubt," he maintains, can only be accomplished by "indulging the false and demeaning assumption that the jurors were too dumb, too suspicious or too emotional to appreciate the difference between 'reasonable doubt' and irrational fantasy or groundless wishful thinking."[95] Nor does Hodes accept the opinion of some that blacks have a different understanding of what is reasonable and what is true based on their experiences with the police. "But that only makes matters worse, it seems to me, for it either relativizes truth (which is an extraordinarily dangerous proposition for any minority to embrace) or it relativizes rationality and wrongfully presumes that blacks have lost the capacity for logical thought, leaving them to fall back on mysticism and the intuitions of victimhood."[96]

Defenders of the *Simpson* verdict claimed that the backlash against the jury was clouded by negative media coverage of the defense evidence. According to Toobin, however, overall media coverage was more favorable to the defense than it should have been. He maintained that:

---

94. Ibid., 1100–1.
95. Ibid., 1103.
96. Ibid., 1103–4.

Fear of being called racist transcended everything in that newsroom. This extended, I think, even to discussions of the evidence. The safe course for those of us covering the case was to nitpick along with the defense attorneys. Sure, Simpson cut his left hand on the night of the murders, and DNA tests showed conclusively that it was Simpson's blood to the left of the footprints leaving the scene, but could those blood samples have been contaminated? It was likewise settled that Nicole's blood was on a sock found in Simpson's bedroom, and that Ron Goldman's blood was found in Simpson's Bronco, but perhaps those samples had been planted? Hair consistent with Simpson's was found in the knit cap at the murder scene and on Ron Goldman's shirt, but hair matches are not one hundred percent dispositive. The gloves that Nicole bought for Simpson in 1990 were almost certainly the ones used by her killer, but maybe somehow not. Our caution and fear, however, misled. The case against Simpson was simply overwhelming. When we said otherwise, we lied to the audience that trusted us.[97]

Whatever the cause of the enormous backlash to the verdict, it dramatically changed Simpson's life. He was no longer welcome in Brentwood. Hertz as well as the other companies that had used him in their advertising terminated his services. His agents dropped him and he was no longer welcome at the exclusive Riviera Country Club. Before the verdict was announced, his business managers had arranged with a pay-for-view network to have a two-hour live TV show, with O. J. being interviewed by Larry King and taking phone calls from viewers. When word was leaked that Larry King was considering being part of this program, his network, CNN, reacted to the public outcry, cable operators across the country refused to carry any program that would profit Simpson, and the project was cancelled. The extent of Simpson's isolation was dramatized when his own defense lawyer, Robert Shapiro, declared in an interview with

---

97. Jeffrey Toobin, "A Horrible Human Event," *New Yorker*, October 23, 1995, reprinted in Frontline, http://www.pbs.org/wgbh/pages/frontline/oj/highlights/toobin.html.

Barbara Walters that "we not only played the race card, we dealt it from the bottom of the deck."[98]

O. J.'s descent into oblivion continued with the result of the wrongful death civil case brought by the parents of Nicole Simpson and Ron Goldman. The presiding judge, Hiroshi Fujisaki, became, in the words of *USA Today*, "the man who finally pulled the plug on the circus antics in the O. J. Simpson case."

Judge Fujisaki banned TV cameras and audio feeds from the courtroom, imposed a gag order on the lawyers, and eliminated any mention of race; he controlled the courtroom and kept the case moving. This time, no evidence of police conspiracy was presented. In the criminal case, Simpson invoked his right not to testify. In the civil case, he had to answer questions at the pretrial depositions as well as at the trial itself. Another big difference was the burden of proof required in a civil case, which is the "preponderance of the evidence" rather than the higher "beyond a reasonable doubt" for the criminal trial. The civil trial, which lasted four months, ended with the jury, composed of nine whites, one black, one Hispanic, and one person of mixed Asian and African ancestry, unanimously awarding $33.5 million in compensatory and punitive damages. The court ordered Simpson to turn over his assets, his 1968 Heisman trophy, his paintings, and his golf clubs. The Rockingham estate was auctioned off and eventually was demolished by the new owner.

In September 2007 in Las Vegas, things got even worse for O. J. He had learned that a group of collectible dealers had some of his memorabilia in a hotel room. In order to prevent the Goldmans from acquiring them to help satisfy their judgment, O. J. and five accomplices entered the hotel room, prevented the occupants from leaving, then left with O. J.'s memorabilia and with other items as well. He was later arrested and charged with armed robbery, kidnapping, and conspiracy. On October 3, 2008, thirteen years to the day since his acquittal in Los Angeles, Simpson was convicted and sentenced to a minimum of nine years with a maximum of thirty-three years in

---

98. Toobin, *The Run of His Life*, 438.

prison. He is currently serving his sentence in Lovelock Correctional Center in Nevada and will be eligible for parole in 2017.

Losers in the *Simpson* case, Marcia Clark and Chris Darden were winners financially. Each received lucrative book deals and each left the district attorney's office. Clark became a fiction writer and has published four novels. Darden also became a writer and is a frequent commentator for CNN, Court TV, and NBC.

The *Simpson* acquittal elevated Johnnie Cochran to national fame. He expanded his law firm into fifteen states. Cochran was stricken with brain cancer and passed away in 2005 at the age of sixty-seven.

F. Lee Bailey ran into difficulty shortly after the case ended. He was disbarred in Florida and Massachusetts for mishandling a client's money and was also pursued by the IRS for owing two million dollars in back taxes.

Mark Fuhrman managed to rehabilitate himself. Fuhrman pled *nolo contendere*, that is, no contest, to a charge of perjury and received three years' probation and a $200 fine. His book, *Murder in Brentwood*, became a *New York Times* best seller. He demonstrated his skill as a detective by investigating the then-unsolved 1975 murder of teenager Martha Moxley in Greenwich, Connecticut, and determined that the murderer was Michael Skakel, the nephew of Robert Kennedy's widow, Ethel. Skakel was convicted in 2002. Author of nine books, Fuhrman is a frequent commentator and analyst on various TV news shows.

The *Simpson* trial left Judge Ito's heretofore excellent reputation in shambles. Ito was almost universally criticized for poor and inconsistent decisions, for entertaining celebrities in his chambers while keeping the sequestered jurors waiting, and for not exercising control over the incessant "sidebar" arguments of counsel outside the presence of the jury. A trial that should have taken two months took eight months. In the first fifty days, the jury heard an average of two hours of testimony a day and at one point sat for eleven consecutive days hearing no testimony at all while the lawyers argued fine legal details. *Newsweek* put his picture on their cover under the headline "What a Mess." In the years following the *Simpson* verdict, the advice given by senior judges at judicial teaching seminars was

"Don't be an Ito."[99] He continued to serve on the bench until 2014, when he retired.

The disappointment of most Americans with the result of the *Simpson* trial led to calls for major changes to the criminal justice system, such as abandoning trial by jury in favor of the continental system of professional judges, the lowering of the burden of proof so that defendants could be convicted on a standard less demanding than "beyond a reasonable doubt" (to something like "clear and convincing evidence"), and allowing the jury to draw adverse inferences if the defendants invoke their privilege not to testify. Some critics suggested that the English system of press control be adopted to prohibit the media and also lawyers, interested parties, and witnesses from revealing any information while the trial is in progress. Others wanted to eliminate the exclusionary rule that prevents the introduction of reliable evidence that was wrongfully obtained by the police and/or prohibit lawyers from making political or racial appeals to the jury. Aside from the unconstitutionality of many of these proposals, most of these are structured to change the balance between prosecution and defense and make convictions easier. None of those so-called reforms were adopted. As Oliver Wendell Holmes warned years ago:

> Great cases, like hard cases, make bad law. For great cases are called great, not by reason of their importance in shaping the law of the future, but because of some accident of immediate overwhelming interest which appeals to the feelings and distorts the judgment.[100]

---

99. A few examples of the criticism Ito received are Chapter III, "A Judicial Error," of Bugliosi, *Outrage*, 79–111; Murray Richtel, "The Simpson Trial: A Timid Judge and a Lawless Verdict," 67 U.Colo. L. Rev. 977 (1996); Kourlis, "Not Jury Nullification," 1109; Ronald Allen, "The Simpson Affair, Reform of the Criminal Justice Process, and Magic Bullets," *University of Colorado Law Review* 67 (1996): 989, 1011–4 (describing Judge Ito's performance as a "disgrace . . . largely generated by his own fascination with the media coverage of the case"); Cooley, Bess, and Rubin-Jackson, *Madam Foreman*, 205–7 (jurors agreeing that Judge Ito exhibited a lack of control over the trial); Geis and Bienen, *Crimes of the Century*, 207–8.
100. Northern Securities Company v. United States, 193 U.S. 197, 400 (1904); Dershowitz, *Reasonable Doubts*, 196; Geis and Bienen, *Crimes of the Century*, 214.

The *O. J. Simpson* case heightened awareness of issues of domestic abuse and created the political climate to act on laws that had been stalled in the legislative pipeline for years. Congress passed the landmark Violence Against Women Act that earmarks funds for state and federal officials to combat domestic violence. In 1995, thirty-nine state legislatures enacted domestic violence provisions.

The California Legislature enacted a new exception to the rule against hearsay that would allow into evidence a victim's statement describing physical injury or threats even if the victim was unavailable to testify, as long as the statement was made in writing or recorded under circumstances that would indicate its trustworthiness.[101] If this statute had existed at the time of the *Simpson* criminal trial, the prosecution would have been able to admit Nicole's taped call to the Sojourn Battered Women's Shelter.[102]

For a considerable period, judges exercised their discretion to prevent television cameras in the courtroom in high-profile cases. California also adopted a Rule of Professional Conduct that prohibits attorneys from making statements that have a "substantial likelihood of materially prejudicing an adjudicating proceeding."

The *O. J. Simpson* case, the verdict, and the reaction to the verdict lives on for two related reasons. First, because it was a sensational, irresistible soap opera watched by millions, and second, it was a dramatic demonstration that, in our criminal justice system, race matters. That should not have been a surprise to anyone, given massive evidence that in the 1970s and 1980s the LAPD was an arrogant, aggressive paramilitary force that covered up acts of brutality, racism, and corruption. The most egregious example was the acquittal of four white police officers by an all-white jury in Simi Valley, California, in spite of the video showing the officers beating Rodney King, a black motorist, with heavy aluminum batons, fifty-six times in eighty-one seconds.[103]

101. California Evidence Code, Section 1370.
102. But in 2004, The United States Supreme Court strengthened the right of accused defendants to confront witnesses against them under the Sixth Amendment. See Crawford v. Washington, 541 U.S. 36 (2004) and Giles v. California, 554 U.S. 353 (2008). Under these decisions, the effect of the hearsay exception in Section 1370 is largely limited to civil cases.
103. Joe Domanick, *Blue: The LAPD and the Battle to Redeem American Policing* (Simon and

In addition, statistics strongly suggest that black juror protection of black defendants was common in many areas of the country, even in cases involving noncelebrities. In 1993, the national acquittal rate was seventeen percent. In the Bronx, where juries are eighty percent black and Hispanic, the acquittal rate for black defendants was forty-eight percent and for Hispanics thirty-eight percent. In Washington, D.C., where juries are seventy-percent black and defendants in criminal cases are ninety-five percent black, the acquittal rate was twenty-nine percent, and in Detroit, the acquittal rate was thirty percent.[104]

The *Simpson* case is significant because it dramatically brought home, especially to white Americans, that when it comes to belief in law enforcement and the criminal justice system, black people and white people live in different worlds.

Twenty years after the *Simpson* trial, tension between African-Americans and the police persists. Highly publicized conflicts involving police shootings of African-Americans have occurred in Henderson, Missouri, and Charleston, South Carolina; and in Baltimore, Cleveland, and New York City.

Alas, it is hard to disagree with the conclusion of Professor Ronald J. Allen, one of the nation's leading experts in criminal procedure and evidence, that the "O. J. Simpson affair was a disaster from every point of view."[105] It was, we would add, a sensational case that highlighted racial polarization, the power of celebrity and money in the United States, and the defects of a legal system in which so many Americans, with considerable justification, take considerable pride.

Schuster, 2015).
104. Toobin, *The Run of His Life,* 437–8; Bryan Morgan, "The Jury's View," *University of Colorado Law Review* 67 (1996): 983–4. Morgan respects the jury's role and concedes the many instances of bias by white jurors, but he is drawn to the unpleasant conclusion that racial bias—the controlling influence of race on one's actions—was the principal and probably the dispositive reason for the Simpson acquittal and comments that "to the surprise and discomfort of white America, racial bias now seems manifest in the acquittal of defendants of color"; Katheryn Russell-Brown, "Black Protectionism as a Civil Rights Strategy," *Buffalo Law Review* 53 (2005); Professor of Law Russell-Brown explains the tendency of blacks to provide racial support to prominent blacks accused of wrongdoing.
105. Allen, "The Simpson Affair," 989.

Index

prosecutors
  disclosure to defense by, 22–24
  legal and ethical obligations of,
    18–19, 22–24
protections afforded to criminal suspects
  in 1930s, 79–80
  U.S. Supreme Court decisions
    on, 13
Puccio, Thomas, 285–286
pumpkin papers, 123–128, 139–142

Q

quantifying, for clarity and emphasis,
  63–65

R

Rabinowitz, Dorothy, 325–326
race issues. *See* O. J. Simpson trial;
  Scottsboro trials; Skokie affair
Raidor, Betty, 298–299
rape. *See Scottsboro* trials
rebuttal, 59–62
Red Scare. *See* anticommunism
Reed, Stanley, 132
Reese, Marilyn. *See* Sheppard, Marilyn
Reiner, Ira, 304–305
"Report to the Governor in the Matter
  of Sacco and Vanzetti" (Taylor),
  39–40
reputation witnesses, 110
RFLP tests, 346–347
Richter, Fred, 196
right to counsel, 85–86
Ripley, Walter, 27
Riske, Robert, 334–335
Robers, John, 215–216
Roberson, Willie, 82, 98, 102–103
Roberts, Brad, 335
Roddy, Stephen, 82, 84
Roosevelt, Franklin D., 111
Rosen, William, 130
Rosenzweig, David, 323
Rossbach, Carl, 167
Rossi, David, 334, 335
Rubenstein, Arthur, 282
Rubin, Lael, 305
  2014 reflection on trial, 324
  closing arguments of, 313
  evidence withheld from defense by,
    305–306, 313

opening statement of, 307–308
questioning of Ray Buckey, 312
relationship with *Los Angeles Times*
  editor, 323
withholding of information from
  defense by, 313
Rubin, Robert, 369–370
rule against hearsay, 292
Rule of Professional Conduct, 382
The Run of His Life (Toobin), 354
Russell, Francis, 9, 33
Ryan, Leo, 219

S

Sacco, Nicola. *See also* Sacco and
  Vanzetti trial
  arrest of, 6–7, 17–18
  cross-examination of, 18–22
  draft-dodging by, 18–19
  execution of, 37–38
  judge's bias against, ix, 35–36
  lying by, 7–8
  photos of, 7
  reputation of before arrest, 8
  sculpture memorial of, 2–3
  weapons carried by, 7, 8
Sacco and Vanzetti trial, 39–40
  1977 review of, 39–40
  appeals of, 34
  ballistics experts and, 12–13,
    24–26, 28
  cross-examination questions at,
    12, 18–22
  defense alibi witnesses at, 12
  defense counsel at. *See* Moore,
    Fred
  denial of new trial, 31–33
  executions following, 37–38
  governor-appointed review of,
    36–37
  judge at. *See* Thayer, Webster
  jury deliberation and verdict at,
    26
  jury selection for, 10–11
  Massachusetts' apology about, 2
  motions for new trial, 27–28,
    30–31
  mystery at heart of, 3
  new evidence discovered after,
    27–28